Play = Learning

PLAY = LEARNING

How Play Motivates and Enhances Children's Cognitive and Social-Emotional Growth

Edited by

Dorothy G. Singer
Roberta Michnick Golinkoff
Kathy Hirsh-Pasek

2006

OXFORD
UNIVERSITY PRESS

Oxford University Press, Inc., publishes works that further
Oxford University's objective of excellence
in research, scholarship, and education.

Oxford New York
Auckland Cape Town Dar es Salaam Hong Kong Karachi
Kuala Lumpur Madrid Melborne Mexico City Nairobi
New Delhi Shanghai Taipei Toronto

With offices in
Argentina Austria Brazil Chile Czech Republic France Greece
Guatemala Hungary Italy Japan Poland Portugal Singapore
South Korea Switzerland Thailand Turkey Ukraine Vietnam

Published by Oxford University Press, Inc.
198 Madison Avenue, New York, New York 10016

www.oup.com

Library of Congress Cataloging-in-Publication Data
Play = learning : how play motivates and enhances children's cognitive and social-emotional growth / edited by Dorothy G. Singer, Roberta Michnick Golinkoff, and Kathy Hirsh–Pasek.
p. cm.
Includes index.
ISBN-13 978-0-19-530438-1
1. Play—Psychological aspects. 2. Play—Social aspects. I. Title: Play equals learning. II. Singer, Dorothy G. III. Golinkoff, Roberta M. IV. Hirsh–Pasek, Kathy.
BF717.P578 2006
155.4'18—dc22 2005027315

9 8 7 6 5 4

Printed in the United States of America
on acid-free paper

To Jerry, my favorite play partner.
—Dorothy G. Singer

To my childhood friends wherever you are, with whom I spent many happy hours at play, and to my grownup friend, Larry, who helps me feel the joy of childhood.
—Roberta Michnick Golinkoff

To my parents, who encouraged me to play and think "out of the box."
To my husband, Jeff, and our three sons (Josh, Benj, and Mike), who taught me firsthand that play is the royal road to learning and innovation!
—Kathy Hirsh-Pasek

Acknowledgments

This book grew out of the material our authors submitted for our conference, Play = Learning, held June 10–11, 2005, at Yale University. This conference was made possible through the generous support of Fisher-Price, Inc., and through the auspices of Yale University. Laurie Oravec, former Director of Public Relations at Fisher-Price, Inc., was a guiding force throughout the preparation and realization of the conference. We thank Laurie and Fisher-Price, Inc. We also thank Catharine Carlin and Jennifer Rappaport at Oxford University Press for their continued support during the process of organizing this book and for their confidence in us.

We thank Jane Erickson, who spent numerous hours typing endless lists to make sure that we reached those people interested in early childcare and play; Vanessa De Nicola, Anna Rainey, and Deena Skolnick for their efforts during the play conference; and Brittania Weatherspoon for her excellent word-processing skills in preparing the materials for this book and for her help before and during the conference.

Finally, we thank all the researchers—past and present—who studied the benefits of play and reaffirmed what children everywhere always know: Play is the joyous feature of childhood.

Dorothy G. Singer
Roberta Michnick Golinkoff
Kathy Hirsh-Pasek

Contents

Contributors

EDITORS

Dorothy G. Singer is Senior Research Scientist, Department of Psychology, Yale University. She is also Co-Director, with Jerome L. Singer, of the Yale University Family Television Research and Consultation Center. An expert on early childhood development, television effects on youth, and parent training in imaginative play, she has written 20 books and more than 150 articles. Her latest books are *Handbook of Children and the Media*; *Make-Believe: Games and Activities for Imaginative Play*; *Imagination and Play in the Electronic Age*; *Handbook of Children, Culture, and Violence*; and *Children's Play: Roots of Reading* (edited by E. Zigler, D. Singer, and S. Bishop-Josef); the last book was selected for CHOICE's Outstanding Academic Title list. Dr. Singer is a Fellow of the American Psychological Association (APA) and received the award for Distinguished Scientific Contributions to the Media by Division 46 of APA in 2004.

Roberta Michnick Golinkoff holds the H. Rodney Sharp Chair in the School of Education at the University of Delaware, with joint appointments in Psychology and Linguistics. A Guggenheim Fellow and a James McKeen Cattell Award winner, she has written dozens of journal articles, chapters, and academic books. Her latest book, *Action Meets Word: How Children Learn Verbs* (OUP 2005), edited with Kathy Hirsh-Pasek, continues her work on how children learn language. Committed to dissemination, she lectures internationally and wrote two popular press books, also with Kathy Hirsh-Pasek. *How Babies Talk: The Magic and Mystery of Language Development in the First Three Years of Life* was called a "godsend" by Steven Pinker. The second book is called *Einstein Never Used Flash Cards:*

How Our Children Really Learn and Why They Need to Play More and Memorize Less. Its mantra is the source of the name for the present book, Play = Learning.

Kathy Hirsh-Pasek is the Stanley and Debra Lefkowitz Professor in the Department of Psychology at Temple University, where she serves as Director of the Infant Language Laboratory. Her research in the areas of early language development and infant cognition, funded by the National Science Foundation and the National Institutes of Health and Human Development, has resulted in seven books and numerous publications. She is a Fellow of the American Psychological Association and the American Psychological Society, serves as an associate editor of *Child Development*, and is treasurer of the International Society for Infant Studies. Her recent book written with Roberta Golinkoff, *Einstein Never Used Flashcards*, won the prestigious Books for a Better Life Prize awarded by the Multiple Sclerosis Society. Professor Hirsh-Pasek has published more than 100 professional articles and has given more than 80 invited lectures around the world.

AUTHORS

Harvey F. Bellin, an alumnus of Yale College and Yale School of Drama (MFA, Directing), is President of The Media Group of Connecticut, Inc., and a former Research Affiliate of the Yale University Department of Psychology. He was awarded an Outstanding Director Emmy by the New York City Chapter of NATAS. Since 1997, he has collaborated with Prof. Jerome Singer and Dr. Dorothy Singer of Yale University under U.S. Department of Education grants to develop three video-based programs of make-believe games to strengthen the school-readiness skills of at-risk preschoolers from poor families. He was Project Director of five other U.S. Department of Education grants, coproducer of the PBS series *The Shakespeare Hour Hosted by Walter Matthau*, and producer/director of award-winning cultural programs about Asia, Europe, the Middle East, and the former Soviet Union.

Laura E. Berk, PhD, is Distinguished Professor of Psychology at Illinois State University. She has published widely in the fields of early childhood development and education, focusing on the effects of school environments on children's development, the social origins and functional significance of children's private speech, and the role of make-believe play in the development of self-regulation. Her books include *Private Speech: From Social Interaction to Self-Regulation*; *Scaffolding Children's Learning: Vygotsky and Early Childhood Education*; and *Awakening Children's Minds: How Parents and Teachers Can Make a Difference*. She is the author of three textbooks in child and human development: *Child Development*; *Infants, Children, and Adolescents*; and *Development Through the Lifespan*.

Sandra J. Bishop-Josef is Assistant Director of Yale University's Edward Zigler Center in Child Development and Social Policy and an Associate Research Scientist at the Yale Child Study Center. She directs the Zigler Center's fellowship training program. Bishop-Josef's primary research interests are in the area of child abuse and neglect. She is also interested in early childhood intervention programs and other services children receive. Bishop-Josef coedited a volume with Edward Zigler and Dorothy Singer titled *Children's Play: The Roots of Reading*, which was selected for CHOICE's Outstanding Academic Title list.

James Black received a PhD in neuroscience and an MD from the University of Illinois at Urbana-Champaign. He then did a psychiatry residency at the University of Utah. He is currently Assistant Professor of Psychiatry at Southern Illinois School of Medicine. He has done research in neural plasticity and the effects of experience on development. Recent research includes studies of how children cope with traumatic events. His clinical work concentrates on neuropsychiatry, trauma, and attachment.

Carolyn Brockmeyer is a doctoral student in Developmental Psychology at Lehigh University. She is interested in narrative development during the preschool years, specifically how narrative activity may foster social competence, including social perspective-taking skills.

James F. Christie is a Professor of Curriculum and Instruction at Arizona State University, where he teaches courses in language, literacy, and early childhood education. His research interests include early literacy development and children's play. His publications include the coauthored books *Play, Development, and Early Education*; *Building a Foundation for Preschool Literacy*; *Teaching Language and Literacy* (2nd ed.); and *Play and Literacy in Early Education*. He is a member of the Early Literacy Development Commission of the International Reading Association and past president of the Association for the Study of Play. He is currently project codirector for the Arizona Centers of Excellence in Early Education Early Reading First project.

Herbert P. Ginsburg, PhD, is the Jacob H. Schiff Professor of Psychology and Education at Teachers College, Columbia University. His research interests include the development of mathematical thinking (with particular attention to young children and disadvantaged populations) and the assessment of cognitive function. He has conducted basic research on the development of mathematical thinking and developed mathematics curricula for young children, tests of mathematical thinking, and video workshops to enhance teachers' understanding of students' learning of mathematics. Currently he is exploring how computer technology can be used to help teachers assess children's mathematical knowledge.

Wendy Haight received her BA from Reed College and her PhD in Educational Psychology from the University of Chicago. She currently is Associate Professor of Social Work at the University of Illinois, Urbana-Champaign, where she directs the PhD program. She has written extensively on caregiver–child pretend play in various cultural communities. Her current research focuses on the role of caregivers in helping children to interpret traumatic events.

Robyn M. Holmes received her PhD from Rutgers University and is Associate Professor of Psychology at Monmouth University. Her teaching and research interests are in children's play and toys, social cognition, and cross-cultural and qualitative approaches. She has published numerous articles and chapters on children's play and authored two books: *How Young Children Perceive Race* and *Fieldwork with Children*. Most recently, she has been studying children's recess behaviors and cheating during play.

Trisha D. Mann earned a BS in Psychology from Illinois State University and is a doctoral student in School Psychology at Illinois State University. Her research focuses on children's museums as community contexts for promoting parent–child engagement.

Judith McDowell received a BS in Education in 1994 and an MEd in 1996 from Temple University. She has certifications in early child, elementary, and special education and taught in an early intervention program. She has been a Head Start teacher in Philadelphia since 1994 and currently is a consultant for the University of Pennsylvannia on early childhood curriculum. She has been implementing storytelling and story-acting activity in her Head Start classroom for 3 years.

Ageliki Nicolopoulou received her PhD in Developmental Psychology from the University of California at Berkeley and is Associate Professor of Psychology at Lehigh University. She is a sociocultural developmental psychologist whose work focuses on the role of narrative and play in development, socialization, and education. Her other research interests include the influence of the peer group and peer culture as social contexts for children's development, the foundations of emergent literacy, and the developmental interplay between the construction of reality and the formation of identity, including gender identity. She is guest editor of a special issue of *Cognitive Development* (2005) on "Play and narrative in the process of development: Commonalities, differences, and interrelations."

Amy T. Ogan earned a BS in Psychology from the University of Iowa, was a preschool teacher before entering graduate school, and is a doctoral candidate in School Psychology at Illinois State University. She is currently completing her dissertation, which addresses the influence of make-believe play on the development of self-regulation among Head Start preschoolers.

Teresa Ostler is a Licensed Clinical Psychologist and Associate Professor of Social Work at the University of Illinois at Urbana-Champaign. She received her PhD in Developmental Psychology from the University of California at Berkeley. Her research focuses on parents with mental illness and on parent–child attachment. She is currently working to implement an intervention to support the mental health of children exposed to parent methamphetamine abuse.

Anthony D. Pellegrini is Professor of Psychological Foundations of Education in the Department of Educational Psychology, University of Minnesota, Twin Cities Campus. He has research interests in methodological issues in the general area of human development, specifically in direct observations. He is especially involved in the development of play and dominance. His research has been funded by the National Institutes of Health, the Spencer Foundation, and the W. T. Grant Foundation. He is a Fellow of the American Psychological Association and has been awarded a fellowship from the British Psychological Society.

Melissa Allen Preissler is a Lecturer in the Department of Psychology at the University of Edinburgh. She recently completed a Postdoctoral Fellowship jointly in the Psychology Department at Yale University and in the Developmental Disabilities Clinic of the Yale Child Study Center. She received her PhD in Cognitive Psychology at New York University in 2003 after a fellowship at Harvard University. Her research explores the symbolic understanding of pictures and words by children with autism and normally developing toddlers, and early language acquisition.

Mitchel Resnick, Professor at the MIT Media Laboratory, explores how people (especially children) can use new technologies to learn new things in new ways. His research group helped develop the ideas and technologies underlying the LEGO Mindstorms robotics construction kit. He cofounded the Computer Clubhouse project, an international network of after-school learning centers for youth from low-income communities. Resnick earned a BA in physics at Princeton University (1978), and MS and PhD degrees in computer science at MIT (1988, 1992). He is author of *Turtles, Termites, and Traffic Jams* (1994), coauthor of *Adventures in Modeling* (2001), and coeditor of *Constructionism in Practice* (1996).

Kathleen A. Roskos at John Carroll University teaches courses in reading instruction and reading diagnosis. Formerly an elementary classroom teacher, Dr. Roskos has served in a variety of educational administration roles, including director of federal programs in the public schools and department chair in higher education. She recently completed 2 years of public service as the Director of the Ohio Literacy Initiative at the Ohio Department of Education, providing leadership in P–12 literacy policy and programs. Dr. Roskos studies early literacy development, teacher cognition, and the design of professional education for teachers and has published research articles on these topics in leading journals. She is currently a member of the e-Learning Committee and the Early Childhood Commission of the International Reading Association and a leader in the Literacy Development for Young Children SIG of that organization.

Kathryn Sheridan received her Bachelor's and Master's degrees in Social Work from the University of Alabama. She is currently a doctoral student in Social Work at the University of Illinois at Urbana-Champaign. Her research interests include foster children's perspectives of the traumatic events they have experienced, as well as risk and protective factors.

Jerome L. Singer received his doctorate in Clinical Psychology from the University of Pennsylvania. He is Professor Emeritus of Psychology at Yale University, where he served for many years as Director of the Graduate Program in Clinical Psychology and also as Director of Graduate Studies in Psychology. He is a specialist in research on the psychology of imagination and daydreaming. Dr. Singer has authored more than 250 technical articles on thought processes, imagery, personality, and psychotherapy, as well as on children's play and the effects of television. He is a Past President of the Eastern Psychological Association and of the Divisions of Personality-Social Psychology and the Psychology of Aesthetics, Creativity, and the Arts of the American Psychological Association. Recent books, among his 20, include *The House of Make-Believe*; *Repression and Dissociation*; *Imagination and Play in the Electronic Age*; and *Imagery in Psychotherapy.*

Deborah S. Weber is Manager for the Fisher-Price Child Research Department, which is the toy industry's most respected center for research on childhood development and play. This center is dedicated to the progression of research and practice, thereby impacting the conception and development of innovative toys and children's products. Dr. Weber holds bachelor's, master's, and doctorate degrees in early childhood and elementary education. She received her bachelor's and master's degree at St. Bonaventure University and her PhD from the State University of New York at Buffalo.

Edward F. Zigler is Sterling Professor of Psychology, Emeritus, at Yale University. He holds a PhD in clinical psychology from the University of Texas at Austin. He was the first Director of the Office of Child Development (now the Administration on Children, Youth, and Families) and Chief of the U.S. Children's Bureau. He was a member of the national planning committees of the Head Start, Follow Thru, and Early Head Start programs. Dr. Zigler founded and is Director Emeritus of Yale's Edward Zigler Center in Child Development and Social Policy. He founded the School of the 21st Century model, which has been adopted by more than 1,300 schools in 20 states.

Play = Learning

1

Why Play = Learning: A Challenge for Parents and Educators

ROBERTA MICHNICK GOLINKOFF, KATHY HIRSH-PASEK,
AND DOROTHY G. SINGER

Computers are useless. They only give you answers!
—Pablo Picasso

Imagine a world in which children are encouraged to parrot answers, to fill in the blanks, and to not go beyond the facts. Imagine a world in which one size fits all (as in today's educational standards), and no size fits any. Madeleine L'Engle (1962) describes just such a world in her classic book, *A Wrinkle in Time*.

> Below them the town was laid out in harsh angular patterns. The houses in the outskirts were all exactly alike, small square boxes painted gray. . . . In front of all the houses children were playing. Some were skipping ropes, some were bouncing balls. Meg felt vaguely that something was wrong with their play. . . .
>
> "Look!" Charles Wallace said suddenly. "They're skipping and bouncing in rhythm! Everyone's doing it at exactly the same moment."
>
> This was so. As the skipping rope hit the pavement, so did the ball. As the rope curved over the head of the jumping child, the child with the ball caught the ball. Down came the ropes. Down came the balls. Over and over again. . . . All in rhythm. All identical. Like the houses. Like the paths. Like the flowers. (p. 103)

From the living room to the classroom, children are being increasingly programmed and structured—as are the teachers who teach them. There is little time for play; the focus is on memorization of the "facts." Indeed, play is viewed as a waste of time when more important "work," the work of memorizing and parroting, could be done. As the pressure on children in school increases, paradoxically their ability to relax and just have fun through play is being restricted.

Today, for example, many schools have reduced or eliminated recess time (see chapter 3). This is unfortunate, because during recess, children engage in rough-and-tumble play (pouncing, chasing, and wrestling), which is distinct from aggression (Gordon, Kollack-Walker, Akil, & Panksepp, 2002). In Finland, recess is an important part of the schedule, and children return to classrooms refreshed and ready to learn; indeed, Finnish children score high on reading tests (Alvarez, 2005). Research finds that rough-and-tumble play not only is a physical release but also "may facilitate friendships and promote cooperative pro-social behaviors and attitudes" (Scott & Panksepp, 2003, p. 549). Children who play together learn to work together.

Class time across the country is now spent in either assessment or assessment preparation—in having children learn to fill in the blanks with rote answers. The classrooms that used to display children's work and drawings now devote their walls to "testing tips" designed to help children do well on standardized assessments. The multibillion-dollar educational toy industry sells toys that teach isolated facts to children young enough to push their buttons and ring their bells. There exists a booming tutoring industry for the preschool set so that Johnny can enter *kindergarten* at the head of his class. Schools have either dropped or cut back on creative curricula such as music and art. These cultural activities are considered unnecessary flourishes in an educational system that is obsessively focused on core academic topics such as reading and math.

According to a recent statement in the *Wall Street Journal*, "President Bush's No Child Left Behind program pushed districts to require more from younger pupils. As a result, in many districts, skills once thought appropriate for first or second graders are being taught in kindergarten, while kindergarten skills have been bumped down to preschool" (Kronholz, 2005, p. B1). Is it any wonder that preschoolers are being expelled as a disciplinary measure at unprecedented rates (Gilliam, 2005)? Gilliam's national survey of 3,898 prekindergarten classrooms reveals that 10.4% of teachers reported expelling at least one preschooler within the past 12 months of the study. Rates were found to be highest for older preschoolers and African Americans. More boys were expelled than were girls, and the boys were having more behavioral problems in school. The highest rates for expulsion were in faith-affiliated centers and for-profit childcare. Are these children being expelled because the school expectations have changed and they have little time for play?

Our living rooms and classrooms have become pressure cookers, and children are getting less opportunity to be active physical players. In fact, some have suggested that children suffer from a "nature deficit disorder" (Louv, 2005) because they spend so little time outside at play. Is it any wonder that third graders in New York City (according to the *New York Times*; Schwartz, 2005) wake up crying and with stomachaches because they know they are to take a high-stakes test that day? Parents praise videos like *Baby Einstein* for having beautiful trees, apparently forgetting that these are available for endless inspection, and for free, in the real world. Obesity and childhood hypertension are on the increase in the 0 to 6 sets. The Mayo Clinic Web site offers a chilling view on the long-term effects of childhood obesity.

> Over the past 30 years, the rate of obesity in the US has more than doubled for preschoolers and adolescents, and it has more than tripled for children ages 6 to 11. Obese children get a head start on health problems such as diabetes and heart disease, often carrying these problems into an obese adulthood. . . . Obesity may soon top smoking as the nation's most preventable cause of death. (Mayo Clinic, 2005)

Obesity in children seems an inevitable outcome of the fact that even children under 2 are spending an average of 2 hours a day watching television (Rideout, Vandewater, & Wartella, 2003). This does not include the extra 40 minutes a day they spend watching videos. Children as young as 3 months are already viewing television and VCRs (see chapter 9). A report from the American Psychological Society in 2003 (Schwartz, 2005) tells us that 25% of sixth graders watch 40 or more hours of television per week, effectively turning media viewing into a full-time job. A statement by Anderson et al. (2003) captures the dramatic situation American children find themselves in: "Children ages 0–6 spend more time on entertainment media than on reading, being read to, and playing outside combined" (p. 100).

THE PROBLEM HAS NO BORDERS

Children in other Western countries are also playing less with peers and parents. In the past, schools could count on children arriving with some literacy skills that they acquired in play with parents and other adults. In England, children are now starting school unable even to recite a simple rhyme. A survey entitled "Young Children's Skills on Entry to Education," administered by the British government's basic skills agency (Smithers, 2003), was given to more than 700 teachers. Teachers claim that half of all children now start school at 4 or 5 unable to speak audibly, be understood by others, respond to simple instructions, recognize their own names, or even count to 5. Smithers states that learning nursery rhymes on a parent or caregiver's lap has traditionally been seen as an important first step toward literacy and numeracy skills, as well as key to phonological awareness.

The article laments the lack of adult participation and playful learning in these children's lives. At the same time, television and computers seem to serve as substitutes for parental guidance. Several chapters in this book attest to the importance of parental or teacher guidance in children's play as a way to foster learning (see, for example, chapters 8, 6, and 5).

In Ireland, Ready, Steady, Learn is a program organized in response to the lack of playtime in schools, health care, and childcare facilities. A million pounds has now been allocated to local authorities to expand play facilities.

From a conference in London, with researchers from Sweden, Austria, Italy, Australia, and Brazil, a strong message emerged about the importance of play to children's lives and learning (Hartmann, 2002). Teachers were trying to encourage more imaginative play in the classrooms. Despite the strong evidence in favor of play and the international attention, teachers in Brazil continue to believe that the classroom is best used for learning only and that the playground is for play.

In a five-country (France, Germany, Great Britain, Japan, and the United States) study conducted by LEGO on parents' beliefs about play, 94% of the parents agreed that time spent playing is time spent learning (LEGO Learning Institute, 2002). Nonetheless, parents felt that more time should be given to cognitive tasks at the *expense of free time* when play occurs. Parents in this study seem confused about whether play is really a way to learn. The same finding emerged in a more recent survey conducted by Fisher-Price that asked parents to rank the benefits of play. Parents ranked "learning through play" as number 12 on a list of 14, while "releasing energy" was rated as number 1 (Glick Gryfe, 2005). Many parents do not seem to appreciate that children can learn as they play and that through play, children are motivated to learn the basic skills they will need for success in school.

Zigler and Bishop-Josef (chapter 2) wrote, "Play is under siege." As a result, the academic, social, artistic, and creative skills that flow naturally from ordinary, everyday, unstructured play are also threatened. This book returns play to center stage, flying in the face of trends all around us that minimize and disparage it. Here we review the evidence that play, especially guided play, offers a road to learning. Children need play alongside more traditional learning to build social and cognitive skills. In short, these chapters set forth the evidence that play prepares children to not only be better people but also be better prepared to work in what Tom Friedman (2005) calls today's "flat world," where everyone has ready access to the facts.

Florida (2002) estimates that 30% of the workforce now is part of what he calls the "creative class." Even working- and service-class jobs require the generation of ideas rather than mere physical labor: "The nation's geographic center of gravity has shifted away from traditional industrial regions to new axes of creativity and innovation" (p. 11). In his new book, *A Whole New Mind: Moving From the Information Age to the Conceptual Age* (2005), Daniel Pink makes a similar argument. He writes:

> The last few decades have belonged to a certain kind of person with a certain kind of mind—computer programmers who could crank code, lawyers who could craft contracts, MBAs who could crunch numbers. But the keys to the kingdom are changing hands. The future belongs to a very different kind of person with a very different kind of mind—creators and empathizers, pattern recognizers and meaning makers. These people—artists, inventors, designers, storytellers, caregivers, consolers, big picture thinkers—will now reap society's richest rewards and share its greatest joys. (Pink, 2005)

The world is moving toward an emerging creative class that values conceptual knowledge and original thinking. Ironically, our educational system is going in the opposite direction, as if we were educating children for the 19th century instead of the 21st. Instead of encouraging creativity, thinking outside the box, or coloring outside the lines, we are requiring children to memorize information, even in the face of the fact that information constantly changes. This is not to say that we do not need to know facts; we do. But the power of knowledge comes from *weaving* those facts together in new and imaginative ways. And facts *change*. We no longer believe the world is flat, or that the element phlogiston makes up the universe, or that ulcers come from stress. This book confronts the prevailing popular "fact" that play is immaterial to children's development. Play is crucial to children's mental health, and it prepares children for school. It offers both social and cognitive advantages for children and the adults they will become.

WHY PLAY IS IMPORTANT TO CHILDREN'S EMOTIONAL HEALTH

Vygotsky said many years ago that play helps children work out the rules for social interaction and allows children to be at their best. Research supports what Vygotsky wrote in 1932: "In play it is as though he were a head taller than himself" (Vygotsky, 1930–1935/1978, p. 102), as though the child were trying to jump above his normal behavior competencies. Play is important for building social competence and confidence in dealing with peers, a life skill that is essential for functioning in school (Howes, 1992; Howes & Matheson, 1992; Raver, 2002; Singer & Singer, 2005), as well as in life on the job.

For children who have difficult life circumstances, emotional problems, or developmental delays, play may be even more critical. Haight, Black, Jacobsen, and Sheridan (chapter 11) demonstrate how children who have been traumatized can use pretend play with their mothers to work through the effects of the stress. As Haight et al. write, children can gain immeasurably from "constructing meaning from emotionally challenging experiences" (p. 210) through pretend play. Relatedly, children with autism have limited ability to engage in symbolic play (see chapter 12). Research suggests that play-based interventions hold promise for helping these children overcome some of their social limitations.

Play is also critical to self-regulation and children's ability to manage their own behavior and emotions. As Berk, Mann, and Ogan (chapter 5) state, "Self-regulation is central to our conception of what it means to be human—the foundation for choice and decision making, for mastery of higher cognitive processes, and for morality" (p. 74). For example, when a child learns to inhibit her reach to the light socket when told "no," to delay gratification (dessert is after dinner), or to calm herself when she is upset, she is manifesting the development of self-regulation. Play is the place where children practice these skills.

An example of how this occurs is when children play the role of the teacher in pretend play. To do this, they must adopt another perspective and practice the rules that operate in the classroom. They are also internalizing the words that help them control their own outbursts, such as when they imperiously tell a "pupil" to take turns and sit down. When children acting as teacher scold the "pupils," they are mastering their own reactions to when they were last scolded. Make-believe play is rule based, and children work at following the rules. They also use play as a way to work though their own emotions, as demonstrated by one child experiencing trauma (a mother dying of cancer) and another child learning self-control and more adaptive behavior. That little boy fought with other children in school and behaved aggressively at home (Singer & Singer, 2005).

As Priessler (chapter 12) indicated, "Pretend play bridges the gap between real events in the changing world and imagination within one's head" (p. 233). Play seems to serve as a buffer for children who often need to cope with change and digest baffling new experiences. This fact was illustrated in a study on movie viewing. Children exposed to a stressful movie scene were allowed to have a free play period either before or after viewing the film. Both of the groups allowed to play declined on measures of stress and anxiety compared with a group that was not allowed to play (Barnett & Storm, 1981). Even on the first day of preschool, children who played more evidenced less anxiety about their transition (Barnett, 1984).

This message about play holds not only for preschoolers but also for older children. Middle schoolers are suffering from increased pressure and the lack of downtime needed to absorb the events of the day and regroup their emotions. Research by Luthar and Latendresse (2005) suggests that "we need to raise awareness of the potential cost of overscheduled, competitive lifestyles" (p. 52) in that even affluent teenagers show serious problems in anxiety, depression, and substance abuse. No one is immune to the effects of missing relaxed family time. Play and unscheduled downtime are central to our emotional well-being throughout our lives.

THE GOOD OLD DAYS WHEN PLAY WAS VALUED

It was not always the case that play was perceived as outmoded and a waste of time for young children. Many theorists wrote about the utility of play for children's development. Piaget (1951), in particular, viewed play as an adaptive behavior that was instrumental in furthering children's thinking. Engaging in what Piaget called "functional assimilation," children might count sets of small objects over and over again, not because they were told to do so but because they apparently gained pleasure from consolidating and practicing this burgeoning skill (see chapter 8). For Piaget and Vygotsky (see chapters 5 and 6), play was an opportunity for children to learn more about their world, to stretch to accommodate new ideas, and to foster their imaginations.

Despite extensive evidence on the value of play, some began to question its utility when it appeared that Americans were falling behind in education. Zigler and Bishop-Josef (chapter 2) describe how the launching of the Soviet Sputnik in the 1950s can be identified with the time when play began to be repudiated and cognitive skills overemphasized. When Head Start was conceived in 1965, it was seen as a "whole child" program, supporting emotional, cognitive, and physical development, among other areas. It, too, began to tip toward a concentration on cognitive achievement. As Zigler and Bishop-Josef point out, assuming that cognitive skills can be considered in isolation and not intertwined with the physical, social, and emotional systems "is shortsighted, if not futile" (p. 22). What it takes to achieve in school is bound up with a child's emotional and physical status. A hungry child or a child suffering from emotional trauma is unlikely to be able to concentrate on the three R's.

In today's world, the pressure on the educational establishment is intense. Teachers and administrators know that children need to learn playfully and that children learn best in meaningful contexts. Yet, many teachers feel compelled to homogenize and narrow their offerings to be responsive to the testing movement (see chapter 4). Kagan and Lowenstein (2004) put it best when they wrote, "A scan of current literature might easily lead one to believe that the achievement of school readiness through children's play is an oxymoron" (p. 59).

WHAT DO THE DATA TELL US ABOUT THE ROLE OF PLAY IN CHILDREN'S LIVES?

The data are incontrovertible. They have been telling the same story throughout the last 40 years of research. When children are in environments where learning is occurring in a meaningful context, where they have choices, and where they are encouraged to follow their interests, learning takes place best (Hirsh-Pasek & Golinkoff, 2003). Ironically, as Hirsh-Pasek and Golinkoff argued, we have adopted a metaphor of the child as "empty vessel": pour in the facts and the child will passively absorb the material. However, the research tells us exactly the opposite. In preschool, when children are pressured to learn in schools with "academic" as opposed to developmentally appropriate curricula, they report being more anxious and perfectionistic (Rescorla, 1991) than their more playful peers. They are no more ahead in first grade in academic achievement. Such programs also have the effect of reducing children's motivation and making them have lower expectations for their academic abilities, less pride in their achievements, and more dependency on adults (Stipek, Feiler, Daniels, & Milburn, 1995)—regardless of social class. Children who have been schooled to think that there is one right answer and that learning is memorization are also dependent on adults for their learning. They have not learned *how to learn*. Ironically, these are the children we hope will join the creative class in the 21st century and keep the United States at the forefront of ingenuity and innovation.

On the other hand, there is also evidence that children learn what they are taught. Children who experience "direction instruction" (e.g., Bereiter, 1986) with emphasis on drill and practice can learn lessons and even achieve general cognitive gains (Bowman, Donovan, & Burns, 2001). Differences arise in variables that matter for socialization and for instilling a love of learning. Children in the direct instruction programs had higher rates of delinquency, were less willing to help other children, and were more likely to experience emotional problems (p. 139). Hart, Yang, Charlesworth, and Burts (2003) confirmed these findings in a longitudinal study that directly compared children who received direct instruction with those who received developmentally appropriate pedagogical practices. Results showed that through the third grade, children receiving direct instruction experienced more stress than children receiving developmentally appropriate curricula. Furthermore, stress seemed to play a causal role in Hart et al.'s model, as it predicted the appearance of hyperactive and distractible behaviors, as well as greater hostility and aggression. Importantly, these findings emerged regardless of gender, race, and socioeconomic status. Being placed in a direct instruction classroom also hindered boys' achievement, mediated by the stress of being in such a classroom. These children grew more slowly in reading (vocabulary and comprehension) and language expression than did their peers in more developmentally appropriate classrooms.

Findings from the Cost Quality Study add to the power of developmentally appropriate pedagogy based in play over a "back to basics" pedagogy (Peisner-Feinberg et al., 1999). With a large subject base of 812 children from kindergarten to second grade, Howes and Byler (2005) noted that children experiencing developmentally appropriate pedagogy experienced higher levels of academic achievement, scoring higher on receptive language, mathematics, and reading in second grade. Furthermore, these data defied a common assumption about how poor children learn best. There was no evidence that poor children did better in back-to-basics programs (see also Peisner-Feinberg et al., 1999).

In sum, treating children like empty vessels whose heads can be filled with knowledge because we select what they will learn and teach it directly leads to problems in two domains. First, studies show that children in these programs often learn less academically than their peers who are not being taught concepts directly but in a more playful manner. Second, these programs have the unintended social consequences of creating students who are less likely to experience empathy with their peers, more likely to show evidence of stress-induced hyperactivity, and more likely to engage in delinquent acts.

CONCLUSIONS

What can we do to stem the tide of well-meaning parents who cart their children to endless adult-structured activities in the belief that they are enabling their children to achieve their fullest potential? What can we do to encourage debate on the learning strategies that really promote children's learning? We can call attention to the fact that *play = learning*. This prologue reviews just the tip of the iceberg of research on the importance of play to diverse areas of children's development. The data that speak to the value of play are presented in the chapters that follow. The evidence is compelling: play promotes learning, and guided play is a powerful teaching tool. It is imperative that we not only attend to this message but also take seriously Kagan and Lowenstein's (2004) call to action: "The challenge ahead is not to blithely romanticize or to falsely criticize play; it is to discern the purposes for and the conditions under which play is an optimally useful pedagogical strategy, fully realizing the heterogeneous effects on children's development and their school readiness" (p. 59). It is in this spirit that this book presents the next generation of findings about play across the spectrum of development.

References

Alvarez, L. (2005, April 9). Educators flocking to Finland, land of literate children. *New York Times,* p. A4.

Anderson, C. A., Berkowitz, L., Donnerstein, E., Huesmann, L. R., Johnson, J. D., Linz, D., et al. (2003). The influence of media violence on youth. *Psychological Science in the Public Interest, 4*(3).

Barnett, L. A. (1984). Research note: Young children's resolution of distress through play. *Journal of Child Psychology and Psychiatry, 25*, 477–483.

Barnett, L. A., & Storm, B. (1981). Play, pleasure, and pain: The reduction of anxiety through play. *Leisure Sciences, 4*, 161–175.

Bereiter, C. (1986). Does direct instruction cause delinquency? *Early Childhood Research Quarterly, 1*, 289–292.

Bowman, B. T., Donovan, S., & Burns, S. (2001). *Eager to learn: Educating our preschoolers*. Report of the National Research Council, Committee on Early Childhood Pedagogy, Commission on Behavioral and Social Sciences Education. Washington, DC: Academic Press.

Florida, R. (2002). *The rise of the creative class: And how it's transforming work, leisure, community and everyday life*. New York: Basic Books.

Friedman, T. L. (2005). *The world is flat: A brief history of the twenty-first century*. New York: Farrar, Straus and Giroux.

Gilliam, W. (2005). Prekindergarteners left behind: Expulsion rates in state prekindergarten systems. New Haven, CT: Yale Child Study Center.

Glick Gryfe, R. (2005). *How to change the conversation: A custom study conducted for Fisher-Price by Yankelovich*. New York: Fisher-Price.

Hart, C., Yang, C., Charlesworth, R., & Burts, D. (2003). *Kindergarten teaching practices: Associations with later child academic and social/emotional adjustment to school*. SRCD Symposium presentation, Tampa, FL.

Hartmann, W. (2002, August). *Toy culture in preschool education and children's toy preferences in Viennese kindergartens (Austria) and in German-speaking kindergartens in South Tyrol (Italy)*. Paper presented in the Symposium on Toy Culture in Preschool Education and Children's Toy Preferences: Common Features and Differences in Europe and Across the World, World Congress. London.

Hirsh-Pasek, K., & Golinkoff, R. M. (2003). *Einstein never used flash cards: How our children really learn and why they need to play more and memorize less*. Emmaus, PA: Rodale.

Howes, C. (1992). *The collaborative construction of pretend: Social pretend play functions*. Albany: State University of New York Press.

Howes, C., & Byler, P. (2005). *Pedagogy from child care to second grade: Influences of developmentally appropriate practices*. Manuscript in preparation.

Howes, C., & Matheson, C. (1992). Sequences in the development of competent play with peers: Social and social pretend play. *Developmental Psychology, 28*, 961–974.

Kagan, S., & Lowenstein, A. (2004). School readiness and children's play: Contemporary oxymoron or compatible option? In E. Zigler, D. G. Singer, & S. Bishop-Josef (Eds.), *Children's play: The roots of reading* (pp. 59–76). Washington, DC: Zero to Three Press.

Kronholz, J. (2005, July 12). Preschoolers' prep—Courses help kids get ready for kindergarten, which is like first grade used to be. *Wall Street Journal*, pp. B1, B4.

LEGO Learning Institute. (2002). *Time for playful learning: A cross-cultural study of parental values and attitudes towards children's time for play*. Billund, Denmark: LEGO Learning Institute. Retrieved from http://www.legolearning.net.

L'Engle, M. (1962). *A wrinkle in time*. New York: Dell.

Louv, R. (2005). *Last child in the woods: Saving our children from nature deficit disorder*. Chapel Hill, NC: Algonquin.

Luthar, S. S., & Latendresse, S. J. (2005). Children of the affluent: Challenges to well-being. *Current Directions in Psychological Science, 14*, 49–53.

Mayo Clinic. (2005, April 19). *Childhood obesity: What parents can do*. Retrieved November 14, 2005, from http://www.mayoclinic.com/health/childhood-obesity/FL00058

Peisner-Feinberg, E. S., Burchinal, M. R., Clifford, R. M., Culkin, M. L., Howes, C., Kagan, S. L., et al. (1999). *The children of the cost, quality, and outcomes study go to school: Executive summary*. Chapel Hill, NC: University of North Carolina, Frank Porter Graham Child Development Center.

Piaget, J. (1951). *Play, dreams, and imitation in childhood.* New York: Norton. (Original work published 1936.)

Pink, D. H. (2005). *A whole new mind: Moving from the information age to the conceptual age.* New York: Penguin.

Raver, C. (2002). *Emotions matter: Making the case for the role of young children's emotional development for early school readiness* (No. XVI). Ann Arbor, MI: Society for Research in Child Development.

Ready, Steady, Learn. (2005). Dublin, Ireland: National Children's Office.

Rescorla, L. (1991). Early academics: Introduction to the debate. In L. Rescorla, M. Hyson, & K. Hirsh-Pasek (Eds.), *Early academics: Challenge or pressure?* (pp. 5–13). San Francisco: Jossey-Bass.

Rideout, V. J., Vandewater, E. A., & Wartella, E. A. (2003). *Zero to six: Electronic media in the lives of infants, toddlers and preschoolers.* Menlo Park, CA: The Kaiser Family Foundation.

Schwartz, J. (2005, June 14). She's studying, he's playing. *The New York Times*, p. Fl.

Scott, E., & Panksepp, J. (2003). Rough-and-tumble play in human children. *Aggressive Behavior, 29*, 539–551.

Singer, D., & Singer, J. L. (2005). *Imagination and play in the electronic age.* Cambridge, MA: Harvard University Press.

Singer, D. G., & Singer, J. L. (1990). *The house of make-believe: Children's play and the developing imagination.* Cambridge, MA: Harvard University Press.

Smithers, R. (2003, March 4). Silence of the little lambs: Talking skills in decline. *The Guardian,* p. 3.

Stipek, D. J., Feiler, R., Daniels, D., & Milburn, S. (1995). Effects of different instructional approaches on young children's achievement and motivation. *Child Development, 66*, 209–223.

Vygotsky, L. S. (1978). *Mind in society: The development of higher mental processes* (M. Cole, V. John-Steiner, S. Scribner, & E. Souberman, Eds. and trans.). Cambridge, MA: Harvard University Press. (Original work published 1930–1935.)

Zigler, E., Singer, D. G., & Bishop-Josef, S. (Eds.). (2004). *Children's play: The roots of reading.* Washington, DC: Zero to Three Press.

PART I

Challenges to Play

2

The Cognitive Child Versus the Whole Child: Lessons From 40 Years of Head Start

EDWARD F. ZIGLER AND SANDRA J. BISHOP-JOSEF

Children's play has come under renewed attack. Some have argued that in the current policy environment, play has become a "four-letter word" (Hirsh-Pasek & Golinkoff, 2003, p. 8). Many preschools and elementary schools have reduced or even eliminated play from their schedules (Bodrova & Leong, 2003; Brandon, 2002; Johnson, 1998; Murline, 2000; Vail, 2003). In some locations, dress-up areas and blocks are being removed from preschool classrooms, and recess periods in elementary schools are being shortened or omitted (Steinhauer, 2005; Vail, 2003). In Atlanta, an elementary school was built—without a playground (Axtman, 2004). In response to a bill before the Connecticut legislature, opponents argued that mandating a daily 20-minute recess to help prevent obesity would "cut into needed time for academics" (Hladky, 2005, p. A4). In sum, Bodrova and Leong (2003) described the current situation as "the disappearance of play from early childhood classrooms" (p. 12).

Play is being replaced by lessons focused on cognitive development, particularly literacy and reading, to match the content of standardized testing (Brandon, 2002; Fromberg, 1990; Johnson, 1998; Steinhauer, 2005; Vail, 2003). One expert stated: "We are not allowing normal, creative, interactive play. We are wanting kids to sit down and write their names at 3 and do rote tasks that are extremely boring at a young age" (Adele Brodkin, quoted in Steinhauer, 2005, p. 4). Brodkin argued that these inappropriate expectations are likely to be responsible for the recent trend of young children being expelled from preschool. The lessons addressing cognitive development often involve "children sitting at tables engaged in whole-class activities" (Whitehurst, 2001, p. 16), instead of activities such as making Play-Doh gifts, with the teacher engaging the children in conversations about their work (contrasting example of "child-centered approach" provided by Whitehurst, 2001, p. 9). Alphabet drills and "quiet desk work" are also increasingly used (Steinhauer, 2005). Some teachers have argued, "The instruction techniques that early childhood education experts say are ideal for learning frequently are derided as 'just play' by administrators and policymakers pushing what they consider to be more academically oriented curricula" (Brandon, 2002, p. 1).

The policy change away from play and toward cognitive development resulted partially from findings showing the poor academic achievement of many American children, in comparison with students from other nations (Elkind, 2001). The change also reflects an attempt to eliminate the well-documented achievement gap between children from low socioeconomic backgrounds and minority families and those from higher income, nonminority backgrounds (Raver & Zigler, 2004).

The George W. Bush administration has done much to fuel the current attack on play. The president has spoken often about reforming education, including preschool education, by focusing on cognitive development, literacy, and "numeracy." Mrs. Bush, a former librarian, hosted a White House Summit on Early Childhood Cognitive Development—not child development or even the whole of cognitive development. The focus was on literacy, one cognitive skill out of many related to school success. In the 2001 reauthorization, the Elementary and Secondary Education Act (Pub. L. No. 89–10), first passed in 1965, was renamed "The No Child Left Behind Act" (Pub. L. No. 107–110). The new law added the president's initiative that all children be able to read by third grade (Bush, 2003). The reading mandate and accompanying testing resulted in further emphasis on literacy training in the early elementary grades.

Parents of young children are also increasingly demanding preschool content that they view as "academic" rather than play (Vail, 2003). For example, one preschool director commented about parents: "They agree in theory that play is important, but they say, 'Could you just throw in the worksheets, so I can see what they are learning?'" (Vail, 2003). Another noted: "All parents want now are worksheets, and they want them in their babies' hands as early as possible" (Bodrova & Leong, 2003, p. 12). A recent article in the National Association for the Education of Young Children's (NAEYC) journal provided guidance for teachers who need to defend play-based preschool environments from attacks by individuals, including parents, who question their value (Stegelin, 2005). As parents are the "customers" of early childhood programs, programs are likely to eventually succumb to parental pressure and change curricula to reflect parental preferences, even if these are ill advised, such as devaluing play.

The focus on cognition and literacy also found its way into policies and proposals for Head Start. The Bush administration initially wanted to change Head Start from a comprehensive intervention to a literacy program (Raver & Zigler, 2004; Steinberg, 2002; Strauss, 2003; Zigler, 2003). However, changing the law governing Head Start would have required considerable time. To move the program in the desired direction more quickly, the administration imposed new protocols on how the program should be run (decisions that are within its power). For example, a new national reporting system (NRS) was instituted that requires standardized testing of Head Start preschoolers twice a year to assess their cognitive development (language, preliteracy, and premath skills). The results of the testing will be used to determine whether centers are performing adequately; one fear is that funding decisions will be based on children's test scores. Another fear is that teachers will "teach to the test," focusing only on the narrow range of skills assessed by the NRS. Recent data support the validity of this latter fear: the U.S. Government Accountability Office (GAO, 2005) found that at least 18% of Head Start programs have changed their instruction to correspond to the content of the NRS standardized testing. The GAO stated that this could prove detrimental to children if teachers omit other equally important skills from their curricula and called for studies to examine the impact of the changes.

In addition, as part of his early childhood initiative "Good Start, Grow Smart," President Bush announced a national program to train all Head Start teachers on strategies to promote literacy (U.S. Department of Health and Human Services [DHHS], 2002). In response, DHHS developed the Strategic Teacher Education Program (STEP), which included training on a literacy curriculum developed by the Center for Improving the Readiness of Children for Learning and Education (CIRCLE). Training was held in June 2002 for 3,000 Head Start teachers, and a follow-up training was conducted in November 2002 (Advisory Committee on Head Start Research & Evaluation, 2003). Although the training was supposed to be voluntary, Head Start personnel reported pressure to participate (Strauss, 2002). Some argued that the training essentially establishes a national curriculum, thereby violating the "local control" tradition that was designed to ensure that Head Start is responsive to the needs identified in each local community.

During 2003, Congress began work to reauthorize Head Start. The reauthorization process typically adjusts program details to keep budgets and services current. This time, however, Congress sought to redesign Head Start. A version of a bill later passed in the House (H.R. 2210) removed language in the law relating to what has always been one focus of Head Start, social and emotional development. Most occurrences of these words were replaced with the word *literacy*. This version also stopped assessments of children's social and emotional functioning in ongoing national evaluations of Head Start (Schumacher, Greenberg, & Mezey, 2003). Instead, representatives wanted assessments of whether children meet specified goals on preliteracy and premath tests. The bill also proposed block granting Head Start to as many as eight states (Zigler & Styfco, 2004). For 40 years, Head Start has been the only federal program with a funding stream that goes directly from the federal government to local grantees. Local grantees receive the federal funds, not the state, thereby avoiding state control of Head Start. The proposed legislation changed this funding pattern to allow up to eight states to receive block grants for Head Start, rather than providing the federal funding directly to local grantees. The assessment and block grant goals prevailed in the bill that eventually passed the House (by one vote), although the obliteration of language pertaining to social and emotional competence and evaluations did not.

The Senate also introduced a Head Start bill, the Head Start Improvements for School Readiness Act (S. 1940). This bill did not call for drastic changes like those in the House bill (Schumacher & Greenberg, 2004). However, the Senate bill included a detailed list of items that all Head Start children must learn. Congress was unable to pass a bill reauthorizing Head Start during the 108th session, so efforts began anew in the 109th Congress. Based on the experience of the 108th session, it is likely in the upcoming reauthorization that Head Start's defining whole child approach (encompassing physical health and social and emotional development, as well as cognitive development) will again be pitted against an exclusive focus on cognitive development (literacy and math). The resolution of this controversy will influence the use of play (which some inaccurately view as relevant only to social and emotional development) as a learning mechanism in Head Start.

Many experts have criticized the proposed changes to Head Start policy that overemphasize cognitive development and standardized testing, arguing that they are inappropriate (Raver & Zigler, 2004; Steinberg, 2002; Stipek, 2004; Strauss, 2003). David Elkind (2001), in a piece reminiscent of Piaget's constructivist views entitled "Young Einsteins: Much Too Early," argued that young children learn best through direct interaction with their environment. Before a certain age, they simply are not capable of the level of reasoning necessary for formal instruction in reading and mathematics. Elkind believed this fact of development explained why the pioneers of early childhood education developed hands-on models of learning. Elkind's article was accompanied by a counterpoint by Whitehurst (2001) titled "Young Einsteins: Much Too Late." Whitehurst, who was subsequently appointed director of the Institute of Education Sciences at the U.S. Department of Education by President Bush, claimed that "content-centered" approaches (i.e., academically oriented) are more likely to facilitate children's literacy learning. Raver and Zigler (2004) disagreed, criticizing the emphasis on cognitive development and standardized testing as being far too narrow and unsupported by scientific evidence on how children learn. They advocated continued attention to, and assessment of, children's social and emotional development, viewing this domain as synergistic with intellectual development. With regard to the Elkind–Whitehurst debate, the authors of this chapter agree with Stipek (2004) that quality preschool education requires pursuing both hands-on, play-based learning and direct instruction of academic skills simultaneously. Kagan and Lowenstein (2004), in a comprehensive review of the literature on school readiness and play, reached the same conclusion. Without taking sides on whether emotion or cognition should be primary, more than 300 scholars signed a letter protesting the plan to carry out standardized testing in Head Start and questioning the validity of the proposed assessments (Raver & Zigler, 2004; see also Meisels & Atkins-Burnett, 2004.). The concerns of these scholars were borne out by the recent GAO study (2005) that severely criticized the NRS. The GAO found that the reliability and validity of the NRS have not been established and argued, therefore, that "results from the first year of the NRS are of limited value for accountability purposes." Critics have also questioned the wisdom of Congress "micro-managing" Head Start, which has always been a program run at the local level and tailored to meet the needs of children and families in each particular locality.

A HISTORICAL PERSPECTIVE

Similar repudiation of play and overemphasis on cognitive skills have occurred since the 1950s. We have presented this history in detail elsewhere (Zigler & Bishop-Josef, 2004), so we will provide only a brief discussion here.

American attitudes toward education were seriously affected by the Soviet Union's launch of Sputnik in 1957 (Zigler, 1984). The Soviets' beating the United States into space was traumatic for Americans, and many perceived the Soviet feat as evidence that the more rigorous Soviet education system was more effective than ours. A return to the three R's was touted as the way to build American superiority in the global arena. This emphasis on cognitive development had nothing to do with new knowledge about child development or education. Rather, it was a result of overreaction to a historical event. Admiral Hyman G. Rickover, a key spokesperson, made the provocative assertion that young children in the Soviet Union were being trained in mathematics while American children were busy finger painting. Thus, the battle line was clearly drawn between "academic" pursuits and play.

By the 1960s, the emphasis on cognition was accompanied by an "environmental mystique" (Zigler, 1970). This view held that minimal environmental interventions could yield dramatic increases in children's cognitive functioning. The environmental formulation was propagated through the popular press and bookstores filled with titles such as *Give Your Child a Superior Mind* (Engelmann & Engelmann, 1966). Another guiding principle of this environmental approach was that intervention programs are most effective if they are administered during a critical period—the earlier the better (Bloom, 1964). This questionable argument fueled the infatuation with cognitive development and compelled parents and educators to feverishly teach children as much as possible, as early as possible. Play, previously considered the work of children, became suspect. Instead, drill and exposure to educational gadgetry were seen as the activities worthy of children's time and attention.

Even Head Start fell victim to the excessive focus on cognitive skills and naive environmentalism (Zigler, 1970). From its inception in 1965, Head Start has been a comprehensive, whole child program, with components to support physical and mental health, nutrition, social and emotional development, early education and cognitive development, social services for children's families, and community and parental involvement (Zigler & Styfco, 2001). The founders of Head Start believed that preparing children who live in poverty for school requires meeting all of their needs, not just focusing on their academic skills. As will be discussed later, play has a prominent place in Head Start curricula. However, when researchers began to evaluate early intervention programs, they were drawn to assessments of cognitive functioning, particularly IQ test scores (Zigler & Trickett, 1978). The researchers ignored the rich, comprehensive nature of the Head Start intervention and focused on one narrow outcome. Part of the reason was the zeitgeist of the time.

Evaluators also became enthralled with the results: relatively minor interventions—even 6 to 8 weeks of Head Start—seemed to produce large increases in children's IQs. These gains were soon found to be caused by improvements in motivation rather than cognitive functioning (Zigler & Butterfield, 1968). Yet findings such as these did not (and still do not) deter the use of IQ as a primary measure of Head Start's effectiveness (Raver & Zigler, 1991; Zigler & Trickett, 1978). This practice is understandable in that measures of IQ were readily available, easy to administer and score, and deemed reliable and valid, whereas measures of socioemotional constructs were and still are less well developed. Also, IQ was a construct that policy makers and the public could easily understand, and it was known to be related to many other behaviors, particularly school performance.

Soon, researchers lost faith in IQ as a measure of Head Start's success (Raver & Zigler, 1991), when the 1969 Westinghouse Report (Westinghouse Learning Corporation and Ohio University, 1969) found that Head Start children failed to sustain their IQ advantage once they moved to elementary school. This report nearly proved fatal to Head Start, because some concluded that this failure to sustain IQ gains meant that Head Start was ineffective. However, investigators began to understand that Head Start children's rapid IQ gains could be explained by motivational factors (e.g., less fear of the test and tester), rather than by true improvement in cognitive ability (Zigler & Trickett, 1978). Experts also pointed out the numerous difficulties and biases in using IQ to evaluate comprehensive intervention programs (e.g., Zigler & Trickett, 1978).

In the early 1970s, the Office of Child Development (OCD; now the Administration on Children, Youth, and Families, ACYF) articulated everyday social competence as the overriding goal of Head Start and encouraged broader evaluations to measure more accurately the program's effectiveness (Raver & Zigler, 1991). However, no accepted definition was available of social competence, much less established measures. Therefore, OCD funded the Measures Project in 1977, a multisite study to develop a battery of measures of the factors making up social competence, including but not limited to appropriate cognitive measures. Zigler and Trickett (1978) also suggested approaches to assessing social competence that included measures of motivational and emotional variables, physical health and well-being, achievement, and formal cognitive ability.

Thus, by the late 1970s to early 1980s, the naive cognitive-environmental view had largely been rejected, and a renewed appreciation of the whole child and the value of play was becoming evident. Books by David Elkind, *The Hurried Child* (1981) and *Miseducation: Preschoolers at Risk* (1987), argued that children were being pushed too hard, too early, especially with respect to intellectual tasks. Children were being rushed through childhood, Elkind stated, with little time allowed for being a child and experiencing age-appropriate activities, including play. He saw the consequences of this pressure as severe, ranging from stress to behavior problems and even to suicide. Elkind's books were very popular and important in moving both professionals and the general public toward a view that social and emotional development is a valuable part of child development that strongly affects intellectual growth. There was also a renewed appreciation for the value of play. The "risks" associated with academic activities in preschool can be overstated, however. The pendulum had certainly swung too far when many Head Start teachers refused to even put letters of the alphabet on the walls of Head Start classrooms. Like Stipek (2004), we are seeking a middle ground where all the current views are mined for value and incorporated into a combined approach to children's preschool education.

During the 1980s, however, the pendulum had already started to swing back in the opposite direction. In 1982, the Reagan administration cut most of the funding for the Measures Project, supporting only the site that was developing measures of cognitive functioning. During the Reagan and George H. W. Bush years, the Head Start administration was again focusing almost exclusively on cognitive measures to assess the program's effectiveness (Raver & Zigler, 1991). Further, the cognitive measurement system that emanated from the Measures Project (Head Start Measures Battery) was accompanied by a curriculum, which led to concerns about "teaching to the test" and worries that play would be devalued.

The tide began to shift yet again during the next decade (Zigler, 1994). For example, in 1995, the National Educational Goals Panel, a semigovernmental group of federal and state policy makers, officially defined school readiness as having five dimensions: (a) physical well-being and motor development, (b) social and emotional development, (c) approaches to learning, (d) language development, and (e) cognition and general knowledge (Kagan, Moore, & Bredekamp, 1995). This definition emphasized that these factors are inextricably linked and must be considered in their totality as indicators of school readiness. The 1998 reauthorization of Head Start explicitly stated that the goal of the program is "school readiness," similarly defining *readiness* in terms of physical and mental health, social and emotional development, parental involvement, and preacademic skills (Raver & Zigler, 2004). Finally, a sensible middle ground seemed to have been reached, a consensus that learning is fostered by more than cognitive training. However, the tide turned again shortly thereafter, culminating in the recent attack on play and the prescribed focus on academics described early in this chapter. Once again, the emphasis on cognition was accompanied by a simplistic environmentalism, as when new mothers were given Mozart CDs in the hospital, with the prescription to play them for their infants to increase their intelligence (Jones & Zigler, 2002).

This brief historical narrative demonstrates that the current disenchantment with play is a step backward in our nation's history. It is also a clear illustration of the swinging pendulum that is often evident in American education, where prevailing political winds allow one extreme view to quickly rise to ascendancy, only to be replaced by another view. Clearly, what is needed is a balanced approach that is based on knowledge derived from the best child development research and sound educational practice.

THE WHOLE CHILD APPROACH

Proponents of the whole child approach do not deny the importance of cognitive skills, including literacy. President George W. Bush's initiative to ensure that every American child will be a proficient reader is laudable. However, reading is only one aspect of cognitive development, and cognitive development is only one aspect of human development. Cognitive skills are very important, but they are so intertwined with the physical, social, and emotional systems that it is shortsighted, if not futile, to dwell on the intellect and exclude its partners.

Consider what goes into literacy. It involves mastery of the alphabet, phonemes, and other basic word skills, for certain. But a prerequisite to achieving literacy is good physical health. The child who is frequently absent from school because of illness or who has vision or hearing problems will have difficulty learning to read, as will children who suffer emotional problems such as depression or posttraumatic stress disorder. By the same token, a child who begins kindergarten knowing letters and sounds may be cognitively prepared, but if he or she does not understand how to listen, share, take turns, and get along with teachers and classmates, this lack of socialization will hinder further learning (Raver, 2002). To succeed in reading and at school, a child must receive appropriate education, of course, but he or she must also be physically and mentally healthy, have reasonable social skills, and have curiosity, confidence, and motivation to succeed. This broader view was endorsed in the authoritative book *From Neurons to Neighborhoods* (Shonkoff & Phillips, 2000), in which the finest child development thinkers in the nation pointed out the importance of emotional and motivational factors in human development and learning.

The position that social and emotional factors are essential for cognitive development, including literacy, is not new. The founders of Head Start recognized the importance of these factors 40 years ago, when they designed the program in 1965. Since that time, a body of research has demonstrated the importance of emotional and social factors for school readiness (Raver, 2002; Shonkoff & Phillips, 2000). For example, emotional self-regulation has been found to be an especially important component of learning (Raver & Zigler, 1991). Children must be able to focus their attention on the task at hand, filtering out distractions. They must be able to control their emotions when in the classroom, during both individual and group activities. They must be able to organize their behavior and listen to the teacher. All of these are essentially noncognitive factors that foster learning. Further, this type of emotional self-regulation can be developed through play when children take turns, regulate one another's behavior, and learn to cooperate (Bredekamp, 2004).

Play also provides opportunities for acquiring many cognitive skills. Although play is often thought of in terms of "free play," dictated by the child, play can also be educationally focused, directed by the teacher or parent to reach specific educational goals. Through both forms of play, children can learn vocabulary, language skills, concepts, problem solving, perspective taking, representational skills, memory, and creativity (e.g., Davidson, 1998; Newman, 1990; Russ, Robins, & Christiano, 1999; Singer, Singer, Plaskon, & Schweder, 2003). Play has also been found to contribute to early literacy development (Christie, 1998; Owocki, 1999).

In addition, play has been shown to contribute to social development, including social skills such as turn taking, collaboration and following rules, empathy, self-regulation, self-confidence, impulse control, and motivation (e.g., Corsaro,

1988; Klugman & Smilansky, 1990; Krafft & Berk, 1998). These factors have an impact on cognitive development and are just as important in learning to read as the ability to recognize letters or sounds.

THEORY REGARDING CHILDREN'S PLAY AND DEVELOPMENT

The current attack on play contradicts sound developmental theory. The two preeminent theorists of cognitive development of the 20th century, Jean Piaget and Lev Vygotsky, both stressed the essential role of play for cognitive development.

Jean Piaget (1896–1980) was a Swiss psychologist who studied cognitive development for more than 50 years, beginning in the 1920s (Zigler & Finn-Stevenson, 1993). Piaget developed his theory of cognitive development after conducting extensive observations of his own children, including their play. He argued that children actively acquire knowledge through interacting with the physical environment. In particular, cognitive development occurs through the complementary processes of assimilation and accommodation. In assimilation, the child interprets the environment in terms of his or her present way of thinking. For example, a child using a box as if it were a car is assimilating the box to his or her mental concept of a car. Accommodation, in contrast, consists of the child changing and expanding on what he or she already knows. When the child encounters something in the environment that he or she does not understand, the child has to expand, through accommodation, his or her view of the world and thereby restore equilibrium. Play, according to Piaget (1932), provides the child with a multitude of opportunities to interact with materials in the environment and construct his or her own knowledge about the world. Thus, play is one of the primary contexts in which cognitive development occurs.

Lev Vygotsky (1896–1934) was a Russian psychologist and theorist of cognitive development (see chapter 5) and a contemporary of Piaget. Vygotsky emphasized sociocultural influences on development, particularly how interactions with people—parents, teachers, and peers—foster cognitive development. He argued that development occurs within the "zone of proximal development," when tasks that are difficult for children to learn alone can be mastered if a child is guided by someone who is skilled at the task. The zone of proximal development has a lower limit (what the child can do alone) and an upper limit (what the child is capable of with guidance). In interacting with more skilled partners, the child can be taught the upper limit of the zone. Vygotsky (1978a, 1978b) claimed that play serves as the primary context for cognitive development: "Play is the source of development and creates the zone of proximal development" (1978a, p. 138). In play, the child interacts with others (more skilled peers, teachers, and parents) and can learn from them. Further, Vygotsky argued, when children use objects to represent other objects in play (e.g., using a block as a telephone), they inadvertently set the stage for abstract thought. Play allows children to understand that an object (telephone) can be represented by another object (block), separating the actual physical object from its meaning. Children can then take the step to thinking in the absence of any object. Once the child has developed representational abilities through play, he or she is able to use these abilities to develop reading and writing (where sounds are represented by symbols). In addition, following the rules inherent in all play leads children to develop self-regulation, which is essential for success in the structured environment of the school classroom.

PRACTICE CONCERNING CHILDREN'S PLAY AND DEVELOPMENT

Recognizing the vital importance of play for children's development, experts have designed curricula that use play to enhance cognitive development, as well as teach preliteracy and literacy skills (e.g., Bodrova & Leong, 2001, 2003; Bruce, 2001; Gronlund, 2001; Owocki, 1999; Sawyers & Rogers, 1988; Singer et al., 2003). For example, Bodrova and Leong's (2001, 2003) "Tools of the Mind" preschool and kindergarten classrooms, based on Vygotsky's theory of cognitive development and the work of his student Elkonin, use sociodramatic play to foster literacy. These classrooms contain dramatic play areas where children spend a substantial amount of time daily, and dramatic play permeates many classroom activities. Teachers support children's play by helping them create imaginary situations, providing props, and expanding possible play roles. Children, with the teacher's assistance, develop written play plans, including the theme, the roles, and the rules that will govern the play. Preliminary evaluations of the Tools of the Mind curriculum support its effectiveness (Bodrova & Leong, 2001; Bodrova, Leong, Norford, & Paynter, 2003). In one study, children who spent 50 to 60 minutes of a 2½-hour program engaging in supported sociodramatic play scored higher on literacy skills than did children in control classrooms (Bodrova & Leong, 2001). Thus, play, rather than detracting from academic learning, actually supported it.

Other experts have also developed play-based curricula and provided evidence of their beneficial effects on cognitive development. For example, Learninggames (Sparling & Lewis, 2003) offers caregivers (and parents) activities to enhance child development, including cognitive development, from birth to age 5. The Learninggames curriculum was developed in the Carolina Abecedarian Project, which provided an early education program to poor children from infancy through age 5. Longitudinal results indicated that children in the project had higher scores on tests of cognitive ability from preschool to age 21 and higher reading and math achievement from elementary school to age 21, completed more years of education, and were more likely to attend college than children in the control group (Campbell, Ramey, Pungello, Sparling, & Miller-Johnson, 2002).

The Singers' Learning Through Play/Circle of Make-Believe project (Singer & Singer, 2004) uses videotapes and a manual to train parents and caregivers of low-income children to play pretend games involving school readiness concepts with the children. Results from several studies indicated that children who engaged in the pretend games with their parents and caregivers had school readiness scores superior to those of a comparison group.

CHILDREN'S PLAY IN THE CONTEXT OF HEAD START

Performance Standards

As discussed previously, from its very inception, Head Start has embodied a focus on the whole child, with components addressing physical health, nutrition, social and emotional development, education, services for children's families, and community and parental involvement. Included in this comprehensive approach is recognition of the importance of play for child development. Several of the Head Start performance standards for education and early childhood development (USDHHS, 1998; 45 CFR, 1304.21) include a focus on play.

Performance standard 1304.21 (a) (4) describes the various means by which Head Start programs must "provide for the development of each child's cognitive and language skills" (USDHHS, 1998, p. 68). This standard identifies play as one of the primary strategies for promoting children's cognitive and language skills and requires that Head Start programs support "each child's learning, using various strategies, including experimentation, inquiry, observation, play and exploration" (1304.21 (a) (4) (i); USDHHS, 1998, p. 68). With regard to literacy and numeracy, in particular, this standard requires that programs support "emerging literacy and numeracy development through materials and activities according to the developmental level of each child" (1304.21 (a) (4) (iv); USDHHS, 1998, p. 70). The guidance section for this standard lists ways adults can support the development of literacy and numeracy, including "games, dramatic play, fingerplays, puzzles, blocks" (p. 71). The standard also mentions play as a means of promoting the development of language skills and urges adults in Head Start to encourage "dramatic play in which children act out familiar activities, such as going to the grocery store or the library, and using the telephone" (1304.21 (a) (4) (iii); USDHHS, 1998, p. 70). Thus the performance standard regarding cognitive and language development includes several explicit references to how play can be used to support this development.

Play is also mentioned in the Head Start performance standard concerning physical development (1304.21 (a) (5); USDHSS, 1998). This standard requires Head Start programs to "promote each child's physical development by providing sufficient time, indoor and outdoor space, equipment, materials and adult guidance for active play and movement that support the development of gross motor skills" (p. 71). The standard further states: "A child's gross motor development is important to overall health. As such, that development is important to the achievement of cognitive skills" (p. 71), again linking play and cognitive development.

Curricula

The curricula used in Head Start also demonstrate an understanding of the value of play and its essential role in children's learning. The Head Start performance standards require that programs implement a curriculum (1304.3(a) (5); USDHHS, 1998). *Curriculum* is defined as a written plan that includes:

1. The goals for children's development and learning
2. The experiences through which they will achieve these goals
3. What staff and parents do to help children achieve these goals
4. The materials needed to support the implementation of the curriculum

Any curriculum used in Head Start must meet these definitional criteria. The curriculum also must provide for "the development of cognitive skills by encouraging each child to organize his or her experiences, to understand concepts, and to develop age appropriate literacy, numeracy, reasoning, problem solving and decision making skills which form a foundation for school readiness and later school success" (1304.21 (c) (1) (ii); USDHHS, 1998, p. 79). The guidance for this standard lists various ways adults in Head Start can support children's cognitive development, including "supporting play as a way for children to organize their experiences and understand concepts" (p. 79). Thus, when discussing the Head Start curriculum, the performance standards again include a focus on play.

The Head Start performance standards do not prescribe any particular curriculum. Programs are free to write their own curriculum, use a locally developed curriculum, or purchase a published curriculum. A GAO study (U.S. General Accounting Office, 2003) found that most Head Start programs were compliant in implementing a curriculum. Further, the majority (58%) of Head Start programs used one of two published curricula: either the Creative Curriculum (36%) or the High Scope curriculum (22%).

Creative Curriculum

The Creative Curriculum for Preschool (Dodge, Colker, & Heroman, 2002) focuses on children's active learning through play and stresses the importance of social and emotional development for learning. Each classroom has 11 interest areas: blocks, dramatic play, toys and games, art, library, discovery, sand and water, music and movement, cooking, computers, and outdoors. The curriculum has six content areas (literacy, mathematics, science, social studies, the arts, and technology), and learning in each of these content areas occurs in each of the interest areas. For example, literacy activities are infused throughout each of the 11 interest areas, rather than just in the library area or during book reading activities (Heroman & Jones, 2004). Teachers label toy boxes with drawings of the toys they contain, as well as with the words naming the toys. The cooking area has picture-and-word instructions for activities like washing hands. The daily schedule is posted with both pictures and words outlining the day's activities.

Several of the interest areas include a focus on play (Dodge et al., 2002). For example, the dramatic play area encourages children to engage in imaginative play. This play can be used to promote cognitive development, including literacy and numeracy. For example, vocabulary development is enhanced when the teacher introduces props for the play scenarios and teaches children the props' names (e.g., stethoscope and tongue depressor for playing "doctor's office"). Prewriting skills can be developed through using writing tools and paper of various kinds (e.g., prescription pads). Premath skills can also be developed in the dramatic play area (e.g., providing a height chart and scale for the doctor's office). Play is incorporated into the outdoor interest area and used in the service of cognitive development. For example, to promote preliteracy skills, teachers can ask children to explore outdoors and record on clipboards what plants they observe. Later, in the classroom, children can use resource books to find pictures of what they discovered outside. They can also make charts and graphs to organize their observations, which promotes premath skills.

The Creative Curriculum is based on research in child development and children's learning. Preliminary research has also supported the curriculum's effectiveness. One study evaluated the use of the curriculum in the Department of Defense's Sure Start preschool program (Abbott-Shim, 2000). Examining 10 randomly selected classrooms, researchers found that children made significant gains on receptive vocabulary, language production, print awareness, and mathematical problem solving over the course of 1 year of participation in the Sure Start preschool. However, this study did not have a comparison group. Several randomized controlled studies of the Creative Curriculum are also currently in progress through the U.S. Department of Education's preschool curriculum evaluation research grants program ("Research Studies on the Effectiveness of the Creative Curriculum," 2002), so more rigorous evidence of the curriculum's effectiveness is forthcoming.

High Scope Curriculum

The High Scope curriculum (Hohmann & Weikart, 1995) encourages children to pursue their own interests and takes advantage of children's natural desire to communicate what is meaningful to them to others. It is based on Piaget's theory of cognitive development, particularly his central idea that children actively acquire knowledge through interacting with the physical environment, which includes play. The curriculum includes 58 key experiences for children, grouped into 10 categories: creative representation, language and literacy, initiative and social relations, movement, music, classification, seriation, number, space, and time. Like the Creative Curriculum, the High Scope classroom is divided into various interest areas, including blocks, house, toy, book, sand and water, and outdoors. Also similar to Creative Curriculum, literacy and numeracy learning occurs in all of the interest areas. The High Scope curriculum stresses the need for a daily routine, including a "plan-do-review" sequence. Children plan what activities they want to engage in, engage in these activities during "work" times (or, more accurately, "play" times), and end by recalling and reflecting on what they have done. In each of these phases, there are opportunities for gaining preliteracy skills. For example, children can describe their plans to the teacher or make a drawing of their plans. During the work time, children locate toys by going to bins labeled with both a picture of the toys and their names. In reviewing the activity, children are required to use words to describe what they have done.

The High Scope curriculum was developed in the early 1960s for the High Scope Perry Preschool Project, one of the most studied preschool intervention programs. Therefore, there is considerable longitudinal evidence available on the curriculum's effectiveness. Low-income 3- and 4-year-olds (N = 123) were randomly assigned to the Perry Preschool Project or a no-preschool comparison group. Researchers have followed the children over time, assessing them every year from ages 3 to 11, and then at ages 14, 15, 19, 27, and 40. The most recent study at age 40 found that Perry Preschool attendees were more likely to have graduated from high school and have a job, had higher earnings, and had committed fewer crimes than the comparison group (Schweinhart, 2004). Preschool attendees performed better on intellectual and language tests during early childhood, on school achievement tests between age 9 and 14, and on literacy tests at age 19 and 27. A cost-benefit analysis determined that the project returned $17 for every dollar invested. Schweinhart and colleagues determined that the program cost $15,166 per participant and had an economic return to society of $258,888. The savings to society came in the form of reduced costs for crime, special education, and welfare, as well as increased tax revenue from participants' increased wages.

Marcon (1999) also found evidence for the value of child-initiated curricula and play for later school outcomes. Her study evaluated three approaches to preschool education: child initiated, academically focused, and a combination. She found that although children who had been in more academically focused preschools were less likely to be held back, by fourth grade they had significantly lower grades than children who had experienced more child-initiated preschool models.

Impact of Head Start on School Readiness and Educational Success

The question of whether Head Start affects children's school readiness and educational success has been a matter of long-standing debate. This debate may have been fueled, in part, by the fact that Head Start focuses on the whole child, its performance standards demonstrate an appreciation for the key role of play in children's learning, and programs typically employ curricula with a strong emphasis on play. Head Start is not a place where children are given rote memorization tasks or taught to some external test of narrow cognitive ability (although the recent adoption of the NRS has raised concerns about teaching to the test). Rather, children learn through active engagement with people and materials in the very rich classroom environment, including substantial time in both free and structured play (Dodge et al., 2002; Hohmann & Weikart, 1995; Zigler & Styfco, 2001).

Barnett (2004) conducted a critical review of the extensive body of research examining Head Start and other preschool programs' effects on children's cognitive development. He concluded: "The weight of the evidence indicates that a wide range of preschool programs including Head Start can increase IQ scores during the early childhood years, improve achievement, and prevent grade retention and special education" (p. 242). Barnett cited many methodological shortcomings in studies to date, however, and called for better research designs in future studies.

One such better designed study has demonstrated positive effects of Head Start on children's literacy development. This study, using random assignment to Head Start versus a comparison group, found that Head Start children developed preliteracy skills significantly faster than children in the comparison group (Abbott-Shim, Lambert, & McCarty, 2003). For both receptive vocabulary (the Peabody

Picture Vocabulary Test) and phonemic awareness (Early Phonemic Awareness Profile), the comparison group showed only normal maturation from pretest to posttest, whereas Head Start children had rates of growth that were significantly faster than the comparison group.

The FACES study (Head Start Family and Child Experiences Survey; Administration for Children & Families, Office of Planning, Research & Evaluation [ACF OPRE], 1997, 2003) also offers evidence of Head Start's effects on school readiness. FACES provides information on outcomes for nationally representative samples of children served by Head Start. There have been three waves of the FACES study, in 1997, 2000, and 2003. Results to date indicate that children show substantial gains on measures of school readiness, particularly vocabulary and early writing skills, over the course of participating in 1 year of Head Start. These children continue to show gains in vocabulary, early writing skills, and early math skills in kindergarten. Further, the gains that children made in Head Start predicted their achievement in kindergarten (ACF OPRE, 2003).

More definitive data on the question of Head Start's effects on school readiness will be forthcoming in the near future. The 1998 reauthorization of Head Start mandated a rigorous national study to examine the impact of the program. In 2000, the Department of Health and Human Services awarded a contract for the study, and data collection began in 2002 (ACF OPRE, 2000). The study includes randomized assignment to Head Start or a control group and follows a nationally representative sample of 5,000 children from ages 3 and 4 through the end of first grade. The study's final report is due in December 2006.

At this point, however, there is already converging evidence that Head Start, although it is designed to provide comprehensive services to meet the needs of the whole child and includes a focus on play in its performance standards and curricula, has significant impact on children's cognitive development and school readiness, including important preliteracy skills. The available data do not allow us to determine if play, per se, is linked to school readiness outcomes among Head Start children. Head Start is a comprehensive program, and studies have not examined the impact of its individual components, including play. But because Head Start curricula embody a strong emphasis on play, it is not unreasonable to assume that play accounts, at least in part, for the positive school readiness outcomes found.

CONCLUSION

Four decades of research and practice offer unequivocal evidence for the critical importance of play for children's development. Play has been found to contribute to development in the domains of social, emotional, and cognitive development, including language, numeracy, and literacy. Play is children's work (Zigler, 1987). Thus, the current attack on play defies the evidence and is misguided.

In response to the renewed focus on cognitive skills, many organizations have advocated for the important role of play in children's development. For example, the NAEYC, the leading organization of early childhood educators, developed a position statement on "principles of child development and learning that inform developmentally appropriate practice." The statement includes the item "Play is an important vehicle for children's social, emotional, and cognitive development, as well as a reflection of their development" (NAEYC, 1996). Articles in NAEYC's professional journal also promote the benefits of play (e.g., Stone, 1995). In addition, several organizations have been founded to advocate for the importance of play. These include Playing for Keeps (http://www.playingforkeeps.org), Alliance for Childhood (http://www.allianceforchildhood.net), American Association for the Child's Right to Play (http://www.ipausa.org), and Play Matters (http://www.playmatters.net), founded by Docia Zavitkovsky, a former president of NAEYC.

Defending play should not be necessary, just as mustering support for cognitive training should not be required. Research demonstrates the two-way relationship between the two, which leads back to the position advocated in this chapter and, in fact, back to the time before any formal study of child development: To foster learning, parents, teachers, and policy makers must focus on the whole child. An important point to emphasize is that those who espouse the whole child approach view *all* systems of development (including cognitive development) as synergistic and, in that regard, as the proper focus of child rearing and education. In contrast, those who believe that the cognitive system merits the most attention are essentially rejecting the needs of the rest of the child. By ignoring the contributions of the physical and psychological systems to learning, they promote an educational system designed to fail. To be fair, their extreme view that only cognitive skills are important may be simply a backlash reaction to extreme views that only socioemotional health is important. Both extremes are unfounded and likely to be detrimental to optimal child learning and development.

There is reason to hope that the tide will again turn and an appreciation for the value of play will be reborn. We are optimistic that the rigorous randomized control trials currently in the field (the Department of Education's Preschool Curriculum Evaluation studies and the Head Start national impact study) will provide strong evidence for the value of both play-focused curricula and Head Start for children's school readiness and school success. There is also a beginning backlash to attacks on play in the policy arena: legislators in Virginia and Michigan have recently passed laws mandating daily recess periods, and other states have similar legislation pending (Axtman, 2004). A new article in the *Archives of Pediatric and Adolescent Medicine*, published by the American Medical Association, focused on "resurrecting free play in young children" by arguing that beyond its benefits for physical health, play enhances child well-being, including attention, affiliation, and affect (Burdette & Whitaker, 2005). We add our voices to these in advocating for a renewed focus on the whole child, including an appreciation for the essential role of play, in both education and parental child rearing.

References

Abbott-Shim, M. (2000). *Summary of the Sure Start program evaluation.* Retrieved February 28, 2005, from http://www.teachingstrategies.com/pages/document.cfm?pagedocid=86

Abbott-Shim, M., Lambert, R., & McCarty, F. (2003). A comparison of school readiness outcomes for children randomly assigned to a Head Start program and the program's wait list. *Journal of Education for Students Placed at Risk, 8*, 191–214.

Administration for Children & Families, Office of Planning, Research & Evaluation. (1997). *Head Start Family and Child Experiences Survey (FACES), 1997–2008.* Retrieved February 26, 2005, from http://www.acf.hhs.gov/programs/opre/hs/faces/index.html

Administration for Children & Families, Office of Planning, Research & Evaluation. (2000). *Head Start Impact Study 2000–2006.* Retrieved February 26, 2005, from http://www.acf.hhs.gov/programs/opre/hs/impact_study/index.html

Administration for Children & Families, Office of Planning, Research & Evaluation. (2003, April). *Head Start FACES 2000: A whole-child perspective on program performance. Executive summary.* Retrieved February 26, 2005, from http://www.acf.hhs.gov/programs/opre/hs/faces/reports/executive_summary/exe_sum.html

Advisory Committee on Head Start Research & Evaluation. (2003). An overview of Head Start literacy, mentor-coaching, and Strategic Teacher Education Program (STEP). Retrieved May 25, 2005, from http://www.acf.hhs.gov/programs/hsb/research/hsreac/jun2003/jun03_step_overview.htm

Axtman, L. (2004, November 16). Recess backlash: Parents say it pays to play. *Christian Science Monitor*, p. 3.

Barnett, W. S. (2004). Does Head Start have lasting cognitive effects? In E. Zigler & S. Styfco (Eds.), *The Head Start debates* (pp. 221–249). Baltimore: Paul H. Brookes.

Bloom, B. S. (1964). *Stability and change in human characteristics.* New York: Wiley.

Bodrova, E., & Leong, D. J. (2001). *Tools of the mind: A case study implementing the Vygotskian approach in American early childhood and primary classrooms.* Geneva, Switzerland: International Bureau of Education.

Bodrova, E., & Leong, D. J. (2003). Chopsticks and counting chips: Do play and foundational skills need to compete for the teacher's attention in an early childhood classroom? *Young Children, 58,* 10–17.

Bodrova, E., Leong, D. J., Norford, J. S., & Paynter, D. E. (2003). It only looks like child's play. *Journal of Staff Development, 24,* 47–51.

Brandon, K. (2002, October 20). Kindergarten less playful as pressure to achieve grows. *Chicago Tribune*, p. 1.

Bredekamp, S. (2004). Play and school readiness. In E. F. Zigler, D. G. Singer, & S. J. Bishop-Josef (Eds.), *Children's play: The roots of reading* (pp. 159–174). Washington, DC: Zero to Three Press.

Bruce, T. (2001). *Learning through play: Babies, toddlers, and the foundation years.* London: Hodder & Stoughton.

Burdette, H. L., & Whitaker, R. C. (2005). Resurrecting free play in young children Looking beyond fitness and fatness to attention, affiliation, and affect. *Archives of Pediatric and Adolescent Medicine, 159*, 46–50.

Bush, G. W. (2003, January 8). *Remarks by the president on the first anniversary of the No Child Left Behind Act.* Retrieved September 10, 2003, from http://www.whitehouse.gov/news/releases/2003/01/20030108–4.html

Campbell, F. A., Ramey, C. T., Pungello, E. P., Sparling, J., & Miller-Johnson, S. (2002). Early childhood education: Young adult outcomes from the Abecedarian Project. *Applied Developmental Science, 6*, 42–57.

Christie, J. F. (1998). Play as a medium for literacy development. In E. P. Frombreg & D. Bergen (Eds.), *Play from birth to twelve and beyond: Contexts, perspectives, and meaning* (pp. 50–55). New York: Garland.

Corsaro, W. A. (1988). Peer culture in the preschool. *Theory into Practice, 27*, 19–24.

Davidson, J. I. F. (1998). Language and play: Natural partners. In E. P. Fromberg & D. Bergen (Eds.), *Play from birth to twelve and beyond: Contexts, perspectives, and meaning* (pp. 175–183). New York: Garland.

Dodge, D. T., Colker, L., & Heroman, C. (2002). *The creative curriculum for preschool* (4th ed.). Washington, DC: Teaching Strategies.

Elementary and Secondary Education Act of 1965, Pub. L. No. 89–10, 64 Stat 1100 20 USC 6301.

Elkind, D. (1981). *The hurried child: Growing up too fast, too soon.* Reading, MA: Addison-Wesley.

Elkind, D. (1987). *Miseducation: Preschoolers at risk.* New York: Knopf.

Elkind, D. (2001). Young Einsteins: Much too early. *Education Matters, 1*(2), 9–15.

Engelmann, S., & Engelmann, T. (1966). *Give your child a superior mind.* Riverside, NJ: Simon & Schuster.

Fromberg, D. P. (1990). An agenda for research on play in early childhood education. In E. Klugman & S. Smilanksy (Eds.), *Children's play and learning: Perspectives and policy implications* (pp. 235–249). New York: Teacher's College Press.

Gronlund, G. (2001). Rigorous academics in preschool and kindergarten? Yes! Let me tell you how. *Young Children, 56*, 42–43.

Heroman, C., & Jones, C. (2004). Literacy: The Creative Curriculum approach. Washington, DC: Teaching Strategies, Inc.

Hirsh-Pasek, K., & Golinkoff, R. M. (2003). *Einstein never used flashcards: How our children really learn and why they need to play more and memorize less.* Emmaus, PA: Rodale.

Hladky, G. B. (2005, May 19). House OKs bill to ban junk food sales. *New Haven Register*, pp. 1, A4.

Hohmann, M., & Weikart, D. P. (1995). *Educating young children: Active learning practices for preschool and child care programs* (2nd ed.). Ypsilanti, MI: High/Scope.

Johnson, D. (1998, April 7). Many schools putting an end to child's play. *New York Times*, pp. A1, A16.

Jones, S. M., & Zigler, E. (2002). The Mozart effect: Not learning from history. *Journal of Applied Developmental Psychology, 23*, 355–372.

Kagan, S. L., & Lowenstein, A. E. (2004). School readiness and children's play: Contemporary oxymoron or compatible option? In E. F. Zigler, D. G. Singer, & S. J. Bishop-Josef (Eds.), *Children's play: The roots of reading* (pp. 59–76). Washington, DC: Zero to Three Press.

Kagan, S. L., Moore, E., & Bredekamp, S. (Eds.). (1995). *Reconsidering children's early development and learning: Toward common views and vocabulary* (GPO 1995-396-664). National Education Goals Panel, Goal 1 Technical Planning Group. Washington, DC: U.S. Government Printing Office.

Klugman, E., & Smilansky, S. (1990). *Children's play and learning: Perspectives and policy implications.* New York: Teachers College Press.

Krafft, K. C., & Berk, L. E. (1998). Private speech in two preschools: Significance of open-ended activities and make-believe play for verbal self-regulation. *Early Childhood Research Quarterly, 13*, 637–658.

Marcon, R. (1999). Differential impact of preschool models on development and early learning of inner-city children: A three cohort study. *Developmental Psychology, 35*, 358–375.

Meisels, S. J., & Atkins-Burnett, S. (2004). Public policy viewpoint. The Head Start national reporting system: A critique. *Young Children, 59*, 64–66.

Murline, A. (2000, May). What's your favorite class? Most kids would say recess. Yet many schools are cutting back on unstructured schoolyard play. *U.S. News and World Report, 128*(17), 50–52.

National Association for the Education of Young Children (NAEYC). (1996). *Position statement: Principles of child development and learning that inform developmentally appropriate practice*. Retrieved January 4, 2006, from http://www.naeyc.org/about/positions/dap3.asp

Newman, L. S. (1990). Intentional and unintentional memory in young children: Remembering vs. playing. *Journal of Experimental Child Psychology, 50*, 243–258.

No Child Left Behind Act of 2001, Pub. L. No. 107–110, 115 Stat 1535, 20 USC 6361, Part B, Subpart 1, Sec. 1201.

Owocki, G. (1999). *Literacy through play*. Portsmouth, NH: Heinemann.

Piaget, J. (1932). *Play, dreams, and imitation*. New York: Norton.

Raver, C. C. (2002). Emotions matter: Making the case for the role of young children's emotional development for early school readiness. *Social Policy Report, 16*(3).

Raver, C. C., & Zigler, E. F. (1991). Three steps forward, two steps back: Head Start and the measurement of social competence. *Young Children, 46*, 3–8.

Raver, C. C., & Zigler, E. F. (2004). Public policy viewpoint. Another step back? Assessing readiness in Head Start. *Young Children, 59*, 58–63.

Research studies on the effectiveness of the creative curriculum. (2002). Retrieved February 26, 2005, from http://www.teachingstrategies.com/pages/page.cfm?pageid=188

Russ, S. W., Robins, A. L., & Christiano, B. A. (1999). Pretend play: Longitudinal prediction of creativity and affect in fantasy in children. *Creativity Research Journal, 12*, 129–139.

Sawyers, J. K., & Rogers, C. S. (1988). *Helping young children develop through play: A practical guide for parents, caregivers, and teachers*. Washington, DC: National Association for the Education of Young Children.

Schumacher, R., & Greenberg, M. (2004, January 23). *Head Start reauthorization: A section-by-section analysis of the Senate HELP Committee bill (S. 1940)*. Washington, DC: Center for Law and Social Policy.

Schumacher, R., Greenberg, M., & Mezey, J. (2003, June 2). *Head Start reauthorization: A preliminary analysis of H.R. 2210, the "School Readiness Act of 2003."* Washington, DC: Center for Law and Social Policy.

Schweinhart, L. J. (2004). *The High Scope Perry Preschool study through age 40: Summary, conclusions, and frequently asked questions*. Retrieved February 27, 2005, from http://www.highscope.org/Research/PerryProject/PerryAge40SumWeb.pdf

Shonkoff, J. P., & Phillips, D. A. (Eds.). (2000). *From neurons to neighborhoods: The science of early childhood development*. Washington, DC: National Academy Press.

Singer, D. G., & Singer, J. L. (2004). Encouraging school readiness through guided pretend games. In E. F. Zigler, D. G. Singer, & S. J. Bishop-Josef (Eds.), *Children's play: The roots of reading* (pp. 175–187). Washington, DC: Zero to Three Press.

Singer, D. G., Singer, J. L. Plaskon, S. L., & Schweder, A. E. (2003). A role for play in the preschool curriculum. In S. Olfman (Ed.), *All work and no play: How educational reforms are harming our preschoolers* (pp. 59–101). Westport, CT: Greenwood.

Sparling, J., & Lewis, I. (2003). *Learninggames, the Abecedarian curriculum 36 to 48 months*. Chapel Hill, NC: MindNurture.

Stegelin, D. A. (2005). Making the case for play policy: Research-based reasons to support play-based environments. *Young Children, 60*, 76–85

Steinberg, J. (2002, December 4). For Head Start children, taking a turn at testing. *New York Times*, p. B10.

Steinhauer, J. (2005, May 22). Maybe preschool is the problem. *New York Times*, section 4, pp. 1, 4.

Stipek, D. (2004, May 5). Commentary. Head Start: Can't we have our cake and eat it too? *Education Week, 23*(34), 43, 52.

Stone, S. J. (1995). Wanted: Advocates for play in the primary grades. *Young Children, 50*, 45–54.

Strauss, V. (2002, November 16). Head Start teachers resist new training; sessions on literacy pushed by Bush. *Washington Post*, p. A3.

Strauss, V. (2003, January 17). U.S. to review Head Start program: Bush plan to assess 4-year-olds' progress stirs criticism. *Washington Post*, p. A1.

U.S. Department of Health and Human Services. (1998). *Head Start program performance standards and other regulations.* Title 45 of the Code of Federal Regulations, Parts 1301–1308. Washington, DC: Author.

U.S. Department of Health and Human Services. (2002). *HHS fact sheet. Head Start: Promoting early childhood development.* Retrieved May 25, 2005, from http://fatherhood.hhs.gov/factsheets/fact20020426b.htm

U.S. General Accounting Office. (2003). *Head Start curriculum use and individual child assessment in cognitive and language development* (GAO-03–1049). Washington, DC: Author.

U.S. Government Accountability Office. (2005, May). *Head Start further development could allow results of new test to be used for decision making*. GAO-05–343. Retrieved May 23, 2005, from http://www.gao.gov/new.items/d05343.pdf

Vail, K. (2003, November). Ready to learn. What the Head Start debate about early academics means for your schools. *American School Board Journal, 190*. Retrieved May 25, 2005, from http://www.asbj.com/2003/11/1103coverstory.html

Vygotsky, L. (1978a). Play and its role in the mental development of the child. In J. K. Gardner (Ed.), *Readings in developmental psychology* (pp. 130–139). Boston: Little Brown.

Vygotsky, L. (1978b). The role of play in development. In *Mind in society.* Cambridge, MA: Harvard University Press.

Westinghouse Learning Corporation and Ohio University. (1969). The impact of Head Start: An evaluation of the effects of Head Start on children's cognitive and affective development. Vols. 1 and 2. Report to the Office of Economic Opportunity. Athens, OH: Author.

Whitehurst, G. J. (2001). Young Einsteins: Much too late. *Education Matters, 1*(2), 9, 16–19.

Zigler, E. (1970). The environmental mystique: Training the intellect versus development of the child. *Childhood Education, 46*, 402–412.

Zigler, E. (1984). Foreword. In B. Biber, *Education and psychological development* (pp. ix–xi). New Haven, CT: Yale University Press.

Zigler, E. (1987). Formal schooling for four-year-olds? No. *American Psychologist, 42*, 254–260.

Zigler, E. F. (1994). Foreword. In M. Hyson, *The emotional development of young children: Building an emotion-centered curriculum* (pp. ix–x). New York: Teachers College Press.

Zigler, E. F. (2003). Foreword. In M. Hyson, *The emotional development of young children: Building an emotion-centered curriculum* (2nd ed., pp. x–xi). New York: Teachers College Press.

Zigler, E. F., & Bishop-Josef, S. J. (2004). Play under siege: A historical overview. In

E. F. Zigler, D. G. Singer, & S. J. Bishop-Josef (Eds.), *Children's play: The roots of reading* (pp. 1–13). Washington, DC: Zero to Three Press.

Zigler, E., & Butterfield, E. C. (1968). Motivational aspects of changes in IQ test performance of culturally deprived nursery school children. *Child Development, 39*, 1–14.

Zigler, E. F., & Finn-Stevenson, M. (1993). *Children in a changing world: Development and social issues.* Pacific Grove, CA: Brooks/Cole.

Zigler, E. F., Singer, D. G., & Bishop-Josef, S. J. (Eds.).(2004). *Children's play: The roots of reading*. Washington, DC: Zero to Three Press.

Zigler, E., & Styfco, S. J. (2001). More than the three Rs: The Head Start approach to school readiness. *Education Matters, 1*(2), 12.

Zigler, E., & Styfco, S. J. (2004). Moving Head Start to the states: One experiment too many. *Applied Developmental Science, 8*, 51–55.

Zigler, E., & Trickett, P. (1978). IQ, social competence, and evaluation of early childhood intervention programs. *American Psychologist, 33*, 789–798.

3

The Role of Recess in Primary School

ANTHONY D. PELLEGRINI AND ROBYN M. HOLMES

There can be little doubt that there has been increased emphasis on accountability in both preschool and primary school education over the past 20 years. Opinions regarding the value of this position, however, are certainly diverse. Advocates of the accountability movement rightfully suggest that scarce tax dollars should be spent only on programs that "work." Politicians as different as former President Bill Clinton and President George W. Bush have supported variants of this view.

One of the specific, though less noticed, impacts of accountability has been that children's opportunities for free time (in the form of recess) and corresponding opportunities to interact with their peers have been eliminated or diminished in many school systems across this country, Canada, and the United Kingdom ("No Time for Play," 2001; Pellegrini, 2005). The movement to minimize recess in schools may be popular because politicians and school superintendents see this as a way in which to "get tough on education," provide more "academic time" for students, and improve academic performance. Indeed, it may seem commonsensical to many that reducing recess time has a positive effect on achievement. After all, more time spent in academics should directly translate into improved performance (Brophy & Good, 1974). This view was advanced by the former superintendent of schools in Atlanta, Benjamin Canada, even though there was no empirical or theoretical evidence for the claim ("No Time for Play," 2001).

On the other hand, although many educators and parents recognize the centrality of teaching skills and maximizing the efficient use of relatively scarce classroom time, they also see the necessity of breaks between periods of intense work, when children can both relax and interact with peers, with the hope that they will return to their classrooms after their breaks and work with renewed interest.

There can be common ground between the prorecess and antirecess positions. Many, including us, feel that there is a need for accountability. Our best theory and empirical evidence should be used to guide practice. To do otherwise is to squander the trust and resources of children, families, taxpayers, and educators. Indeed, far too many of the educational policies being recommended for primary school are a form of "folklore," as they have no scientific basis. Yet, what many don't realize is that recess *is* educational. In this chapter, we present both theory and empirical data to support the argument that what goes on during the recess period is "educational" in the traditional sense.

Recess is defined here as an unstructured break time between periods of relatively rigorous academic time. Further, recess can take place either indoors or outdoors and should involve children's free choice of activities and playmates, with minimal adult direction; the role of adults should be to supervise children's safety. For example, adult supervision should prevent children from bullying their peers and using unsafe behaviors on play apparatus, such as standing on a seesaw; only very minimally should adults structure children's play and games. From this view, recess is more characteristic of primary schools than of preschools, which often have "play" as part of the curriculum.

COGNITIVE PERFORMANCE IN SCHOOL

An important goal of primary grades schooling, unlike many preschools and nurseries, is teaching children skills and strategies associated with literacy, mathematics, and science—typically measured by some form of standardized achievement test. *Cognitive performance* is used in this chapter as an umbrella term to cover those skills and strategies associated with school-based learning. The effects of recess breaks on primary school children's satisfaction with school and standardized test performance, as well as more direct measures of cognitive performance—attention to classroom tasks—are assessed. Direct measures of attention to class work, of course, relate to more general cognitive measures, such as achievement test performance: students must attend to their work in order to learn it. As we know from years of research, dating back to the 19th century (e.g., Ebinghaus, 1885/1964; James, 1901), distributing work over a long period of time with breaks interjected, rather than massing it into one period, maximizes attention and more general cognitive performance across the life span.

For young children, a specific form of break from cognitively demanding tasks may be especially effective in maximizing cognitive performance, as suggested by David Bjorklund's cognitive immaturity hypothesis. This position holds that *playful* break times and corresponding peer interaction may be especially important in maximizing performance for primary school children to the extent that such breaks reduce the cognitive interference acquired in earlier instruction (Bjorklund & Green, 1992; Bjorklund & Harnishfeger, 1987; Bjorklund & Pellegrini, 2000). The playful nature of breaks is predicated on the assumption that children's thought processes are different from adults'.

Traditional views of children's cognitive processing (e.g., Piaget, 1983) suggest that young children's cognition is an imperfect version of more mature adult processes. For example, young children's tendencies to make unrealistic estimates of their own capabilities by overestimating their own cognitive (Yussen & Levy, 1975) and social status (Smith & Boulton, 1990) have been framed as a limitation—something to be overcome. The cognitive immaturity hypothesis suggests that these processes are not inferior variants of adult behavior but instead specific adaptations to the niche of childhood that enable young children to effectively learn skills and behaviors (Bjorklund & Pellegrini, 2000). For example, children's overestimation of their own cognitive and social skills enables them to persevere at a task even though, by adult standards, they are not doing it very well. This perseverance may lead to self-perceived success, which may, in turn, lead to higher self-perceived competence and help with learning complicated skills and strategies (Bandura, 1997).

With specific reference to the role of recess, this position holds that *playful*, not structured, breaks may be especially important in maximizing performance because unstructured breaks may reduce the cognitive interference associated with the immediately preceding instruction (e.g., Bjorklund & Harnishfeger, 1987). The immaturity of children's nervous systems and their lack of experiences render them unable to perform higher level cognitive tasks with the same efficiency as older children and adults, and directly influence their educability. From this logic, it follows that young children are especially susceptible to the effects of cognitive interference after sustained periods of structured work (see Dempster, 1992). Breaks during periods of sustained cognitive work should reduce cognitive interference and maximize learning and achievement gains (Toppino, Kasserman, & Mracek, 1991). Further, opportunities for peer interaction during playful breaks not only enable children's feeling of potency and competence but also help children learn and develop the important social skills necessary for successful peer relations both in and out of school.

THE ROLE OF PEER INTERACTION AT RECESS IN PREDICTING FIRST-GRADE ACHIEVEMENT

Playful break times as a recess break provide an interesting venue not only for children to learn and develop social skills but also for assessing young children's cognitive performance. Specifically, unstructured peer interaction is a cognitively and socially very demanding context that is simultaneously very motivating for children. This combination of high cognitive demands and high motivation should lead to children exhibiting higher levels of competence in recess activities than in traditional achievement tests, which are not as motivating (Messick, 1983). Consider the social cognitive demands associated with sustained peer interaction. Children must take others' perspectives, communicate effectively, and follow negotiated rules (Pellegrini, 1982). That children enjoy doing these things means that they are motivated to do the necessary social cognitive work to accomplish such high-level tasks.

Recess as a Demanding and Motivating Context

Children's interactions with peers during playful interaction, relative to interactions with adults, are cognitively and socially more demanding. A number of studies have demonstrated that, when given free choice in a play environment, children who choose to interact with peers rather than adults are more sophisticated on a number of social cognitive dimensions (e.g., Harper & Huie, 1985; Pellegrini, 1984; Wright, 1980). For example, in a university preschool sample, we found that when adults were in children's immediate groups, children's play and oral language production was less sophisticated than when the groups were comprised of children alone (Pellegrini, 1984, 1985). Children's use of oral language with their peers, relative to language used with adults, was more explicit (e.g., pronouns are defined) and more narrative-like (e.g., use of temporal and causal conjunctions such as *and then* and *because*). Children's use of this sort of "literate language" reliably predicts performance on tests of early literacy (Pellegrini & Galda, 1993). Further, children's fantasy more frequently involved their taking a greater variety of roles, including those, such as pretending to be the teacher, where they used language to direct their playmates—a form of language not likely to be observed when teachers are part of the group!

Consistent with Piagetian (1983) theory, the disequilibration characteristic of peer interaction facilitates social and cognitive development. *Disequilibration* is defined as conceptual conflict between what children know and what they encounter. When faced with conceptual conflict, children try to resolve it, and this resolution results in conceptual development. For example, a boy and girl in kindergarten are playing with a doctor's kit. The girl says, " I'll be the doctor and you be sick." That girls can be doctors may conflict with the boy's concept of doctors; this encounter broadens the boy's concept of doctor and what females can do. When individuals disagree, they are confronted with points of view other than their own. For the interaction to continue, they must incorporate (or *accommodate*, to use Piaget's term) the other person's points of view. In short, engaging in sustained social interaction with peers requires a fair amount of social (e.g., cooperation, perspective taking) and cognitive (e.g., ability to communicate clearly) skill.

In comparison, when a child is interacting with an adult, the adult often takes over some of this difficult work, especially if the child is having problems (Vygotsky, 1978). Further, children do not tend to question adults because they are typically socialized not to question or challenge grown-ups. In short, conceptual disagreement, or disequilibration, is more common in peer interaction than in adult–child interaction, which is typically unilateral.

Playful breaks at recess should be a particularly good place to study the ways in which children's social cognitive development is facilitated in playful, peer-interaction contexts. As noted previously, young children are typically motivated to exhibit high levels of competence there because they enjoy interacting with their peers. Consequently, observations in such a highly motivating context should maximize children's exhibition of social and cognitive competence of the sorts noted earlier (Pellegrini, 1984; Waters & Sroufe, 1983; Wright, 1980).

By implication, placing children in such a highly motivating situation is very important from an assessment perspective. It may be that the often-described difference between children's competence as measured in standardized testing situations and their competence as measured in playful situations is due to different levels of motivation to exhibit competence in each situation (Vygotsky, 1978).

Recess Behavior in Kindergarten Predicting First-Grade Achievement

Longitudinal analyses also demonstrate relations between kindergarten children's social behavior at recess on the school playground and measures of first-grade achievement. Kindergarten recess behaviors as a predictor of first-grade achievement is especially important to consider because this is often the transition into full-day schooling and also a period in children's development when social interaction and play may be especially important. More specifically, Pellegrini (1992) examined the relation between kindergarten children's behavior at recess and their performance on a standardized achievement test in first grade. The intent of this research was to show that standardized achievement and aptitude measures alone have limited explanatory and predictive power, especially for young children.

Zigler and Trickett (1978; see also chapter 2) made this point a generation ago in service of a similar cause, namely, to argue against overreliance on standardized measures of cognition, such as IQ tests, in favor of measures of social competence to assess the impact of early intervention programs like Project Head Start. Again, the basis of this argument is that children's optimum performance is not elicited in standardized tests. Instead, peer interaction on the playground at recess may be a more valid assessment context because it is both highly motivating and very demanding. Like Zigler and Trickett's work, the analyses presented here should help to guide legislators and departments of education in their views on teaching and assessing young children.

The results from a 2-year longitudinal study conducted in a public school in Athens, Georgia, support the role of peer interaction at recess in children's achievement (Pellegrini, 1992). This research was motivated in reaction to a law in the state of Georgia (where Pellegrini was living at the time) requiring kindergarten children to pass a standardized achievement test to be promoted to first grade. The school population where the research was carried out was a wide variety of children ranging socioeconomically from very poor to very affluent. Children were observed across 2 years on the school playground during their recess periods. Information on their standardized, academic achievement test performance was available. In this prospective longitudinal study, the Metropolitan Readiness Test (MRT; Nurss & McGauvran, 1976) was used to assess the kindergarten children's general knowledge and achievement in early reading and math concepts. The measure of academic achievement for first graders was the Georgia Criterion-Referenced Test (GCRT), also a test of general knowledge and achievement in early literacy and numeracy concepts.

The results demonstrated that children's recess behavior as kindergarteners was a significant predictor of their first-grade academic achievement, as measured by

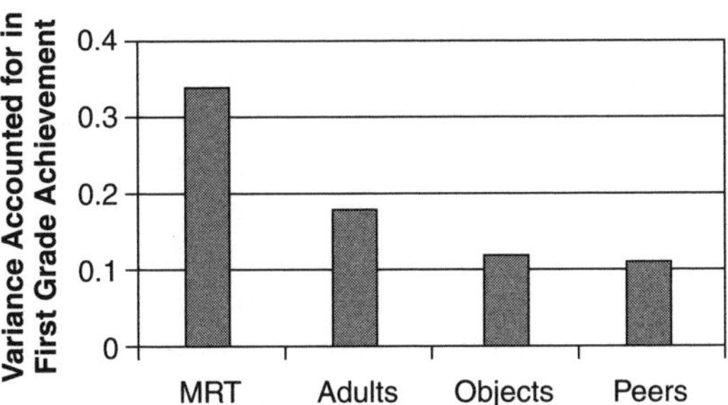

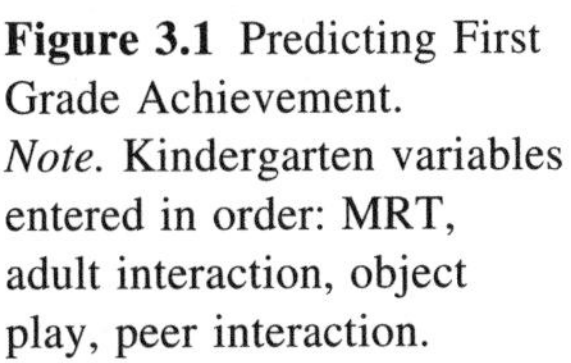
Figure 3.1 Predicting First Grade Achievement.
Note. Kindergarten variables entered in order: MRT, adult interaction, object play, peer interaction.

the GCRT, even after statistically controlling their kindergarten achievement. The measures of recess behavior used were rather gross measures—peer interaction and adult-directed behavior. The peer interactions coded were all forms of cooperative behavior, including play, games, and conversation. Similarly, adult-directed behavior (that is, behavior initiated by a child with an adult) included any overtures to adults by children and positive adult–child interaction. A bar graph, displayed in figure 3.1, represents the variance accounted for in this model. The variables entered, in order, were MRT as a statistical control for kindergarten achievement, adult interaction (which was a *negative* predictor of first-grade achievement), object play, and peer interaction.

In Step 1, the MRT control variable was entered first in predicting first-grade achievement, and it accounted for .34 of the variance in first-grade achievement. Then adult-directed behavior on the playground in kindergarten was entered and it accounted for another, unique .18 of the variance in first-grade achievement, but the relation was negative, not positive. Object play and then peer interaction on the playground in kindergarten each accounted for another and unique .12 and .11, respectively, of the variance in first-grade achievement.

Importantly, peer interaction was positively related to achievement, whereas adult-directed behavior was negatively related to achievement. That is, children who interacted more with peers at recess tended to score higher on the GCRT than children who interacted less with their peers. In fact, children who were involved in high levels of adult-directed behavior at recess tended to score *lower* on these achievement tests than children who interacted less with adults.

These results suggest a number of interesting mechanisms that might have driven the recess advantage. For example, children who chose to interact with adults at recess, rather than with peers, may have lacked the social skills necessary to play with the other children. Evidence from the social competence literature demonstrates that when young children choose to interact with teachers rather than peers in play-oriented contexts, teachers do most of the work in maintaining interaction (Harper & Huie, 1985; Wright, 1980). In comparison, when children interact with peers, they must rely on their own social competence to initiate and sustain interaction. Relatedly, children who choose to interact with adults may be unpopular with their peers. Consequently, they may have been rejected by the peers and by default had only adults with whom to interact. In either case, difficulties in peer relations often forecasts academic difficulties (Coie & Dodge, 1998).

The important point here is that what children do at recess accounts for a statistically significant, and unique, portion of the variation (40%) beyond what standardized tests tell us. These findings support the arguments made by Zigler and Trickett (1978; see also chapter 2) that standardized measures of children's cognition have limited predictive value. Substantially more variance in first-grade achievement is accounted for when children's behavior in a naturalistic and motivating environment is considered. This speaks against the current practice of using one measure (as in the case of No Child Left Behind) to make inferences about children's cognitive performance, especially a measure that focuses exclusively on the academic side.

The varying role of adults in children's cognition in different contexts is consistent with extant research. For example, in free-play situations, adults generally inhibit older preschool children's exhibition of complex forms of play, whereas peers facilitate it (e.g., Dickinson & Moreton, 1991; Pellegrini, 1984; Pellegrini & Galda, 1993). However, in a small-group *teaching* context, such as planning an errand or a classification task, adults are much more effective tutors than are peers (Tudge & Rogoff, 1989). In short, adult guidance is useful in some contexts, like skill teaching, and peer interaction is important in other contexts, where social competence is at stake.

PEER INTERACTION AS THE FOURTH R: THE IMPORTANCE OF PEER INTERACTION FOR ADJUSTMENT TO SCHOOL

The second dimension of the argument made here relates more specially to the importance of peer interaction for children's more general adjustment to primary school. As noted earlier, the observations of recess behavior that were made in the previous reported study were rather gross. These measures told us only about the relative value of peer and adult interaction. In what follows, the role of a specific form of peer interaction, namely, children's games with their peers, in predicting school adjustment will be examined.

At the level of theory, the ability to interact cooperatively with peers, inhibit antisocial behaviors, and form close relationships, such as friendships, are all important developmental tasks for children in the primary grades (Hartup, 1996; Waters & Sroufe, 1983; Zigler & Trickett, 1978). Developmental tasks vary with age (e.g., impulse control during the preschool period and peer group membership during the early primary school years; see chapter 5), and the successful mastery of these tasks constitutes "social competence" for that period and provides the foundation for subsequent development. From this view, mastering the skills necessary for membership in one's school peer group and feeling efficacious in this area should provide a basis for subsequent adjustment to school.

Numerous longitudinal studies and field experiments have documented the importance of children's peer relations in their initial adjustment to elementary school (e.g., Ladd, Kochenderfer, & Coleman, 1996; Pellegrini, 1992; Pellegrini, Kato, Blatchford, & Baines, 2002). For example, Ladd and colleagues (Ladd et al., 1996; Ladd, Price, & Hart, 1988) demonstrated that successful transition from preschool to primary school is fostered when children make the transition with a friend. Friends provide social emotional support for each other in the new and sometimes stressful school environment.

One particular type of peer interaction, playing games with rules such as tag, soccer, and jump rope, is especially important for children making the transition to full-day schooling because these games represent a motivating and important developmental task for that age group (Sutton-Smith, 1971). As Piaget (1965) argued, games are a modal form of interaction for primary school children. Correspondingly, the design features of games are representative of a developmental task for that period. For example, following an externally defined a priori rule is important not only in games but also in the larger arena of social exchange. Sutton-Smith (1971) and others (Pellegrini et al., 2002) have documented empirically the importance of certain forms of games (games of challenge and leadership) for children, and especially boys, making the transition to primary school. Pellegrini and colleagues (2002) defined general facility with games in terms of percent of time spent in games on the playground at recess, as well as peer nominations and teacher ratings of children as "leaders" in games. It was found that playground games predicted boys', but not girls', school adjustment.

This finding is consistent with the theoretical assumption that the social rules and roles that children learn in one niche (with their peers at recess) predict competence in a related niche—adjustment to school more generally. The school playground at recess and the classroom setting are similar to the extent that they encourage rule-governed behavior and cooperative interaction with peers.

The lack of relations between girls' outdoor games and school adjustment may be related to the fact that girls, generally, are less keen than boys on playing outdoors (Harper & Sanders, 1975). This relative lack of enthusiasm for the outdoors as a play venue may be because girls find boys' loud and boisterous behavior outdoors unpleasant and thus segregate themselves from boys into more sedentary groups (Maccoby, 1986; Pellegrini, 2005). It would be interesting to see the degree to which girls' games predict school adjustment in an all-girls' school—where boys' crashing bodies do not inhibit their games. Further, girls' facility with indoor games is also worth examining.

The research just cited also showed how facility with outdoor games during the first part of the school year predicted end-of-year social competence and school adjustment, even after controlling for social competence and school adjustment at the beginning of the year (Pellegrini et al., 2002). Social competence in this study was defined following Sroufe and colleagues (Sroufe, Egelund, & Carlson, 1999) at both the group (being liked by peers) and relationship levels (reciprocal friends). That game facility predicted children's school adjustment is a very important finding for educational policy makers. Games probably provide opportunities to learn and practice the skills necessary for effective social interaction with peers in an important socialization context—early schooling. Further, being facile in one dimension of school, albeit playing games at recess, is probably very important for children's more general feelings of efficacy in school. Feelings of efficacy about school may relate to subsequent achievement motivation, for example, attendance and positive classroom participation.

These results reinforce earlier research where children's peer relations in school predicted school success (e.g., Ladd & Price, 1993), but they also extend this earlier work, in that the majority of the students in the current study were low-income children. It is well known that children, and again boys especially, from economically disadvantaged groups have difficulty adjusting to and succeeding in school (e.g., Ackerman, Brown, & Izard, 2004; Heath, 1983). We demonstrated that their success in one part of the first-grade school day (games at recess) can predict more general school adjustment.

THE ROLE OF RECESS IN COGNITIVE PERFORMANCE: PROXIMAL MEASURES

In the preceding section, the positive role of recess in children's achievement test scores was demonstrated. Recess also has a relatively *immediate* impact on children's cognitive performance. Specifically, in this section we illustrate how children's attention to classroom tasks is facilitated by recess breaks. It is probably this increased attention that is responsible, in part at least, for the positive role of recess in achievement.

Attention is a measure that is consistent with theories suggesting that breaks from concentrated schoolwork should maximize performance. Following the notion of massed versus distributed practice (Ebinghaus, 1885/1964; James, 1901), children are less attentive to classroom tasks during longer seatwork periods than during shorter ones (e.g., Stevenson & Lee, 1990). Correspondingly, children are more physically active and socially interactive on the playground after longer confinement periods than after shorter ones (e.g., Smith & Hagan, 1980). These breaks and the behaviors observed during breaks, in turn, have implications for children's classroom behavior after recess (e.g., Hart, 1993), as well as more distal academic and social cognitive development, as was demonstrated in the previous section. In the studies reported next, attention was measured in terms of children's looking at either their work or, when the teacher was reading to them, at the teacher. Additionally, in some studies children's fidgeting and listlessness were also coded as measures of *in*attention while children did their seatwork.

In what follows, the effects of recess timing on children's attention to classroom work were examined. By recess timing, we mean the amount of time *before* recess that children are forced to be sedentary (or are deprived of social and physical play) and attend to class work. This type of regimen typifies most primary school classrooms (Minuchin & Shapiro, 1983). The school in which this research was conducted allowed the researchers to manipulate the times that children went out for recess, as well as what they did in their classrooms before and after recess. Consequently, these experiments enabled researchers to make *causal* inferences about the effects of recess timing on children's attention to classroom tasks.

The children enrolled in this public elementary school were from varied socioeconomic and ethnic backgrounds. In all of the cases, the children in each of the grades were systematically exposed to different schedules for recess timing.

On some days, they went out to recess at 10 a.m. and on other days at 10:30 a.m. Before and after each recess period, children were read an experimentally manipulated male-preferred (with male characters) or a female-preferred (with female characters) book. During this time, we coded their attention to the task. We also observed and coded their recess behavior.

Our orientation in studying the role of recess timing in children's attention suggests that during that period immediately preceding recess, children's inattention to instructional tasks should increase as a function of duration of the deprivation period. Anecdotal evidence from Japan and Taiwan suggests that children's attention to class work is maximized when instructional periods are relatively short, not long, and intense and when there are frequent breaks between these work periods (Stevenson & Lee, 1990). In these countries, as in the People's Republic of China (Kessen, 1975), children are given a break every 50 minutes or so. When children return from breaks, they seem more attentive and ready to work than before the breaks (see also Lewis, 1995).

In the studies reported next, the effects on attention of both indoor and outdoor recess periods are examined. Examining the effects of indoor recess on children's attention would provide insight into the role of a relatively sedentary break period on subsequent attention. Thus, these results should provide further evaluation of the "blowing off steam" hypothesis (Evans & Pellegrini, 1997). If children's attention is greater after than before the indoor break, the role of physical activity per se should be minimal. Further, and from a policy perspective, educators sometimes use indoor recess as an alternative to outdoor breaks perhaps because teachers or playground supervisors are reluctant to go outdoors during inclement weather, or they may be sensitive to the possibility of lawsuits related to injuries on playground equipment. Results from this experiment should provide insight into the efficacy of indoor breaks.

The first study, to our knowledge, to address directly this issue of outdoor recess activity and postrecess attention found that third-grade children's attention before recess was lower than it was after recess, especially for boys, thus suggesting that recess facilitates attention (Pellegrini & Davis, 1993). However, before accepting these findings at face value and assuming that recess *causes* children to be more or less focused in their studies, we needed to consider that at least one alternative explanation for the results is possible. These results may have been due to the fact that attention was related to the gender role stereotypicality of the tasks on which the children worked. Specifically, in the Pellegrini and Davis (1993) study, children's class work often involved listening to a story. Because the researchers did not systematically monitor the stories read, it may have been the case that some of the stories read were more preferred by girls. Thus, their attention may have been related to the task, not the effect of recess. In the next series of experiments, this confound was removed by systematically varying gender preference of tasks before and after recess.

In Experiment 1 of a new series of experiments, the effects of outdoor recess timing on the classroom behavior of boys and girls in grades K, 2, and 4 were examined (Pellegrini, Huberty, & Jones, 1995). As in all experiments in this series, recess timing varied by 30 minutes. Children's attention (assessed by looking at the book being read to them or at the teacher doing the reading) was assessed before and after recess on male-preferred and female-preferred books.

In Experiment 1, the prerecess results supported the suppositions of Stevenson and Lee (1990), who proposed that children are less attentive during long work periods than during short ones. That is, children were generally more attentive during the short deprivation period, relative to the long period, and older children were more attentive than younger children. For example, fourth-grade children's mean attention scores were greater during the short deprivation time, relative to the long deprivation time. It should not be surprising that children are less attentive as the time they spend on a task increases, nor should it be surprising that their attention to school tasks increases with age. Further, children were more attentive after recess than before. Figure 3.2 displays the prerecess and postrecess *inattention* for grades K, 2, and 4. Note that at each grade level the children were more *inattentive* before than after recess. These data are displayed in figure 3.2.

The prerecess results also support earlier work suggesting that attention to school tasks increases with age (Wittrock, 1986). Further, we found that boys' and girls' attention to the book read to them was influenced by the gender-role stereotypicality of the story. For example, fourth-grade boys in the long timing condition were more attentive to male-preferred stories and less attentive to female-preferred stories, and the pattern was reversed for the girls. This finding is consistent with the extant literature on gender preference for stories (Monson & Sebesta, 1991).

Results from this experiment should be interpreted cautiously, primarily because of the small sample size (20 children per grade and 10 children per sex within each grade) and because there was only one classroom at each grade level. Replication is clearly needed to assure that the results are not aberrational (Lykken, 1968), especially when the results have implications for school policy. Replica-

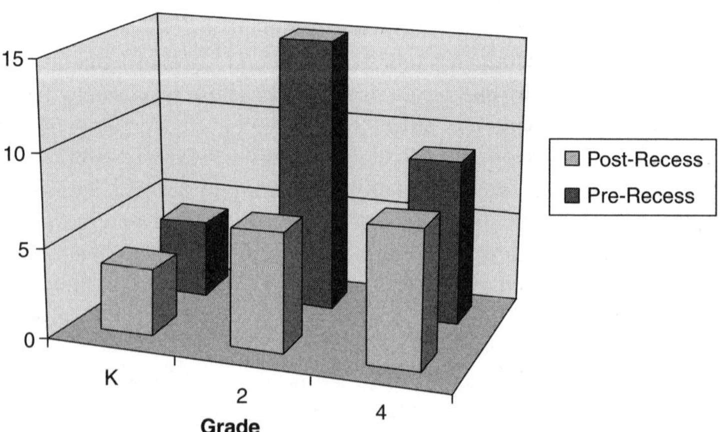

Figure 3.2 Inattention Pre- and Post-Recess

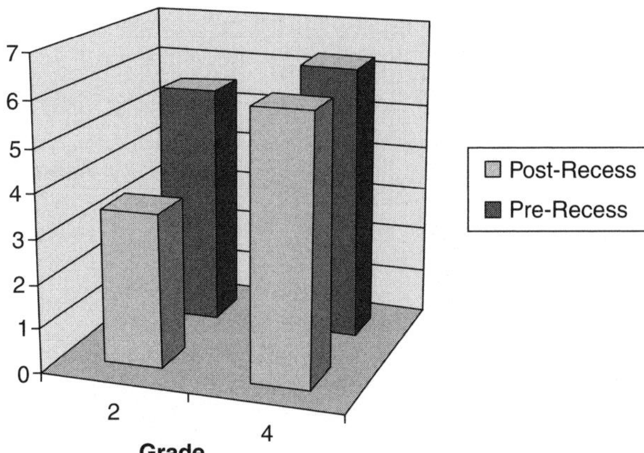

Figure 3.3 Inattention Pre- and Post-Recess

tion is also needed to clarify the effect of condition on physical activity at recess; the results from this experiment were not consistent with the one other experiment involving primary school children. With these needs in mind, we conducted two more experiments (Pellegrini et al., 1995).

In Experiment 2, the same outdoor recess timing and attention procedures were used as in Experiment 1. In Experiment 2, second and fourth graders (one classroom for each grade) were studied in the same school as in Experiment 1. The results from Experiment 2, similar to those from Experiment 1, revealed that children's task attention is affected by recess timing and that timing interacted with dimensions of the task, as well as with children's age and gender. Children generally, but especially second graders, were more attentive after recess than before recess. In addition, a significant difference between prerecess and postrecess attention was observed for second grade only, not for fourth grade. That is, only second graders and not fourth graders were more attentive after recess than before. In figure 3.3, the prerecess and postrecess inattention scores are displayed. The values 1 and 2 indicate second-grade prerecess and postrecess inattention, respectively. Similarly, 3 and 4 represent fourth-grade prerecess and postrecess inattention, respectively. In both cases, note that inattention is lower after recess than before.

In Experiment 3, students in two fourth-grade classrooms were studied, and the same recess timing paradigm employed in the previous experiments was used. The recess period was indoors, however. The same experiment was conducted with two separate, intact classrooms. Such a design was chosen because of the relatively small samples involved in each classroom. This procedure minimizes the probability of obtaining aberrant results if similar results are obtained in both samples—thus replicating each other. The results from this experiment are similar to those from other experiments: attention was greater after the recess period than it was before the break in classroom 2. The result from the indoor recess study was similar to the outdoors results: children are generally more attentive to classroom work after recess than before. Whether recess is indoors or outdoors does not seem to matter. In figure 3.3, these results are displayed with prerecess

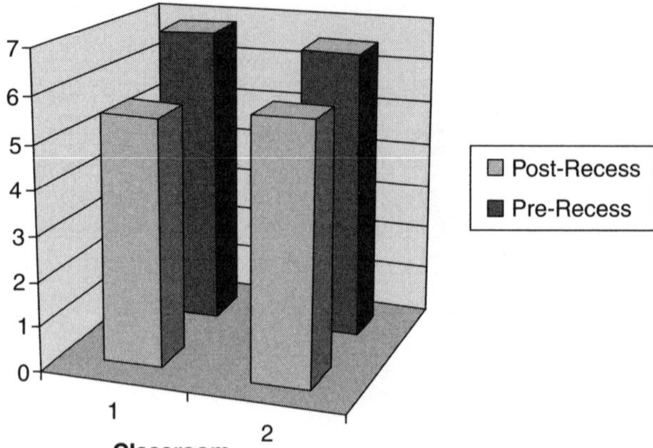

Figure 3.4 Inattention Pre- and Post-Recess

(numbers 1 and 3) and postrecess scores (numbers 2 and 4) of inattention for the two classrooms. Again, note that in both cases, inattention is lower after recess than before, as displayed in figure 3.4.

The resulting message from all of this research is clear. Breaks between periods of intense work maximize children's attention to their class work. More speculatively, this increased attention probably is partially responsible for the positive relations between recess and performance on achievement tests.

What we really still need to know, however, is the degree to which different types of recess regimens relate to attention and achievement. A first step in this direction was already presented, as we found that indoor recess periods, like outdoor periods, seemed to be effective facilitators of children's attention to class work. This result is consistent with mass versus distributed practice as the mechanism responsible for the effects of recess on attention. From this view, the nature of the break is less important than having a break per se. To more thoroughly examine this explanation, researchers should examine different types of breaks after periods of intense cognitive work. For example, does watching a short video or listening to music for a short period facilitate attention? Further, do these effects vary with the age and gender of the child?

Bjorklund's cognitive immaturity hypothesis provides some guidance here (Bjorklund & Pellegrini, 2000). The theory suggests that breaks for preschool and young primary school children should be "playful" and unstructured. Providing time for children to interact with peers or materials on their own terms, that is, with minimal adult direction, should maximize attention to subsequent tasks. The venue, indoors or outdoors, is not important. With older children, merely providing breaks between periods of intense work might suffice to maximize attention. The research on massed versus distributed practice with adults supports this view.

Another crucial aspect of the recess period that needs further research is the duration of the recess period. Should it be 10 minutes, 20 minutes, 30 minutes, or what? We simply do not know. Answers to this question have obvious implications for school policy and scheduling. We explored the issue of recess duration with a sample of preschool children (age 4 and 5) (Holmes, Pellegrini, & Schmidt, unpublished data). Procedurally, children had "circle time" and were read a story before recess. Then they went outdoors for recess periods of 10, 20, or 30 minutes. When they returned to their classrooms, they again sat in a circle and listened to a story read to them by their teachers. Attention was recorded and coded (using scan sampling and instantaneous recording procedures) for whether the child was gazing in the direction of the book or at the teacher reading the book.

Consistent with earlier work with older primary school children (Pellegrini & Davis, 1993; Pellegrini et al., 1995), attention was greater following the recess period than before it, and girls were more attentive than boys to classroom tasks in all conditions. It seems reasonable to conclude that outdoor recess breaks help children attend to classroom tasks.

Regarding the differing durations of recess periods, we found that attention to classroom tasks was greatest following the 20- and 10-minute outdoor play periods, whereas the 30-minute period resulted in higher rates of inattention. These findings are consistent with British anecdotal evidence that children become bored with recess after too long a period, and thus longer periods may become counterproductive (Blatchford, 1998). This work needs to be replicated because it represents only one short-term study with a relatively small sample. The duration of the recess periods is clearly important, as it is one of the persistent questions posed to us by parents and teachers. How long should recess be? Should its duration vary with children's age? Clearly, at this point we have only hints and are not sure.

Although children's attention to classroom instruction is obviously very important, we should not lose sight of the importance of peer interactions for children's successful development as both students and members of society. Developing peer relations is especially important during the preschool and early primary school years (age 3 to 6) (Waters & Sroufe, 1983). Thus, recess periods that encourage opportunities for relatively unfettered peer interaction, as well as exploration of different materials, would maximize both the social and cognitive benefits of recess.

POLICY IMPLICATIONS

Data presented in this chapter provide empirical support for the positive role of recess in the school curriculum. Breaks over the course of the instructional day facilitate primary school children's attention to classroom tasks. That these results were obtained with well-controlled field experiments and replicated a number of times by different groups of researchers should provide confidence in the findings. In terms of specific class performance, the results presented here support the anecdotal evidence from Taiwanese and Japanese schools suggesting that in order to maintain high levels of attention, children need frequent breaks in the course of the day (Stevenson & Lee, 1990). Recall that Stevenson and Lee's study compared the achievement of Asian and American school-age children and found Americans lagging far behind. They found that Asian schools had longer school days and school years but also provided children with breaks every 50 minutes across the entire school day.

This evidence should inform policy and be used to guide those policy makers and politicians seeking to diminish or eliminate recess from the school curriculum.

Like Asian schools, American children's school days and school years should be lengthened. Such a policy would bring the total number of hours American children attend school in a year closer to other countries in the world. This increase should have the corresponding benefit of increasing achievement. Longer school days and years—with frequent breaks—should accomplish this. Additionally, a longer school day and year would ensure that children have a safe place while their parents are at work. Children would be in school, learning and interacting with their peers, rather at home, unsupervised or in expensive after-school care.

Although recess periods alone seem to be important, children also need to interact with peers on their own terms. A physical education class as a substitute for recess does not serve the same purpose (Bjorklund & Pellegrini, 2000; Council on Physical Education for Children, 2001). They need to *play*! This conclusion is supported on a number of fronts. First, at the level of theory, both the cognitive immaturity hypothesis and the massed versus distributed practice theory suggest that after periods of intense effort, children need breaks from instruction. A physical education class is another form of instruction and thus would not provide the sort of interruption needed to maximize instruction. Further, physical education classes typically do not provide the variety of rich opportunities for peer interaction that recess does. The research presented in this chapter pointed to the importance of peer interaction for both social and cognitive outcomes.

Second, the importance of physical education for classroom attention is typically predicated on the idea that children "need to blow off steam" after periods of work and that the vigorous activity associated with physical education should serve this purpose. As noted earlier, the idea of "blowing off steam" is rooted in surplus energy theory—an invalid 19th-century theory (Evans & Pellegrini, 1997).

Third, and related to this last point, earlier research on the role of recess in children's attention found no empirical relation between the levels of children's vigorous activity on the playground at recess and subsequent attention to classroom tasks (Pellegrini & Davis, 1993). Consequently, these results should be used against any effort to use physical education as a substitute for recess.

A fourth implication of this work is that gender preference of classroom tasks is important in children's attention to those tasks. Specifically, research on children's attention consistently shows that boys are less attentive to classroom tasks than girls (Pellegrini et al., 1995), and recess breaks are especially effective in maximizing boys' attention. These findings have implications for school-age boys who are diagnosed with attention-deficit/hyperactivity disorder (ADHD) (Pellegrini & Horvat, 1995). We know, for example, that providing opportunities for more breaks minimizes fidgeting and maximizes attention—two dimensions of ADHD. Teachers and parents should be aware that classroom organization may be responsible for their sons' inattention and fidgeting and that breaks may be a better remedy than Ritalin.

Fifth, the finding that children's competence develops in the context of interacting with peers is especially important because children are rapidly losing these opportunities. There are signs in both the United States and the United Kingdom that children of primary school age have less time available out of school for interacting freely with peers and thus developing social skills and competence (Blatchford, 1998). For example, after school, many American children enter empty homes to wait for their parents to return from work (Steinberg, 1986). There is also a trend in both the United States (Pellegrini, 2005) and in the United Kingdom (Blatchford, 1998; Blatchford & Sumpner, 1998) for recess time to be limited or eliminated from the primary school day. Recess may be one of the few times during the day when children have the opportunity to interact with peers and develop social skills free from adult intervention.

Acknowledgments We acknowledge Mark Van Ryzin for help with constructing the figures in this chapter. The ideas expressed in this chapter also benefited from numerous discussions on the topic across a number of years with Peter Blatchford, Dave Bjorklund, and Peter Smith. We also acknowledge support provided by the Spencer Foundation for a portion of the research reported in the chapter.

References

Ackerman, B., Brown, E., & C. Izard (2004). The relations between contextual risk, earned income, and the school adjustment of children from economically disadvantaged families. *Developmental Psychology*, *40*, 204–216.

Bandura, A. (1997). *Self-efficacy: The exercise of control.* New York: W. H. Freeman.

Bjorklund, D. F., & Green, B. L. (1992). The adaptive nature of cognitive immaturity. *American Psychologist, 47*, 46–54.

Bjorklund, D. F., & Harnishfeger, K. K. (1987). Developmental differences in the mental effort requirements for the use of an organizational strategy in free recall. *Journal of Experimental Child Psychology, 44*, 109–125.

Bjorklund, D. F., & Pellegrini, A. D. (2000). Child development and evolutionary psychology. *Child Development, 71*, 1687–1708.

Blatchford, P. (1998). *Social life in school.* London: Falmer.

Blatchford, P., & Sumpner, C. (1998). What do we know about break time? Results from a national survey of breaktime and lunchtime in primary and secondary schools. *British Educational Research Journal, 24*, 79–94.

Brophy, J., & Good, T. (1974). Teacher-student relationships: Causes and consequences. New York: Holt, Rinehart, and Winston.

Coie, J. D., & Dodge, K. A. (1998). Aggression and antisocial behavior. In N. Eisenberg (Ed.), *Manual of child psychology: Vol. 3. Social, emotional, and personality development* (pp. 779–862). New York: Wiley.

Council on Physical Education for Children. (2001). *Recess in elementary schools: A position paper from the National Association for Sport and Physical Education.* Retrieved September 28, 2000, from http://eric.ed.uiuc.edu/naecs/position/recessplay/html

Dempster, F. N. (1992). The rise and fall of the inhibitory mechanism: Toward a unified theory of cognitive development and aging. *Development Review, 12*, 45–75.

Dickinson, D., & Moreton, J. (1991, April). *Predicting specific kindergarten literacy skills from three-year-olds preschool experience.* Paper presented at the biennial meeting of the Society for Research in Child Development, Seattle, WA.

Ebinghaus, H. (1964). *Memory.* New York: Teachers College Press. (Original work published 1885)

Evans, J., & Pellegrini, A. D. (1997). Surplus energy theory: An endearing but inadequate justification for break time. *Educational Review, 49*, 229–236.

Harper, L., & Huie, K. (1985). The effects of prior group experience, age, and familiarity on the quality and organizational of preschoolers' social relations. *Child Development, 56*, 704–717.

Harper, L., & Sanders, K. (1975). Preschool children's use of space: Sex differences in outdoor play. *Developmental Psychology, 11*, 119.

Hart, C. (1993). Children on playgrounds: Applying current knowledge to future practice and inquiry. In C. Hart (Ed.), *Children on playgrounds: Research perspectives and applications* (pp. 418–432). Albany: State University of New York Press.

Hartup, W. W. (1996). The company they keep: Friendships and their developmental significance. *Child Development, 67*, 1–13.

Heath, S. (1983). *Ways with words.* New York: Cambridge University Press.

Holmes, R. M., Pellegrini, A. D., & Schmidt, T. [Preschool recess attention and attention]. Unpublished raw data.

James, W. (1901). *Talks to teachers on psychology: And to students on some of life's ideals.* New York: Holt.

Kessen, W. (Ed.). (1975). *Childhood in China.* New Haven: Yale University Press.

Ladd, G. W., Kochenderfer, B. J., & Coleman, C. C. (1996). Friendship quality as a predictor of young children's early school adjustment. *Child Development, 67*, 1103–1118.

Ladd, G., & Price, J. (1993). Play styles of peer accepted and peer rejected children on the playground. In C. Hart (Ed.), *Children on playgrounds: Research perspectives and applications* (pp. 130–161). Albany: State University of New York Press.

Ladd, G., Price, J., & Hart, L. (1988). Predicting preschoolers' peer status from their playground behavior. *Child Development, 59*, 986–992.

Lewis, C. (1995). *Educating hearts and minds: Reflections on Japanese preschool and elementary education.* New York: Cambridge University Press.

Lykken, D. (1968). Statistical significance in psychological research. *Psychological Bulletin, 70*, 151–159.

Maccoby, E. E. (1998). *The two sexes: Growing up apart, coming together.* Cambridge, MA: Harvard University Press.

Messick, S. (1983). Assessment of children. In W. Kessen (Ed.), *Handbook of child psychology: Vol. 1. History, theory, and methods* (pp. 477–526). New York: Wiley.

Minuchin, P., & Shapiro, E. (1983). The school as a context for social development. In E. M. Hetherington (Ed.), *Manual of child psychology* (Vol. 4, pp. 197–274). New York: Wiley.

Monson, D., & Sebesta, S. (1991). Reading preferences. In J. Flood, J. Jensen, D. Lapp, & J. Squire (Eds.), *Handbook of research on teaching the English language arts* (pp. 664–673). New York: Macmillan.

No time for play. (2001, June 16). *The Economist*, p. 35.

Nurss, J., & McGauvran, M. (1976). *Metropolitan readiness tests: Levels I and II test and teacher's manual.* New York: Harcourt, Brace, Jovanovich.

Pellegrini, A. (1982). Explorations in preschooler's construction of cohesive test in two play contexts. *Discourse Processes, 5*, 101–108.

Pellegrini, A. D. (1984). The social cognitive ecology of preschool classrooms. *International Journal of Behavioral Development, 7*, 321–332.

Pellegrini, A. D. (1985). Relations between preschool children's play and literate behavior. In L. Galda & A. Pellegrini (Eds.), *Play, language, and story: The development of children's literate behavior.* Norwood, NJ: Ablex.

Pellegrini, A. D. (1992). Kindergarten children's social cognitive status as a predictor of first grade success. *Early Childhood Research Quarterly, 7*, 565–577.

Pellegrini, A. D. (2005). *Recess: Its role in development and education.* Mahwah, NJ: Erlbaum.

Pellegrini, A. D., & Davis, P. (1993). Relations between children's playground and classroom behaviour. *British Journal of Educational Psychology, 63*, 88–95.

Pellegrini, A. D., & Galda, L. (1993). Ten years after: A re-examination of the relations between symbolic play and literacy. *Reading Research Quarterly, 28*, 162–175.

Pellegrini, A. D., Huberty, P. D., & Jones, I. (1995). The effects of recess timing on children's playground and classroom behaviors. *American Educational Research Journal, 32*, 845–864.

Pellegrini, A. D., & Hurvat, M. (1995). A developmental contextual critique of Attention Deficit Hyperactivity Disorder (ADHD). *Educational Researcher, 24,* 13–20.

Pellegrini, A. D., Kato, K., Blatchford, P., & Baines, E. (2002). A short-term longitudinal study of children's playground games across the first year of school: Implications for social competence and adjustment to school. *American Educational Research Journal, 39*, 991–1015.

Piaget, J. (1965). *The moral judgment of the child.* New York: Free Press.

Piaget, J. (1983). Piaget's theory. In W. Kessen (Ed.), *Handbook of child psychology: History, theory, and methods* (pp. 103–128). New York: Wiley.

Smith, P. K., & Boulton, M. (1990). Rough-and-tumble play, aggression, and dominance: Perception and behavior in children's encounters. *Human Development, 33*, 271–282.

Smith, P. K., Hagan, T. (1980). Effects of deprivation on exercise play in nursery school children. *Animal Behaviour, 28,* 922–928.

Sroufe, L. A., Egelund, B., & Carlson, E. A. (1999). One social world: The integrated development of parent–child and peer relationships. In W. A. Collins & B. Laursen (Eds.), *Relationships as developmental contexts. The Minnesota symposia on child psychology* (Vol. 30, pp. 241–261). Mahwah, NJ: Erlbaum.

Steinberg, L. (1986). Latchkey children and susceptibility to peer pressure. *Developmental Psychology, 22*, 433–439.

Stevenson, H. W., & Lee, S. Y. (1990). *Concepts of achievement* (Monographs for the Society for Research in Child Development Serial No. 221, 55, 1–2).

Sutton-Smith, B. (1971). A syntax for play and games. In R. Herron & B. Sutton-Smith (Eds.), *Child's play* (pp. 298–310). New York: Wiley.

Toppino, T. C., Kasserman, J. E., & Mracek, W. A. (1991). The effect of spacing repetitions on the recognition memory of young children and adults. *Journal of Experimental Child Psychology, 51*, 123–138.

Tudge, J., & Rogoff, B. (1989). Peer influences on cognitive development: Piagetian and Vygotskian perspectives. In M. Bornstein & J Bruner (Eds.), Interaction in human development (pp. 17–40). Hillsdale, NJ: Erlbaum.

Vygotsky, L. (1978). Mind in society. Cambridge, MA: Harvard University Press.

Waters, E., & Sroufe, L. A. (1983). Social competence as developmental construct. Developmental Review, 3, 79–97.

Wittrock, M. (1986). Students' thought processes. In M. Wittrock (Ed.), *Handbook of research on teaching* (pp. 297–314). New York: Macmillan.

Wright, M. (1980). Measuring the social competence of preschool children. *Canadian Journal of Behavioral Science, 12*, 17–32.

Yussen, S. R., & Levy, V. M. Jr. (1975). Developmental changes in predicting one's own span of short-term memory. *Journal of Experimental Child Psychology, 19*, 502–508.

Zigler, E., & Trickett, P. (1978). I.Q., social competence, and evaluation of early childhood intervention programs. *American Psychologist, 33,* 789–798.

PART II

School Readiness–School Standards

4

Standards, Science, and the Role of Play in Early Literacy Education

JAMES F. CHRISTIE AND KATHLEEN A. ROSKOS

Play is being shunted aside in early childhood programs in favor of more direct forms of instruction that address the new "pre-K basics" of language, early literacy, and numeracy skills. Although play was once seen as a key promoter of child development, administrators, policy makers, and some teachers increasingly regard play as a waste of instructional time with no clear benefits for high-priority cognitive outcomes, such as prereading skills (Zigler & Bishop-Josef, 2004).

Two majors shifts in policy, originating in the latter decades of the 20th century, have contributed to this dramatic shift in play's status in early learning, especially as it applies in language and literacy domains. One is the powerful movement to prevent reading difficulties, which has given rise to a new perspective on reading instruction that is anchored in a body of "scientifically based reading research" (SBRR) (McCardle & Chhabra, 2004; Snow, Burns, & Griffin, 1998). The other is the standards movement, with its persistent press for accountability, currently manifested in the rise of state-level early childhood academic standards, the development of standardized assessments of academic achievement at the preschool level, and a heavy emphasis on school readiness (Kagan & Lowenstein, 2004). The combination of the SBRR and standards converges to form current conceptions of "excellent instruction." Excellent instruction, as framed by the SBRR perspective and related academic standards, has little, if anything, in common with play (or so it seems).

In this chapter, we attempt to show how play can further the ambitious goal of achieving excellent early literacy instruction for all children—instruction that encompasses research evidence, strong standards, and play in the early childhood classroom. We start with early literacy policy, examining the role of play in a standards-based context and exploring its potential to assist children to meet more rigorous early literacy expectations. Standards increase accountability for emergent literacy instruction, thus creating new pressures for play's role as a medium for learning and a shift from unfocused free play to "educational" play—play activities that are linked to educational goals, objectives, and outcomes. We then turn our attention to relationships between the "science of play" and the "science of early literacy," noting the overlap between these two complex areas of preschool development and learning, and making the case for research-based connections between play and core literacy skills. Closing the chapter, we urge the more vigorous advocacy of educational play in early childhood programs and propose several strategies that can better secure play's position in early literacy instruction across preschool, day care, and prekindergarten settings.

EARLY LITERACY POLICY, STANDARDS, AND PLAY

Early literacy policy is a new topic in the field of early childhood, introduced into the national policy arena at the turn of this century (Roskos & Vukelich, 2006). Research on children's rapidly developing brains in the first years of life, their emerging print knowledge and skills, and the influence of rich early literacy experiences (e.g., being read to) on later reading achievement demonstrated the early onset of literacy development in young children (Bowman, Donovan, & Burns, 2001; Shonkoff & Phillips, 2000; Snow et al., 1998). As scientific research converged on a new realization of an earlier, longer developmental path to literacy, it also revealed a difficult social problem. Some infants, toddlers, and preschoolers receive high-quality, education-oriented care filled with literacy experiences at home or in childcare that prepare them for school and successful reading achievement. Many others do not, and they enter school with deficits (e.g., weak vocabulary) that are extremely difficult to remedy and that put them at risk for reading failure. The psychological, social, and economic consequences of reading failure are well documented (Snow et al., 1998) as having serious implications for an information-based society over the long term (Heckman, 2002). Effective, research-based early literacy instruction for all young children offers a strong preventive measure for reducing the incidence of reading failure.

Spread into the policy environment, this movement to prevent reading disabilities through early instruction formed the basis of an ambitious federal early reading policy, Good Start, Grow Smart (2002), which called for early learning content guidelines linked to reliable, valid assessments in Head Start and childcare in general. One component of this initiative was a strong recommendation that, in order to receive federal education funds, the states voluntarily needed to adopt early childhood standards for early literacy and mathematics that were "science-based" with firm support from empirical research studies. *Standards* were defined as statements about specific child outcomes, and the guidelines specified that early literacy standards should focus on the "science-based" outcomes in oral language, background knowledge, phonological processing, and print knowledge.

Good Start, Grow Smart accelerated the movement to establish state early childhood standards. The number of states with early childhood standards increased from 18 in 2000 to 35 in 2004 (Neuman & Roskos, 2005). By 2005, 43 states had pre-K standards, most of which specify "science-based" early literacy outcomes for young children. This development has led to a decidedly mixed reaction in the early childhood education community.

Standards are static expectations, outcome statements, or "amounts" meant to satisfy established criteria (e.g., what children should know and be able to do at certain age levels) (Marzano & Kendall, 1998). They are durable end points, that is, models or examples of what should be, that share a consensus of acceptance. Standard setting inevitably raises concerns about what is expected because so much is at stake for educators, families, and students in meeting rigorous standards. Expectations that are too high can frustrate learning, and those too low can squander it. Establishing academic standards is an especially sensitive endeavor in the preschool years, given the young age of the learners, the diversity of their early learning experiences, and the variability of early development (Burns, Midgette, Leong, & Bodrova, 2003; Scott-Little, Kagan, & Frelow, 2003).

Many early educators fear that early literacy standards will result in a K–3 literacy curriculum that is being pushed down into preschool programs and that teachers will be required to teach to the standards in highly structured and scripted ways (Vukelich & Christie, 2004). Traditionally, early education has emphasized the integration of content areas, not isolated subject learning in well-defined instructional groups (Schickedanz, Pergantis, Kanosky, Blaney, & Ottinger, 1997). It has focused on the whole child's cognitive, physical, and social-emotional development, with high regard for individual differences in learning and development (Bowman, Donovan, & Burns, 2001; Bredekamp & Copple, 1997). A "pushed-down" early literacy curriculum, however, threatens developmentally appropriate forms of teaching that honor children's personal inventions, discoveries, and meanings, including play (Zigler & Bishop-Joseph, 2004). Moreover, in the 2-hour time frame of many programs, it might lead to the neglect of other important areas of development that are necessary for school readiness (e.g., social-emotional skills; Shonkoff, 2004).

Other policy makers and early educators view standards as critical framers of content and curriculum, professional development, and assessments in building a coherent education system that promotes the development of school readiness skills for all children (Good Start, Grow Smart, 2002; Schweinhart, 2003). If standards are high-quality, age-appropriate, research-based indicators (Neuman, Roskos, & Vukelich, 2003), they can guide preschool teachers' decision making about early literacy curriculum, instruction, and assessment. As clear instructional goals, performance indicators can help cohere daily instruction, thus leading to better curriculum alignment, which has been found to improve students' achievement in K–3 basic skills (Cohen & Hill, 2001; Grissmer, Flanagan, Kawata, & Williamson, 2000).

Although it is too soon to assess the influence of a standards-based architecture on preschool literacy education, it is not too soon to recognize the growing influence of early literacy standards in shaping preschool language and literacy teaching practices. A good example is the Early Reading First program (NCLB, 2001). Between 2002 and 2005, Early Reading First has funded approximately

120 projects designed to increase low-income preschool children's academic readiness by means of SBRR early literacy instruction. The latest round of Early Reading First guidelines, for example, specifies that programs should ensure that children develop (a) recognition, leading to automatic recognition, of letters of the alphabet; (b) knowledge of letter sounds, the blending of sounds, and the use of increasingly complex vocabulary; (c) an understanding that written language is composed of phonemes and letters, each representing one or more speech sounds that in combination make up syllables, words, and sentences; (d) spoken language, including vocabulary and oral comprehension abilities; and (e) knowledge of the purposes and conventions of print.

Is there room for play in these policies and the standards-based, SBRR early literacy programs they promulgate? Some answer with a firm "no" because the very nature of play seems at odds with the rigors of skill instruction called for in literacy programs like Early Reading First. In a dynamic view of development, play is not an end state, terminus, or outcome (Bronfenbrenner & Ceci, 1994; Thelen & Smith, 1995). It is a process recognizable as a pattern of activity with certain salient features, such as positive affect, nonliterality, means-over-ends orientation, flexibility, and autonomy (King, 1979; Rubin, Fein, & Vandenberg, 1983; Smith & Vollstedt, 1985). Play can be guided, but not scripted; it can be assembled, but not tightly structured; it can be educationally significant, but often indirectly. Given its fluidity, flexibility, and unpredictability, play may be difficult to systematically control in the pursuit of serious skill sets for which the program and teacher will be held accountable. Time allocated to play, therefore, can be viewed as inefficient and better spent on more specific literacy activities where the educational benefits are scientifically clear (e.g., learning alphabet letter names), especially for children at risk of having difficulties in learning to read (Zigler, Singer, & Bishop-Josef, 2004).

Other educators may not be so quick to relegate play to the very edges of the preschool day in reaching the goal of excellent early literacy instruction for all children. To instruct (as in *to tell*), they would argue, is not enough and can reduce learning to isolated skills. Considerable research, in fact, supports a more integrated view of skill development and learning that involves exploration, selective copying toward mastery, a "push" to test the limits of behavior, and sheer playful repetition of skill sequences in space and time to initiate a developmental cascade (Bronfenbrenner & Ceci, 1994; Bruner, 1972; Thelen & Smith, 1995; Vygotsky, 1978). Play provides an ideal context for this combinatorial activity in early childhood. Bruner (1972, p. 689) referred to play as "that special form of violating fixity" so essential for complex skill mastery. Play, with its freedom from insistence on the here and now, introduces the flexibility that converts the rigidities of skill instruction into the realities of skill use by the child. Lacking this, children may be taught, but they may not learn in ways that evolve toward higher levels of skill performance and that, in the end, are educationally significant.

The future role of play lies at this standards–practice nexus. And the important question is not whether play should have a role in the new science- and standards-based early childhood programs. It is more fruitful to ask (a) how play can help children meet important early literacy outcomes that are the building blocks of school reading and writing achievement and (b) which types of play are most effective in accomplishing this. We believe that the answers to these questions reside in the overlap between two extensive lines of inquiry—research on early literacy and research on play. We believe that, just as there is a "science" to early literacy, there also is a "science" to play and its educational applications.

THE SCIENCE OF EARLY LITERACY AND PLAY

Emergent literacy is a relatively young field of inquiry that became a dominant theoretical perspective in the field of early education. During the 1980s, emergent literacy researchers conducted a series of descriptive studies that showed that children begin learning about reading and writing at a very early age by observing and interacting with adults and other children in literacy-focused routines such as storybook reading and in everyday life activities that involve reading (e.g., menus, signs) and writing (e.g., shopping lists, notes to family members). (For detailed reviews of this first generation of emergent literacy investigations, see Mason, 1984, and Sulzby & Teale, 1991.) The pace of emergent literacy research picked up during the 1990s, providing broad-based support for early literacy programs that had print-rich classroom environments, frequent storybook reading, and opportunities for literacy-enriched play (see Senechal, LeFevre, Colton, & Smith, 2000; Yaden, Rowe, & MacGillivray, 2000).

During the same decade of the 1990s, a "parallel universe" of very different early literacy research was being conducted in the fields of educational psychology and special education (Vukelich & Christie, 2004). This research, which became known as scientifically based reading research (SBRR), was quantitative in nature and used correlational and experimental designs (McCardle & Chhabra, 2004; Snow et al., 1998). SBRR investigations have identified core early literacy knowledge and skills that are highly predictive of reading achievement, namely, oral language, phonological awareness, alphabet letter knowledge, and print awareness (Neuman & Dickinson, 2001; Snow et al., 1998). Background knowledge has also been identified as having a key role in children's reading acquisition (Neuman, 2001). SBRR researchers have identified "science-based" instructional strategies, such as dialogic reading (Whitehurst et al., 1994), that appear to be effective in teaching these skills. The SBRR perspective fit well with the new policy focus on reading disabilities, and the movement to establish early childhood standards has arguably supplanted emergent literacy as the dominant view of early reading development and instruction.

Play theory and research in early childhood have a longer history than their counterparts in early literacy, reaching back to the beginnings of the 20th century, when psychologists Karl Groos (1898) and G. Stanley Hall (1907) began making connections between play and development. From 1880 to 1979, no fewer than 739 scholarly articles and books were written about children's play (Sutton-Smith, 1985). The pace accelerated in the 1980s, stimulated by Rubin et al.'s (1983) chapter in the *Handbook of Child Psychology*.

Research-based evidence on the role of play in early child development in general and on its role in language acquisition and social competence in particular is considerable (see Johnson, Christie, & Wardle, 2005). The theoretical formulations of both Piaget (1966) and Vygotsky (1966) address the significance of play in the development of symbolic thinking as a cornerstone of cognition. More so than Piaget, Vygotsky attributed a key role in the development of language and thought to make-believe play, which he described as a "particular feature of the preschool age" with profound implications in future development (p. 17). Vygotsky (1966, p. 16) argued that play "contains all the developmental tendencies in a condensed form" (physical, cognitive, emotional) and thus creates a zone of proximal development that *pulls* the child forward. For this reason, play activity is essential in the preschool years because it *leads* development, giving rise to abstract thinking (thought separate from action or object), self-awareness, and self-regulation. Play, in other words, is a process particularly influential at the preschool age for achieving cycles of self-organization and development that contribute to cognition. It is a mechanism of developmental change.

Jerome Bruner (1972) argued that play is a necessary point of departure for learning the symbolic means of culture, namely, language, and that play contributes to children's ability to solve problems by increasing their behavioral options. Singer and Singer (1990, 2005) have developed a cognitive-affective framework in which play mediates a reciprocal relationship between these two important realms of development. Children who are more imaginative in their play are more open to their affect system and are thus able to develop a more elaborate and richer storehouse of affect-laden symbols and memories. Together, these theories have motivated a rich body of investigative work on the role of play in children's early development and learning.

Beginning in the late 1980s, researchers began investigating *direct* connections between play and literacy (Christie, 2003). Research on the play–literacy interface exploded during the 1990s (see Roskos & Christie, 2004), and it became the most heavily researched aspect of early literacy during that decade (Yaden et al., 2000).

In searching for links between literacy and play, we examined all three areas of inquiry: basic research on early literacy, basic research on play, and studies on direct links between literacy and play.

- *Oral Language*. Sociodramatic play occurs when groups of children adopt roles and act out make-believe stories and situations (Johnson et al., 2005). Research has documented firm connections between this advanced form of play and oral language development. Both pretend play and language involve symbolic representation. In language, sound represents objects, actions, attributes, and situations. In play, children use objects and actions, as well as language, to stand for other things. Thus, it is not surprising that symbolic play and language have been found to be related during the toddler years (Bornstein, Vibbert, Tal, & O'Donnel, 1992; Tamis-LeMonda & Bornstein, 1993). In addition, there is evidence that older preschool and kindergarten-age children gain valuable language practice by engaging in sociodramatic play. (Garvey, 1974)

Sociodramatic play also places heavy linguistics demands on children and prods them to use their maximum language abilities. Children must make intentional use of lexical and syntactical features of language in order to (a) signify the person, object, and situational transformations that occur in pretense play and (b) identify and elaborate on play themes as they unfold during the play episode. Bruner (1983) contends that "the most complicated grammatical and pragmatic forms of language appear first in play activity" (p. 65).

Findings from a more recent longitudinal study in the United States have shown that rich language used in play has an impact on literacy development. The Home School Study of Language and Literacy Development (Dickinson & Tabors, 2001) examined the home and school literacy environments of low-income children from age 3 through kindergarten. The study reported consistent relationships between the language that children used during play and their performance on literacy and language measures. For example, at age 3, children who engaged in more pretend talk during play were more likely to perform well on assessments of receptive vocabulary and narrative production (also see Singer & Singer, 1981). Dickinson and Tabors (2001) also reported consistent links between play and long-term language growth. For example, the total number of words and the variety of words that children used during free play in preschool were positively related to their performance on language measures administered in kindergarten.

- *Phonological Awareness*. Phonological awareness refers to conscious awareness of the sounds of language. This awareness is a prerequisite for learning the alphabetic principle that letters represent the sounds of language. Phonological awareness in the early years is one of the strongest predictors of later success in learning to read (Snow et al., 1998), and it is always a key objective of SBBR early literacy programs.

Researchers have observed that infants and toddlers frequently play with the sounds of language. For example, Weir (1976, pp. 610–611) reported that her own 2½-year-old child playfully repeated strings of words containing related sounds ("*Babette / back here / wet*") exploring both rhyme (words that end with the same sound) and alliteration (words that begin with the same sound). According to Cazden (1976), when children use language to *communicate*, the form and structure of language are transparent. They just focus on the meaning of what is being said. However, when children *play* with language, the structural features of language become opaque. This creates opportunities for children to become aware of phonological, syntactic, and lexical aspects of language.

The learning potential of language play is supported by Fernandez-Fein and Baker's (1997) findings that children's knowledge of nursery rhymes and the frequency that they engage in word play were both strong predictors of children's phonological awareness. It is not surprising, therefore, that many research-based strategies for promoting phonological awareness in preschool and kindergarten use playful activities such as singing songs, reciting nursery rhymes, reading books that play with the sounds of language, and gamelike activities (e.g., Adams, Foorman, Lundberg, & Beeler, 1998). Hirsh-Pasek and Golinkoff's (2003) intriguingly titled book, *Einstein Never Used Flash Cards*, contains additional suggestions of informal games that parents and early educators can use to help children learn phonemic awareness and other early literacy skills in an enjoyable, playful manner.

- *Print Awareness*. Literacy-enriched play centers contain theme-related reading and writing materials. For example, a doctor play center might contain pencils, pens, prescription pads, an appointment book, patient folders, wall signs ("Please sign in"), and insurance cards. Research has shown that, when available, these literacy tools and props result in marked increases in the amounts of emergent reading and writing activity during play (Neuman & Roskos, 1992). In addition, several studies have shown that when children play in print-enriched settings, they often learn to read the words that are present (Neuman & Roskos, 1993; Vukelich, 1994). In the doctor play example, children would be more likely to recognize the words *please*, *sign*, and *in* than children who were not exposed to these words in the context of play.
- *Background Knowledge*. Sara Smilansky (1968) has proposed that sociodramatic play helps children integrate experiences that seem unrelated at first, such as selecting menu items and paying money to a cashier in restaurant play. Several research studies have supported this claim. For example, Saltz, Dixon, and Johnson (1977) found that sociodramatic play and thematic fantasy play (i.e., adult-facilitated role enactment of fairy tales) helped preschool children connect separate events into logical sequences. More recently, Gmitrova and Gmitrova (2003) demonstrated a link between teacher-guided play of 3- to 6-year-olds and their manifestation of conceptual development. With small groups of children, teachers were able to gently enter the playing process and shift the children's cognitive behaviors to a higher conceptual level by "using the powerful natural engine of the free play" (p. 245).

Singer and Singer (2004) have created the Circle of Make-Believe, an interactive video-based program for parents and other caregivers of 3- to 5-year-olds that contains seven different "learning games" illustrated on video (demonstrated by real people: actual parents, preschooler, and teachers), which use play activity to build background knowledge and other school readiness skills such as alphabet recognition and counting. For example, in "Where Is My Kitten?" children use a kitten puppet (a cat face drawn on a paper plate) and pretend binoculars to practice words that describe spatial relationships: *on top of* and *under*, *in front of* and *behind*. Data from a study conducted in eight states indicated that children who engaged in the Circle of Make-Believe program made substantial gains on a readiness skills measure that included letter, shape, and number recognition.

Our brief review of play-literacy research highlights the science that suggests play in early childhood contains critical components (oral language, phonological awareness, print knowledge, and background knowledge) that are linked to later literacy achievement. And this is necessary because early educators need an empirical basis for choosing learning activities that aim to develop children's early literacy. Consider, for example, the common early literacy standard of alphabet knowledge (knowledge of letter names and sounds), one of the best predictors of future reading achievement (Byrne & Field-Barnsley, 1993; Ehri & Sweet, 1991). Instruction often involves drawing children's attention to selected letters during storybook reading, brief lessons with posters containing illustrations of objects that begin with the same letter, alphabet "word walls," or writing activities. As such, this pointing out of letters may not hold much meaning for young children, although they often attentively follow the teacher's lead. Literacy-enriched play settings, however, provide an effective venue for children to use their emerging knowledge of the alphabet. Let's say the letter *t* has been the focus of instruction, which by itself holds little real meaning for the child. But in the context of a taxi play center this bit of linguistic information can grow more relevant. Here children can practice and consolidate their name and sound knowledge. Couple these props with sensitive teacher scaffolding ("Why don't you make a sign for your taxi stand?"), and children are presented with meaningful, highly contextualized opportunities to recognize and write the letter *t*. This linking of immediate play activity and distant literacy standards rarely occurs by happenstance. Rather, it reflects thoughtful planning by a knowledgeable teacher who understands the interests and needs of children.

As another example, one of the authors recently visited a preschool classroom that was part an Early Reading First project. The teacher was using a blend of SBBR instructional techniques and academically linked play. During large group circle time, she and the children sang a song that had to do with building a tree house. The teacher paused to point out the words that rhymed in the story and then encouraged the children to come up with other words that ended with the same rhyming sound. She also focused on several tool-related vocabulary terms: *hammer* and *nail*. Next, the teacher did a shared reading lesson with a big book about building a doghouse. Before reading the book with the children, she did a "picture walk," engaging the children in a discussion about objects in the photos in this informational book. The teacher focused children's attention on several tool vocabulary terms: *hammer*, *nail*, *saw*, *measuring tape*, and *safety goggles*. Then the teacher read the book and encouraged the children to read along. Some were able to do so because of the simple text and picture clues. During center time, children had the option of playing in a dramatic play center that was set up as a house construction site. There was a "house" made out of large cardboard boxes. In addition, there were toy tools (hammers, saw, measuring tape, level), safety goggles, hard hats, some golf tees that were used as make-believe nails, and several signs ("Hard Hat Area," "Danger," "Construction Site"). Two girls and a boy spent 30 minutes in the center, using the toy tools to measure, plan, and build the house. During this play, they used the target vocabulary repeatedly and also explored the uses of the tools. The dramatic play center was used as a means to provide children with an opportunity to practice and consolidate the vocabulary and concepts that were being taught in the instructional part of the curriculum.

Play and standards can indeed coexist, and play-based strategies are legitimate practices in the early childhood curriculum. Play's role, however, is tenuous at best, and its position shaky. Unless more vigorous steps are taken, it may not survive this round of educational reform that has reached so deep into the everyday practice of early childhood teachers.

POLICY RECOMMENDATIONS

Three steps can strengthen play's status in this era of early childhood standards: a shift toward "blended" curricula that integrate direct instruction with educational play activities, improved teacher education, and increased play advocacy.

1. Blended Early Literacy Programs

We need to move away from the old either/or mentality that separates play from academic instruction. Kagan and Lowenstein (2004) conclude that:

> The literature is clear: Diverse strategies that combine play and more structured efforts are effective accelerators of children's readiness for school and long-term development. Apparently, just as children need intentionality in their exposure to all dimensions of development, so too may they need exposure to play-based and child-initiated as well as teacher-directed pedagogical strategies. Clearly, no single strategy can be expected to work for all children, all the time. (p. 72)

We agree and therefore favor blended early literacy programs that provide both focused instruction and related play activities. Design features of blended programs include large-group shared reading, small-group instruction, and content-rich language experiences to model, demonstrate, clarify, and apply core literacy skills. Theme-related dramatic play centers, linked conceptually to language and literacy content, allow more reading and writing, listening, and talking that help establish new concepts and skills in action. Time, play props, materials, and equipment are organized to help children grasp and practice early literacy skills on a developmental basis and are highly supportive of learning through doing.

Blended programs align well with an integrated view of skill development. Content-related play experiences provide children with enjoyable opportunities to explore, copy, and repeat skills and concepts that are initially introduced through instruction. In addition, these programs also fit with the principle of *equifinality*. The equifinality hypothesis contends that specific positive outcomes can happen in multiple ways in an open system (Sackett, Sameroff, Cairns, & Suomi, 1981). As a result, there are multiple avenues or routes to the same developmental destination (Martin & Caro, 1985). Although direct instruction can facilitate core literacy skills and concepts, there are also other means for obtaining the same outcomes, including play.

The Early Reading First grant example described in the previous section is a good example of the equifinality principle. In this classroom, some children learned vocabulary words as a result of teacher instruction during shared reading of books that contain these terms. Other children learned the vocabulary during play as a result of interactions with peers or a teacher during play. We witnessed collaborative peer learning in action when a 4-year-old female "construction worker" strenuously reprimanded a male coworker for not wearing safety goggles when using a toy power saw. Initially, the boy put down the saw and walked away (with his feelings hurt a bit). Back on the job with the saw a few minutes later, the boy had the goggles on and the term *safety goggles* also firmly entrenched in his lexicon because of his interaction with his bossy playmate.

2. Improved Teacher Education

Dunn, Beach, and Kontos (2000) surveyed the play settings in 24 childcare centers and discovered that these areas contained few functional, theme-related literacy materials. In fact, few opportunities existed for any type of literacy activity during free play periods. These findings suggest that the teachers did not believe that it was important to link literacy and play, that they were not familiar with the literacy-enriched play setting strategy, or both. Similarly, McLane (2003) had 90 Head Start teachers complete a questionnaire that focused on their beliefs about play's role in development and education. Although a majority of the teachers viewed play as making important contributions to children's social, emotional, and language development, only 6% believed that play contributed to literacy development.

These findings indicate a need for early childhood teacher education programs and professional development efforts to focus on increasing early childhood teachers' knowledge of the connections between play, early literacy learning, and pre-K academic standards. In addition, teachers need to learn how to plan and implement play experiences that will help children learn core academic content. Play has to be used in a thoughtful, intentional teaching strategy. Bredekamp points out that:

> For children to benefit fully from play, teachers must take their own roles seriously. Early childhood educators cannot wander about the classroom operating on the vague assumption that children learn through play while, at the same time, lamenting the challenges to play coming from parents and administrators. Instead, teachers must recognize play as one of the key teaching and learning contexts in the early childhood classroom, must acquire skills themselves in research-based effective teaching strategies such as scaffolding language use during play, and must incorporate play along with other more directive teaching throughout the preschool day. (2004, p. 171)

Equipping teachers to be mindful and strategic in using play to help children learn academically requires that play be front and center in early childhood teacher education programs. To affect practice, coverage of play in teacher preparation programs needs to move beyond traditional lectures and textbook readings. Future teachers also need opportunities to plan and use play-related strategies to promote learning the academic outcomes specified in state early childhood standards, as well as time to reflect on how children respond to play-based teaching.

3. Increased Play Advocacy

A major cause of the current "antiplay" shift across all levels of schooling is the widespread belief by many educators, parents, administrators, politicians, and education policy makers that play is not educational. This belief leads to the unfortunate conclusion that, in order to free up time for more productive educational strategies such as direct instruction, we must reduce or eliminate play and play opportunities (Jones, 2003). To counter this trend, early childhood educators and play researchers need to be more vigorous advocates for educational play (Hewit, 2001). This advocacy needs to occur at the home, local school, and national levels.

On the home front, Hirsh-Pasek and Golinkoff recommend a "new three R's" for parents who are trying to balance the pressures to boost their young children's achievement with children's need for authentic, playful learning:

- *Reflect*. Ask yourself, Why am I enrolling 4-year-old Johnny in the class? Does Johnny really like (art, yoga, computer science, music, fill in the blank), or do I feel pressure to make sure that Johnny has a leg up on other children his age? . . .
- *Resist*. It takes courage to resist the forces that tell us that earlier is better. . . .
- *Re-center*. . . . Each time you engage in a teachable moment with your child—each time you play with your child—you are seeing child development in action. You are connecting with your child and have become a more sensitive and responsive parent. (2003, pp. 259–260)

If parents can come to believe in the educational value of play, they will be much less likely to put pressure on teachers and policy makers to remove play from the early childhood curriculum.

At the school level, early childhood teachers can make a valuable contribution to this effort by clearly documenting the learning opportunities that occur during classroom play. As the old saying goes, a picture can be worth a thousand words. With the advent of digital photography, teachers can take photos that illustrate the literacy learning opportunities in play, such as children reading menus, writing down orders, and using coupons to get reduced rates on meals at a restaurant play center. These photos can be displayed on classroom walls and in newsletters sent home to parents. This play documentation can also serve as an assessment tool. For example, samples of play-related writing can be saved in folders or more elaborate "portfolios" and used to document children's writing development to parents.

At the national level, educators and researchers need to do a better job of disseminating findings that demonstrate that play is a means to promote academic achievement (Johnson, 1994). As the studies cited here illustrate, there is a robust body of research supporting the connection between play and early literacy. Research also has highlighted effective play-based teaching strategies, such as games, literacy-enriched play settings, and appropriate forms of teacher scaffolding. This research needs to be presented to preservice and in-service teachers, administrators, and educational policy makers. Books such as *Einstein Never Used Flash Cards* (Hirsh-Pasek & Golinkoff, 2003) are ideal for this purpose. Jim Johnson (1994) recommends we also utilize radio (e.g., National Public Radio), television, and the Internet to spread the word about the educational value of play.

SUMMARY

We believe that play can and must hold its central role in early literacy education, even in this era of science and standards. However, this is not going to be an easy task. Even though robust theoretical and research connections exist between play and core early literacy skills and dispositions, there are strong antiplay forces at work—most prominently a pervasive attitude that play is not educational. Overcoming these challenges and biases will require a multipronged effort by teachers, teacher educators, and researchers. New blended curricula that integrate multiple forms of instruction with academically connected play need to be adopted, implemented, and evaluated. We also need to improve early childhood teacher education programs so that new teachers are truly play experts, well versed in play theory, play research, and (most important of all) how to use play to help children learn standards-based academic content. Finally, we need to increase our advocacy and marketing of play so that parents, administrators, and policy makers are cognizant of the educational benefits of play and play's impressive research base. Tongue in cheek, Brian Sutton-Smith (1995, p. 283), the famous play theorist, once remarked that play is a "medium for propaganda for one propaedeutic sort or another." And in this instance, we gladly use it to argue for the preservation of play in children's early literacy learning—for without it, learning to read and write can be very dreary indeed.

Reference

Adams, M., Foorman, B., Lundberg, I., & Beeler, T. (1998). The elusive phoneme: Why phonemic awareness is so important and how to help children develop it. *American Educator, 21*(1–2), 18–29.

Bornstein, M., Vibbert, M., Tal, J., & O'Donnel, K. (1992). Toddler language and play in the second year: Stability, covariation, and influences of parenting. *First Language, 12*, 323–338.

Bowman, B., Donovan, M., & Burns, M. (2001). *Eager to learn: Educating our preschoolers*. Washington, DC: National Academy Press.

Bredekamp, S. (2004). Play and school readiness. In E. Zigler, D. Singer, & S. Bishop-Josef (Eds.), *Children's play: The roots of reading* (pp. 159–174). Washington, DC: Zero to Three Press.

Bredekamp, S., & Copple, C. (1997). *Developmentally appropriate practice in early childhood programs* (Rev. ed.). Washington, DC: NAEYC.

Bronfenbrenner, U., & Ceci, S. J. (1994). Nature–nurture reconceptualized in developmental perspective: A bioecological model. *Psychological Review, 101*, 568–586.

Bruner, J. (1972). *Beyond the information given: Studies in the psychology of knowing*. New York: Norton.

Bruner, J. (1983). Play, thought, and language. *Peabody Journal of Education, 60*(3), 60–69.

Burns, M. S., Midgette, K., Leong, D., & Bodrova, E. (2001). *Prekindergarten benchmarks for language and literacy: Progress made and challenges to be met*. Aurora, CO: McREL.

Byrne, B., & Field-Barnsley, R. (1993). Evaluation of a program to teach phonemic awareness to young children: A 1-year follow-up. *Journal of Educational Psychology, 85*(1), 104–111.

Cazden, C. (1976). Play with language and meta-linguistic awareness: One dimension of language experience. In J. Bruner, A. Jolly, & K. Sylva (Eds.), *Play and its role in development and evolution* (pp. 603–608). New York: Basic Books.

Christie, J. (2003, February). *The story behind play and literacy*. Paper presented at the annual conference of the Association for the Study of Play, Charleston, SC.

Cohen, D., & Hill, H. (2001). *Learning policy*. New Haven, CT: Yale University Press.

Dickinson, D., & Tabors, P. (2001). *Beginning literacy with language: Young children learning at home and school*. Baltimore: Paul H. Brookes.

Dunn, L., Beach, S., & Kontos, S. (2000). Supporting literacy in early childhood programs: A challenge for the future. In K. Roskos & J. Christie (Eds.), *Play and literacy in early childhood: Research from multiple perspectives* (pp. 91–105). Mahwah, NJ: Erlbaum.

Ehri, L., & Sweet, J. (1991). Fingerpoint-reading of memorized texts: What enables beginners to process print? *Reading Research Quarterly, 24*, 442–462.

Fernandez-Fein, S., & Baker, L. (1997). Rhyme and alliteration sensitivity and relevant experiences among preschoolers from diverse backgrounds. *Journal of Literacy Research, 29*, 433–459.

Garvey, C. (1974). Some properties of social play. *Merrill-Palmer Quarterly, 20*, 163–180.

Gmitrova, V., & Gmitrova, J. (2003). The impact of teacher-directed and child-directed pretend play on cognitive competence in kindergarten children. *Early Childhood Education Journal, 30*(4), 241–246.

Good Start, Grow Smart. (2002, April). U.S. Department of Education.

Grissmer, D., Flanagan, A., Kawata, J., & Williamson, S. (2000). *Improving student achievement: What NAEP state test scores tell us*. Santa Monica, CA: RAND.

Groos, K. (1898). *The play of animals* (E. L. Baldwin, Trans.). New York: Appleton.

Hall, G. S. (1907). *Youth: Its education, regimen, and hygiene*. New York: Appleton.

Heckman, J. (2002). Human capital: Investing in parents to facilitate positive outcomes in young children. Opening session remarks. In *The first eight years: Pathways to the future* (Summary of conference proceeding, pp. 6–15). Washington, DC: The Head Start Bureau, Mailman School of Health & Society for Research in Child Development.

Hewit, S. (2001). Can play-based curriculum survive the standards storm? A teacher educator's perspective. *Play, Policy, & Practice Connections, 6*(2), 3–5.

Hirsh-Pasek, K., & Golinkoff, R. (2003). *Einstein never used flash cards: How our children really learn and why they need to play more and memorize less*. Emmaus, PA: Rodale.

Johnson, J. (1994). The challenge of incorporating research on play into the practice of preschool education. *Journal of Applied Developmental Psychology, 15*, 603–618.

Johnson, J., Christie, J., & Wardle, F. (2005). *Play, development, and early education*. New York: Allyn & Bacon.

Jones, E. (2003). Viewpoint: Playing to get smart. *Young Children, 58*(3), 32–36.

Kagan, S., & Lowenstein, A. (2004). School readiness and children's play: Contemporary oxymoron or compatible option? In E. Zigler, D. Singer, & S. Bishop-Josef (Eds.), *Children's play: The roots of reading* (pp. 59–76). Washington, DC: Zero to Three Press.

King, N. (1979). Play: The kindergartners' perspective. *Elementary School Journal, 80*, 81–87.

Martin, P., & Caro, T. (1985). On the functions of play and its role in behavioral development. In J. Rosenblatt, C. Beer, M. Busnel, & P. Slater (Eds.), *Advances in the study of behavior* (Vol. 15, pp. 59–103). New York: Academic Press.

Marzano, R., & Kendall, J. (1998)). *Implementing standards-based education* Washington, DC: National Education Association.

Mason, J. (1984). Early reading from a developmental perspective. In P. D. Pearson (Ed.), *Handbook of reading research* (pp. 505–543). New York: Longman.

McCardle, P., & Chhabra, V. (2004). *The voice of evidence in reading research.* Baltimore: Brookes.

McLane, J. (2003). *"Does not." "Does, too." Thinking about play in the early childhood classroom* (Occasional Paper, Number 4). Chicago: Erikson Institute.

NCLB. (2001). *No Child Left Behind: Reauthorization of the Elementary and Secondary Education Act Legislation and Policies.* Retrieved November 18, 2005, from http://www.ed.gov/about/offices/list/oese/legislation.html#leg

Neuman, S. (2001). The role of knowledge in early literacy. *Reading Research Quarterly, 36*, 468–475.

Neuman, S., & Dickinson, D. (Eds.). (2001). *The handbook of early literacy research.* New York: Guilford.

Neuman, S., & Roskos, K. (1992). Literacy objects as cultural tools: Effects on children's literacy behaviors during play. *Reading Research Quarterly, 27*, 203–223.

Neuman, S., & Roskos, K. (1993). Access to print for children of poverty: Differential effects of adult mediation and literacy-enriched play settings on environmental and functional print tasks. *American Educational Research Journal, 30*, 95–122.

Neuman, S., & Roskos, K. (2005). The state of the state prekindergarten standards. *Early Childhood Research Quarterly, 20*, 125–145.

Neuman, S., Roskos, K., & Vukelich, C. (2003, December). *Meeting the school readiness challenge for low-income children: An evaluation of prekindergarten standards in 35 states.* Paper presented at the annual meeting of the National Reading Conference, Scottsdale, AZ.

Piaget, J. (1962). *Play, dreams and imitation in childhood.* New York: Norton.

Roskos, K., & Christie, J. (2004). Examining the play–literacy interface: A critical review and future directions. In E. Zigler, D. Singer, & S. Bishop-Josef (Eds.), *Children's play: The roots of reading* (pp. 95–123). Washington, DC: Zero to Three Press.

Roskos, K., & Vukelich, C. (2006). Early literacy policy and pedagogy. In D. Dickinson & S. Neuman (Eds.), *Handbook of Early Literacy Research II* (pp. 295–310). New York: Guilford.

Rubin, K., Fein, G., & Vandenberg, B. (1983). Play. In P. H. Mussen (Ed.), *Handbook of child psychology: Vol. 4. Socialization, personality, and social development* (4th ed., pp. 693–774). New York: Wiley.

Sackett, G., Sameroff, A., Cairns, R., & Suomi, S. (1981). Continuity in behavioral development: Theoretical and empirical issues. In K. Immelmann, G. Barrow, L. Petrinovich, & M. Main (Eds.), *Behavioral development* (pp. 23–57). New York: Cambridge University Press.

Saltz, E., Dixon, D., & Johnson, J. (1977). Training disadvantaged preschoolers on various fantasy activities: Effects on cognitive functioning and impulse control. *Child Development, 48*, 367–380.

Schickedanz, J., Pergantis, M. L., Kanosky, J., Blaney, A., & Ottinger, J. (1997). *Curriculum in early childhood.* Boston: Allyn & Bacon.

Schweinhart, L. (2003). *Making validated educational models central in preschool standards.* New Brunswick, NJ: National Institute in Early Education and Research.

Scott-Little, C., Kagan, S., & Frelow, V. (2003). *Standards for preschool children's learning and development: Who has standards, how were they developed and how are they used.* Raleigh, NC: SERVE.

Senechal, M., LeFevre, J., Colton, K. V., & Smith, B. L. (2000). On refining theoretical models of emergent literacy. *Journal of School Psychology, 39*(5), 439–460.

Shonkoff, J. (2004). *Science, policy, and the young developing child: Closing the gap between what we know and what we do.* Chicago: Ounce of Prevention Fund.

Shonkoff, J., & Phillips, D. (2000). *From neurons to neighborhoods: The science of early childhood development.* Washington, DC: National Academy Press.

Singer, D., & Singer, J. (1990). *The house of make-believe: Children's play and developing imagination.* Cambridge, MA: Harvard University Press.

Singer, D., & Singer, J. (2004). Encouraging school readiness through guided pretend games. In E. Zigler, D. Singer, & S. Bishop-Josef (Eds.), *Children's play: The roots of reading* (pp. 175–187). Washington, DC: Zero to Three Press.

Singer, D., & Singer, J. (2005). *Imagination and play in the electronic age.* Cambridge, MA: Harvard University Press.

Singer, J., & Singer, D. (1981). *Imagination and aggression of preschoolers.* New York: Erlbaum.

Smilansky, S. (1968). *The effects of sociodramatic play on disadvantaged preschool children.* New York: Wiley.

Smith, P., & Vollstedt, R. (1985). On defining play: An empirical study of the relationship between play and various play criteria. *Child Development, 56*, 1042–1050.

Snow, C., Burns, M. S., & Griffin, P. (1998). *Preventing reading difficulties in young children.* Washington, DC: National Academy Press.

Sulzby, E., & Teale, W. (1991). Emergent literacy. In R. Barr, M. Kamil, P. Mosenthal, & P. D. Pearson (Eds.), *Handbook of reading research* (Vol. 2, pp. 727–757). New York: Longman.

Sutton-Smith, B. (1985). Play research: State of the art. In J. Frost & S. Sunderlin (Eds.), *When children play* (pp. 9–16). Wheaton, MD: Association for Childhood Education International.

Sutton-Smith, B. (1995). Conclusion: The persuasive rhetorics of play. In A. D. Pellegrini (Ed.), *The future of play theory* (pp. 275–296). Albany: State University of New York Press.

Tamis-LeMonda, C., & Bornstein, M. (1993). Play and its relations to other mental functions in the child. In M. Bornstein & A. O'Reilly (Eds.), *The role of play in the development of thought: New directions in child development* (Vol. 59, pp. 17–27). San Francisco: Jossey-Bass.

Thelen, E., & Smith, L. B. (1995). *A dynamic systems approach to the development of cognition and action.* Cambridge, MA: MIT Press.

Vukelich, C. (1994). Effects of play interventions on young children's reading of environmental print. *Early Childhood Research Quarterly, 9*, 153–170.

Vukelich, C., & Christie, J. (2004). *Building a foundation for preschool literacy: Effective instruction for children's reading and writing development.* Newark, DE: International Reading Association.

Vygosky, L. (1966). Play and its role in mental development. *Soviet Psychology, 5*, 6–18.

Vygotsky, L. (1978). *Mind in society: The development of psychological processes*. Cambridge, MA: Harvard University Press.

Weir, R. (1976). Playing with language. In J. Bruner, A. Jolly, & K. Sylva (Eds.), *Play and its role in development and evolution* (pp. 609–618). New York: Basic Books.

Whitehurst, G., Epstein, J., Angell, A., Payne, A., Crone, D., & Fischel, J. (1994). Outcomes of an emergent literacy intervention in Head Start. *Journal of Educational Psychology, 86*, 542–555.

Yaden, D., Rowe, D., & MacGillivray, L. (2000). Emergent literacy: A matter (polyphony) of perspectives. In M. Kamil, P. Mosenthal, P. D. Pearson, & R. Barr (Eds.), *Handbook of reading research* (Vol. 3, pp. 425–454). Mahwah, NJ: Erlbaum.

Zigler, E., & Bishop-Josef, S. (2004). Play under siege: A historical overview. In E. Zigler, D. Singer, & S. Bishop-Josef (Eds.), *Children's play: The roots of reading* (pp. 1–14). Washington, DC: Zero to Three Press.

Zigler, E., Singer, D., & Bishop-Josef, S. (Eds.). (2004). *Children's play: The roots of reading*. Washington, DC: Zero to Three Press.

5

Make-Believe Play: Wellspring for Development of Self-Regulation

LAURA E. BERK, TRISHA D. MANN, AND AMY T. OGAN

The early childhood years are a crucial time for the development of self-regulation —an array of complex mental capacities that includes impulse and emotion control, self-guidance of thought and behavior, planning, self-reliance, and socially responsible behavior (Bronson, 2001; Kopp, 1991). By the end of the preschool years, well-regulated children can wait for a turn, resist the temptation to grab a desired object from another child, clean up after a play period with little or no adult prompting, willingly help another child or adult with a task, and persist at a challenging activity. Such children also actively try to control negative emotion, often by talking to themselves ("I'll get a chance soon") or changing their goals (when one activity isn't possible, turning to another).

As these examples illustrate, self-regulation is central to our conception of what it means to be human—the foundation for choice and decision making, for mastery of higher cognitive processes, and for morality. Self-regulatory capacities are also essential for children to meet the academic and social requirements of school. The human need for complex, flexible regulatory systems that can cope with a wide array of environmental conditions means that the development of self-regulation begins early, takes place over an extended time period, and requires substantial external support.

Early childhood is also the "high season" of imaginative play (Singer & Singer, 1990), when make-believe evolves from simple imitative acts into elaborate plots involving complex coordination of roles. In this chapter, we present wide-ranging evidence that pretense is pivotal in children's advancing mastery over their own thinking, emotions, and behavior. Our work is grounded in the sociocultural theory of eminent Russian developmental psychologist Lev Vygotsky (1896–1934), who viewed social experiences—including make-believe play—as prime catalysts of development. We begin by reviewing central Vygotskian concepts and related research, key to understanding Vygotsky's view of the role of make-believe in self-regulatory development. Then we turn to Vygotskian ideas about the function of pretense and to supportive evidence. We conclude with the importance of encouraging and enriching children's make-believe in families, early childhood programs, and communities and of providing developmentally appropriate play interventions for children who are deficient in self-regulatory skills.

EARLY CHILDHOOD: A CRUCIAL PERIOD FOR DEVELOPMENT OF SELF-REGULATION

Self-regulation begins with control of arousal and modulation of sensory stimulation in the early months of life and extends to emergence of compliance and impulse control in the second year (Kopp, 1982). During the preschool years, children start to use cognitive strategies to control their emotions and impulses, learn to act in accord with social and moral standards, and make strides in directing and monitoring their thinking and behavior in pursuit of self-chosen goals and the expectations of others (Flavell, Miller, & Miller, 2002; Luria, 1961; Mischel, 1996; Vygotsky, 1934/1986). The diverse aspects of self-regulation are interrelated. Impulse control, emotion regulation, cognitive regulation, and the capacity to act in accord with social and moral standards contribute to one another. Self-regulation is a crowning achievement of early childhood (Bronson, 2001; Eisenberg, Smith, Sadovsky, & Spinrad, 2004).

Methods that permit study of the relationship between brain functioning and behavior (such as functional magnetic resonance imaging) suggest that massive changes in the cerebral cortex, especially the frontal lobes, underlie gains in self-regulation (see, for example, Gerardi-Caulton, 2000; Rothbart, Ellis, Rueda, & Posner, 2003). Formation of synapses in the frontal lobes peaks during the preschool years, reaching nearly double the adult value around age 4, with pruning of synapses just underway—neurological developments that signify a period of high plasticity, or "readiness" for learning (Nelson, 2002; Rothbart & Bates, 1998; Thompson et al., 2000). The neurological underpinnings of self-regulation (and other higher cognitive functions), however, do not simply "mature" in the young child. Instead, mounting evidence indicates that they result from dynamic interchanges between brain activity and experience (Huttenlocher, 2002; Johnson, 1998). Appropriate environmental supports are essential for the cerebral organization that gives rise to self-regulation.

Gains in behavioral self-control between 18 and 30 months, as indexed by the child's increasing capacity to delay gratification (e.g., wait to eat a raisin or open a gift), correlate with early language progress (Vaughn, Kopp, & Krakow, 1984). Indeed, the earliest manifestations of self-control, in the form of compliance, require that toddlers have developed sufficient language to comprehend a caregiver's verbal directives. Compliance, in turn, quickly leads to the first self-directed verbal commands in the service of self-control, evident in, for example, the toddler who exclaims, "No, can't!" and then inhibits her reach toward a light socket. Large individual differences in self-control are apparent early and remain modestly stable into middle childhood and adolescence, with language development remaining a significant predictor of maturity (Cournoyer, Solomon, & Trudel, 1998; Kochanska, Murray, & Coy, 1997; Shoda, Mischel, & Peake, 1990).

In accord with these findings, diverse theories grant language a facilitating role in the development of self-regulation (Mischel, 1996; Piaget, 1936/1951; Skinner, 1957; Vygotsky, 1934/1986). Among them, however, Vygotsky's sociocultural perspective is unique in regarding language as the prime catalyst of self-regulatory development.

VYGOTSKY'S THEORY: ADULT-CHILD DIALOGUES ENGENDER SELF-REGULATION

According to Vygotsky, cooperative dialogues between children and more knowledgeable members of their society are essential for children to acquire uniquely human, higher cognitive processes, including management of attention and behavior, reflection on experiences and ideas, and strategies for solving cognitive and social problems. Any complex form of thinking first appears in social communication, between the child and more expert representatives of his or her culture as they engage in joint activities (Vygotsky (1930–1935/1978). Only later does it appear within the child as an autonomous capacity or skill. Because language is our primary avenue of communication with others and the central means through which we represent experience, once children become capable of thinking with words, their capacity to make contact with, and to be influenced by, more expert minds greatly expands. Eventually, children take the communication jointly generated in these dialogues and turn it toward the self. As a result, language (as we will see later when we take up private, or self-directed, speech) becomes an indispensable mental tool for guiding and managing thought and behavior.

For Vygotsky (1930–1935/1978), communication with more mature cultural members promotes development by providing the child with experiences in his or her zone of proximal development—a vital Vygotskian concept that refers to tasks that offer an appropriate degree of challenge in that the child can accomplish them with social support. Contemporary followers of Vygotsky point out that adult and child jointly create this zone through at least two communicative ingredients.

First, for information, ideas, and skills to move from the social-interactive plane to the internal-thinking plane, adult and child must strive for *intersubjectivity,* or shared understanding, which grows out of each partner's sensitivity to the other's perspective (Newson & Newson, 1975). Intersubjectivity is itself a developmental process. Because infants and young children are still acquiring communication skills, the younger the child, the greater the adult's responsibility for making mental contact and sustaining interaction through sensitively adjusted verbal and nonverbal cues (Ratner & Stettner, 1991). The development of spoken language enables greater clarification of purpose between participants in a dialogue and, thus, brings a vastly expanded potential for intersubjectivity. By 2 to 3 years, children can clearly state their thoughts and feelings and respond in a timely and relevant fashion in a dialogue—capacities that improve with experience (Whitington & Ward, 1999). As the adult adjusts her communication to the child's level, the child stretches up to grasp the adult's viewpoint, yielding a "meeting of minds" that fuels children's learning.

Intersubjectivity makes possible a second interactive feature that creates the zone of proximal development: *scaffolding*, a metaphor that captures effective adult support as children engage in challenging endeavors (Wood, 1989). In scaffolding, the child is viewed as an edifice, actively under construction; the adult provides a dynamic, flexible scaffold, or framework, that assists the child in mastering new competencies. To promote development, the adult varies his assistance to fit the child's changing level of performance by adjusting the task so its demands are appropriate and by tailoring the degree of intervention to the child's current learning needs (Berk & Winsler, 1995). A major goal of scaffolding is to promote self-regulation by offering strategies for successful mastery and relinquishing assistance once the child can function autonomously.

Studies of children of diverse ages engaged in a wide variety of tasks reveal that adult encouragement, emotional support, and scaffolding predict increased effort and more successful performance when children attempt challenging tasks on their own (Diaz, Neal, & Vachio, 1991; Landry, Miller-Loncar, Smith, & Swank, 2002; Neitzel & Stright, 2003; Pratt, Kerig, Cowan, & Cowan, 1988; Roberts & Barnes, 1992). Moreover, scaffolding is linked to children's use of private speech—a major sign that children are adopting socially generated strategies and using them to regulate their own thinking and behavior (Behrend, Rosengren, & Perlmutter, 1989, 1992; Berk & Spuhl, 1995).

VYGOTSKY'S VIEW OF MAKE-BELIEVE PLAY: VITAL CONTEXT FOR DEVELOPMENT OF SELF-REGULATION

Vygotsky regarded make-believe play as the paramount early childhood context for development of self-regulation. Consistent with this view, make-believe is rich in collaborative dialogues and development-enhancing consequences. As soon as toddlers have the language skills to engage in pretense, warm, involved parents often join in and scaffold their play.

Consider Kevin, who takes charge of his 2½-year-old daughter Sophie on weekday afternoons: On arriving home from child care, Sophie usually grabs Kevin's hand and leads him to the family room rug, filled with building toys and make-believe props. One afternoon, Sophie moved a toy horse and cow inside a small, enclosed fence that she and Kevin had put together the day before. Then she turned the animals on their sides and moved them toward each other.

> "Why are the horse and cow lying down?" Kevin inquired.
>
> "'Cause they're tired," Sophie answered, pushing the two animals closer together.
>
> "Oh, yes," Kevin affirmed. Then building on Sophie's theme, he placed a teddy bear on another part of the rug and offered, "I think Ted's tired, too. I'm going to start a bed over here for some other animals."

> Sophie turned toward the teddy bear, lifted his paw, and exclaimed, "She wants a lollipop to hold in her hand!"
>
> "A lollipop in her hand? We haven't got any lollipops, have we?" answered Kevin. "Maybe this could be a make-believe lollipop," suggested Kevin, placing a round piece on the end of a long Tinkertoy stick and handing the structure to Sophie.
>
> "That's a lollipop," agreed Sophie, placing it in the paw of the teddy bear.
>
> "Can she suck that while she's going off to sleep?" asked Kevin. "Do you think that's what she wants?"
>
> "It's a pacifier," explained Sophie, renaming the object.
>
> "A pacifier, do you think? The pacifier might help her get to sleep," Kevin confirmed.
>
> "This long, long pacifier," Sophie answered, picking up the Tinkertoy structure, looking at its long stick, and pausing as if to decide what to do next.
>
> "Leprechaun is looking pretty tired," suggested Kevin, laying Sophie's stuffed leprechaun next to the teddy bear. "What do you think?"
>
> "He wants a lollipop, too!"
>
> "Oh, he wants a lollipop as well. What are we going to use for a lollipop for the leprechaun?" asked Kevin.
>
> Pressing the teddy bear's and the leprechaun's arms together and the lollipop-turned-pacifier between them, Sophie readily arrived at a solution. "He's sharing," she affirmed.
>
> "Oh, they'll share! All right," Kevin agreed. (Adapted from Berk, 2001, pp. 107–108)

Eminent developmental theorists of the 20th century accorded make-believe play a significant role in development, variously regarding it as a means through which preschoolers practice and solidify symbolic schemes (Piaget, 1936/1951), as a form of wish fulfillment that assists children in mastering fears and anxieties (Freud, 1959), and as an avenue for exploring social roles and gaining a sense of their future (Erikson, 1950). Acknowledging these functions, Vygotsky moved beyond them, elevating make-believe to a "leading factor in development"—a unique, broadly influential zone of proximal development in which children experiment with a wide array of challenging skills and acquire culturally valued competencies (Vygotsky, 1930–1935/1978, p. 101). Foremost among those abilities is a greatly strengthened capacity for self-regulation. Vygotsky stated:

> [Make-believe] play creates a zone of proximal development in the child. In play, the child always behaves beyond his average age, above his daily behavior; in play it is as though he were a head taller than himself. As in the focus of a magnifying glass, play contains all developmental tendencies in a condensed form and is itself a major source of development. (p. 102)

Careful observations of children at play reveal what Vygotsky meant when he asserted that make-believe play creates a zone of proximal development in which the child is "a head taller than herself." In Sophie's play with her father, she satisfied both the teddy bear's and the leprechaun's desire for a lollipop, when just one toy lollipop was available, by having them share—a remarkably mature response for a 2-year-old. In everyday life, Western toddlers and preschoolers find sharing to be difficult (Fasig, 2000; Levine, 1983). As another illustration, consider 5-year-old

David, who cannot sit still and pay attention during circle time in kindergarten for more than 2 minutes. Yet when pretending to be a cooperative member of the class while playing school with his friends, David can sit and attend for as long as 10 minutes. Play provides the roles, rules, and scenarios that enable David to focus and sustain interest at a higher level than he does in nonpretend activities. Indeed, during the preschool years, as goal-directed play becomes more complex, often in the form of make-believe, children's attention spans increase and their distractibility declines (Choi & Anderson, 1991; Ruff & Capozzoli, 2003).

Unique Features of Make-Believe Play

Vygotsky (1930–1935/1978) asserted that the distinctive features of make-believe play—those that make it unique among children's experiences—clarify just how it leads development forward. He concluded that two crucial elements distinguish make-believe from other childhood activities.

First, the creation of imaginary situations in play helps children separate mental representations from the objects and events for which they stand. Once preschoolers realize that words, gestures, and other symbols are distinct from external reality, they are on their way to using those symbols as tools for overcoming impulse and managing their own behavior. As a result, children strengthen their *internal capacity* to become civilized and socially responsible. Second, a careful look at children's play scenarios reveals that make-believe play is, above all, rule-based play. Drawing on experiences in their families and communities, children continuously devise and follow social rules in pretense. In doing so, they strive to bring their behavior in line with social expectations, thereby strengthening their sensitivity to *external pressures* to act in socially desirable ways.

These complementary ingredients of make-believe play suggest that it is a supreme contributor to the development of self-regulation—one that extends the impact of adult teaching and example more than any other context of the preschool years (Berk, 2001). Let's examine these features of pretense more closely.

Overcoming Impulsive Action

Between 1 and 2½ years of age, as children acquire language, the ability to comply with others' directives, and limited self-control, caregivers increasingly insist that children engage in socially appropriate conduct: respect property, treat others kindly, obey safety rules, delay gratification, participate in simple chores, and use good manners (Gralinski & Kopp, 1993). During the very period when children must learn to subordinate their desires to social life, imaginative play flourishes. For Vygotsky (1930–1935/1978), this synchrony between socialization and make-believe is no coincidence. The young, immature child colors on walls, drops toys on the spot when another activity engages him, runs after a ball that rolls into the street, grabs an attractive object from a playmate, and cannot wait patiently while his mother is on the phone. Make-believe play, Vygotsky asserted, helps preschoolers conquer these impulses by giving the child repeated practice in "acting independently of what he sees" (p. 101).

According to Vygotsky, the object substitutions in make-believe are crucial in helping children use thought to guide behavior. By changing an object's usual meaning—making a Tinkertoy stand for a lollipop or a folded blanket for a sleeping baby—children detach ideas from the stimuli around them. Sophie, for example, used the image of a lollipop to alter the Tinkertoy's identity. In doing so, she controlled the lollipop's very existence, as well as the teddy bear's, the leprechaun's, and her own actions toward it.

Toddlers' efforts at make-believe reveal that distinguishing mental symbols from their real-world referents is initially quite difficult. Children younger than age 2 generally use only realistic-looking objects while pretending—a toy telephone to talk into or a cup to drink from (Tomasello, Striano, & Rochat, 1999). Around age 2, children start to pretend with less realistic toys. During the third year, they flexibly imagine objects and events without support from the real world, as when they exclaim, "I'm launching the rocket!" while gesturing with their hands or without acting out the event at all (O'Reilly, 1995; Striano, Tomasello, & Rochat, 2001).

Vygotsky maintained that in separating symbols from objects, make-believe play helps children choose deliberately among alternative courses of action. In play, Sophie imagined that both the teddy bear and the leprechaun wanted a lollipop, considered possibilities (whether to give the lollipop to one, create a second lollipop, or have them share), and decided the eventual outcome.

Acquiring and Enacting the Rules of Social Life

Vygotsky, like Erikson, regarded make-believe as a vital early childhood context for learning about social roles. Vygotsky (1930–1935/1978), however, was more explicit about how pretense fosters children's eager, willing participation in social life. Children's imaginative play, Vygotsky pointed out, contains a paradox. In play, preschoolers seem to do what they most feel like doing, and to an outside observer, their play appears free and spontaneous. Nevertheless, pretend play demands that children act against their immediate impulses because they must subject themselves to the rules of the make-believe scene. For example, a child pretending to go to sleep follows the rules of bedtime behavior, another child imagining herself to be a mother conforms to the rules of parental behavior, and still another child playing astronaut obeys the rules of shuttle launch and space walk.

In this sense, make-believe is not really "free play," as it often is assumed to be. Instead, its essence is self-restraint—voluntarily following social rules. While pretending, Vygotsky (1930–1935/1978) explained, children repeatedly face conflicts between the rules of the make-believe situation and what they would do if they could act impulsively, and they usually decide in favor of the rules. When tired, Sophie's teddy bear and leprechaun do not stay up doing just as they please. Instead, they obey their caregivers and go to bed. With only one lollipop, rather than quarreling and grabbing, the teddy bear and the leprechaun share.

According to Vygotsky (1930–1935/1978), children's greatest self-control occurs during make-believe, when at their own initiative they renounce a momentary attraction in favor of rule-governed behavior. The paradox of make-believe is that when children subordinate their actions to rules in everyday life, they usually give up something they want—instead of keeping a toy for themselves, they share it; instead of watching more TV, they go to bed. During pretense, however, renouncing impulse and following social rules, rather than frustrating or disappointing the child, is central to the pleasure of playing. Thus, subordinating immediate desires to the rules of make-believe becomes "a new form of desire" (p. 100)—one that responds to the child's need to become an accepted member of her culture.

Indeed, informal observations of children's pretense suggest that they rarely violate the rules of their social world. As preschoolers increasingly participate in sociodramatic play with peers, the complex negotiations they engage in to create play scenes, as well as the settings, actions, and conversations of those scenes, continually draw on cultural rules, conventions, and models of cooperation (Vygotsky, 1933, as cited by Ortega, 2003).

RESEARCH ON MAKE-BELIEVE PLAY AND SELF-REGULATION

In line with Vygotsky's emphasis on the development-enhancing, forward-moving consequences of make-believe, research confirms that preschoolers' involvement in pretense is linked to wide-ranging favorable outcomes, including language and literacy development, understanding of mental states (false belief, emotions, and others' perspectives), ability to distinguish appearance from reality, social competence, and divergent thinking (see, for example, Bergen & Mauer, 2000; Connolly & Doyle, 1984; Dansky, 1980; Ervin-Tripp, 1991; Kavanaugh & Engel, 1998; Lindsey & Colwell, 2003; Lloyd & Howe, 2003; Roskos & Neuman, 1998; Schwebel, Rosen, & Singer, 1999; Singer & Singer, 1990, 2005; Taylor & Carlson, 1997). Given that self-regulatory capacities are prerequisite to, and benefit from, these indicators of cognitive and social maturity (Bronson, 2001), the evidence is compatible with the notion that make-believe play contributes importantly to self-regulation.

Yet these studies do not directly answer the question of whether participation in make-believe play fosters a self-regulated child. An emerging literature, including several of our own studies, supports the contributing role of make-believe.

Make-Believe Play and Private Speech

In Vygotsky's (1930–1935/1978) theory, language is not only a major means through which culturally adaptive cognitive processes are transmitted to children but also the primary vehicle for self-regulation. If Vygotsky theory is correct that make-believe assists children in overcoming impulse and managing their own behavior, then we might expect children's pretense to be especially rich in self-regulating language.

During the preschool years, private speech (or speech directed to the self) can be observed frequently; it accounts for 20 to 60% of preschoolers' utterances during play and other activities (Berk, 1992). Vygotsky explained that as more expert partners interact with children in ways that enhance their knowledge and understanding, children integrate those dialogues into their private speech. Over time, they weave into their self-talk an increasingly rich tapestry of voices from their social world (Wertsch, 1993)—a process that ensures transfer of values, strategies, and skills from the minds of one generation to the minds of the next.

Research confirms that private speech signifies that children are taking over the support provided by others and using it to guide and control their own thinking and behavior (see, for example, Furrow, 1992). Although self-talk takes many forms, in most instances preschoolers appear to be working through ideas, surmounting obstacles, mastering cognitive or social skills, or managing intense emotion (Berk, 1992, 2001). Many studies support the self-regulating function of private speech. For example, private speech increases under conditions of challenge. Moreover, preschoolers and young school-age children who make self-guiding comments while working on challenging tasks are more attentive and involved and perform better than their less talkative age-mates (Berk & Spuhl, 1995; Bivens & Berk, 1990; Winsler, Diaz, & Montero, 1997). In one investigation, 4- and 5-year-olds judged by their preschool teachers as good at regulating emotion used more private speech during free play, art, and puzzle activities than did classmates who were rated as poorly regulated (Broderick, 2001).

In a series of investigations, we examined the relationship of make-believe play to preschoolers' use of private speech. In the most extensive of these studies, Krafft and Berk (1998) observed children during free-choice periods in two preschools that differed sharply in encouragement of imaginative play: the Y Preschool (called this because it is sponsored by the YWCA) and the Montessori Preschool. In the Y Preschool, play formed the basis of the daily program. Children had easy access to a wide variety of pretend-play props, and each classroom contained two centers especially conducive to sociodramatic play—a block-building area and a playhouse. The Montessori preschool, in contrast, actively discouraged make-believe (although not all Montessori schools do). Spurred by Montessori principles advocating realistic activities, the teachers set up "workstations" from which children selected table activities; typical options were puzzles, letter tracing, small construction blocks, containers with water for pouring, picture books, and materials for drawing and writing. When the Montessori children lapsed into make-believe, teachers often interrupted to draw them back to workstation pursuits.

Time sampling observations were collected on 59 middle-socioeconomic-status (SES) 3- to 5-year-olds (approximately half in each preschool), with each child observed for 80 30-second intervals equally divided across 4 days. The Montessori children, despite teacher discouragement, did engage in pretense, but at a sharply reduced rate; Y preschoolers displayed nearly 3 times as much make-believe play (see table 5.1). Private speech showed a parallel trend: Children in the Y preschool engaged in substantially more self-talk than their Montessori counterparts—in particular, role play verbalizations, which take the self or an object (such as a puppet or doll) as a partner, and self-guiding speech, in which the child thinks out loud by commenting on her activity and formulating plans for action (refer again to table 5.1). Moreover, with verbal ability controlled (a correlate of both pretense

Table 5.1 Relationship of Type of Preschool to Make-Believe Play and Private Speech

	Montessori Preschool		Y Preschool		
	M	*SD*	M	*SD*	*F*(1,52)
Make-believe play	11.6	8.2	32.6	15.9	49.8**
Total private speech	17.1	9.3	34.8	13.5	25.4**
Role-play private speech	3.5	4.8	12.6	9.3	20.3**
Describing own activity/self-guidance	3.2	3.1	4.6	3.4	4.5*

Note. Means indicate number of observation intervals, out of 80, in which make-believe play and private speech occurred.
$^*p < .05$. $^{**}p < .01$.

and private speech), among children's free-choice pursuits, fantasy play emerged as the strongest correlate of total private speech ($r = .59$, $p <.01$) and the two private speech subtypes just mentioned ($r = .74$, $p <.001$ and $r = .27$, $p <.05$).

These results indicate that the more children engaged in make-believe, the more they talked to themselves to work out pretend characters' actions and to guide their thought and behavior during realistic tasks. Moreover, the two subtypes of private speech were positively correlated, $r = .42$, $p <.01$. Overall, the findings suggest that private speech, so rich in the make-believe context, may carry over and facilitate children's self-talk when they face real-world challenges.

As noted earlier, private speech increases with task difficulty; once preschoolers become more proficient at the puzzle, picture arrangement, and other problem-solving tasks in which private speech has most often been observed, their audible, self-directed speech declines by abbreviating and becoming less audible (Duncan & Pratt, 1997; Patrick & Abravanel, 2000; see also Berk, 1992, 2001, for reviews). Yet private speech follows a decidedly different age-related course during make-believe play. Gillingham and Berk (1995) videotaped 30 middle-SES 2½- to 6-year-olds during a 9-minute play period in a laboratory liberally equipped with fantasy-play props. Children's private speech was coded into remarks (a word, phrase, or sentence uttered without pause), and the amount of time they spent in two broad play categories was recorded: (a) simple play, involving inspection and manipulation of toys, and (b) complex play, largely make-believe. Although make-believe was the dominant form of play for children of all ages, it increased sharply and linearly between 2½ and 6. As in Krafft and Berk's research, the incidence of task-relevant private speech during make-believe was high, averaging 2.3 remarks per minute. Moreover, instead of diminishing, private speech remained at a comparably high level throughout the entire age range.

Our interpretation of this sustained high incidence of private speech during make-believe across the preschool years is that children continually set challenges for themselves during pretense. In line with Vygotsky's theory, make-believe play creates a zone of proximal development in which preschoolers frequently call on self-directed language to work out their imaginings and bring behavior under the control of thought.

Make-Believe Play and Emotional Self-Regulation

Psychoanalytic theorists, and others, contend that pretend play, by offering children the opportunity to enact and modify an unlimited variety of emotional experiences, enables them to master negative affect in a safe context (Bretherton & Beeghly, 1989; Fein, 1989). The first systematic research to test this assumption reported confirming findings. Barnett and Storm (1981) randomly assigned 20 preschoolers to view a stressful movie scene (Lassie and her master became lost in a storm) and compared their subsequent play behavior with that of 20 controls, who viewed the scene and its positive resolution (Lassie and her master were safely reunited). Initial anxiety levels of the two groups, based on a physiological measure (palm sweating) and a self-report (selecting from very happy to very sad faces the one that represented how the child felt), were comparable, but as expected, anxiety in the stressful-movie group rose much more following viewing. However, children in the movie-stressor group declined sharply in anxiety and negative emotion after the play period, during which they spent more time enacting events related to the Lassie scene than control children did. In a second investigation, Barnett (1984) observed 74 3-year-olds as they exhibited distress at the departure of their mother on the first day of preschool. High- and low-anxious children, distinguished on the basis of observations (clinging, pleading, crying) and physiological reaction (palm sweating), participated in either a free-play or a story-reading session. Relative to the other children, anxious children in the play condition engaged in more play thematically directed at resolving conflict, and they also showed a greater decline in physiological anxiety.

Recent findings are consistent with the notion that make-believe play is among the socialization experiences that contribute to an emotionally well-regulated child. High levels of sociodramatic play and conflict-resolution themes in play narratives are linked to good emotional self-regulation in preschoolers (Fantuzzo, Sekino, & Cohen, 2004; Lemche et al., 2003). Although many studies indicate that emotional self-regulation is essential for socially competent play behavior (Eisenberg, 1998, 2003), fewer have addressed the role of make-believe play in the development of emotional self-regulation. In one suggestive (but not conclusive) investigation, children who positively resolved an experimenter-induced, emotionally arousing make-believe event in a laboratory (a hungry crocodile puppet threatened to eat all the toys) so play could continue were rated by their parents as having more effective emotion-regulation skills in everyday life (Galyer & Evans, 2001). Additional evidence, reviewed in a later section, indicates that the thematic content of children's pretense has much to do with its power to enhance children's emotional (and other) self-regulatory skills.

Make-Believe Play and Socially Responsible Behavior

In two investigations, we explored whether participation in make-believe play influences preschoolers' performance on two naturalistic measures of self-regulation that tap socially responsible behavior: (a) the extent to which the child independently cleans up materials after free choice time in preschool (Alessandri,

1992; Kochanska, Murray, Jacques, Koenig, & Vandegeest, 1996) and (b) the child's attentiveness and cooperativeness during circle time (Huston-Stein, Friedrick-Cofer, & Susman, 1977).

In the first of these studies (Elias & Berk, 2002), 51 middle-SES 3- and 4-year-olds were observed in their preschool classrooms during the fall (Time 1) and the spring (Time 2) of the school year. During the fall, each child's play in the block and housekeeping areas was observed for four 10-minute periods, each on a separate day, with time-sampling codes assessing the quantity and maturity of fantasy pursuits, based on the Smilansky Scale (Smilansky & Shefatya, 1990). In addition, during both the fall and the spring, observers rated children's behavior for self-regulatory maturity during four cleanup and four circle-time periods. We reasoned that a short-term prospective design, investigating relationships between play at Time 1 and change in self-regulatory competence from Time 1 to Time 2, would offer strong support for the beneficial effect of play on self-regulation.

In addition, during the fall, parents (either the mother or the father, depending on who served as the principal caregiver) were asked to rate their child's temperament on the Children's Behavior Questionnaire (CBQ; Rothbart, Ahadi, & Hersey, 1994). A high CBQ score indicates impulsivity; as early as the preschool years, impulsivity predicts greater likelihood of later externalizing behavior problems, including attention-deficit/hyperactivity disorder (ADHD) and conduct disorder (Barkley, 2003). We were particularly interested in whether make-believe play might strengthen self-regulation among these at-risk preschoolers, who tend to be delayed in development of both play and private speech (Alessandri, 1992; Berk, 2001; Berk & Landau, 1993; Berk & Potts, 1991).

Results confirmed the contribution of make-believe to future self-regulation: Controlling for verbal ability and fall self-regulation scores, time spent in complex sociodramatic play (involving object substitutions with language or toys that are not replicas of the object itself, peer interaction directed toward maintaining a joint make-believe goal, and verbal dialogue for pretend characters) was positively correlated with spring cleanup performance, $r = .32$, $p < .05$. (Similar results were not obtained for circle time; in this adult-directed activity, the teachers did much regulating of children's behavior by prompting those who were distracted to attend and participate, thereby making it difficult to access children's *self*-regulation.) Furthermore, as anticipated, children in the highest quartile in impulsivity scored lower than children in the lowest quartile in both cleanup and circle time self-regulation, as well as on a teacher rating of self-control. Yet when relationships between complex sociodramatic play and spring cleanup performance were computed separately for high-impulsive and low-impulsive preschoolers, the high-impulsive subgroup showed a strong positive correlation mirroring the relationship obtained for the sample as a whole, $r = .81$, $p < .01$; in contrast, play and cleanup performance were unrelated for the low-impulsive children, $r = .01$, n.s., with the difference between the correlations reaching significance, $Z = 1.9$, $p < .05$.

Our findings revealed that preschoolers who more often engaged in complex sociodramatic play showed greater improvement in social responsibility over the next 5 to 6 months. The sociodramatic play–self-regulation association was particularly strong for children judged by their parents to be highly impulsive—that is, who were poorly regulated to begin with. Children most in need of enhancing their self-regulatory abilities were especially sensitive to the benefits of sociodramatic play.

In a second investigation, Harris and Berk (2003) focused on low-SES preschoolers, who often display language, cognitive, and self-regulatory deficits (Campbell, 1995). As with highly impulsive children in the Elias and Berk study, we reasoned that if, as Vygotsky's theory suggests, make-believe fosters self-regulation, then fantasy play experiences—in particular, sociodramatic play—may be especially important for self-regulatory development among children from impoverished families.

Participants were 19 4-year-olds in two Head Start classrooms. Again, we used a short-term prospective design, observing children's play and self-regulation, as assessed by cleanup performance, in the winter (Time 1) and reobserving cleanup performance 4 months later during the late spring (Time 2). Cross-study comparisons revealed that in comparison with middle-SES children, the Head Start participants scored low in language development and engaged in less make-believe play and less mature, cooperative play; in fact, they displayed only about one fourth of the joint, cooperative engagement typically observed among their middle-SES counterparts (Robinson, Anderson, Porter, Hart, & Wouden-Miller, 2003; Rubin, Watson, & Jambor, 1978).

Moreover, no form of make-believe play, including sociodramatic play, was positively associated with self-regulation in the Head Start sample. To the contrary, controlling for verbal ability and winter cleanup performance, sociodramatic play was negatively, but nonsignificantly, associated with late-spring cleanup performance, $r = -.25$. The observers informally noted that when the children gathered socially for pretense, they frequently enacted violent themes (e.g., fights, killings, robberies, and imprisonments), which may have contributed both to their low incidence of play cooperation and to the lack of predictability from make-believe to self-regulation.

The Importance of Make-Believe Themes

Indeed, other evidence suggests that the content of pretense is vitally important in the make-believe play–self-regulation relationship. Dunn and Hughes (2001) recruited a sample of 80 preschoolers, half of whom were labeled "hard to manage" because, on the basis of maternal ratings, they scored above the 90th percentile in hyperactivity and above the 90th percentile in conduct disorder; the other half, the controls, scored below the 50th percentile on both measures. At age 4, with their closest friend, the children visited a playroom equipped with fantasy play props for two 20-minute sessions. Their play was videotaped and coded for pretend themes and interactive behavior. The children also responded to an additional battery of tasks; several assessed "executive function," or self-regulatory, competencies, including inhibitory control (capacity to suppress maladaptive responses), planning, and flexibility of attention. Two years later, at age 6, the children were given a measure of sociomoral maturity, in which they responded to stories designed to reveal their understanding of the emotional consequences of prosocial acts and transgressions.

Interactions involving violent themes were 3 times more frequent in the play of the hard-to-manage children than for the control children. Moreover, engaging in much fantasizing containing violence was linked to poorer performance on executive function measures, with correlations in the .20s, $p < .05$, that remained significant after the researchers controlled for language ability. Thematically violent play also predicted negative social behavior: the more such pretense children exhibited, the more conflict-ridden, poorly coordinated, and antisocial their interactions with their friend became, with correlations ranging from the .30s to the .40s, $p < .05$. Children high in violent pretense appeared particularly deficient in emotional self-regulation; they were more often angry, less often positive, more often bullied and teased, and more often broke rules outside the make-believe scenarios. Moreover, their violent make-believe did not occur at the instigation of, nor was it exacerbated by, the behavior of their play partners; the correlation between the violent pretense of the participants and their friends was nonsignificant.

Impressive evidence for the potential of violent imaginative play to undermine self-regulation emerged in a prospective analysis, in which the investigators examined the relationship between make-believe with themes of violence at age 4 and moral sensibilities 2 years later. Children high in violent pretense were less likely as 6-year-olds to respond empathically toward victims who had been harmed by others and, in their accounts of perpetrators' feelings, more often gave hedonistic answers ("He'll be happy because he got what he wanted") and external answers ("He'll be sad because the teacher will be cross") than remorseful answers ("He'll feel sad because he hurt someone"). Violent make-believe themes made a significant, unique contribution to later individual differences in moral maturity, even after verbal ability and a variety of other 4-year-old measures, including antisocial interaction and emotional self-regulation, were controlled, $r^2 = .22$, $p < .05$.

When predictions from violent make-believe were examined separately for the hard-to-manage and the control children, the patterns of correlations were similar, although they were not significant for the controls, who rarely generated violent images during pretense. The researchers noted that control children were especially likely to engage in play involving elaborate narrative stories, such as Little Red Riding Hood, Peter Pan, and Sleeping Beauty, as well as fantastic role play in which children transformed themselves into kings, queens, and animals. Indeed, the more children engaged in play of this kind, the higher their verbal ability and the less violent their fantasy themes. Such narrative play—which most preschoolers find highly involving and enjoyable—may be an especially conducive context for self-regulatory development, particularly among children with self-control deficits.

In sum, as Dunn and Hughes's research makes clear, not all make-believe enhances self-regulation. Children draw their play themes from their sociocultural world; those that prevailed in the play of hard-to-manage preschoolers were selfish, inconsiderate, and destructive, perhaps because of a history of unfavorable family and/or media experiences. Consistent with this possibility, in an early study of family and media predictors of preschoolers' play qualities, Singer and Singer

(1981) reported that 3- and 4-year-olds high in aggressive play, compared with children who rarely played aggressively, were exposed to more arguing in their homes (especially physical fighting), were more often physically punished, more often watched action TV shows high in violence, and less often viewed "peaceful" educational TV programs. Furthermore, aggressive children who watched extensive amounts of TV (averaging more than 50 hours per week) tended to come from disorganized homes with few routines (such as bedtime stories) and family activities (such as trips to museums or other cultural activities) that might inspire positive play themes. Taken together, the findings underscore the importance of fostering elaborate, prosocial make-believe during the preschool years, and of intervening when children's play themes become antisocial (see also chapter 11).

ADULT SCAFFOLDING OF CHILDREN'S MAKE-BELIEVE PLAY

Expert partners—in Western societies, typically parents, but also older siblings—scaffold toddlers' and young preschoolers' make-believe. From these interactions, children derive many skills that enhance their play in other contexts. Make-believe, like other complex mental functions, is socially constructed and transferred to children (El'konin, 1978; Garvey, 1990; Smolucha & Smolucha, 1998).

In a longitudinal study tracing the development of make-believe, Haight and Miller (1993) followed nine children from 1 to 4 years of age, repeatedly visiting their homes to gather observations of their pretense. They found that the majority of make-believe was social across the entire age span. From ages 1 to 3, mothers were the children's principal play partners. Over time, mother–child play declined and child–child play increased; by age 4, children played about equally with their mothers and with other children—both siblings and peers.

Furthermore, Haight and Miller and other researchers report clear evidence that mothers teach their toddlers to pretend. During the first half of the second year, mothers initiate almost all make-believe episodes; they also demonstrate many pretend actions toward objects and show children how to use one object to represent another (Miller & Garvey, 1984; Smolucha & Smolucha, 1998). Around age 2, mothers begin to talk about nonexistent fantasy objects, a change that may help children increase the range and complexity of their play symbols during the third year (Kavanaugh, Whitington, & Cerbone, 1983).

While children's play skills are limited, adult scaffolding makes make-believe more interesting, surprising, and absorbing—undoubtedly among the reasons 1- to 3-year-olds prefer to play with their mothers, even when peers and siblings are available (Haight & Miller, 1993). During the second and third years, caregiver support results in more extended and complex pretense (O'Connell & Bretherton, 1984; O'Reilly & Bornstein, 1993; Slade, 1987; Zukow, 1986). As an illustration of the influence of adult scaffolding on the duration and complexity of make-believe, 2½-year-old Sophie and her father Kevin's joint play narrative, excerpted in an earlier section, persisted for nearly an hour—many times longer than Sophie had ever played on her own. Moreover, Haight and Miller found that parent–child make-believe served a wide variety of social purposes, including helping children manage their emotions and impulses and encouraging socially mature behavior.

In Sophie and Kevin's play episode, Kevin sensitively responded to and extended Sophie's play behaviors. He strove for intersubjectivity with Sophie, who readily picked up on Kevin's contributions, which yielded a smoothly functioning, elaborate play dialogue. Adult participation in make-believe that acknowledges and builds on toddlers' play behaviors through demonstrations, suggestions, turn taking, and joint involvement is particularly effective in fostering mature make-believe. In contrast, directions and intrusions (initiating a new activity unrelated to the child's current play) are associated with immature play behavior, in which toddlers merely mouth, touch, and look at toys (Fiese, 1990). In a longitudinal study, Stilson and Harding (1997) found that maternal interactions that suggested play options related to 1½-year-olds' ongoing activity (saying, "Oh, is the doll trying to swim?" as the child puts a doll into a cup) continued to predict extended play sequences and imaginative object substitutions at age 3. In contrast, toddlers whose mothers frequently negated, corrected, and directed ("No, dolls don't go in cups, they go in the doll house") tended to become 3-year-olds who spent much time in simple, immature manipulation of toys. With slightly older children, Shmukler (1981) reported similar findings: During an unstructured play session, 5-year-olds whose mothers gave them "psychological space" to express themselves engaged in more creative, expressive, and socially competent pretense than children whose mothers frequently instructed or otherwise controlled their play.

During the first year, mutually rewarding intersubjective interaction between mother and infant—involving well-organized, face-to-face exchanges of emotion and consistent parental acknowledgment of infant expressiveness—predicts complexity of mother–child pretense and children's use of mental state words (*pretend, feel, imagine*) during play at age 2 (Feldman & Greenbaum, 1997). Parental behaviors that assist infants in "connecting" socially seem to enhance children's later play competence and ability to reflect on and talk with others about thoughts and feelings. In sum, quality of adult–child social engagement, both within and outside make-believe, has much to do with the potential of such play to blossom into a cognitively and socially constructive force that leads development forward.

SUPPORTING MAKE-BELIEVE PLAY AND SELF-REGULATION IN EARLY CHILDHOOD

Children devote less time to make-believe in village cultures, where beginning in toddlerhood, they observe and—as soon as their capacities permit—participate in the daily activities of adults (Gaskins, 2000; Morelli, Rogoff, & Angelillo, 2003). In Western societies, children are largely excluded from adult pursuits. The ubiquitous and compelling nature of Western children's make-believe suggests that it substitutes for their restricted access to the adult world. In make-believe, children come to appreciate society's norms and, in striving to uphold those norms, learn to regulate emotion, thought, and behavior in the service of constructive social goals.

Moreover, the features of make-believe—child controlled, rich in social engagement and language, and attuned to the child's interests—are ideal for stimulating changes in the cerebral cortex that underlie the development of self-regulation (Thompson, 2004). The young brain undergoes *experience-expectant growth*—growth that results from exploration of the environment and from opportunities to communicate with and share daily routines with caregivers. Such growth lays the foundation for later-occurring *experience-dependent growth*, which gives rise to specialized skills through intensive effort and practice (Greenough & Black, 1992; Huttenlocher, 2002). Children's engagement in pretense is consistent with the experience-expectant processes known to prepare the brain for later systematic, focused learning, the kind that will take place in school.

Clearly, efforts to foster young children's make-believe are vital. We offer the following recommendations for policy and practice:

1. *Community contexts and expert child-rearing advice that promote make-believe play.* Surveys of nationally representative samples reveal that compared with American parents of a generation ago, today's overly busy, pressured parents spend fewer leisure hours conversing and playing with their children (Hofferth & Sandberg, 1999; Schor, 2002). Preschools, childcare centers, recreation programs, and children's museums are in a prime position to disseminate research-based information to parents about the importance of scaffolding young children's play and to arrange opportunities for adult–child playful collaboration.

In a recent study, we recorded how adults and children representing a socioeconomic cross-section of a Midwestern small city spent time while visiting a local children's museum (Mann, Braswell, & Berk, 2005). A range of museum exhibits—a post office, a grocery store, a flower shop, a farm, a kitchen, medical offices, a train depot, a gas station—represented the child's community. Many other exhibits offered additional experiences with construction, science, art, and literacy (for example, a robotics table, a paint wall, and reading and poetry corners). Posted on walls were messages encouraging parents to engage with their children. We observed each of 160 adult–child dyads for 10 minutes, coding every 30 seconds for the child's activity (make-believe, construction, art, physical play, onlooker, transition, disengaged) and adult action toward the child (directing to an activity, imparting exhibit-related information, jointly engaging in the activity, disciplining, watching, giving affection, or absence from the child's activity).

The majority of child visitors (63%) were preschoolers and kindergartners between ages 3 and 6; the remaining visitors were evenly divided between toddlers (18%) and 7- to 12-year-old schoolchildren (19%). Most children (62%) came with their mothers, 16% came with their fathers, and 22% with other adults, mostly grandmothers. Across the entire age range, make-believe was the most common activity, consuming 38% of children's time. The next most frequent activity was physical play (30%), followed by construction and art, which occurred considerably less often (12 and 10%, respectively). Only rarely were children passive onlookers (5%) or in transition or disengaged (5%). Furthermore, children took the lead in selecting activities; adults were seen directing them less than 4% of the time. The most frequently observed adult action, by far, was joint activity

(47%), followed by watching the child at play (28%). Irrespective of their child's age, parents spent slightly more than half the time jointly engaged, less often watching and imparting information than other adults, *F*s = 2.3 and 3.5, $p < .05$.

As our museum study illustrates, in a relaxed, encouraging context, parents readily pretend with their children—and do so as often with school-age youngsters as with toddlers and preschoolers! Today's parents may be especially receptive to information on how and why to engage in such play. Survey results indicate that 61% are critical of their own efforts—judge the job they are doing with their own children as "fair" or "poor" (Public Agenda, 2002; see also chapter 9). Moreover, in recent years, parental reports of child problematic behaviors, from lack of interest in school to emotional and behavior problems, have risen—a circumstance that has magnified parents' desire for expert counsel on how to rear children effectively (Vandivere, Gallagher, & Moore, 2004). Clearly, make-believe play merits a center-stage role in the early childhood, parenting-advice literature.

2. *Teaching through play in early childhood classrooms.* The increasing focus of American education on test score gains and the associated narrowing of experiences in many preschool and primary classrooms to academic tutoring are undermining children's self-regulatory capacities. When preschoolers and kindergartners spend much time sitting and doing worksheets, as opposed to actively engaging in play-based learning, they become inattentive and restless, express doubt about their abilities, prefer less challenging tasks, and are less advanced in motor, academic, language, and social skills at the end of the school year. Follow-ups through third grade reveal lasting, negative consequences, including poorer study habits and achievement and a rise in distractibility, hyperactivity, and peer aggression over time (Burts et al., 1992; Hart et al., 1998; Hart, Yang, Charlesworth, & Burts, 2003; Hirsh-Pasek & Golinkoff, 2003; Singer & Singer, 2005).

Most preschool and primary teachers know, on the basis of their training and experience, that play is a vital source of learning. When asked, they report that play promotes a wide range of favorable outcomes, including self-confidence and self-esteem, independence, responsibility, language, and social skills. Yet they also say that increasing pressures for curriculum coverage and for test-based evidence of children's academic progress lead, at best, to competition between teacher-directed instruction and play and, at worst, to play being squeezed out of classroom activities. Moreover, despite teachers' certainty about the importance of play, their conceptions of play and academic work are often bipolar, with play deemed enjoyable and academic work deemed serious (Bennett, Wood, & Rogers, 1999; Owles, 2000).

Furthermore, teachers often adopt a noninterventionist approach to children's play. In doing so, they discover that many children—especially those with little history of collaborative make-believe—need assistance in generating positive play themes, following through with play plans, negotiating with peers, and resolving conflicts. Unfortunately, children who stand to benefit most from teacher-scaffolded play are the least likely to receive it. School administrators and teachers tend to prefer academic tutoring for economically disadvantaged children, despite its established negative impact on academic and social adjustment (Stipek & Byler, 1997).

Combating the rising tide of developmentally inappropriate practice and restoring play to a central position in early childhood education will require vigorous, unified efforts on the part of leaders in the fields of child development and education (Zigler & Bishop-Josef, 2004). Play researchers can contribute greatly by disseminating their findings in understandable, applied ways to administrators, teachers, and the general public. Connecting with practitioners and everyday citizens has yet to become an esteemed endeavor among scholars of child development, but some investigators are nevertheless doing so, and fortunately so, as a groundswell of scholarly voices is indispensable for reestablishing and ensuring children's access to play-based learning.

3. *Make-believe play interventions for children with self-regulatory deficits.* In Elias and Berk's (2002) research, the relationship between sociodramatic play and gains in self-regulation was especially strong for highly impulsive preschoolers. Such children, who often display limited, thematically antisocial pretense, benefit greatly from adult-scaffolded play interventions. An extensive literature on play training, mostly conducted with low-SES preschoolers, reveals that children with weak play skills who receive adult encouragement to engage in make-believe, relative to alternative-activity or no-play controls, show gains in sociodramatic play, imaginativeness of play content, mental test scores, impulse control, coherence of storytelling, and capacity to empathize with others (Dansky, 1980; Feitelson & Ross, 1973; Freyberg, 1973; Saltz & Johnson, 1977).

At the same time, play training is beneficial only when the strategies interveners use are developmentally appropriate. In one of our investigations (Ogan, 2005), 38 4- and 5-year-olds enrolled in a Head Start program whose pretense was high in antisocial themes (on average, the children enacted an antisocial event once every 6 minutes in free play) were given a battery of seven self-regulation measures tapping their capacity to control their own behavior (speed up, slow down, or inhibit), cooperate with others (take turns and share with a partner), and plan the best way to gather items in a play grocery store (see Gauvain & Rogoff, 1989; Kochanska et al., 1996; Murray & Kochanska, 2002). Then the children were randomly assigned to one of two conditions, in which they received eight weekly 30-minute individual play-training sessions: (a) adult-directed make-believe, in which a research assistant presented the child with a prosocial play theme, coached the child in enacting the theme with specific instructions, and corrected any socially inappropriate behavior by showing the child how to reenact events in alternative ways, and (b) adult-supported make-believe, in which a research assistant permitted the child to create a make-believe scenario, joined in at the invitation of the child, and interrupted the child's play only when it became antisocial. After each play-training session, children were given a period of free play with the toys. Then, immediately after the conclusion of play training and at a 1-month follow-up, the battery of self-regulation measures was readministered.

Findings confirmed the benefits of sensitive, responsive adult scaffolding of make-believe, discussed earlier in this chapter. First, adult direction constricted the children's spontaneous play; children in the adult-directed condition spent less free-play time in make-believe and more than twice as much time unoccupied as did children in the adult-supported condition. Second, immediate and follow-up gains in self-regulation consistently favored the adult-supported condition. Children receiving gentle encouragement to pretend, by an adult who capitalized on the child's contribution, showed greater improvement on diverse measures of self-regulation, including modulation of speed of behavior, inhibition of impulse, and planning.

In sum, a wealth of evidence justifies protecting, supporting, and enlarging the young child's "house of make-believe" (Singer & Singer, 1990). Imaginative play provides a firm foundation for all aspects of psychological development. Rich opportunities for make-believe, sensitively nurtured by parents, caregivers, and teachers, are among the best ways to ensure that young children acquire the self-regulatory skills essential for succeeding in school, academically and socially.

References

Alessandri, S. M. (1992). Attention, play, and social behavior in ADHD preschoolers. *Journal of Abnormal Child Psychology, 20,* 289–302.

Barkley, R. G. (2003). Attention-deficit/hyperactivity disorder. In E. J. Mash & R. A. Barkley (Eds.), *Child psychopathology* (2nd ed., pp. 75–143). New York: Guilford.

Barnett, L. A. (1984). Research note: Young children's resolution of distress through play. *Journal of Child Psychology and Psychiatry, 25,* 477–483.

Barnett, L. A., & Storm, B. (1981). Play, pleasure, and pain: The reduction of anxiety through play. *Leisure Sciences, 4,* 161–175.

Behrend, D. A., Rosengren, K. S., & Perlmutter, M. (1989). A new look at children's private speech: The effects of age, task difficulty, and parent presence. *International Journal of Behavioral Development, 12,* 305–320.

Behrend, D. A., Rosengren, K. S., & Perlmutter, M. (1992). The relation between private speech and parental interactive style. In R. M. Diaz & L. E. Berk (Eds.), *Private speech: From social interaction to self-regulation* (pp. 85–100). Hillsdale, NJ: Erlbaum.

Bennett, N., Wood, L., & Rogers, S. (1997). *Teaching through play: Teachers' thinking and classroom practice.* Buckingham, UK: Open University Press.

Bergen, D., & Mauer, D. (2000). Symbolic play, phonological awareness, and literacy skills at three age levels. In K. A. Roskos & J. F. Christie (Eds.), *Play and literacy in early childhood: Research from multiple perspectives* (pp. 45–62). Mahwah, NJ: Erlbaum.

Berk, L. E. (1992). Children's private speech: An overview of theory and the status of research. In R. M. Diaz & L. E. Berk (Eds.), *Private speech: From social interaction to self-regulation* (pp. 17–53). Hillsdale, NJ: Erlbaum.

Berk, L. E. (2001). *Awakening children's minds: How parents and teachers can make a difference.* New York: Oxford University Press.

Berk, L. E., & Landau, S. (1993). Private speech of learning disabled and normally achieving children in academic and laboratory contexts. *Child Development, 64,* 556–571.

Berk, L. E., & Potts, M. (1991). Development and functional significance of private speech among attention-deficit hyperactivity disordered and normal boys. *Journal of Abnormal Child Psychology, 19,* 357–377.

Berk, L. E., & Spuhl, S. T. (1995). Maternal interaction, private speech, and task performance in preschool children. *Early Childhood Research Quarterly, 10,* 145–169.

Berk, L. E., & Winsler, A. (1995). *Scaffolding children's learning: Vygotsky and early childhood education.* Washington, DC: National Association for the Education of Young Children.

Bivens, J. A., & Berk, L. E. (1990). A longitudinal study of the development of elementary school children's private speech. *Merrill-Palmer Quarterly, 36,* 443–463.

Bretherton, I., & Beeghly, M. (1989). Pretense: Acting "as if." In J. J. Lockman & N. L. Hazen (Eds.), *Action in social context: Perspectives on early development* (pp. 239–271). New York: Plenum.

Broderick, N. Y. (2001). An investigation of the relationship between private speech and emotion regulation in preschool-age children. *Dissertation Abstracts International: Section B: The Sciences and Engineering, 61*(11–B), 6125.

Bronson, M. B. (2001). *Self-regulation in early childhood: Nature and nurture.* New York: Guilford.

Burts, D. C., Hart, C. H., Charlesworth, R., Fleege, P. O., Mosely, J., & Thomasson, R. H. (1992). Observed activities and stress behaviors of children in developmentally appropriate and inappropriate kindergarten classrooms. *Early Childhood Research Quarterly, 7,* 297–318.

Campbell, S. B. (1995). Behavior problems in preschool children: A review of recent research. *Journal of Child Psychology and Psychiatry, 36,* 113–149.

Choi, H. P., & Anderson, D. R. (1991). A temporal analysis of free toy play and distractibility in young children. *Journal of Experimental Child Psychology, 52,* 41–69.

Connolly, J. A., & Doyle, A. B. (1984). Relations of social fantasy play to social competence in preschoolers. *Developmental Psychology, 20,* 797–806.

Cournoyer, M., Solomon, C. R., & Trudel, M. (1998). I speak then I expect: Language and self-control in the young child at home. *Canadian Journal of Behavioural Science, 30,* 69–81.

Dansky, J. L. (1980). Make-believe: A mediator of the relationship between play and associative fluency. *Child Development, 51,* 576–579.

Diaz, R. M., Neal, C. J., & Vachio, A. (1991). Maternal teaching in the zone of proximal development: A comparison of low- and high-risk dyads. *Merrill-Palmer Quarterly, 37,* 83–108.

Duncan, R. M., & Pratt, M. W. (1997. Microgenetic change in the quantity and quality of preschoolers' private speech. *International Journal of Behavioral Development, 20,* 367–383.

Dunn, J., & Hughes, C. (2001). "I got some swords and you're dead!": Violent fantasy, antisocial behavior, friendship, and moral sensibility in young children. *Child Development, 72,* 491–505.

Eisenberg, N. (1998). The socialization of socioemotional competence. In D. Pushkar, W. M. Bukowski, A. E. Schwartzman, E. M. Stack, & D. R. White (Eds.), *Improving competence across the lifespan* (pp. 59–78). New York: Plenum.

Eisenberg, N. (2003). Prosocial behavior, empathy, and sympathy. In M. H. Bornstein, L. Davidson, C. M. M. Keyes, K. A. Moore, & The Center for Child Well-Being (Eds.), *Well-being: Positive development across the life course* (pp. 253–265). Mahwah, NJ: Erlbaum.

Eisenberg, N., Smith, C. L., Sadovsky, A., & Spinrad, T. L. (2004). Effortful control: Relations with emotion regulation, adjustment, and socialization in childhood. In R. Baumeister & K. D. Vohs (Eds.), *Handbook of self-regulation: Research, theory, and applications* (pp. 259–282). New York: Guilford.

El'konin, D. (197*8). Psikhologia igri* [The psychology of play]. Moscow: Izdatel'stv Pedagogika.

Elias, C. L., & Berk, L. E. (2002). Self-regulation in young children: Is there a role for sociodramatic play? *Early Childhood Research Quarterly, 17,* 1–17.

Erikson, E. H. (1950). *Childhood and society.* New York: Norton.

Ervin-Tripp, S. (1991). Play in language development. In B. Scales, M. Almy, A. Nicolopoulou, & S. Ervin-Tripp (Eds.), *Play and the social context of development in early care and education* (pp. 84–97). New York: Teachers College Press.

Fantuzzo, J., Sekino, Y., & Cohen, H. L. (2004). An examination of the contributions of interactive peer play to salient classroom competencies for urban Head Start children. *Psychology in the Schools, 41,* 323–336.

Fasig, L. G. (2000). Toddlers' understanding of ownership: Implications for self-concept development. *Social Development, 9,* 370–382.

Fein, G. G. (1989). Mind, meaning, and affect: Proposals for a theory of pretense. *Developmental Review, 9,* 345–363.

Feitelson, D., & Ross, G. S. (1973). The neglected factor—play. *Human Development, 16,* 202–223.

Feldman, R., & Greenbaum, C. W. (1997). Affect regulation and synchrony in mother–infant play as precursors to the development of symbolic competence. *Infant Mental Health Journal, 18,* 4–23.

Fiese, B. (1990). Playful relationships: A contextual analysis of mother–toddler interaction and symbolic play. *Child Development, 61,* 1648–1656.

Flavell, J. H., Miller, P. H., & Miller, S. A. (2002). *Cognitive development* (4th ed.). Upper Saddle River, NJ: Prentice Hall.

Freud, S. (1959). Two principles of mental functioning. In *Collected Papers of Sigmund Freud.* New York: HarperCollins.

Freyberg, J. T. (1973). Increasing the imaginative play of urban disadvantaged kindergarten children through systematic training. In J. L. Singer (Ed.), *The child's world of make-believe* (pp. 129–154). New York: Academic Press.

Furrow, D. (1992). Developmental trends in the differentiation of social and private speech. In R. M. Diaz & L. E. Berk (Eds.), *Private speech: From social interaction to self-regulation* (pp. 143–158). Hillsdale, NJ: Erlbaum.

Galyer, K. T., & Evans, I. M. (2001). Pretend play and the development of emotion regulation in preschool children. *Early Child Development and Care, 166,* 93–108.

Garvey, C. (1990). *Play.* Cambridge, MA: Harvard University Press.

Gaskins, S. (2000). Children's daily lives in a Mayan village: A culturally grounded description. *Cross-Cultural Research, 34,* 375–389.

Gauvain, M., & Rogoff, B. (1989). Collaborative problem solving and children's planning skills. *Developmental Psychology, 25,* 139–151.

Gerardi-Caulton, G. (2000). Sensitivity to spatial conflict and the development of self-regulation in children 24–36 months of age. *Developmental Science, 3,* 397–404.

Gillingham, K., and Berk, L. E. (1995). *The role of private speech in the early development of sustained attention.* Poster presented at the biennial meeting of the Society for Research in Child Development, Indianapolis.

Gralinski, J. H., & Kopp, C. B. (1993). Everyday rules for behavior: Mothers' requests to young children. *Developmental Psychology, 29,* 573–584.

Greenough, W. T., & Black, J. E. (1992). Induction of brain structure by experience: Substrates for cognitive development. In M. Gunnar & C. A. Nelson (Eds.), *Minnesota symposia on child psychology* (pp. 155–200). Hillsdale, NJ: Erlbaum.

Haight, W. L., & Miller, P. J. (1993). *Pretending at home: Early development in a sociocultural context.* Albany: State University of New York Press.

Harris, S. K., & Berk, L. E. (2003, April). *Relationship of make-believe play to self-regulation: A study of Head Start children.* Poster presented at the biennial meeting of the Society for Research in Child Development, Tampa, FL.

Hart, C. H., Burts, D. C., Durland, M. A., Charlesworth, R., DeWolf, M., & Fleege, P. O.

(1998). Stress behaviors and activity type participation of preschoolers in more and less developmentally appropriate classrooms: SES and sex differences. *Journal of Research in Childhood Education, 13,* 176–196.

Hart, C. H., Yang, C., Charlesworth, R., & Burts, D. C. (2003, April). *Kindergarten teaching practices: Associations with later child academic and social/emotional adjustment to school.* Poster presented at the biennial meeting of the Society for Research in Child Development, Tampa, FL.

Hirsh-Pasek, K., & Golinkoff, R. M. (2003). *Einstein never used flash cards.* Emmaus, PA: Rodale.

Hofferth, S., & Sandberg, J. (1999). *Changes in American children's use of time, 1981–1997.* In T. Owens & S. Hofferth (Eds.), *Children at the millennium: Where have we come and where are we going?* (pp. 193–229). New York: JAI Press.

Huston-Stein, A., Friedrick-Cofer, L., & Susman, E. J. (1977). The relation of classroom structure to social behavior, imaginative play, and self-regulation of economically disadvantaged children. *Child Development, 48*, 908–916.

Huttenlocher, P. R. (2002). *Neural plasticity: The effects of environment on the development of the cerebral cortex.* Cambridge, MA: Harvard University Press.

Johnson, M. H. (1998). The neural basis of cognitive development. In D. Kuhn & R. S. Siegler (Eds.), *Handbook of child psychology: Vol. 2. Cognition, perception, and language* (5th ed., pp. 1–49). New York: Wiley.

Kavanaugh, R. D., & Engel, S. (1998). The development of pretense and narrative in early childhood. In O. N. Saracho & B. Spodek (Eds.), *Multiple perspectives on play in early childhood education* (pp. 80–99). Albany: State University of New York Press.

Kavanaugh, R. D., Whitington, S., & Cerbone, M. J. (1983). Mother's use of fantasy in speech to young children. *Journal of Child Language, 10*, 45–55.

Kochanska, G., Murray, K., & Coy, K. C. (1997). Inhibitory control as a contributor to conscience in childhood: From toddler to school age. *Child Development, 68*, 263–277.

Kochanska, G., Murray, K., Jacques, T. Y., Koenig, A. L., & Vandegeest, K. A. (1996). Inhibitory control in young children and its role in emerging internalization. *Child Development, 67*, 490–507.

Kopp, C. B. (1982). Antecedents of self-regulation: A developmental perspective. *Developmental Psychology, 18*, 199–214.

Kopp, C. B. (1991). Young children's progression to self-regulation. In M. Bullock (Ed.), *Contributions to human development: Vol. 22. The development of intentional action: Cognitive, motivational, and interactive processes* (pp. 38–54). Basel, Switzerland: Karger.

Krafft, K. C., & Berk, L. E. (1998). Private speech in two preschools: Significance of open-ended activities and make-believe play for verbal regulation. *Early Childhood Research Quarterly, 13*, 637–658.

Landry, S. H., Miller-Loncar, C. L., Smith, K. E., & Swank, P. R. (2002). The role of early parenting in children's development of executive processes. *Developmental Neuropsychology, 21*, 15–41.

Lemche, E., Lennertz, I., Orthmann, C., Ari, A., Grote, K., Hafker, J., et al. (2003). Emotion-regulatory process in evoked play narratives: Their relation with mental representations and family interactions. *Praxis der Kinderpsychologie und Kinderpsychiatrie, 52*, 156–171.

Levine, L. E. (1983). Mine: Self-definition in 2-year-old boys. *Developmental Psychology, 19*, 544–549.

Lindsey, E. W., & Colwell, M. J. (2003). Preschoolers' emotional competence: Links to pretend and physical play. *Child Study Journal, 33,* 39–52.

Lloyd, B., & Howe, N. (2003). Solitary play and convergent and divergent thinking skills in preschool children. *Early Childhood Research Quarterly, 18,* 22–41.

Luria, A. R. (1961). *The role of speech in the regulation of normal and abnormal behavior.* London: Pergamon.

Mann, T. D., Braswell, G., & Berk, L. E. (2005, April). *A community children's museum as a context for parent–child engagement.* Poster presented at the biennial meeting of the Society for Research in Child Development, Atlanta, GA.

Miller, P., & Garvey, C. (1984). Mother–baby role play: Its origins in social support. In I. Bretherton (Ed.), *Symbolic play* (pp. 101–130). New York: Academic Press.

Mischel, W. (1996). From good intentions to willpower. In P. M. Gollwitzer & J. A. Bargh (Eds.), *The psychology of action* (pp. 197–218). New York: Guilford.

Morelli, G. A., Rogoff, B., & Angelillo, C. (2003). Cultural variation in young children's access to work or involvement in specialized child-focused activities. *International Journal of Behavioral Development, 27,* 264–274.

Murray, K. T., & Kochanska, G. (2002). Effortful control: Factor structure and relation to externalizing and internalizing behaviors. *Journal of Abnormal Child Psychology, 30,* 503–514.

Neitzel, C., & Stright, A. D. (2003). Mothers' scaffolding of children's problem solving: Establishing a foundation of academic self-regulatory competence. *Journal of Family Psychology, 17,* 147–159.

Nelson, C. A. (2002). Neural development and lifelong plasticity. In R. M. Lerner, F. Jacobs, & D. Wertlieb (Eds.), *Handbook of applied developmental science* (Vol. 1, pp. 31–60). Thousand Oaks, CA: Sage.

Newson, J., & Newson, E. (1975). Intersubjectivity and the transmission of culture: On the social origins of symbolic functioning. *Bulletin of the British Psychological Society, 28,* 437–446.

O'Connell, B., & Bretherton, I. (1984). Toddlers' play alone and with mother: The role of maternal guidance. In I. Bretherton (Ed.), *Symbolic play* (pp. 337–368). New York: Academic Press.

Ogan, A. T. (2005). *An investigation of the effects of make-believe play training on the development of self-regulation in Head Start children.* Unpublished doctoral dissertation, Illinois State University, Normal.

O'Reilly, A. W. (1995). Using representations: Comprehension and production of actions with imagined objects. *Child Development, 66,* 999–1010.

O'Reilly, A. W., & Bornstein, M. H. (1993). Caregiver–child interaction in play. In M. H. Bornstein & A. W. O'Reilly (Eds.), *New directions for child development* (No. 59, pp. 55–66). San Francisco: Jossey-Bass.

Ortega, R. (2003). Play, activity, and thought: Reflections on Piaget's and Vygotsky's theories. In D. E. Lytle (Ed.), *Play and educational theory and practice* (pp. 99–115). Westport, CT: Praeger.

Owles, C. S. (2000). *Living, learning, and literacy in an early childhood classroom: The successes and struggles of one good teacher.* Unpublished doctoral dissertation, University of Illinois, Champaign–Urbana.

Patrick, E., & Abravanel, E. (2000). The self-regulatory nature of preschool children's private speech in a naturalistic setting. *Applied Psycholinguistics, 21,* 45–61.

Piaget, J. (1951). *Play, dreams, and imitation in childhood.* New York: Norton. (Original work published 1936)

Pratt, M. W., Kerig, P., Cowan, P. A., & Cowan, C. P. (1988). Mothers and fathers teaching 3-year-olds: Authoritative parents and adult scaffolding of young children's learning. *Developmental Psychology, 24*, 832–839.

Public Agenda. (2002). *A lot easier said than done: Parents talk about raising children in today's America.* Retrieved from http://www.publicagenda.org/specials/parents/parents.htm

Ratner, H. H., & Stettner, L. J. (1991). Thinking and feeling: Putting Humpty Dumpty together again. *Merrill-Palmer Quarterly, 37*, 1–26.

Roberts, R. N., & Barnes, M. L. (1992). "Let momma show you how": Maternal–child interactions and their effects on children's cognitive performance. *Journal of Applied Developmental Psychology, 13*, 363–376.

Robinson, C. C., Anderson, G. T., Porter, C. L., Hart, C. H., & Wouden-Miller, M. (2003). Sequential transition patterns of preschoolers' social interactions during child-initiated play: Is parallel-aware play a bi-directional bridge to other play states? *Early Childhood Research Quarterly, 18*, 3–21.

Roskos, K., & Neuman, S. B. (1998). Play as an opportunity for literacy. In O. N. Saracho & B. Spodek (Eds.), *Multiple perspectives on play in early childhood education* (pp. 101–115). Albany: State University of New York Press.

Rothbart, M. K., Ahadi, S. A., & Hersey, K. L. (1994). Temperament and social behavior in childhood. *Merrill-Palmer Quarterly, 40*, 21–29.

Rothbart, M. K., & Bates, J. E. (1998). Temperament. In N. Eisenberg (Ed.), *Handbook of child psychology: Vol. 3. Social, emotional, and personality development* (5th ed., pp. 105–176). New York: Wiley.

Rothbart, M. K., Ellis, L. K., Rueda, M. R., & Posner, M. I. (2003). Developing mechanisms of temperamental effortful control. *Journal of Personality, 71*, 1113–1143.

Rubin, K. H., Watson, K. S., & Jambor, T. W. (1978). Free-play behaviors in preschool and kindergarten children. *Child Development, 49*, 534–536.

Ruff, H. A., & Capozzoli, M. C. (2003). Development of attention and distractibility in the first 4 years of life. *Developmental Psychology, 39*, 877–890.

Saltz, E., & Johnson, J. (1977). Training disadvantaged preschoolers on various fantasy activities: Effects on cognitive functioning and impulse control. *Child Development, 48*, 367–380.

Schor, J. B. (2002). Time crunch among American parents. In S. A. Hewlett, N. Rankin, & C. West (Eds.), *Taking parenting public: The case for a new social movement* (pp. 83–102). Lanham, MD: Rowman & Littlefield.

Schwebel, D. C., Rosen, C. S., & Singer, J. L. (1999). Preschoolers' pretend play and theory of mind: The roles of jointly constructed pretense. *British Journal of Developmental Psychology, 17*, 333–348.

Shmukler, D. (1981). Mother–child interaction and its relationship to the predisposition of imaginative play. *Genetic Psychology Monographs, 104*, 215–235.

Shoda, Y., Mischel, W., & Peake, P. K. (1990). Predicting adolescent cognitive and self-regulatory competencies from preschool delay of gratification: Identifying diagnostic conditions. *Developmental Psychology, 26*, 978–986.

Singer, D. G., & Singer, J. L. (1990). *The house of make-believe.* Cambridge, MA: Harvard University Press.

Singer, D. G., & Singer, J. L. (2005). *Imagination and play in the electronic age.* Cambridge, MA: Harvard University Press.

Singer, J. L., & Singer, D. G. (1981). *Television, imagination, and aggression: A study of preschoolers.* Hillsdale, NJ: Erlbaum.

Skinner, B. F. (1957). *Verbal behavior.* New York: Appleton-Century-Crofts.

Slade, A. (1987). A longitudinal study of maternal involvement and symbolic play during the toddler period. *Child Development, 58*, 367–375.

Smilansky, S., & Shefatya, L. (1990). *Facilitating play: A medium for promoting cognitive, socioemotional and academic development in young children.* Gaithersburg, MD: Psychosocial and Educational Publications.

Smolucha, L., & Smolucha, F. (1998). The social origins of mind: Post-Piagetian perspectives on pretend play. In O. N. Saracho & B. Spodek (Eds.), *Multiple perspectives on play in early childhood education* (pp. 34–58). Albany: State University of New York Press.

Stilson, S. R., & Harding, C. G. (1997). Early social context as it relates to symbolic play: A longitudinal investigation. *Merrill-Palmer Quarterly, 43*, 682–693.

Stipek, D. J., & Byler, P. (1997). Early childhood education teachers: Do they practice what they preach? *Early Childhood Research Quarterly, 12*, 305–326.

Striano, T., Tomasello, M., & Rochat, P. (2001). Social and object support for early symbolic play. *Developmental Science, 4*, 442–455.

Taylor, M., & Carlson, S. M. (1997). The relation between individual differences in fantasy and theory of mind. *Child Development, 68*, 436–455.

Thompson, P. M., Giedd, J. N., Woods, R. P., MacDonald, D., Evans, A. C., & Toga, A. W. (2000). Growth patterns in the developing brain detected by using continuum mechanical tensor maps. *Nature, 404*, 190–192.

Thompson, R. A. (2004). Development in the first years of life. In E. F. Zigler, D. G. Singer, & S. J. Bishop-Josef (Eds.), *Children's play: The roots of reading* (pp. 15–31). Washington, DC: Zero to Three Press.

Tomasello, M., Striano, T., & Rochat, P. (1999). Do young children use objects as symbols? *British Journal of Developmental Psychology, 17*, 563–584.

Vandivere, S., Gallagher, M., & Moore, K. A. (2004). *Changes in children's well-being and family environments. Snapshots of America's Families III,* No. 10. New York: Urban Institute. Retrieved from http://www.urban.org/url.cfm?ID=310912

Vaughn, B. E., Kopp, C. E., & Krakow, J. B. (1984). The emergence and consolidation of self-control from eighteen to thirty months of age: Normative trends and individual differences. *Child Development, 50*, 971–975.

Vygotsky, L. S. (1933). Fragment from notes for lectures on the psychology of preschool children. In D. B. El'konin, *Psicología del juego* [Psychology of play] (pp. 269–282). Madrid: Pablo del Rio.

Vygotsky, L. S. (1978). *Mind in society: The development of higher mental processes* (M. Cole, V. John-Steiner, S. Scribner, & E. Souberman, Eds. and Trans.). Cambridge, MA: Harvard University Press. (Original work published 1930–1935)

Vygotsky, L. S. (1986). *Thought and language* (A. Kozulin, Trans.). Cambridge, MA: MIT Press. (Original work published 1934)

Wertsch, J. V. (1993). *Voices of the mind: A sociocultural approach to mental action.* Cambridge, MA: Harvard University Press.

Whitington, V., & Ward, C. (1999). Intersubjectivity in caregiver–child communication. In L. E. Berk (Ed.), *Landscapes of development* (pp. 109–120). Belmont, CA: Wadsworth.

Winsler, A., Diaz, R. M., & Montero, I. (1997). The role of private speech in the transition from collaborative to independent task performance in young children. *Early Childhood Research Quarterly, 12*, 59–79.

Wood, D. J. (1989). Social interaction as tutoring. In M. H. Bornstein & J. S. Bruner (Eds.), *Interaction in human development* (pp. 59–80). Hillsdale, NJ: Erlbaum.

Zigler, E. F., & Bishop-Josef, J. (2004). Play under siege: A historical overview. In E. F. Zigler, D. G. Singer, & S. J. Bishop-Josef (Eds.), *Children's play: The roots of reading* (pp. 1–13). Washington, DC: Zero to Three Press.

Zukow, P. G. (1986). The relationship between interaction with the caregiver and the emergence of play activities during the one-word period. *British Journal of Developmental Psychology, 4*, 223–234.

6

My Magic Story Car: Video-Based Play Intervention to Strengthen Emergent Literacy of At-Risk Preschoolers

HARVEY F. BELLIN AND DOROTHY G. SINGER

Elisha and Max are in their make-believe library in their day care center pretending to read a book about building castles. Elisha counts the blocks as she hands them to Max, who repeats the numbers as he places each block in the structure. Max is growing impatient, however, and says that he will be the castle's "big green dragon." Elisha responds, "Okay, I will be the princess with a purple dress, but let's finish making the castle." Juan joins them and wants to play. Max agrees and offers Juan a role as the prince. But Juan wants to be the green dragon. Much negotiating takes place. Finally, Juan agrees to assume this role, but he insists on wearing a gold crown.

Through their make-believe play, these 4-year-olds are developing basic cognitive and social skills. They count; name colors; pretend to read; use vocabulary, expressive language, and socialized speech; and practice cooperation and sharing. They are also practicing eye–hand coordination and learning about spatial relationships. They are improvising a simple "script" about a prince, princess, and dragon based on a mixture of fairy tales that were read to them and a library game they had played in the *My Magic Story Car* program described in this chapter. Learning happens as they improvise their pretend game.

As Joan Almon, the coordinator of the Alliance for Childhood's branch in the United States says, "Creative play is like a spring that bubbles up from deep within a child. It is refreshing and enlivening. It is a *natural part of the makeup of every healthy child*. The child's love of learning is intimately linked with a zest for play" (Almon, 2003, p. 18).

This chapter focuses on *My Magic Story Car*, a video-based program that strengthens emergent literacy skills of at-risk preschool children from low-income families through one of the most effective available modalities—make-believe play. Research documents how make-believe play, a natural feature of early childhood development peaking at ages 3 to 5, is an intrinsically motivating modality for engaging preschoolers in activities to enhance a plethora of cognitive, socioemotional, and motor skills (Segal, 2004; Simms, 2003; Singer & Singer, 1990, 2005). Through play, children practice vocabulary and new ways to express themselves. They verbalize plot sequences with increasingly complex situations that often evoke correcting responses from adults or peers. The narrative sequences of imaginative play can also enhance socioemotional skills such as cause-and-effect thinking, empathy, cooperation, patience, civility, and self-regulation. (See chapter 5; Bowman, 2004; Howes & Wishard, 2004; Singer & Singer, 1990, 2005).

Numerous studies, summarized by J. L. Singer (2002), support the value of training parents and other caregivers to use imaginative play to strengthen preschoolers' cognitive skills through simple activities such as playing games, reading, storytelling, explaining things in ways that strengthen a child's ability to find verbal labels for their milieu, providing basic toys that lend themselves to varied "plot lines" (e.g., puppets and blocks), and singing rhymes that help a child notice similar sounds. Intergenerational play is also mutually reinforcing for parents and other caregivers and an effective means of engaging adults as full partners in children's development.

Singer and Singer (2001) developed a comprehensive set of learning games to strengthen these skills among 3- to 5-year-olds. The games require no previous training and use inexpensive, common household objects such as bags, boxes, and socks. Several of these games were adapted into a new video-based program, *My Magic Story Car,* that uses play to address a crucial national priority—strengthening the emergent literacy of preschool children from poor families who are at an increased risk of starting school lacking the skills they need to learn to read.

EMERGENT LITERACY AND SOCIOECONOMIC RISK FACTORS

Reading is a uniquely empowering skill and a prerequisite survival skill for a full and productive life in 21st-century America. The crucial foundations for reading, "emergent literacy," are developed in the early childhood years before school entry. However, research starting with a pivotal 1996 report by the Carnegie Task Force on Learning in the Primary Grades has shown that a significant number of U.S. children, particularly children from poor families, start school lacking skills necessary for learning to read (Carnegie, 1996). Their academic achievement gap widens in the elementary school years, their prospects for high school graduation diminish, and their likelihood for later success plummets. In fact, reading scores in 10th grade can be predicted with accuracy on the basis of a child's knowledge of the alphabet in kindergarten (Whitehurst, 2001).

The socioeconomic status (SES) of children's families is one of the strongest predictors of performance differences in children entering school (Whitehurst, 2001). A significant number of young children are vulnerable to this economic risk factor: nearly 20% (19.8%) of children under age 6 in the United States (4.7 million children) live in poverty (childstats.gov, 2005), and 42% (9.6 million children) live in low-income families (National Center for Children in Poverty, 2005). More than half (52.9%) of preschool children in female-householder families with no father present live in poverty—more than 5 times the rate of their counterparts in married-couple families (9.6%) (DeNavas-Walt, Proctor, & Mills, 2004; U.S. Census Bureau, 2004).

In a major study of the impact of family SES on children's early academic achievement, the National Center for Education Statistics (NCES) Early Childhood Longitudinal Study, *Kindergarten Class of 1998–99*, has followed 22,000 children from kindergarten through fifth grade. In nearly every measure NCES assessed—kindergartners' reading and mathematics scores, general knowledge, social skills, approaches to learning, and preschool educational opportunities in the home—consistently lower scores were found for kindergartners with risk factors associated with low SES: (a) household income below the poverty level, (b) single-mother household, (c) low maternal education, and (d) non-English primary home language (U.S. Department of Education, 2002, 2004).

Fifty-two percent of kindergartners whose mothers did not graduate from high school scored in the lowest quartile on reading tests, as did 49% of children whose families had received public assistance and 36% of children in single-mother households. When children in the NCES longitudinal study completed third grade, the higher the number of their family risk factors, the smaller the gains children experienced in both reading and mathematics. In fact, the reading and mathematics achievement gaps of children with multiple risk factors increased from the start of kindergarten to the end of third grade (U.S. Department of Education, 2004).

Additional factors place preschool children from poor families at risk of difficulties in learning to read when they start school:

- Children who do not engage in rich language interactions with their parents will have low levels of vocabulary and conceptual development, and this will affect their later reading and academic achievement (Whitehurst, 2001). The *Meaningful Differences* study by Hart and Risley (1995) recorded naturally occurring conversations in the homes of professional, working-class, and welfare families with young children for 2½ years. They found that professional parents exchanged nearly 300 more spoken words per hour with their children than did welfare parents. As a result, by age 3, professional families' children had larger recorded vocabularies than welfare families' parents. By first grade, linguistically advantaged children are likely to have vocabularies 4 times the size of their linguistically disadvantaged peers, and these differences widen in elementary school (Whitehurst, 2001).
- Reading aloud daily to preschoolers promotes language acquisition and correlates with literacy development and later success in school. Preschoolers who are read to at least 3 times a week are almost twice as likely to score in the top 25% in reading in kindergarten and first grade than children read to less than 3 times a week. In 2001, only 48% of preschoolers in families living below the poverty line were read aloud to every day, compared with 61% of children in families at or above the poverty line (U.S. Department of Education, 2002).

- An additional risk factor is the quality of childcare for many poor preschoolers. Their primary arrangements are more likely to be parental (45%), relative care (26%), or nonrelative home care (10%) with caregivers who are less likely to have been trained in child development (childstats.gov, 2005). And the 27% of poor preschoolers in center-based programs often have teachers who do not know how to provide children with the emergent literacy opportunities and experiences that can compensate for the lack of language stimulation at home (Whitehurst, 2001).

In summary, children from low-SES families enter kindergarten at increased risk for lacking the emergent literacy skills needed to learn how to read, but recent research offers strategies for reliable interventions.

STRATEGIES FOR ENHANCING PRESCHOOLERS' EMERGENT LITERACY

A vast outpouring of studies ranging from brain science to early childhood pedagogy show a strong consensus about developmentally appropriate interventions for preventing reading difficulties among children from low-SES families (National Research Council, 1998, 2000; RAND Reading Study Group, 2002; Roskos, Christie, & Richgels, 2003; U.S. Department of Education, 2000, 2002, 2004; U.S. Department of Health and Human Services, 2005). These and other studies clearly indicate that the precursors to literacy, emergent literacy, start well before school entry, in the first years of life.

Grover J. Whitehurst, Director of the U.S. Department of Education Institute of Education Sciences, has identified two categories of essential emergent literacy skills (Whitehurst, 2001):

1. *Inside-Out Domain*: children's knowledge of the rules for translating written text into spoken words, including (a) phonological awareness, the ability to detect and manipulate the sound structure of oral language (letters, sounds, the links between letters and sounds, and how letters in written language correspond to speech sounds at the level of phonemes), (b) print knowledge (how to use a book, understanding that English text runs from top to bottom and left to right across a page, and the ability to name letters of the alphabet), and (c) emergent writing (pretending to write, learning to write one's name, and using crayons and other writing instruments to draw and later to write letters).
2. *Outside-In Domain*: children's understanding of information outside the printed words they are trying to read, such as (a) meanings of words (vocabulary), (b) comprehension based on knowledge about the world, and (c) understanding narrative and story structure.

These emergent literacy skills occur across a developmental continuum, with strong windows of opportunity at various ages from birth to 5 years (Whitehurst & Lonigan, 1998; Whitehurst, 2001). In a child's first 3 years, parent–child bonding through exploring and playing with books and listening to stories are especially important. Effective techniques for 2- to 3-year-olds include dialogic reading in which the adult does not simply read a story while the child listens; instead, the child is encouraged to talk about the book, and the adult serves as a conversational partner, asking questions and expanding on the child's answers. Skills training for 4- to 5-year-olds includes print knowledge, phonological awareness, letter–sound correspondence, and emergent writing. Whitehurst (2001) prioritizes teaching children phonological awareness, print knowledge, alphabet letter recognition, and emergent writing before they start school. Conceptual and vocabulary skills become important later, once children have mastered the alphabetic code.

A longitudinal study of African American Head Start students by Whitehurst and Storch (2002) demonstrated the equally significant role of home literacy environments in fostering children's emergent literacy and subsequent reading achievement. The findings highlight the importance of factors such as the frequency of shared book reading and trips to a library, the number of age-appropriate books in the home, and parental expectations for their child's learning to read and write. Therefore, providing parents and caregivers with easy and effective ways to enhance children's emergent literacy is another key component of a comprehensive strategy for preventing reading difficulties among at-risk children.

As just outlined, a wealth of evidence-based research highlights the components of effective strategies for strengthening preschoolers' emergent literacy and other school-readiness skills. The question remains of finding effective modalities for delivering these curricula to large numbers of preschool children, and television and video/DVD media have shown very promising results.

APPLYING TV AND VIDEO/DVD MEDIA TO STRENGTHEN PRESCHOOLERS' READY-TO-LEARN SKILLS

A report to Congress, *A Role for Television in Its Enhancement of Children's Readiness to Learn,* prepared for the Corporation for Public Broadcasting by Singer and Singer (1993), laid the foundations for much of today's ready-to-learn television programming for preschoolers, and the subsequent developments have proven quite beneficial.

A national evaluation of the PBS series *Barney & Friends* demonstrated gains by preschool children of all socioeconomic strata and ethnicities when examples of cognitive and social skills in the television programs were reinforced by play with adult caregivers (Singer & Singer, 1998). Teenagers who regularly watched programs such as *Sesame Street* and *Mr. Rogers' Neighborhood* before starting school scored higher in English, math, and science than their peers who had rarely viewed these educational programs (Huston, Anderson, Wright, Linebarger, & Schmitt, 2001). Early childhood education television programming continues to expand through additional outlets such as the Nickelodeon cable channel's Noggin commercial-free company (Umstead, 2003).

However, many at-risk preschoolers are not exposed to these programs. Therefore, under U.S. Department of Education grants, Bellin, Singer, and Singer developed a series of video/DVD programs of playful learning games to deliver cognitive and socioemotional skills training directly to at-risk preschoolers in any childcare setting—parent and relative care, nonrelative home care, nursery schools, prekindergartens, day care, and Head Start centers. The first two programs were:

- *Learning through Play for School Readiness.* A video program and facilitator's manual for training parents and other caregivers to engage preschool children from low-SES families in playing make-believe games that resulted in measurable gains in children's cognitive and socioemotional skills (Bellin, Singer, & Singer, 1999).
- *Circle of Make-Believe.* A video program of playful learning games for 3- to 5-year-olds from low-SES families and an instructions and materials booklet for adults. It requires *no training* sessions for parents or other caregivers. The program is designed for use anytime, anyplace, in any childcare setting to strengthen children's cognitive and social-emotional skills (Bellin, Singer, & Singer, 2001).

Both programs were extensively tested in representative childcare settings for underprivileged preschoolers. *Learning Through Play for School Readiness* was tested with 463 preschoolers in the care of 310 parents and teachers in low-SES communities in California, Connecticut, and Georgia. *Circle of Make-Believe* was tested with 546 preschoolers in the care of 260 parents, teachers, and home care providers in low-SES urban and rural communities in Alabama, California, Connecticut, Maryland, Minnesota, Ohio, Wisconsin, and Wyoming. The results of these 5 years of testing indicated (Bellin, Singer, & Singer, 1999, 2001):

- Video-based programs are an effective medium for empowering parents, teachers, and other caregivers of children from poor families with reliable, easily replicated interventions for use in any childcare setting.
- Developmentally appropriate video-based programs of make-believe play, a natural feature of early childhood development, can be effective, intrinsically motivating modalities to engage preschoolers from low-SES families in playing games designed to strengthen specific school-readiness skills.
- When preschoolers from low-SES families played the programs' learning games for just 2 weeks, they showed measurable gains in targeted cognitive skills, such as enhanced vocabulary and counting, and socioemotional skills, such as politeness and emotional literacy.
- After the testing period, children continued to use skills modeled in the learning games on their own without adult intervention; that is, they appear to have gained ownership of these skills.

MY MAGIC STORY CAR: PROGRAM DESIGN

The preceding findings—the efficacy of learning through make-believe play, the consensus of research on the requisite skills of emergent literacy, and the use of video-based media to deliver easily replicable interventions to any childcare setting—were incorporated into a new video-based program to strengthen emergent literacy skills of at-risk 4- to 5-year-olds from poor families, *My Magic Story Car* (Bellin, Singer, & Singer, 2006).

The program's title, *My Magic Story Car*, is derived from the findings of the researchers' previous video-based programs that indicated preschool children's fascination with driving make-believe vehicles. In this program, adults help children assemble their own magic story cars (chairs, cushions, or cardboard boxes decorated with alphabet letters) with a "license plate" on which children are assisted in writing their names or initials. Children in the video and young viewers drive their magic story cars to play five learning games with make-believe narratives designed to strengthen specific emergent literacy and socioemotional skills.

The five *My Magic Story Car* games and their targeted emergent skills are:

1. *Rhyme Store Game*. Children practice rhyming and then use rhymes to buy toy animals at a discount in the Rhyme Store. *Targeted Skills*: Phonological awareness: rhymes (words that end with the same sound) and enhanced vocabulary.
2. *Lost Puppy Game*. Children "drive" to a library, get library cards, and borrow a book that tells how to help a sad lost puppy go home. They must guess the first letter and then the name of the puppy's owner. The child playing the puppy barks positive or negative feedback to the children's choice of letters. *Targeted Skills*: Print knowledge: naming alphabet letters, using a library, emergent writing (writing one's name on a library card), enhanced emergent literacy vocabulary, and dialogic reading.
3. *Octopus Treasure Game*. To raise funds for a neighborhood playground, children transform their cars into submarines to retrieve a treasure in a sunken ship. A giant octopus guarding the ship requires them to answer several compound-word riddles to win the treasure. *Targeted Skills*: Phonological awareness: compound words (words composed of two other words), enhanced vocabulary, and knowledge of the world (undersea nature).
4. *Birthday Presents Game*. Children match pictures of birthday presents that start with the same first letter and sound. At the party, they give the birthday person these sets of presents, as well as the special present of learning alphabet letters. *Targeted Skills*: Phonological awareness: alliteration (words that start with the same sound); print knowledge: naming alphabet letters; and emergent writing (drawing with crayons).
5. *Trip to Mars Game*. In response to a make-believe inquiry from children on Mars, an adult helps children make their own book about their life on earth. Children change their cars into spaceships, fly the book to Mars, and teach Martian children (who have never seen books) how to use the book. *Targeted Skills*: Print knowledge: parts of a book and direction in which text is read; emergent literacy vocabulary (e.g., "author" and "title"); and general knowledge (planets, space travel).

MY MAGIC STORY CAR: PROGRAM COMPONENTS

The *My Magic Story Car* program presents the five learning games in two components:

(a) *Printed Manuals for Parents and Caregivers* with comprehensive instructions in user-friendly text that is clear to low-SES adults, including those with limited literacy skills or for whom English is a second language; materials needed for playing each game, so that no purchases are necessary; tips on helping preschoolers prepare to become good readers; and resource lists.

(b) *Video/DVD Program for Preschool Children* with engaging depictions of playing the five learning games that interweave live action, playful animations, and interactive challenges to preschoolers. Viewers stop the program after watching each game and then play that game themselves with the guidelines and materials in the printed manuals. The video component incorporates several approaches that proved effective in the researchers' previous programs, *Learning Through Play for School Readiness* and *Circle of Make-Believe*:

- *Video Production with "Real People."* The video/DVD features children playing the five games with their parents or teachers. Testing indicated that seeing "real people" (not actors), with whom they can identify having fun and engaging in the learning games, motivates and empowers child and adult viewers with confidence that the activities are easy to do, require no special training, and can be done by anyone, anytime, anyplace: "If they can do it, I can do it."
- *Computer-Generated Animation.* The live-action sequences are punctuated with playful, age-appropriate, computer-generated animations. The animations provide entertainment value, reinforce the program's playful learning environment, and help children visualize imaginative story elements, such as the giant octopus that guards a submerged treasure in the Octopus Treasure game and the make-believe Martian children encountered in the Trip to Mars game.
- *Real-Time Interactivity.* A key feature of the video/DVD program is engaging young viewers in the learning games as active participants, rather than passive observers. The program's youthful narrator punctuates each game with tips and real-time interactive challenges in which young viewers are invited to answer questions that reinforce skills modeled in the program. For example, in the Rhyme Store game, children make rhymes to buy toy animals at discount prices. Children in the video take turns identifying pictures of an animal (e.g., *cat*) and two other items that rhyme with that word (e.g., *bat*, *hat*). They must then say a fourth word that rhymes with all three pictures. The narrator challenges young

viewers to say the fourth rhyming word before children in the video respond: "Can you say another word that rhymes with *cat*, *bat*, and *hat*?" Also, children in the video have to say aloud the first letter of a key word in each game to start their Magic Story Car engines and play that game (e.g., Puppy, Mars). In each case, the narrator challenges young viewers to say that first letter before children in the video respond.

- *Original Musical Score.* The upbeat, lively, very contemporary *My Magic Story Car* theme song and musical score helps to engage young viewers and maintain their attention.
- *DVD and Videocassette Versions.* The program was developed in both videocassette and DVD formats. The DVD format, with its menus and buttons, provides easy, user-directed, nonlinear access to each game whenever children want to see it. It is a considerably better interface than linear videocassettes, in which it is often difficult to locate the exact starting point of a particular game. The rapid adoption of inexpensive DVD players in low-income communities is a very positive trend for this program's potential efficacy and long-term viability (see Testing: Participants' Use of Information Technologies).

TESTING *MY MAGIC STORY CAR*: RESEARCH QUESTIONS

To assess the program's efficacy in enhancing the emergent literacy of 4- to 5-year-olds from poor families, *My Magic Story Car* was tested in low-SES communities in six states with a representative sample of 434 preschoolers in the care of 259 parents, teachers, and home care providers. The program was tested in two phases:

(a) Year one local testing (New Haven, CT) in representative parent, teacher, and home care settings.
(b) Year two national testing in five geographically and demographically diverse additional states (California, Illinois, New York, Ohio, and South Carolina).

Each phase of the testing addressed the following research questions:

- Can representative parents, home care providers, and teachers of 4- to 5-year-olds from low-SES families use the video-based program in their respective childcare settings without any prior training, and do they find it effective?
- Does the program engage preschoolers and motivate them to play the learning games?
- After playing the program's games for just 2 weeks, do preschoolers demonstrate measurable gains in the targeted emergent literacy knowledge and skills embedded in the learning games?

- After playing the program's games for just 2 weeks, do adults show gains in their own skills for enhancing the emergent literacy of children in their care?
- After the 2-week test period, do preschoolers continue to play the games on their own without adult intervention, engage other children in playing the games, and/or incorporate skills demonstrated in the games into their daily activities?

TESTING *MY MAGIC STORY CAR*: PARTICIPANTS

Participants in Year One (Local) Testing

Following the positive outcomes of testing a prototype program, in the first year of the study the program was tested in representative inner city childcare settings in New Haven, Connecticut, using random assignment, before and after measures, and statistical controls. Testing was conducted with 267 participants, 179 preschool children in the care of 91 adults (33 parents, 35 teachers, and 23 home care providers).

The mean age of the 179 participating children was 4.07 years (SD = 0.40). Each parent tested the program with one child. Teachers tested it with a mean of 2.74 preschoolers, and home care providers tested it with a mean of 2.04 preschoolers.

Demographic features of participating parents reflected those of the program's targeted communities: nearly all were mothers (92%), and more than half (56%) were unmarried. Eighteen percent spoke Spanish as their first language, and some parents presented the program to their child in a mixture of English and Spanish. Participating teachers and home care providers reflected the greatly varied levels of educational attainment and teaching experience among these professions in low-income communities.

For ethical reasons, participants were not asked to identify their race or ethnicity or that of children in their care. However, to test the program in settings representative of targeted end users, participants were recruited from predominantly African American and Hispanic preschools.

Participants in Year Two (National) Testing

The second year of the study focused on the extent that positive outcomes from year one testing in Connecticut (discussed later) could be replicated in representative low-income childcare settings in five other states. Through the cooperation of other universities, participants were recruited in Los Angeles, Chicago, New York City, Cleveland, Ohio, and Greenville, South Carolina. Testing was conducted with 303 participants, 180 preschool children in the care of 123 adults (44 parents, 45 teachers, and 34 home care providers).

Demographic features of the national testing participants were similar to those of the participants in year one local testing. The mean age of the 180 participating children was 4.00 years. Eleven percent of children spoke a first language other than English. Ninety-one percent of participating parents were mothers. Once again, for ethical reasons, participants were not asked to identify their race or ethnicity or that of children in their care; however, participants were recruited from predominantly African American and Hispanic preschools and communities in order to test the program in settings representative of targeted end users.

Participants' Use of Information Technologies

Data gathered on adult participants' access to information technologies reflected positive national trends of increasing computer access in low-SES communities (U.S. Department of Commerce, 2002). Among year one (local testing) participants, 62% percent of parents, 83% of teachers, and 78% of home care providers had some access to computers. One year later, participants in national testing reflected even stronger gains in access to computers. Eighty-nine percent of adult participants (89% of parents, 87% of teachers, and 91% of home care providers) had some access to computers. About half of participants in both years (56%, 44%) used computers at home, about a fourth (21%, 29%) accessed computers at work, about 15% (13%, 17%) in public libraries, and the remainder (10%, 8%) in other settings.

Participants' use of DVD players reflected the accelerated adoption of this technology in all segments of the U.S. population. In 2002, only 2% of adult participants (1 of 50) had requested a DVD copy of the program's prototype version; 98% had requested videocassettes. By 2004, the first year of the full study, nearly a third (32%) of adult participants requested the program in DVD rather than videocassette format. In 2005, the second year of the full study, 60% of participants in national testing requested the program in DVD format. As noted previously, low-income communities' rapid adoption of inexpensive DVD technology is a positive trend for enhanced use of *My Magic Story Car*. The DVD format, with its menus and buttons, provides easy, user-directed, nonlinear access to each game anytime children want to see it, and it is a considerably better interface than linear videocassettes.

TESTING *MY MAGIC STORY CAR*: METHODOLOGY

In both years of the study, adult participants and parents of preschoolers in the care of participating teachers and home care providers signed informed consent forms. All participants were assigned code numbers to preserve their anonymity.

Testing in the first year of the study was conducted in representative inner city childcare settings in New Haven, Connecticut, using random assignment, before and after measures, and statistical controls.

A written instrument and telephone interviews were employed to assess children's preintervention emergent literacy skills, including the number of alphabet letters the child can name, print knowledge (e.g., parts of a book, direction in which English text is read, the meaning of terms such as *author* and *title*), phonological awareness (e.g., child's ability to make rhymes), and emergent writing (e.g., child's ability to write his or her name). Adults' current practices to foster emergent literacy (e.g., frequency of taking children to a library) were also assessed prior to intervention.

Participants were randomly assigned to an experimental group ($N = 136$, 45 adults and 91 children) that used the program with children in their care for 2 weeks or a control group ($N = 131$, 46 adults and 85 children) that did not receive this intervention. The two groups were evenly matched in terms of demographic features and children's preintervention scores on the multiple emergent literacy measures.

The video/DVD for children and printed manuals for adults were distributed to parents, teachers, and home care providers in the experimental group. To simulate how the final version of *My Magic Story Car* would be used in childcare settings, participants had no prior training in how to use the program. Participants were simply asked to present the program to children in their care and play its emergent literacy learning games for 2 weeks. After the 2-week test period, experimental group outcomes were recorded on three instruments:

- Children's postintervention emergent literacy skills: Children's scores for the same skills previously scored on the preintervention instrument and telephone interviews (e.g., the number of letters the child can name).
- Record of play form: A log of the frequency (times/week) and amount of time spent playing the games, which games were played most often and were "favorite games," and the extent to which children continued to play the games on their own without adult intervention.
- Feedback form: Participating adults rated the program's usefulness on a 5-point scale and provided qualitative comments on any enhancements in children's emergent literacy and/or their own practices for fostering emergent literacy after using the program.

Experimental group adults also attended one of several 90-minute focus groups to provide additional qualitative feedback on their experiences when using the program with children in their care and to offer suggestions for any refinements needed.

For ethical reasons, to increase the number of participants testing the program, and to examine whether their experiences would replicate the outcomes of the experimental group, the same intervention was then provided for the control group ($N = 46$ childcare settings) subsequent to testing the program with the experimental group. Testing procedures were the same as those conducted with the experimental group, including asking adults to present the program to children for 2 weeks with no prior training in the program's use.

Quantitative and qualitative data were compiled and analyzed to determine (a) whether, as a result of using the program for 2 weeks, experimental group children showed measurable gains in targeted emergent literacy skills when compared with the control group and (b) whether the combined pretest and posttest scores of all participants (experimental and former controls) showed significant gains after the intervention.

Year two national testing in five additional states (California, Illinois, Ohio, New York, and South Carolina) was conducted with similar protocols of assessing children's targeted emergent literacy skills prior to intervention; asking parents, teachers, and home care providers to present the program to children in their care for 2 weeks with no prior training in the program's use; assessing children's targeted emergent literacy skills after the intervention; and conducting focus groups to compile adults' qualitative feedback. However, because of logistical considerations, national testing participants were not divided into experimental and control groups. Instead, all national testing participants received the same intervention at the same time.

TESTING *MY MAGIC STORY CAR*: FINDINGS

Assessments of Program Efficacy and Use

The data indicated that participating low-SES parents, teachers, and home care providers were able to use the program with no prior training.

Participants also had no difficulties in providing children some form of the "magic story cars" needed for playing the learning games. The majority reported they had used cushions, pillows, chairs, or decorated cardboard boxes. Some participants evolved rather creative solutions, such as giving children laundry baskets, mop buckets, diaper boxes, carpet squares, or large stuffed animals to drive as their magic story cars.

Adult participants were asked to rate the usefulness of *My Magic Story Car* and gave it very high scores. They rated the video/DVD and printed manuals on a 5-point scale, in which 1 = not useful, 2 = somewhat useful, 3 = fairly useful, 4 = very useful, and 5 = extremely useful. In year one, 85% of participants scored both the video/DVD and the printed manuals 4 (very useful) or 5 (extremely useful) on the 5-point scale. Among year two national testing participants, 85% rated the video/DVD and 82% rated the printed manuals 4 (very useful) or 5 (extremely useful).

As one measure of the extent to which the program engaged and motivated children, participants recorded how much time children spent playing the emergent literacy games during the 2-week test period. Their responses indicated that despite the adults' hectic schedules, participants devoted considerable time engaging in the games. In year one (local) testing, children in home care played the games for 9.5 hours (means), children played the games with parents 7.7 hours (means), and those with teachers played 4.4 hours (means). Teachers attributed their lower number of hours playing the games to their more limited opportunities within the highly structured school schedule.

Year two testing employed slightly different measures, which also indicated that the 303 national testing participants devoted considerable time to playing the games. On average, participants played the games 4.5 per week, with 95% of the sessions lasting 20 minutes or more and over half of the sessions (53%) lasting 30 minutes or more.

Outcomes for Children

In year one (Connecticut) testing, enhancements to children's emergent literacy were assessed in two ways: (a) comparisons of experimental group postintervention sores with control group preintervention scores and (b) comparison of all participants' (experimental group and former control group) cumulative postintervention scores with their cumulative preintervention scores. In year two national testing, preintervention and postintervention scores were recorded for all participants without dividing them into experimental and control groups. The following summarizes the outcomes.

Print Knowledge: Naming Alphabet Letters

The video presentations of the Lost Puppy game, Birthday Presents game, and to some extent all the games in the program show young children naming alphabet letters to solve challenges in the games' make-believe narratives. The video also provides young viewers many interactive challenges for practicing this important skill. Before and after testing indicated significant gains in children's ability to name alphabet letters after they played the program's emergent literacy games for just 2 weeks.

Year One (Local Testing) Results After exposure to the program for 2 weeks, experimental group children's mean postintervention score of knowing 16.79 letters ($p \leq .01$) was more than a third higher than control group children's mean preintervention score of knowing 12.32 alphabet letters. The most significant difference was among children in home care settings, where the experimental group's postintervention mean score of knowing 16.35 letters ($p \leq .01$) was more than two thirds higher than the control group's preintervention mean score of knowing 9.73 letters.

After the control group also used the program and played its games for 2 weeks, their before and after scores were combined with those of the experimental group children. Again, there were significant gains in the postintervention scores for all participants (experimental and former controls): a postintervention gain from a mean of knowing 12.35 letters to a mean of knowing 17.51 letters ($p \leq .01$). The largest gain was among home care children, who increased their ability to name alphabet letters by more than 50%, from a mean of identifying 10.93 letters to a mean of identifying 16.57 letters ($p \leq .01$).

Year Two (National Testing) Results It is important to note that year two national testing occurred later in the academic year (April–May) than year one local testing (November–December). Therefore, many children had higher preintervention scores and somewhat lower rates of gain than year one participants for skills such as the identifying alphabet letters. Nonetheless, after children participating in year two national testing played the games for just 2 weeks, they showed a statistically significant postintervention gain from a mean of knowing 14.21 letters to a mean of being able to identify 17.19 letters ($p \leq .001$).

Print Knowledge: Literacy-Related Words (Author, Title, Library, Borrow)

The Trip to Mars game and the Lost Puppy game incorporate definitions and narrative examples of the words *author*, *title*, *library*, and *borrow* (as in *borrowing* library books). Before and after test scores indicated significant gains in children's understanding and use of these four words.

Year One (Local Testing) Results Experimental group children's postintervention mean score, correctly identifying 2.98 of the 4 literacy-related words ($p \leq .01$), was more than two thirds higher than control group children's preintervention mean score (correctly identifying 1.76 of the 4 words). Experimental group children in home care settings showed particularly strong gains; their postintervention mean score of knowing 3.35 of the 4 words ($p \leq .01$) was more than double the home care control group's score of knowing only 1.57 of the 4 words.

After the control group also used the program and their outcomes were combined with those of experimental children, even stronger gains were evident: a postintervention score of knowing 3.08 of the 4 words ($p \leq .001$), which nearly doubled their preintervention score of knowing only 1.58 of the 4 words.

Year Two (National Testing) Results Preschoolers who participated in national testing in five additional states also demonstrated statistically significant gains in their understanding of the literacy-related words *author*, *title*, *library*, and *borrow*. Their postintervention score of knowing 2.48 of the 4 words ($p \leq .001$) was more than three fourths higher than their preintervention score of identifying only 1.37 of the 4 words.

Print Knowledge: Book Use

The Trip to Mars game and to some extent the Lost Puppy game provide young viewers interactive challenges to practice how to use books and identify the parts of books.

Year One (Local Testing) Results In year one, preschoolers were scored for their understanding of three elements of print knowledge: (a) identifying a book's front cover, (b) identifying a book's back cover, and (c) indicating the direction in which we read English text (top to bottom, left to right).

Children also showed gains in this skill after exposure to the program. The experimental group children's postintervention mean score, correctly answering 2.80 of the 3 book use questions ($p \leq .01$), contrasted with the control group children's mean score of 2.16 correct answers to the 3 questions. After the control group also played the program's games for 2 weeks, and their scores were combined with the outcomes of the experimental group, the mean postintervention score for all participants (experimental and former controls) increased from a mean of 2.25 correct answers to a mean of 2.76 correct answers to the 3 book use questions ($p \leq .01$).

Year Two (National Testing) Results As noted previously, because national testing was conducted later in the school year than year one local testing, children began with higher preintervention scores and therefore showed smaller resultant gains for this measure. On average, children participating in national testing demonstrated a modest gain in their correct answers to four book knowledge questions: (a) identifying a book's front cover, (b) identifying a book's back cover, (c) identifying which elements of a printed page are "words," and (d) indicating the direction in which we read English text. Their preintervention mean score, correctly answering 3.37 of the 4 questions, rose to a postintervention mean score of 3.69 correct answers to the 4 book use questions ($p \leq .001$) after playing the program's games.

Phonological Awareness: Rhyming

The Rhyme Store game demonstrates rhyming and gives young viewers many interactive challenges to practice rhyming. Preintervention and postintervention testing indicated statistically significant gains in children's abilities to rhyme after exposure to the program for just 2 weeks.

Year One (Local Testing) Results The experimental group children's postintervention score, a mean of 77.8% who could make rhymes, was 16.7% higher than the control group children's preintervention mean score of 61.1% who could rhyme. After the control group also used the program for 2 weeks and their scores were combined with those of the experimental group children, the mean postintervention score for all participants (experimental and former controls) increased by 27.84%, from a mean of 56.5% to a mean of 84.4% of children who could make rhymes.

Year Two (National Testing) Results Children who played the program's games in five additional states showed an even stronger 33% mean gain, an increase from 43% to 76% of children who could make rhymes after exposure to the program for 2 weeks.

Phonological Awareness: Compound Words

The primary learning objective of the Octopus Treasure game is providing young viewers interactive challenges to practice recognizing and manipulating compound words such as *cowboy*, *sunshine*, and *popcorn*.

Children's abilities to recognize and manipulate compound words were not full assessed until year two national testing. The year two national testing instrument included a set of eight questions to score children's understanding of compound words before and after intervention (e.g., "What two words do you hear when I say the word *doorbell*? What word is left when I take the word *door* away from the word *doorbell*?).

Understanding compound words is the program's most challenging emergent literacy skill, because it pushes the envelope of preschoolers' developmental levels. Several participants noted children experienced difficulties on their first attempts with compound words; however, the vast majority experienced gains in this skill after playing the game again. Before exposure to the program, children had a mean score of correctly answering less than half, only 3.73, of the 8 compound word questions. After playing the games for 2 weeks, children's mean score rose by more than 50% to a mean of correctly answering 5.57 of the 8 compound word questions ($p \leq .001$).

Participants' qualitative feedback reinforced these findings. For example, one teacher noted: "I have seen a change in the children's vocabulary. They are using words from the games. They loved compound words. They broke up words by syllable. They also tried to put two words together, like *dollhouse*, *doghouse*, *classroom*, *basketball*, *bathtub*, *bathroom*, and *boxcar*. I was amazed and excited about their progress."

Phonological Awareness: Letter Sounds

The primary emergent literacy objective of the Birthday Presents game is providing young viewers interactive challenges to practice alliterations—words that begin with the same sound (and letter). Children in the video and young viewers are asked to match sets of make-believe birthday presents that begin with the same sound and letter, such as *ball*, *bat*, *balloon*, and *book*. At the same time, they practice naming alphabet letters.

Children's abilities to recognize and manipulate letter sounds were not fully assessed until year two national testing. In three questions on the national testing instruments, two words that start with the same sound, (e.g., *dog* and *doll*) were read aloud to a child, who was asked to say those two words aloud and then say another word that begins with the same sound. After playing the program's games for 2 weeks, participating children showed a statistically significant gain in this skill, going from a preintervention mean of correctly answering 1.33 of the 3 letter sound questions to a postintervention mean of correctly answering 1.99 of the 3 letter sound questions ($p \leq .001$).

Emergent Writing: Child Can Write His or Her Name

The program provides children opportunities to practice emergent writing when they play the Lost Puppy game (writing their names on library cards), the Trip to Mars game (writing their name as the "author" of a book for children on Mars), and when writing their names on "license plates" for their magic story cars.

Writing is a complex skill involving cognitive as well as motor skills that develop over a longer time frame than other emergent literacy variables such as learning the meanings of the book-related words *title*, *author*, *library*, and *borrow*. Nonetheless, in both years of testing, children showed statistically significant gains in emergent writing after using the program for just 2 weeks.

Year One (Local Testing) Results The percentage of experimental group children who could write their names after playing the games (74.2%) was 13.6% higher than the percentage of controls who could write their names before using the program (60.6%). After the control group also used the program and their scores were combined with those of the experimental group children, the mean postintervention score for all participants (experimental and former controls) increased by 12.3%, from a preintervention mean of 59.6% to a postintervention mean of 71.9% of children who could write their names.

Year Two (National Testing) Results Children who participated in national testing showed a comparable 15% postintervention gain. After exposure to the program, their mean score increased from 43% to 58% of children who could write their names.

Gains in Children's Knowledge of and Interest in Libraries

One objective of the Lost Puppy game is to motivate children to want to use libraries and to obtain their own library cards. Participants' feedback indicated strong increases in children's (and parents') interest in libraries and books after playing the program's games, as illustrated in these representative examples:

- We have a library with Spanish and English books and a writing area. These areas of the classroom were not popular, but now the children compete to have a turn there. (Teacher)
- They set up chairs to play library on their own. (Home care provider)
- I invited the parents of the children to come and watch it (the video). And one of the parents right away, that afternoon, when they were leaving, took their child to a library. (Teacher)
- I have heard kids asking their moms if they can go to the library after school. (Teacher)
- More than anything I try to make more time to go to the library. She [daughter] keeps saying, "Mom, come on, let's go to the library, come on!" (Parent)

Ongoing Outcomes of Playing the Games

An important measure of the product's efficacy is the extent to which, after playing the games for 2 weeks with adults, children continued playing the games on their own without adult intervention, engaged other children in playing the games, and/or incorporated skills they learned in the games into their daily activities.

Year One (Local Testing) Results Adult participants ($N = 91$) rated the extent to which children ($N = 176$) continued playing the games on their own on a 5-point scale, in which 1 = not at all, 3 = sometimes, and 5 = many times. Sixty-five percent of all adult participants (73% of home care providers, 70% of parents, and 54% of teachers) reported that children continued to play the games on their own; that is, they gave scores of 3 (sometimes) to 5 (many times) for this measure.

Year Two (National Testing) Results Adults participating in national testing ($N = 123$) reported somewhat higher scores for this measure. Sixty-eight percent of participants (84% of home care providers, 82% of parents, and 49% of teachers) reported that children continued to play the games on their own without adult intervention after the 2-week test period. In both years, teachers attributed their lower scores for this measure to children's more limited free time during the highly structured hours they spend with teachers.

Participants' qualitative feedback from both years included these comments:

- They play the games by themselves and with each other. They imitate me as a teacher; they teach letters and sounds to the other kids. (Teacher)
- The big surprise was taking the children to a real library. They told the librarian where the front and back covers of the book were. (Home care provider)
- My son was afraid to say the alphabet when he was in school. Now he spells words that he sees wherever we go. When we were at a store, he spelled the word E-X-I-T. (Parent)
- He taught the rhyme game and the lost puppy to his friends in Sunday school. (Parent)

Outcomes for Adults

Qualitative feedback from written instruments and focus groups indicated that many parents, teachers, and home care providers made meaningful gains in their own skills for fostering emergent literacy after using the program for just 2 weeks.

For example, a teacher noted: "Participating in the project made me more aware of teaching children about reading left to right. Before, I just assumed that everyone would know that. Now I am more aware of the sounds of letters. It was great to watch the children become authors, to write their own words, and to see the sense of pride and accomplishment that followed."

Another teacher commented: "Before, I actually didn't know how to do a lot of activities with alphabets because we weren't suppose to teach that to the children —like you're suppose to teach them in kindergarten or in elementary school. So we didn't know how to be more creative with letters or reading, but now we just do it at all, all the time." And a parent reported: "I realized that a lot of things that I did not think she was ready for or things I did not think she even thought about, she knew. When she shows interest, that makes me show more interest."

A home care provider offered this insight: "I think I'd kind of lost touch with some of the real simple things that you can do with children. I had watched one of my grandchildren one Christmas tear the wrappings off, throw the present out, and hop in the box. Well, this [program] brought all of that back. Because children do like simple things, and I think that's why they enjoyed it. Because they could decorate their box. They could get in it. That was their own little space. Each one knew which one was theirs, even the 16-month-old. And the little group couldn't wait to see who was going to be the puppy and show the others ones, you know, how you read the book and which way you went to read it, you know, and who it was written by, and they enjoyed that. . . . I think the best way they can learn is through play."

One of the best summaries of the program's ultimate purpose was provided by a mother from Puerto Rico at the end of a focus group session. She offered her thanks for being including in the testing, which gave her new skills for helping her young son learn. She sadly recalled that when she was a child, her parents were not involved in her education, and she didn't want to do that to her children. Now, even when she comes home from work exhausted, she reads books to her children every night. She concluded: "I know how much it means to them, how good it is for them, and how good it is for me too."

CONCLUSIONS

A significant number of U.S. children, particularly children from poor families, start kindergarten lacking the skills needed to learn reading. *My Magic Story Car* is a video-based program that untrained parents and other caregivers can use in any childcare setting to engage 4- and 5-year-olds from low-income families in make-believe games that strengthen their emergent literacy skills. The program addresses its objective by interweaving three elements: (a) make-believe play as an intrinsically motivating modality for engaging preschoolers in learning activities, (b) empirical studies of the requisite skills of emergent literacy, and (c) video-based programs as an effective medium for empowering parents and caregivers of poor children with easily replicated, reliable interventions for implementation in any childcare setting.

In just 2 weeks, children in the study showed significant gains in key emergent literacy skills embedded in the game's make-believe narratives, such as phonological awareness and print knowledge. Children also showed increased knowledge of and interest in books and libraries, and adults reported that using the program led to gains in their own skills for fostering children's emergent literacy. After the 2-week test period, the vast majority of children (66%–68%) continued to play the games on their own without adult intervention, incorporate skills modeled in the games into their daily activities, and teach the games to other children.

Reading is a prerequisite survival skill for a full and productive life in 21st-century America. Providing parents, teachers, and other caregivers of disadvantaged preschoolers an engaging, empirically tested, easily replicated, no-prior-training-required program for strengthening emergent literacy can help to kindle a spark in young children, a spark of each child's vast potential that can brighten when he or she enters school and continue glowing through a lifetime of learning. *My Magic Story Car* demonstrates that one of the most effective ways of kindling this spark is also among the most natural, entertaining, amusing, rewarding, and exhilarating of all human experiences—make-believe play.

Few activities surpass the intrinsic power and pure enjoyment of play—for adults as well as young children. We can be transformed by "playing" an instrument, experiencing a "play" at the theater, participating in or observing the "plays" of competitive sports, or "playing" a hand of cards. Many of our most rigorous intellectual disciplines, such as the protocols of experimental sciences and the "what if" scenarios of economics, politics, and war games, are, in reality, simply highly structured forms of play. To the extent that we are wise enough to leverage the natural potency of play in our pedagogy and other practices, the more effective we can become in all species of human endeavors.

Perhaps, it is little wonder that the approaches at the heart of the program outlined in this chapter have proven effective in democratizing and leveling the emergent literacy playing field for at-risk, disadvantaged preschoolers. As Shakespeare's Hamlet said: "The play's the thing" (*Hamlet*, II:2).

Acknowledgments The program was developed under a U.S. Department of Education Institute of Education Sciences SBIR grant by Dr. Dorothy Singer and Prof. Emeritus Jerome Singer, Directors of the Yale University Family Television Research Center, and Harvey Bellin, President of The Media Group of Connecticut, Inc., and formerly Department of Psychology, Yale University.

References

Almon, J. (2003). The vital role of play in early childhood education. In S. Olfman (Ed.), *All work and no play: How educational reforms are harming our preschoolers* (pp. 17–41). Westport, CT: Praeger.

Bellin, H. F., Singer, D. G., & Singer, J. L. (1999). *Learning through play for school readiness*. Unpublished report to the U.S. Department of Education Early Childhood Institute.

Bellin, H. F., Singer, D. G., & Singer, J. L. (2001). *Circle of make-believe*. Unpublished report to the U.S. Department of Education Early Childhood Institute.

Bellin, H. F., Singer, D. G., & Singer, J. L. (2006). *My Magic Story Car*. Unpublished report to the U.S. Department of Education Institute of Education Sciences.

Bowman, B. (2004). Play in the multicultural world of children: Implications for adults. In E. F. Zigler, D. G. Singer, & S. J. Bishop-Josef (Eds.), *Children's play: Roots of reading* (pp. 125–141). Washington, DC: Zero to Three.

Carnegie Task Force on Learning in the Primary Grades. (1996). *Years of promise: A comprehensive learning strategy for America's children*. New York: Carnegie.

Childstats.gov. Federal Interagency Forum on Child and Family Statistics. (2005). *America's children: Key national indicators of well-being, 2005*. Retrieved December 3, 2005, from http://www.childstats.gov

DeNavas-Walt, C., Proctor, B. D. & Mills, R. J. (2004). U.S. Census Bureau, Current Population Reports, P60–226, *Income, Poverty, and Health Insurance Coverage in the United States: 2003*. Washington, DC: U.S. Government Printing Office.

Hart, B., & Risley, T. R. (1995). *Meaningful differences in everyday experiences of young American children*. Baltimore: Paul H. Brooks.

Howes, C., & Wishard, A. G. (2004). Revisiting shared meaning: Looking through the lens of culture and linking shared pretend play through proto-narrative development to emergent literacy. In E. F. Zigler, D. G. Singer, & S. J. Bishop-Josef (Eds.), *Children's play: Roots of reading* (pp. 143–158). Washington, DC: Zero to Three.

Huston, A. C., Anderson, D. R., Wright, J. C., Linebarger, D. L., & Schmitt, K. L. (2001). *Sesame Street* viewers as adolescents: The recontact study. In S. M. Fisch & R. T. Truglio (Eds.), *"G" is for growing* (pp. 131–143). Mahwah, NJ: Erlbaum.

National Center for Children in Poverty. (2005). *Basic facts about low-income children:*

Birth to age 6 (p. 1). Retrieved December 3, 2005, from http://www.nccp.org/pub_ycp05.html

National Research Council. (1998). *Preventing reading difficulties in young children*. Washington, DC: National Academy Press. Retrieved December 3, 2005, from http://stills.nap.edu/html/prdyc

National Research Council. (2000). *Eager to learn: Educating our preschoolers*. Washington, DC: National Academy Press. Retrieved December 3, 2005, from http://books.nap.edu/openbook/0309068363/html/index.html

RAND Reading Study Group. (2002). *Reading for understanding: Toward an R&D program in reading comprehension*. Retrieved December 3, 2005, from http://www.rand.org/multi/achievementforall/reading/

Roskos, K. A., Christie, J. F., & Richgels, D. J. (2003). The essentials of early literacy instruction. *Young Children, 58*(2), 30–39.

Segal, M. (2004). The roots and fruits of pretending. In E. F. Zigler, D. G. Singer, & S. J. Bishop-Josef (Eds.), *Children's play: Roots of reading* (pp. 33–48). Washington, DC: Zero to Three.

Simms, E. M. (2003). Play and the transformation of feeling: Niki's case. In S. Olfman (Ed.), *All work and no play: How educational reforms are harming our preschoolers* (pp. 177–191). Westport, CT: Praeger.

Singer, D. G., & Singer, J. L. (1990). *The house of make-believe: Children's play and the developing imagination*. Cambridge, MA: Harvard University Press.

Singer, D. G., & Singer, J. L. (2001). *Make believe: Games and activities to foster imaginative play in young children*. Washington, DC: Magination.

Singer, D. G., & Singer, J. L. (2005). *Imagination and play in the electronic age*. Cambridge, MA: Harvard University Press.

Singer, J. L. (2002). Cognitive and affective implications of imaginative play in childhood. In M. Lewis (Ed.), *Child and adolescent psychiatry: A comprehensive textbook* (3rd ed., pp. 252–263). Philadelphia: Lippincott, Williams & Wilkins.

Singer, J. L., & Singer, D. G. (1993). A role for television in its enhancement of children's readiness to learn. Corporation for Public Broadcasting report to the Congress of the United States. Published as *Public broadcasting: Ready to teach. A report to the 103rd Congress and the American people*. Pursuant to Public Law, 102–356. Washington, DC: Corporation for Public Broadcasting.

Singer, J. L., & Singer, D. G. (1998). *Barney & Friends* as entertainment and education: Evaluating the quality and effectiveness of a television series for preschool children. In J.K. Asamen & G. Berry (Eds.), *Research paradigms, television, and social behavior* (pp. 305–367). Beverly Hills, CA: Sage.

Umstead, R. T. (2003). Noggin finds new pre-K focus. *Multichannel News*, February 24. Retrieved January 10, 2006, from http//www.multichannel.com/article/CA278768.html?display=Top+ST.

U.S. Census Bureau. (2004). *Annual demographic survey: CPS 2004 annual social and economic supplement*. Retrieved December 3, 2005, from http://pubdb3.census.gov/macro/032004/pov/toc.htm

U.S. Department of Commerce. National Telecommunications & Information Administration (NTIA). (2002). *A nation online: How Americans are expanding their use of the Internet.* Retrieved December 3, 2005, from http://www.ntia.doc.gov/ntiahome/dn/index.html

U.S. Department of Education. National Center for Education Statistics (NCES). (2000). *The Kindergarten Year*. (NCES 20123). Retrieved January 9, 2006, from http://nces.ed.gov/pubsearch/pubsinfo.asp?pubid=2001023

U.S. Department of Education. National Center for Education Statistics (NCES). (2002). *Children's reading and mathematical achievement in kindergarten and first grade.* Retrieved December 3, 2005, at http://nces.ed.gov/pubs2002/kindergarten//

U.S. Department of Education. National Center for Education Statistics (NCES). (2004). *From kindergarten through third grade: Children's beginning school experiences* (NCES 2004–007). Retrieved December 3, 2005, from http://nces.ed.gov/programs/quarterly/vol_6/6_3/2_1.asp

U.S. Department of Health and Human Services, Administration for Children and Families (May 2005). *Head Start Impact Study: First Year Findings.* Washington, DC. Retrieved January 9, 2006, from http://www.acf.hhs.gov/programs/opre/hs/impact_study/index.html

Whitehurst, G. J. (2001, July 26). Address to White House summit on early childhood cognitive development, Washington, DC. Retrieved December 3, 2005, from http://www.ed.gov/news/pressreleases/2001/07/07262001_whitehurst.html

Whitehurst, G. J., & Lonigan, C. J. (1998). Child development and emergent literacy. *Child Development, 68*, 848–872.

Whitehurst, G. J., & Storch, S. A. (2002). A structural model supporting home literacy activities with African American children. In B. Bowman (Ed.), *Love to read.* Washington, DC: National Black Child Development Institute.

7

Narrative Play and Emergent Literacy: Storytelling and Story-Acting Meet Journal Writing

AGELIKI NICOLOPOULOU, JUDITH MCDOWELL, AND CAROLYN BROCKMEYER

Debates about early childhood curricula tend to pit teacher-centered and skill-oriented approaches against child-centered or play-oriented approaches (e.g., Golbeck, 2001; Stipek et al., 1998; Stipek, Feiler, Daniels, & Milburn, 1995). Current trends emphasize the need for teacher-directed instruction focusing on the transmission of specific academic skills, especially for low-income children. Increasingly, only lip service is paid to the significance and value of play for young children.

We recognize the value of teacher-directed and skill-oriented literacy activities for young children, but the discussion has become too one-sided and unbalanced. Years of developmental research have demonstrated that young children have different interests, cognitive styles, and ways of grasping the world from adults, with important implications for their modes of learning. Thus, we should not be quick to fill up preschool classrooms exclusively with adult-centered skill-based activities that may be foreign to a child's perspective. We need to balance these didactic skill-based activities with more child-centered activities within the preschool curriculum.

Furthermore, this polarization of teacher-directed and child-centered approaches often poses a false dichotomy. Increasing evidence suggests that early childhood education is most effective when it successfully combines both kinds of educational activities (e.g., Graue, Clemens, Reynolds, & Niles, 2004). We hope to contribute to this line of inquiry by showing how teacher-directed and skill-oriented activities themselves can become even more engaging, meaningful, and valuable for children when they are linked to child-centered and play-oriented activities. Thus, we advocate a genuine integration between didactic and child-centered approaches in ways that allow them to complement and support each other.

PLAY, NARRATIVE, AND EMERGENT LITERACY

To create successful child-centered activities, it is important to tap the significance and developmental value of symbolic play for young children. Play engages them in ways that simultaneously draw on and mobilize imagination, emotion, cognition, and group life (Nicolopoulou, 1993). We agree with the teacher-researcher Vivian Paley (2004, p. 8) that, in early childhood, "fantasy play is the glue that binds together all other pursuits, including the early teaching of reading and writing skills." This does not involve simply alternating between direct instructional activities and unstructured play. The challenge is to integrate the play element *into* the curriculum in ways that are structured but foster the children's own participation and initiative, so that children infuse them with their own interests and concerns.

For promoting early literacy-related skills, activities that systematically integrate symbolic play and narrative can be especially valuable and effective. Play and narrative are closely intertwined in young children's experience and development; in fact, symbolic or pretend play consists mostly of enacted narratives (for some discussion of relevant issues, see Nicolopoulou 1993, 1997a, 2002, in press, which suggest, among other things, that Vygotsky's [1933/1967] analysis of play offers important theoretical resources for grasping the developmental interplay between play and narrative). And a growing body of research has argued convincingly that children's acquisition of narrative skills in their preschool years is an important foundation of emergent literacy (e.g., Dickinson & Tabors, 2001; McCabe & Bliss, 2003; Snow, 1991; Wells, 1985, 1986). Training children in the kinds of technical skills related most obviously and directly to literacy—such as letter and word recognition and phonological processing—is important but not sufficient. Children must also master a broader range of linguistic and cognitive skills, and these become increasingly important as the child moves from simple decoding to reading for meaning and comprehension (Dickinson & Tabors, 2001; Roth, Speece, & Cooper, 2002; Whitehurst & Lonigan, 1998, 2001). The argument advanced by these scholars (with some differences of terminology and emphasis) is that the skills required and promoted by young children's narrative activity form part of an interconnected and mutually supportive cluster of *decontextualized* oral language skills that play a critical role in facilitating children's achievement of literacy and their overall school success.

Language use is "decontextualized," in the technical sense used in this research, to the extent that it involves explicitly constructing, conveying, and comprehending information in ways that are not embedded in the supportive framework of conversational interaction and do not rely on implicit shared background knowledge and nonverbal cues. Decontextualized discourse thus raises greater demands than "contextualized" discourse for semantic clarity, planning, and linguistic self-monitoring. Examples of decontextualized language use include various forms of coherent extended discourse such as narratives, explanations, and other monologues, as well as metalinguistic operations such as giving formal definitions and monitoring the grammatical correctness of speech (e.g., Snow, 1983, 1991). There is solid evidence that "skill at the decontextualized uses of language predict[s] literacy and school achievement better than skill at other challenging tasks that are not specifically decontextualized" (Snow & Dickinson, 1991, p. 185).

For young children, stories are an especially important mode of decontextualized discourse because they pose the challenge of explicitly building up a scenario or picture of the world by using only words. To put it another way, freestanding stories are *self-contextualizing* (Wells, 1985, p. 253) to a greater extent than other forms of discourse that young children typically experience and construct. The experience of narratives—both listening to them and telling them—helps to bring home to children "the symbolic potential of language: its power to create possible and imaginary worlds through words" (Wells, 1986, p. 156; cf. Bruner, 1986). In the process, narrative discourse can be especially effective in helping the child prepare to grasp "the disembedded and sustained characteristics" of written texts and "the more disembedded uses of spoken language that the school curriculum demands" (Wells, 1986, pp. 250, 253). And unlike many other forms of decontextualized language use, narrative is an important and engaging activity for children from an early age (for an overview of research in the area of children and narratives, see Nicolopoulou, 1997a). Thus, preschool activities that mobilize this enthusiasm by integrating play and narrative can play an important part in laying the foundations of emergent literacy and of school readiness more generally.

A CONCRETE ILLUSTRATION: EVIDENCE FROM A HEAD START CLASSROOM

This chapter presents a concrete example to illustrate and support these claims, based on a teacher–researcher collaboration in a Head Start preschool classroom. The first author, Nicolopoulou, helped to introduce, guide, and monitor a practice of spontaneous storytelling and group story-acting, which integrates narrative and play elements, in the classroom of the second author, McDowell. The third author, Brockmeyer, is a graduate student who assisted in this research. Observations reported here are drawn from the first year and a half of our collaboration, the spring semester of 2003 and the 2003–2004 school year. The evidence indicates that the storytelling and story-acting practice successfully engaged these low-income preschool children and promoted their learning and development—findings that are consistent with previous studies by the first author (e.g., Nicolopoulou, 2002). More unexpectedly, we discovered that introducing this narrative- and play-based activity into the classroom transformed a more directly literacy-oriented activity that was already part of the curriculum, journal writing, and made it more engaging and educationally effective. The present chapter focuses on this strikingly suggestive outcome. Our analysis draws on a rich and diverse body of data, including the children's stories, their journal entries, our observational field notes as researchers, and the teacher's own weekly journal and periodic assessments of the children.

The Classroom, the Children, and the Community

This Head Start classroom is one of five located in the lower level of an elementary school in a large urban center in the northeastern United States. This is a neighborhood school in a low-income, disadvantaged area of the city. The student population is almost 100% African American. The neighborhood is isolated from the rest of the city and has high rates of unemployment, crime, and infant mortality. Drug use and other illegal activities flourish, and there are frequent shootings. Housing is generally substandard, the few available jobs tend to be low-paying, health care facilities are inadequate, and few services are available.

To qualify for Head Start, a family's annual income must be below the poverty line established by the federal government: $15,000 for a family of three. Most of the Head Start children live in single-parent families, have very young mothers, or are raised by grandparents. In addition, some mothers have children close in age, so children as young as 4 or 5 may be expected to take care of themselves and their younger siblings. A number of the parents are in jail or have been in jail. A large percentage of the children in this Head Start center also have had a family member shot or killed in violent incidents. The school itself can be a dangerous place for young children. The school playground is a barren, uneven cement yard with no trees in sight. Teachers often take the children to a nearby playground with some old rusting and colorless play equipment, where they must be mindful of glass shards or other remnants of street parties.

Each Head Start class has about 19 children of mixed ages, ranging from 3 to 4 at the beginning of the school year. Each year, some children who entered the class as 3-year-olds continue the following year as 4-year-olds, usually in the same teacher's classroom. The two classes studied were similar in makeup, with roughly equal numbers of 3- and 4-year-olds. During the first year (2002–2003), there were 9 3-year-olds (5 girls and 4 boys) and 10 4-year-olds (5 boys and 5 girls). During the second year (2003–2004), there were 10 3-year-olds (7 girls and 3 boys) and 9 4-year-olds (4 girls and 5 boys). All 5 Head Start classes follow the same curriculum, which combines the citywide school district curriculum and Head Start performance standards. In the past 10 years, promoting language and literacy development has been an increasingly central focus.

The Storytelling and Story-Acting Practice: A Play- and Narrative-Based Activity

The practice of spontaneous story composition and group dramatization examined here was pioneered by Vivian Paley (1986, 1990, 2004) and has been used, with variations, in a wide range of preschool and kindergarten classrooms in the United States and abroad (in addition to Paley's own accounts, see Cooper, 1993; Fein, Ardila-Rey, & Groth, 2000; London Bubble Theatre, 2001; McLane &

McNamee, 1990; McNamee, 1990, 1992; Nicolopoulou, 1996, 1997b, 2002). We introduced it into this classroom as a regular part of the curriculum for the spring semester of 2003, and it was then continued for the entire 2003–2004 school year. In both classes, it was used an average of 2 days per week. (It can also be conducted more frequently, and in some preschools it is a daily activity.)

This activity offers children an opportunity to compose and tell stories at their own initiative, which they dictate to a designated teacher, and then to act out their stories later that day in collaboration with other children whom they choose. In this classroom, the storytelling part of the activity takes place right after breakfast. The teacher or a teacher's aide sits at a designated storytelling table with the classroom storybook and makes herself available to take the children's stories. Any child who wishes can dictate a story to this teacher, who writes it down as the child tells it with minimal intervention. These storytelling events are self-initiated and voluntary. No child is pressured to tell a story, children are allowed to tell any kind of story they wish, and teachers are discouraged from using this opportunity to correct children's grammar, vocabulary, or narrative structure. As in other classrooms where this storytelling and story-acting practice is used, there are always children ready to tell stories. The teacher usually takes between two and four stories per day, depending mostly on how much time is made available for storytelling.

The story-acting part of the practice takes place during group time, when the entire class is assembled sitting in a semicircle. All stories dictated during that day are read aloud and enacted in the order they were told. First the teacher reads the story to the class; then the child author picks a character in the story to play and chooses other children for the remaining roles; then the story is read aloud a second time by the teacher while the child author and other children act it out, with the rest of the class as an audience. When this practice is established as a regular part of classroom activities, all children in the class typically participate in three interrelated roles: composing and dictating stories, taking part in the group enactment of stories (their own and those of other children), and listening to and watching the performance of the stories of the other children in the class.

Impact and Significance of the Storytelling and Story-Acting Practice

This is an apparently simple technique with complex and powerful effects. Both theoretical considerations and extensive experience suggest that the combination of story*telling* and story-*acting* components is key to its operation and educational effectiveness. Children typically enjoy storytelling for its own sake, but the prospect of having their story acted out, together with other children whom they choose, offers a powerful additional motivation to compose and dictate stories. Furthermore, one result of the fact that the stories are read to and dramatized for the entire class at group time is that children tell their stories not only to adults but also primarily to each other; they do so, not in one-to-one interaction, but in a shared public setting. The *public* and *peer-oriented* dimension of this activity helps to create a *community of storytellers* in the classroom, enmeshed in the ongoing context of the classroom culture and the children's everyday peer-group life. In classes using this activity, children regularly borrow and reuse themes, characters, plotlines, and other narrative elements from each others' stories; however, they do not simply copy these elements but appropriate them *selectively* and then flexibly adapt them in composing their own stories (e.g., Nicolopoulou, 1997b, 2002; Nicolopoulou, Scales, & Weintraub, 1994; Paley, 1986, 1988; Richner & Nicolopoulou, 2001). Thus, participating in this practice helps the children form and sustain a shared culture of peer-group *collaboration*, *experimentation*, and *mutual cross-fertilization* that serves as powerful matrix for learning and development.

Although this is a structured and teacher-facilitated activity, it is simultaneously child-centered. The children's storytelling is *voluntary*, *self-initiated*, and *relatively spontaneous*; each child is able to participate according to his or her own individual interests, pace, inclination, and developmental rhythms. At the same time, this activity draws on the power of peer-group processes and their emotional and social-relational importance for children (Maccoby, 1998). In addition, the group story-acting integrates a significant *play* element into this narrative activity—not only in terms of the children's involvement in narrative enactment itself (which is a central feature of pretend play) but also in terms of other kinds of peer interactions that typically accompany children's social pretend play (including the selection of actors for role playing and the turn taking involved in alternating between participation as actors, actor-authors, and audience members).

Thus, this activity engages and mobilizes a range of children's interests and motivations in an integrated way, including play, fantasy, and friendship. There are strong indications that it helps to promote oral language skills that serve as key foundations of emergent literacy, as well as other important dimensions of school readiness. In addition to the accounts and examinations of this storytelling and story-acting practice mentioned earlier, there have been some efforts to systematically evaluate its effects on young children's learning and development and to clarify the developmental mechanisms involved (e.g., Groth, 1999; McNamee, 1987; and work by Nicolopoulou cited later). Overall, this work provides evidence for three basic findings.

First, both middle-class and low-income children show consistent enthusiasm for and engagement with this activity (e.g., Cooper, 1993; Nicolopoulou, 1996, 1997b, 2002; Nicolopoulou & Richner 1999; Nicolopoulou et al., 1994; Paley, 1990, 2004). Second, participation in this activity significantly enhances the development of narrative skills for both middle-class and low-income preschool children (McLane & McNamee, 1990; McNamee, 1987; Nicolopoulou, 1996, 2002; Nicolopoulou & Richner, 1999), and there is evidence that it also promotes the development of a wider range of decontextualized oral language skills, although this has so far been tested only with low-income Head Start preschoolers (Nicolopoulou, 2002; Nicolopoulou & Richner, 1999). Third, this activity promotes preschoolers' literacy awareness. Children display fascination with the process of having their words (and other children's) written down on paper and in various ways show that they are actively thinking about the connections between thoughts, spoken words, marks on paper, the arrangement of text on the page, and the transformations of spoken to written representation and back (e.g., Cooper, 1993; Fein et al., 2000; Groth & Darling, 2001). In addition, preliminary evidence suggests that participation in this activity also promotes some important dimensions of young children's social competence (including capacities for cooperation, social understanding, and self-regulation), but that line of research is still in process.

Patterns of Storytelling in This Head Start Classroom

As indicated earlier, the storytelling and story-acting practice was conducted for one semester during the 2002–2003 school year (i.e., spring 2003) and both semesters during the 2003–2004 school year. During the spring semester of the first year, the 19 children in the class generated a total of 84 stories. Every child told at least 1 story, and 6 of them told between 6 and 16 stories apiece. During the second year, the 19 children in the class generated 177 stories, slightly more than double the previous amount. Again, every child told at least 1 story, and 11 told between 6 and 24 stories over the course of the year. In both years, the children telling substantial numbers of stories included both girls and boys. This point is worth noting, because the teachers' experience in this Head Start program is that the boys tend to be considerably more reluctant than the girls to participate in writing-related activities.

Children tended to compose longer stories over time; within the same classroom, older children tended to compose longer stories than younger children. At times, children made it explicitly clear that they regarded telling longer stories as a conscious goal and a desirable achievement, proudly declaring that "I told a long story" or "I filled up the whole page." When they encountered the one-page limit for a dictated story, some children even asked the teacher to write around the edges to make sure that they filled up the whole page. In these and other ways, the children displayed a keen awareness of the relationship between their oral compositions and the written record of their story in the storybook.

We will focus here on the *types* of stories told by the children and their transformations over time. Some of the key distinctive features of the children's storytelling in this Head Start classroom can be highlighted by contrast with patterns in other classrooms where this storytelling and story-acting practice has been observed. These have mostly been in preschools serving children from middle-class backgrounds, and in these classrooms the children overwhelmingly choose to tell fictional or imaginary stories, rather than "factual" accounts of personal experience like those presented in show-and-tell or sharing time (Nicolopoulou, 2002; Paley, 1990, 2004). They also tell their stories overwhelmingly in the third person (even when they insert themselves or their friends into the stories as characters). Research in narrative development suggests that the connection between these two characteristics is not accidental. Middle-class 2-year-olds seem to begin by telling mostly first-person personal narratives, but they soon move toward a wider range of narrative forms, including fantasy narratives and fictionalization of the self (Nelson, 1996). And when young children have extensive exposure to book reading and to literacy-oriented modes of discourse, they grasp at an early age that stories are typically told in the third person unless they are accounts of their own experience, thus establishing a distinction between the "author" of the story and the characters within it (e.g., Scollon & Scollon, 1981).

There is less research on this storytelling and story-acting practice in preschools with children from low-income and otherwise disadvantaged backgrounds. The available information indicates that fictional stories predominate there as well, but intriguing variations have also appeared. One example is provided by a Head Start class previously studied by Nicolopoulou, in a different state from the classroom discussed in this chapter; the location was semirural rather than urban, and the racial and ethnic backgrounds of the children were White and some Hispanic, with no African Americans (Nicolopoulou, 2002; Nicolopoulou & Richner, 1999). These children were eager to participate in both storytelling and story-acting, but for the first 3 weeks they did not display effective familiarity with some of the basic, minimal conventions for telling a coherent and self-contextualizing story. They simply listed a string of characters and sometimes mentioned other relevant elements, usually without providing any explicit actions or descriptions for the characters, relating them to each other, or constructing coherent sequences of actions and events. This phase of protonarrative groping ended with the emergence of a shared fictional genre that was rapidly adopted, elaborated, and modified in various ways by all the children in the class. This narrative paradigm was a third-person fictional scenario that centered on a wedding, featuring the two linked characters of Wedding Boy and Wedding Girl, combined with aggressive violence by animals or other characters. The other kinds of stories told in the class were also third-person fictional narratives.

The Head Start classroom examined in the present study displayed a different pattern. All the children were able to tell simple but coherent freestanding stories from the start, and the length and complexity of their stories increased over time. This was true for both the spring 2003 semester and the 2003–2004 school year and for both younger and older children in each class. On the other hand, these were usually not third-person fictional stories. At the beginning, most stories took the form of personal narratives told in the first person—featuring the child, family members, and friends—and third-person narratives always remained a minority. Here is the first story told by one of the 3-year-olds in spring 2003:

> I went to the movies. I was watching Scooby-Doo at the movies. And my friend was at the movies with me. And we were eating popcorn and chips and my mom was with us too. And my god-mom too. I have two god-moms. And Rose was with me too. The end. (Taylor, 3–4; 2/28/03)

And here is one of the earliest stories in that class, told by one of the older children:

> I went walking and my brother went to the store and we went to the playground. After we went home and drunk some ice tea. We went to the park with our dad. Then mom said, "Let's take a ride around your uncle's house." Then we went to ride our bike at our uncle's house and then we went to the swimming pool and then we went to our bed. Then we went to the Spiderman movie at the movie theater. (Damian, 5–4; 2/11/03)

However, to describe these simply as narratives of personal experience would be incomplete and misleading. The story just quoted, for example, may appear to be a realistic story about events from the child's everyday life. But as the previous discussion should have made clear, many of these children do not actually have the "normal" carefree lives they portray in stories like this one. As the classroom teacher, the second author had extensive information about the children and their families and was able to confirm that many of the incidents described in such stories did not occur and in some cases could not have occurred. Children who described outings with their fathers had fathers who did not live with them, whom they saw infrequently at most, or who were in jail, and it was very rare for any of these children to be taken for an outing in the park by an adult male. Children described visiting certain friends' houses for sleepovers when, in fact, this never occurred. To a considerable extent, the children used such stories to portray stylized or idealized pictures of their everyday lives, disguised as factual accounts. So their stories often had a significant fictional dimension—usually including an element of wish-fulfillment fantasizing—despite being framed in apparently realistic terms.

Furthermore, even when the children included more obvious fantasy elements in their stories—such as cartoon action heroes, dinosaurs, or fairy tale characters—they often continued to present the stories in the form of first-person personal narratives. The fantasy characters were portrayed as doing things together with the author and his or her friends. For example, here is another story by the older child just quoted:

> Me and Spiderman and Batman went to the movies. Then we played together. Then we do flip flops together. Then Batman flied up to his car. Then I sprayed my webs up there. Then we all drive the car. A real car. Then we beat up the bad guys. Then Batman flied away and I swung away with my webs. Then we sat together. Then we saved the world. Then we got in the house and we watched scary movies. We watched "Scream." Then we heard the bad guys. We saw the bad guys movie and how they beat the world up. Then we saved the world. Then a dinosaur hurt the world and we had to flip the dinosaur over to his country. Then we played the guitar. Then we made an iced tea stand. Then we were in the woods. Then we broke our toy. When we heard the bad guys say, "let's take over the world," we saved the world once again. Then we saw them doing karate. That's the end. (Damian, 5–4; 2/28/03)

Over time, there was an increasing tendency toward third-person storytelling, but consistent use of the third person never became predominant. Instead, many stories took a transitional form, with an unstable mixture of first-person and third-person storytelling.

To capture these developmental patterns in the children's storytelling, we coded all stories told during the 2003–2004 school year in terms of two dimensions: the type of narrative voice used (first person, third person, or mixed) and the type of world depicted. The second variable had three categories: (1) *actual*, involving accounts of past events that happened or could have happened; (2) *wishful-possible*, describing activities and events that are realistically possible in the everyday world of children and families, but which we knew the child had never actually experienced (e.g., all the children visited the teacher's home and had dinner with her, or the storyteller described visiting the home of other children in the class to play or have sleepovers when we knew this had not occurred); and (3) *wishful-impossible*, describing events that could not have occurred (e.g., the teacher was one child's baby, the children drove the teacher to her home, the child swung on his Spider Man webs) and/or including fantasy characters from books, TV, or movies.

Overall, both boys and girls told substantially more first-person than third-person stories (figure 7.1), but there was a shift away from first-person stories over the course of the year, with an increase in the proportions of mixed and third-person stories. Between the fall and spring semesters, the proportion of first-person stories decreased from 50% to 24% for the girls and from 69% to 35% for the boys, whereas the proportion of third-person stories increased from 0% to 28% for the girls and from 8% to 25% for the boys. The existence of gender-related differences in these results is not surprising, because gender differences of one sort or another have consistently been found in previous research on young children's spontaneous storytelling (e.g., Nicolopoulou, 1996, 1997b, 2002; Nicolopoulou et al., 1994; Richner & Nicolopoulou, 2001), but in this case there is no need to explore them further, because the basic tendencies point very clearly in the same direction.

With respect to the type of world depicted in their stories (figure 7.2), both boys and girls showed clear shifts in the direction of more fictional or imaginary stories, though only a minority of their stories were framed in a straightforward third-personal fictional form, even when the content had a substantial fantasy element. For both boys and girls, only a minority of their stories were "actual" personal narratives. In the fall, this proportion was higher for the boys—39% as opposed to 11% for the girls—but by the spring the proportions had decreased to

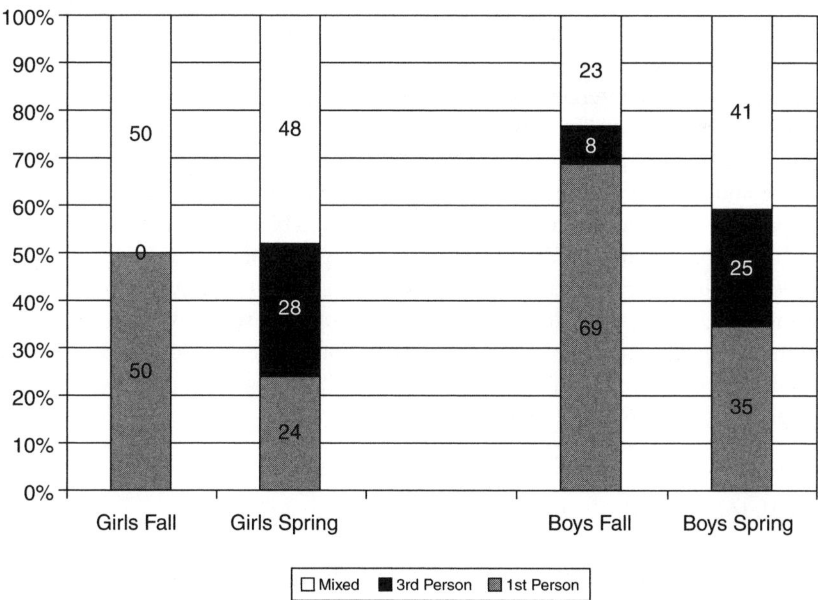

Figure 7.1 Story-Voice (2003–2004 Stories)

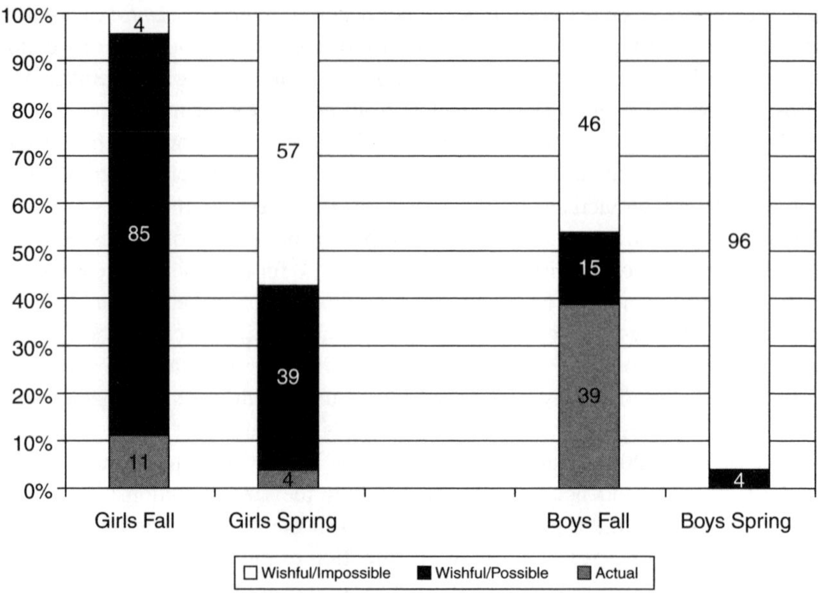

Figure 7.2 Type of World (2003–2004 Stories)

0% for the boys and 4% for the girls. Between the fall and the spring, the girls' stories shifted from a solid preponderance of wishful-possible stories, with 85% wishful-possible and 4% wishful-impossible, to a dominant role for wishful-impossible stories, with 57% wishful-impossible and 39% wishful-possible. By comparison, the boys shifted more directly from "actual" personal narratives to wishful-impossible narratives. They told 46% wishful-impossible stories in the fall—a much higher percentage than the girls—and 15% wishful-possible. In the spring, 96% of their stories were wishful-impossible and 4% wishful-possible.

There are good reasons to believe that the children's participation in the storytelling and story-acting practice promoted these developments, though it is not yet possible to demonstrate this with the data available. What the results do indicate clearly is that the children were actively engaged in this narrative- and play-based activity, that the character of the stories they told changed substantially in the process, and that the direction of this development was toward the increased prominence of what Wells (1985, p. 253) and others have described as a central and distinctive function of narrative language: "its power to create possible and imaginary worlds through words."

JOURNAL WRITING: A LITERACY-ORIENTED ACTIVITY

As noted earlier, for more than a decade this Head Start program has placed increasing emphasis on children's acquisition of literacy-related skills. Since 1997, one technique used for this purpose is a version of journal writing widely used in kindergarten, first-grade, and elementary classes (Feldgus & Cardonick, 1999). This is intended to promote basic skills for both reading (e.g., letter recognition, letter and sound knowledge, word concept) and writing (e.g., print knowledge and fine motor skills).

Because few of these Head Start children have mastered reading and writing, this journal writing activity focuses on children's drawings, accompanied by teacher-assisted written descriptions, interpretations, and identifications of these drawings. The intention is to introduce writing through drawing (an approach discussed in more general terms by, e.g., Dyson, 1989). The activity takes place daily at the beginning of the day. As the children finish eating breakfast, individual children are invited to come to a designated journal writing table, where the teacher or an assistant is ready to facilitate the activity. In this classroom, the journal writing table is across the room from the table used for story dictation.

Each child has his or her own journal book, constructed by the teacher with two pieces of colored construction paper as covers, with the child's name written on the front cover in large capital letters, and 10 to 15 sheets of white paper inside. Between journal writing sessions, the books are kept by the teacher. The adult first indicates a new journal page by writing the date in the upper-right corner of the page (e.g., "March 5, 2003"). The child then uses colored markers to make a journal entry on this dated page—by drawing a picture, scribbling, or both. When the journal entry is finished, the child brings the journal back to the adult, and together they compose a written account of the entry. The adult asks the child to explain the pictures and other markings and writes down the child's answers at the bottom of the journal page. (If the child does not answer, the adult writes down simple descriptions of the items drawn on the page, while reading these aloud to the child as she does so.)

Some children (most often girls) are always eager to do journal writing; others (most often boys) sometimes need a bit more persuasion. But all the children in this Head Start classroom participate in this activity, and each usually fills up several journal books during the year. As explained later, we were able to examine the journal books of eight children from the 2002–2003 school year. The mean number of journal entries by the girls during the year was 25, versus 19 entries for the boys. These quantities are roughly typical for most years in this classroom.

The Development of Children's Journal Entries

The development of the children's journal entries typically passes through several characteristic phases. Because a number of children enter this Head Start classroom as 3-year-olds and continue the next year as 4-year-olds, it is possible to sketch out a 2-year overview. At the beginning, the journal entries are just free-form scribbles. The children do not yet depict recognizable objects. When the adult asks them to talk about their pictures, the children often remain silent, so the adult provides descriptions of the child's drawing and writes them down, being careful not to impute representational meanings: "This is a red picture." "Takia is using the color blue."

Within a few months, the children's scribbles become more differentiated and organized. They often draw circles and ellipses that are cleared of the whorls and lines that used to fill their scribbled drawings. Over several months, children complexify their drawings by adding distinct figures inside the circle or ellipses, including dots, smaller circles, or lines. They now also begin to interpret these drawings as "things" and to give representational meanings to them, such as "persons," "my pop pop," or "a motorcycle." At times, they bring their pictures to the adult, saying gleefully, "Look, I made a monster."

In the next phase, especially among late 4- and beginning 5-year-olds, children begin to adopt stereotypic pictorial depictions: a house is a pentagon, a sun is a circle with lines extending from its surface, a flower is a circle surrounded by ellipses, and so on. Children know what they have depicted, telling the adult, "This is a house," and they often announce in advance what they are going to make to the adult and others nearby. Finally, they begin to combine representations of people and things to make simple scenes: "This is a house, a girl, the sun, and the letters."

Starting about the same time that the children recognize that their lines can represent things, we also see the beginnings of *kid writing*. This is the term used by Feldgus and Cardonick (1999) to capture the range of young children's early writing efforts, from imitative protowriting to rudimentary forms of actual writing. Kid writing includes any marks intended to represent letters, words, or phrases. In this classroom, it occurs most frequently among 4- and 5-year-olds, though it may begin earlier.

As children's drawings become more defined and organized, they begin to include some kid writing. At first, the children do lines or squiggles that imitate adult writing. These are placed near the date written by the adult or within the parallel lines at the bottom of the page where the adult writes what the child says. As the year goes on, children begin to intersperse their drawings with recognizable letters. Kid writing is encouraged as part of this activity. The adult may ask the child what he or she wrote and then write the response under the kid writing. At times, some children may become fascinated with kid writing, and their journal entry may consist mainly of letters rather than pictures.

When Storytelling and Story-Acting Meet Journal Writing

The big surprise for us was the impact that storytelling and story-acting had on journal writing. There were strong indications that children's participation in the storytelling and story-acting practice increased their engagement with the journal writing activity, enriched its operation, and enhanced its effectiveness. These effects became apparent during the 2003–2004 school year, especially during the spring semester, when the children themselves established a link between the two activities.

From Journal Descriptions to Stories

The most striking change began in February of 2004, when the children started to narrativize their journal entries. Rather than the simple descriptions that the children typically gave for their pictures—"This is a house, a girl, the sun, the letters"

(Danaja, 5–2; 2/17/04, Journal entry)—many of them now used the drawing as the basis for a story. For example, the girl just quoted did a drawing, similar to the previous one, that depicted a house, two sliding boards, a tree, a flower, and a girl. However, instead of simply describing these objects, the child told the teacher the following story:

> Sliding Board
>
> Me and Fatimah is going to the store. Then we went to get the bad boys. Then we went to get Taylor. And Taylor ran away from us. Then we went to get Danaja. Then we went to Miss Judy's house. Miss Judy took a picture of us. Then we spent the night over Miss Judy's house. The bad boy beat us up. (Danaja, 5–3; 3/8/04, Journal entry)

This tendency was not restricted to one or two children. During the spring, child after child began to shift from offering the typical descriptions that this teacher had heard children tell year after year to telling full-blown stories. In the process, the length and complexity of their journal entries increased substantially. In January 2004, another child made this characteristic journal entry: "This is the grass, and the sky, and my cousin, and me, and the sky, and the apple tree" (Taylor, 4–7; 1/6/04, Journal entry). In February this child, after drawing two hands, told the teacher the following story about her picture:

> This is me and my cousin and first it started to snow and we picked snow up and then we put our hands up and then we had a snowball fight. Then we went inside the house and we had some hot chocolate together, then marshmallows. And then we went upstairs and watched a scary movie. And then we went to sleep and when we woke up all my friends came over to my house and then we went to the playground then we went to the store and got some candy and then we went home and ate it and then we went to sleep. The end. (Taylor, 4–9; 2/24/04, Journal entry)

Even the boys, who in previous years were typically less interested in journal writing (and in some cases had to be actively coaxed in order to elicit journal entries), became more active and enthusiastic about this activity. Again, this change coincided with a shift from journal descriptions to journal stories. For example, one 4-year-old boy who had given descriptions of his pictures in the fall—"This is a happy face" (4–4; 9/25/03, Journal entry) or "Daryl and Joshua are playing together" (4–5; 10/16/03, Journal entry)—began to shift to narratives in February:

> I was a Power Ranger. Then they go home. Then Daryl said to me, "Who are you?" We saw bad guys. Yazid and Niger are the bad guys. Fatimah and Brent are the power rangers. But Fatimah is not the power ranger. Fatimah was the bad guy. Then we saw Lawrence and he was the bad guy. Me and Daryl wacked Lawrence. Then we wacked Fatimah. Then we punched Fatimah. I pushed my watch and my hands turning green then I pushed my time watch. Then my arms turned red and green. Then Daryl's hands turn green. Then his arms turned red. The end. (Joshua, 4–9; 2/18/04, Journal entry)

Overall, 14 of the 19 children in this class told stories for their journal entries (and the 5 who did not were, for one reason or another, the least involved in classroom activities in general). In the previous 7 years that McDowell had used this journal writing activity in her class, she had never observed children providing stories rather than simple descriptions for their journal entries. The most plausible explanation is that the storytelling and story-acting practice provided a model for the children in creating stories and improved their narrative skills, and that as they mastered this storytelling mode they were able to apply it flexibly to the journal writing activity, which, in turn, increased their enthusiasm for journal writing. In addition, as this pattern became evident, the teacher and her aide began letting children act out their journal stories in the story-acting part of the storytelling and story-acting practice, and these public presentations undoubtedly helped encourage other children to narrativize their own journal entries. In this respect as well, integrating the two activities helped to catalyze a transformation in the journal writing activity.

Greater Interest and Engagement in Journal Writing: A Comparison

As we have noted, one aspect of this transformation was that children became more interested and engaged in the journal writing activity. In comparison with the 2002–2003 school year, in 2003–2004 there was a surge in the number of journal entries by the girls and an even more dramatic increase by the boys.

Because these phenomena became apparent to us only during the 2003–2004 school year, we had not systematically examined the children's journals the previous year, and most of the journals from the 2002–2003 class were no longer available for analysis in the present study. However, eight children from that class had continued in the 2003–2004 class, and their journals had been retained by the teacher. Therefore, in order to carry out a systematic comparison, we selected a sample of eight other children from the 2003–2004 class who had not been in Head Start the previous year and who matched the age distribution of the first sample in 2002–2003. Comparing these samples from the two classes, we found that in the 2002–2003 class the average number of journal entries per child was 25 for the girls and 19 for the boys, and the corresponding figures for in 2003–2004 class were 39 for the girls and 46 for the boys.

These children not only made more journal entries in 2003–2004 but also showed a stronger interest in the journal writing activity in other ways. Several of them began to decorate the covers of their journal books, and a few (mostly girls) even created their own journal books—actions that McDowell had observed very rarely in all the previous years of using this journal writing activity in her classroom. The children also appeared to spend more time on their journals and to draw more detailed pictures. But at this point we do not yet have comparative data to confirm (or disconfirm) these impressions systematically.

Enhancing Writing

Another comparison brings out an association between the integration of these two activities and an increase in the children's literacy awareness and print knowledge. This involves the use of kid writing by the young 3-year-olds (3 to 3½) in the samples from the two classes (2 girls and 2 boys from 2002–2003 versus 4 girls and 1 boy from 2003–2004). In the 2002–2003 sample, only 2 children (both girls) included kid writing in any of their journal entries. In the 2003–2004 sample, all 5 children included kid writing in many of their stories.

Overall, the percentage of journal entries with kid writing (mean proportions) for this age group increased from 16% in 2002–2003 to 53% in 2003–2004. A more detailed comparison by semesters is even more suggestive. Spring 2003 and fall 2004 were the two semesters in which the storytelling and story-acting practice was in use for one semester. In fall 2002 it had not been introduced, and in spring 2004 it had been in use for two semesters. A comparison reveals sharp differences between these three categories in the percentages of journal entries with kid writing: fall 2002, 7%; spring 2003, 25%; fall 2003, 28%; spring 2004, 64%. Other indicators also show a clear increase in writing skills and print knowledge for the young children in the 2003–2004 class. Higher proportions of these children were writing alphabet letters, using invented spelling, writing from left to right, and using a return sweep when writing.

A new form of narrative kid writing also emerged. On days when the teacher did not have time to write down a story to go with a child's drawing and had to postpone that for another time, some children even began to pretend to write their own stories (that is, several parallel lines of kid writing at the bottom of the page or on the facing page). For example, Daiyonna drew a picture on one page and on the opposite page created several lines of kid writing, after which she announced, "This is Daiyonna's story" (Daiyonna, 5-6; 5/6/04, Journal entry). Again, this was an instance of kid writing never previously observed in this classroom.

Narrative Skills, Narrative Thinking, and Journal Writing

One of the most striking examples of the fruitful integration of storytelling with journal writing was provided by Takia, a girl in her second year of Head Start who was receiving services for significant cognitive and speech delays (as her often disconnected stories attested). One day in May 2004, she created her own journal book, using two pieces of purple construction paper for the front and back and four blank pages inside, which she stapled together. She worked diligently the whole morning, first constructing the book on her own and then drawing a series of pictures. After the group story-acting, she continued drawing, and later she brought the book to the teacher to see. She had written "TOT" (kid writing) on the cover and drawn the picture of a figure with a head, body, smiling face, and very long arms. She said it was "Tuney the frog," and this figure was repeated on the first page.

When the teacher praised her initiative, Takia told her that she also had a story, "Tuney the Frog." The teacher sat down and took dictation while Takia told her where to write. She had drawn a picture on most pages of the book, and these pictures were all part of her story. Takia turned the pages as she finished dictating what she wanted on each page. Each drawing had a different topic, but the presence of Tuney throughout the story gives it some continuity.

> First page: Tuney ate the fox. And Tuney said she ain't like no foxes. And she said, "I'm going back home" because she took the letter off the ground.

Second page:	And then she found a yoyo and then she was playing with it at home [picture of yoyo].
Third page:	And a crocodile came out of the egg [picture of egg]
Fourth page:	She [Tuney] said, "Can I have a cup and can I have a bag?" [picture of bag]
Fifth page:	[picture of cup]
Sixth page:	And then they was going to exercise.
Seventh page:	And then she said, "No, you can have a car 'cause I like cars. They're good." It's an airplane car.
Eighth page:	And then Tuney and her mom were looking at the new house. The end.

The story is not especially sophisticated, but for a child like Takia, this represented a remarkable achievement. Amazingly enough, Takia seems to have worked out a story (or some part of it) in her own mind and illustrated it in the journal book before she told it to the teacher. Although this particular example is exceptional, it is a powerful illustration of how the storytelling and story-acting practice can be integrated effectively with the journal writing activity, and how its effects could help to transform and enrich the latter. In the process, the journal writing activity was endowed with new meanings and possibilities for the children involved.

DISCUSSION AND IMPLICATIONS

It would be premature to draw firm conclusions on the basis of the data from just 2 years' classes in one Head Start classroom. But as our preliminary analysis has tried to show, there are good reasons to believe that the children's participation in a narrative- and play-based activity, the storytelling and story-acting practice, transformed the character of their participation in a more directly literacy-oriented activity, journal writing, and substantially increased both its appeal and its educational value. Building on findings from previous research on this storytelling and story-acting practice, our analysis also suggests that the key to understanding these effects lies in the distinctively powerful ways that this storytelling and story-acting practice combines the elements of narrative, play, imagination, and children's peer-group life.

Introducing a narrative element into the journal writing activity seems to have been the crucial catalyst for its transformation and increased effectiveness, and the evidence suggests that this narrativizing tendency was linked to the children's participation in the storytelling and story-acting practice. This participation did more than improve the children's specifically narrative skills. Through composing spontaneous stories and listening to the stories of other children, they gained a stronger understanding of how they could use language to create self-contextualizing possible worlds—thus promoting a cluster of cognitive and language skills that extensive research has identified as among the crucial foundations for emergent literacy—and they applied this orientation to their participation in journal writing.

As the children participated in the storytelling and story-acting activity, they came to understand how they can use language to create self-contextualizing possible worlds (in telling and enacting stories), and this affected the way they approached journal writing. The special appeal of the storytelling and story-acting practice, in turn, stems from the way this narrative-based activity engages and mobilizes a range of children's interests in an integrated way, including elements of play, imagination, and friendship. In addition to tapping children's existing abilities and enthusiasm for narrative expression, it is also a voluntary, child-initiated, and peer group–oriented activity—and it is fun! Children are allowed and encouraged to tell any story they wish, at their own pace, reflecting their interests, concerns, and abilities. This helps children feel that what they have to say is valuable and important and that adults value it. Furthermore, as Paley (2004, p. 5) reminds us, "The dictated story is but a half-told tale. To fulfill its destiny it is dramatized on a pretend stage with the help of the classmates as actors and audience and the teacher as narrator and director." The fact that their stories are acted out for the rest of the class gives children additional motivation for storytelling and helps to create a shared public arena for narrative collaboration, experimentation, and mutual cross-fertilization within the classroom peer-group culture.

These findings bring us back to some larger arguments about early childhood education and development with which we began. Rather than focus in excessively narrow and one-sided ways on teacher-directed, didactic, and skill-based activities, early childhood education needs to balance them with child-centered and play-based activities that successfully build on and mobilize young children's own abilities, motivations, and modes of understanding. And rather than treating these two approaches as mutually exclusive, we should seek to combine them in ways that allow them to complement and enrich each other. As we have argued here, for promoting crucial literacy-related skills in young children, activities that systematically integrate symbolic play with narrative can be especially valuable, effective, and rewarding.

References

Bruner, J. (1986). Actual minds, possible worlds. Cambridge, MA: Harvard University Press.

Cooper, P. (1993). *When stories come to school: Telling, writing, and performing stories in the early childhood classroom.* New York: Teachers & Writers Collaborative.

Dickinson, D. K., & Tabors, P. O. (2001). *Beginning literacy with language.* Baltimore: Paul H. Brookes.

Dyson, A. H. (1989). *Multiple worlds of child writers: Friends learning to write.* New York: Teachers College Press.

Fein, G. G., Ardila-Rey, A. E., & Groth, L. A. (2000). The narrative connection: Stories and literacy. In K. A. Roskos & J. F. Christie (Eds.), *Play and literacy in early childhood: Research from multiple perspectives* (pp. 27–43). Mahwah, NJ: Erlbaum.

Feldgus, E., & Cardonick, I. (1999). *Kid writing: A systematic approach to phonics, journals, and writing workshop*. Bothwell, MA: Wright Group/McGraw Hill.

Golbeck, S. (2001). Instructional models for early childhood: In search of a child-regulated/teacher guided pedagogy. In S. Goldbeck (Ed.), *Psychological perspectives on early childhood education: Reframing dilemmas in research and practice* (pp. 3–34). Mahwah, NJ: Erlbaum.

Graue, E., Clemens, M. A., Reynolds, A. J., & Niles, M. D. (2004). More than teacher directed or child initiated: Preschool curriculum type, parent involvement, and children's outcomes in the child-parent centers. *Education Policy Analysis Archives, 72*, 1–36.

Groth, L. A. (1999). *Sharing original stories: Enactment and discussion in the kindergarten*. Unpublished Ph.D. dissertation, University of Maryland, College Park.

Groth, L. A., & Darling, L. D. (2001). Playing "inside" stories. In A. Göncü & E. Klein (Eds.), *Children in play, story, and school* (pp. 220–237). New York: Guilford.

London Bubble Theatre Company. (2001). *The Helicopter Project resource pack*. [Brochure.] London, UK: London Bubble Theatre Company.

Maccoby, E. E. (1998). An embarrassment of riches: Partnering for high quality research and programs during Head Start expansion. In *Head Start's fourth national research conference: Children and families in an era of rapid change. Creating a shared agenda for researchers, practitioners and policy makers* (pp. 21–29). Washington, DC: Department of Health & Human Services.

McCabe, A., & Bliss, L. S. (2003). *Patterns of narrative discourse: A multicultural, life span approach*. Boston: Allyn & Bacon.

McLane, J. B., & McNamee, G. D. (1990). *Early literacy*. Cambridge, MA: Harvard University Press.

McNamee, G. D. (1987). Social origins of narrative skills. In M. Hickmann (Ed.), *Social and functional approaches to language and thought* (pp. 287–304). Orlando, FL: Academic.

McNamee, G. D. (1990). Learning to read and write in an inner-city setting: A longitudinal study of community change. In L. C. Moll (Ed.), *Vygotsky and education: Instructional implications and applications of sociohistorical psychology* (pp. 287–303). New York: Cambridge University Press.

McNamee, G. D. (1992). Vivian Paley's ideas at work in Head Start. *The Quarterly Newsletter of the Laboratory of Comparative Human Cognition, 14*, 68–70.

Nelson, K. (1996). *Language in cognitive development: The emergence of the mediated mind*. New York: Cambridge University Press.

Nicolopoulou, A. (1993). Play, cognitive development, and the social world: Piaget, Vygotsky, and beyond. *Human Development, 36*, 1–23.

Nicolopoulou, A. (1996). Narrative development in social context. In D. I. Slobin, J. Gerhardt, J. Guo, & A. Kyratzis (Eds.), *Social interaction, social context, and language: Essays in honor of Susan Ervin-Tripp* (pp. 369–390). Mahwah, NJ: Erlbaum.

Nicolopoulou, A. (1997a). Children and narratives: Toward an interpretive and sociocultural approach. In M. Bamberg (Ed.), *Narrative development: Six approaches* (pp. 179–215). Mahwah, NJ: Erlbaum.

Nicolopoulou, A. (1997b). Worldmaking and identity formation in children's narrative play-acting. In B. D. Cox & C. Lightfoot (Eds.), *Sociogenetic perspectives on internalization* (pp. 157–187). Mahwah, NJ: Erlbaum.

Nicolopoulou, A. (2002). Peer-group culture and narrative development. In S. Blum-Kulka & C. E. Snow (Eds.), *Talking to adults: The contribution of multiparty discourse to language acquisition* (pp. 117–152). Mahwah, NJ: Erlbaum.

Nicolopoulou, A. (in press). The interplay of play and narrative in children's development: Theoretical reflections and concrete examples. In A. Göncü & S. Gaskins (Eds.), *Play and Development*. Mahwah, NJ: Erlbaum.

Nicolopoulou, A., & Richner, E. S. (1999, September). *Narrative development and emergent literacy in social context: Integrating peer-group practices in the education of low-income children*. Paper presented in an invited symposium on "the collaborative classroom as a context for development" at the ninth European Conference on Developmental Psychology, Spetses, Greece.

Nicolopoulou, A., Scales, B., & Weintraub, J. (1994). Gender differences and symbolic imagination in the stories of four-year-olds. In A. H. Dyson & C. Genishi (Eds.), *The need for story: Cultural diversity in classroom and community* (pp. 102–123). Urbana, IL: NCTE.

Paley, V. G. (1986). *Mollie is three: Growing up in school*. Chicago: University of Chicago Press.

Paley, V. G. (1988). *Bad guys don't have birthdays: Fantasy play at four*. Chicago: University of Chicago Press.

Paley, V. G. (1990). *The boy who would be a helicopter: The uses of storytelling in the classroom*. Cambridge, MA: Harvard University Press.

Paley, V. G. (2004). *A child's work: The importance of fantasy play*. Chicago: Chicago University Press.

Richner, E. S., & Nicolopoulou, A. (2001). The narrative construction of differing conceptions of the person in the development of young children's social understanding. *Early Education & Development, 12*, 393–432.

Roth, F. P., Speece, D. L., and Cooper, D. L. (2002). A longitudinal analysis of the connection between oral language and early reading. *Journal of Educational Research, 95*, 259–272.

Scollon, R., & Scollon, S. B. K. (1981). *Narrative, literacy, and face in interethnic communication*. Norwood, NJ: Ablex.

Snow, C. E. (1983). Literacy and language: Relationships during the preschool years. *Harvard Educational Review, 53*, 165–189.

Snow, C. E. (1991). The theoretical basis for relationships between language and literacy in development. *Journal of Research in Childhood Education, 6*, 5–10.

Snow, C. E., & Dickinson, D. K. (1991). Skills that aren't basic in a new conception of literacy. In E. M. Jennings & A. C. Purves (Eds.), *Literate systems and individual lives: Perspectives on literacy and schooling* (pp. 179–191). Albany: State University of New York Press.

Stipek, D. J., Feiler, R., Byler, P., Ryan, R., Milburn, S., & Salmon, J. M. (1998). Good beginnings: What difference does the program make in preparing young children for school? *Journal of Applied Developmental Psychology, 19*, 41–66.

Stipek, D., Feiler, R., Daniels, D., & Milburn, S. (1995). Effects of differential instructional approaches on young children's achievement and motivation. *Child Development, 66*, 209–223.

Vygotsky, L. S. (1967). Play and its role in the mental development of the child. *Soviet Psychology, 12*, 6–18. (Translation of a stenographic record of a lecture given in Russian in 1933)

Wells, G. (1985). Preschool literacy-related activities and success in school. In D. R. Olson, N. Torrance, & A. Hildyard (Eds.), *Literacy, language, and learning: The nature and consequences of reading and writing* (pp. 229–255). New York: Cambridge University Press.

Wells, G. (1986). *The meaning makers: Children learning language and using language to learn*. Portsmouth, NH: Heinemann.

Whitehurst, G. J., & Lonigan, C. J. (1998). Child development and emergent literacy. *Child Development, 69,* 848–872.

Whitehurst, G. J., & Lonigan, C. J. (2001). Emergent literacy: Development from prereaders to readers. In S. B. Newman & D. K. Dickinson (Eds.), *Handbook of early literacy research* (pp. 11–29). New York: Guilford.

8

Mathematical Play and Playful Mathematics: A Guide for Early Education

HERBERT P. GINSBURG

This chapter is about the role of mathematics in children's play and the role of play in early mathematics education. The confluence of environment and biology guarantees that virtually all children acquire major aspects of everyday mathematics (EM). Children's EM is ubiquitous, often competent, and more complex than usually assumed. It involves activities as diverse as perceiving which of two plates of cookies has "more" and reflecting on the issue of what is the largest number. It should therefore come as no surprise that EM is a significant aspect of children's play. Children use informal skills and ideas relating to number, shape, and pattern as they play with blocks or read storybooks. Indeed, EM provides the cognitive foundation for a good deal of play, as well as for other aspects of the child's life. Even more remarkably, spontaneous play may entail explicit mathematical content: young children can enjoy explorations of number and pattern as much as messing around with clay. Further, children also play with the teacher's mathematics—the lessons taught in school. Research on EM provides guidelines for the goals, content, and nature of early childhood mathematics education. If we create and employ a challenging and playful mathematics curriculum, then, as the title of this book suggests, play can indeed produce learning—even mathematics learning.

CHILDREN'S EVERYDAY MATHEMATICS: WHAT IT IS AND WHY ALL CHILDREN DEVELOP IT

Everyday mathematics (EM) refers to what Dewey (1976) in the early part of the 20th century called the child's "crude impulses in counting, measuring, and arranging things in rhythmic series" (p. 282). Vygotsky (1978) also pointed to the phenomenon: "Children's learning begins long before they enter school. . . . They have had to deal with operations of division, addition, subtraction, and the determination of size. Consequently, children have their own preschool arithmetic, which only myopic psychologists could ignore" (p. 84). Vygotsky's reference to arithmetic did not, of course, imply that children's EM is the written, algorithmic arithmetic of the schools. EM seldom takes written form and does not involve conventional procedures for adding or dividing. Instead, EM entails such activities as determining how some cookies should be fairly divided among siblings or judging that adding a toy to a given collection results in "more," which children definitely prefer to "less." Upon a little reflection, every parent realizes that children can do things like this and can be said to possess an EM. But the nature and extent of children's EM are poorly understood.

All children develop some form of EM. It is a fundamental category of mind and is as natural and ubiquitous as crawling. From birth, children in all cultures develop in physical environments containing a multitude of objects and events that can support mathematics learning in everyday life (Ginsburg & Seo, 1999). A large number of parallel bars forms the sides of babies' cribs; stalks of corn in a field are similarly arranged in rows; one collection has a larger number of candies or stones than other; the toy is under the chair, not on top of it; blocks can be cubes, and balls are spheres; in the field, one cow is in front of the tree and another behind it. Although varying in many ways, including the availability of books, schools, and "educational" toys, all environments surely contain objects to count, shapes to discriminate, and locations to identify. The objects and events are not themselves mathematics, but they afford mathematical thinking. The chicks wander around the farmyard. They are chicks, not numbers, but they can be counted. Bars on a crib are pieces of wood, but they can be seen as parallel lines. The chicks and the bars can be the food for mathematical thought. In brief, children are universally provided with common "supporting environments" for at least some aspects of mathematical development (Gelman, Massey, & McManus, 1991, p. 254).

Of course, the existence of mathematical food for thought does not guarantee that it will be ingested, let alone digested. Yet several factors guarantee that virtually all children take advantage of the environmental opportunity and develop key features of everyday mathematical knowledge. First, as Piaget (1952b) maintained, "general heredity," a kind of instinct to learn, ensures that all children "adapt" to their environments and attempt to make sense of them. This thought is echoed in recent theory: "We can think of young children as self-monitoring learning machines who are inclined to learn on the fly, even when they are not in school and regardless of whether they are with adults" (Gelman, 2000, p. 28). Because mathematical thinking is required to make sense of the universal environment, the self-monitoring learning machines tend to learn some mathematical ideas. Children *invent* their own addition methods in the absence of adult instruction (Groen & Resnick, 1977). For example, at first, virtually all children add by "counting all." Shown that Johnny has two apples, and Sally three, 4-year-olds commonly determine the sum by counting, "One, two, three . . . four, five." After using this method for a period of time, children then tend to invent for themselves the more economical method of "counting on from the larger number." Given the same problem, children often begin with the larger set, saying, "three . . . four, five." It is fortunate that children can learn on their own because most parents are unaware of many features of EM, just as psychologists and educators were until the advent of contemporary research on the topic. Thus, in the first half of the 20th century, many educational theorists assumed that "young children started school with no prior mathematical knowledge or experience and that limited instruction" was sufficient for the early grades (Balfanz, 1999, p. 8).

Second, children are either biologically endowed with specific mathematical concepts or biologically primed to learn them. For example, Gelman (2000) proposes that "we are born with number-relevant mental structures that promote the development of principles for counting" (p. 36). Similarly, Geary (1996) argues that all children, regardless of background and culture, are endowed with "biologically primary" abilities, including not only number but also basic geometry. These kinds of abilities are universal to the species (except perhaps for some retarded or otherwise handicapped children) and require only a minimum of environmental support to develop. The evidence for claims like these is mainly of two types. One is that some mathematical concepts seem to emerge very early in infancy and even in animals. Thus, Spelke (2003) shows that 6-month-old infants can discriminate between collections of 6 and 12 dots and reviews other studies showing that "capacities to discriminate between numerosities have been found in nearly every animal tested, from fish to pigeons to rats to primates" (p. 286). The other evidence for the claim is that many everyday mathematical concepts appear to be universal (Klein & Starkey, 1988).

Third, it is often useful to learn mathematical concepts. If you are inadequately nourished, you need to choose more food, rather than less, and if you are gluttonously nourished, you need to choose less food rather than more. If you want to outshine your peers, you need to learn about length ("my tower is higher than yours") and equality ("I have as much as you"). And if you want to buy something, you need to understand and count your money, even in different denominations.

Fourth, the social environment also contributes to the development of mathematical knowledge. Almost all cultures offer children at least one basic mathematical concept and tool—namely, counting. Even groups lacking formal education have developed elaborate counting systems (Zaslavsky, 1973). In many cultures, parents engage in various *informal* activities designed to promote mathematics learning. They count with their children or read books about numbers or shapes. Parents also play mathematics-related board and card games with their children (Saxe, Guberman, & Gearhart, 1987).

Fifth, we use various methods to teach young children mathematics. In some cultures, television shows like *Sesame Street*, computer programs, and toys make elementary mathematics available to young children. Many U.S. states now mandate preschool mathematics instruction, and some schools use mathematics curricula (e.g., Griffin, 2004; Sophian, 2004). Research shows that children can be taught more mathematics than commonly assumed, including symmetry (Zvonkin, 1992) and spatial relations, among other topics (Greenes, 1999).

This confluence of environment and biology guarantees that mathematical ideas of number, space, geometry, and the like are essential parts of children's (and adults') cognitive apparatus. Indeed, EM is so fundamental and familiar that we seldom think of it as mathematics. But knowing that sizes can differ in orderly ways enables the child to select the longer block to create the higher tower. It also enables the child to understand that papa bear is bigger than mama bear, who in turn is bigger than baby bear. Further, a simple idea of covariation (Nunes & Bryant, 1996) allows the child to understand that the bears' sizes are directly related to their beds' sizes: papa bear gets the biggest bed, mamma bear the next biggest, and, of course, baby bear the smallest. It is hard to see how children or adults could survive in the ordinary environment without basic intuitions of more, less, near, far, and the like. Intuitions like these are so essential to human survival that they may well be universal (Klein & Starkey, 1988). Virtually all preschool children can be expected to employ fundamental mathematical ideas.

In brief, all normal children have the capacity, opportunity, and motive to acquire basic mathematical knowledge. It should come as no surprise, then, to learn that EM has a key role in play.

SEVERAL KINDS OF MATHEMATICAL PLAY

Consider three types of mathematical play. EM is deeply embedded within play, play may center on mathematical ideas and objects, and play may center on the mathematics that the teacher has taught.

Mathematics Embedded in Play

EM as the Foundation for Reading

EM manifests itself in many unexpected activities, one of them being make-believe reading. Preschool children sometimes go to the reading area, select a book (perhaps one the teacher has recently read to the group), and play at "reading" it. Of course, they can seldom sound out or recognize individual words. Instead, they try to construct a story that resembles what they remember from story time or makes sense of the picture on the page.

Here is an example taken from videotaped observations of children's everyday, unscripted behavior in a day care center. Jessica brings a book to a table where Matthew and Ralph are sitting side by side. Jessica and Ralph are 5, and Matthew is 4. They are all from low-income families, attending a publicly supported day care center. Jessica sits around the corner of the table from Matthew and Ralph. She pretends that she is the teacher and that the lesson is reading; Matthew and Ralph pretend that they are students. She opens the book, picks it up, holds it in her right hand, and tries to show a page to Matthew and Ralph. Before she can say anything, Ralph says to her, "You can't read it like that. You can't see it" (Ginsburg & Seo, 2000).

Ralph's comment reveals at least two important kinds of thinking. First, he is able to engage in *perspective taking*. He considers Jessica's orientation in relation to the book. He notices that from her point of view the book is held at a bad angle and more or less upside down. Second, he knows that it is very hard to read pages from such a perspective. Jessica is responsive to the feedback: she adjusts the orientation of the book so that all of them can see it. "I can see," Ralph says. "Me too," Matthew says.

This shows how EM—understanding something about orientation, perspective, and angle—is a basic component of good "preliteracy." Children need to learn that reading requires viewing the book in the right orientation at a reasonable angle!

Next, as Matthew stands close to Ralph to see the book, Ralph seems annoyed and says to him, "Sit down, Matthew." Matthew returns to his seat. But from there he cannot clearly see the pictures on the book. He moves his chair closer to Ralph's, saying, "Let me get a little bit far." "Little closer," Ralph corrects him. "Little closer, I mean," Matthew says.

This episode shows that as they prepare themselves for the story, Matthew and Ralph spontaneously deal with the idea of *relative distance*. They do not want to keep too close to each other, but they both want to see the book. So they sit side by side, not too close, and yet not too far from the book. Furthermore, they attempt to use the proper language to express these EM ideas. Matthew clearly has the idea of moving closer for a better view. He expresses this idea in terms of what an adult would consider an odd construction, "Let me get a little bit far." Apparently, he means that he wants to be "a little bit far" from the book as opposed to "a lot far." Although this makes perfect sense, Ralph corrects him, pointing out essentially that in this situation we usually talk in terms of greater closeness rather than lesser distance. So children try to express EM ideas in words and sometimes learn from each other the desired conventional language.

Jessica then "reads" the book to Matthew and Ralph by making up a story based on the pictures. She comments on a picture of pumpkins on the page, "That's a lot." Matthew wonders how much is "a lot." He stretches out his arms and asks her, "A lot like this bunch?" Jessica nods her head, indicating agreement. He stretches his arms farther apart and asks her if that also indicates "a lot," saying, "How about this?" Jessica nods again. Matthew stretches his arms even farther and asks, "How about this?" She nods affirmatively yet a third time, indicating that all of the arm gestures indicate "a lot."

Matthew seems to be trying to get a handle on what "a lot" means. He asks whether different "amounts" all indicate a lot. It's like saying, "Is 25 a big number? And 35? And 43, too?" To do this, he has to distinguish among different *relative magnitudes*; he has to know that this arm span is larger than this one, and that the next is even larger still. Further, Mathew attempts to represent an abstract idea—"a lot of pumpkins"—by stretching apart his arms. He enacts the idea with his body.

Jessica continues telling the story: "Put the masks back into that toy box. . . . And then you can take it back out." Matthew repeats, "Take it back out!" So now the children have shifted from ideas about magnitude to the issue of *location*: put things "into" the box and take things "out of" the box.

The children go on to discuss the degree to which a pumpkin was "this tiny scary." My claim is that understanding a story—almost any story!—requires comprehending EM ideas of magnitude, location, quantity, and the like. The same is true for adults reading Shakespeare's sonnets (Ginsburg & Seo, 1999).

Block Play

Children clearly deal with ideas of shape, space, and pattern when they play with blocks (Leeb-Lundberg, 1996), as Froebel had intended when he created this "gift" (Brosterman, 1997). But many educators and parents often fail to appreciate that many different kinds of EM make their appearance in block play.

Chris and Jeff, 4-year-old boys from low-income families, are playing in the block area. In the center, there was a huge structure that towered above the two boys. The structure was about a foot taller than Chris. The boys had built it earlier during their "work time." Both children could touch the very top of the building by reaching high above their heads and standing on their toes. The building consists of a series of quadruple unit blocks stacked one on top of the other. Blocks are placed parallel to one another, and then two more are placed on the top of those on each end to create a series of square shaped levels up from the floor.

Chris and Jeff are sitting next to the block structure and playing with toy people. Jeff says, "I am a boy. I am the strongest boy." To which Chris responds, "I am the strongest boy, too." This competitive concern about relative magnitude continues through most of the segment and eventually seems to bring about a large number of EM activities. For example, Chris soon says, "I can jump very high!" Jeff responds by saying, "I can jump very high than you!"

The children's language carries a tone of one-upmanship; their play stems directly from the desire to say or do something that outweighs what the other just said and did. In a sense, EM forms the cognitive basis for much competition: "I have more *X* than you." The example also illustrates an important point about early EM language: children's ideas are more advanced than their ability to express them in words. When Jeff says, "I can jump very high than you!" his idea is clear, but his linguistic construction is unorthodox. In this case, at least, thought leads language; language does not facilitate thought.

The boys then begin a competitive game in which the challenge is to make toy people jump from higher and higher levels of the building. Chris says, "Put them up high, high, high" and reaches up to the top levels of the building to toss his toy people over the edge. He shows some understanding of various heights and the relationship between the distances at which he can place the toy people on the building. When he says, "High, high up," he places the toy people as high as he can.

The teacher comes over to check on what they are doing. Chris says, "We're putting people up there and they're falling." The teacher replies, "Oh my goodness, what a dreadful idea." Jeff says, "They're sleeping when they are falling." The teacher responds, "Oh I see, it's a fantasy, a pretend game."

The teacher entirely missed the nature of the mathematical activity in which the boys were engaging. Instead, she moralized about the violent nature of the game, calling the boys' activity "a dreadful idea." Jeff countered by making the people less than fully conscious, presumably to lessen the impact of the fall. The teacher let him off the hook by calling the game a fantasy—as if the boys actually thought it was real!

Play Centering on Mathematics

Children do not play only with blocks or dress-up clothes or Legos. They play with mathematics directly.

"We all got one hundred." Steven, a low-socioeconomic-status (SES) African American kindergarten child, is sitting at a round table, playing with very small stringing beads. As he carefully pours the beads in his hand onto the table, Steven considers their number. Instead of saying "many" or "lots of" or "a lot of," like many young children, he says out loud to no one in particular, "Oh, man. I got one hundred." This may be an estimate, an indication of "a lot," or even the biggest number he knows. In any event, he wishes to find out exactly how many he does have and counts to find out. He picks up the beads one by one, and counts, "One, two, three. . . . " When Steven picks out the 10th one, Barbara joins him, "Ten, eleven, twelve. . . . " However, although uttering the number words in sequence, Barbara is not actually enumerating the beads. Instead, she sweeps up beads from the table into her hand. They keep counting. Steven drops the 26th one but ignores it and continues counting, picking up one bead and saying, "twenty-seven." When he takes time to grab the 27th one, Barbara keeps pace with him, saying as he does, "twenty-seven." Steven drops the 30th bead. He pauses for a second and says, "Wait! I made a mistake."

Steven pours the beads in his hands on the table and starts to count them again. He really wants to get it right. "One, two, three. . . . " When he counts "three," Barbara picks out one bead, shows it to him, and says, "I have one." But Steven ignores Barbara's distractions and concentrates all his attention on his counting. When he counts "five," Barbara joins his counting, "five." When he counts "ten," Barbara again shows her beads to Steven, "I got, look. . . . " Steven again ignores her and continues counting. Barbara keeps pace, uttering the same number words. When he counts, "twelve," Barbara shouts meaningless words in his ear, as if she wants to distract his attention. Steven ignores her again, and keeps counting, "nineteen, twenty [at 20, he puts out two beads], twenty-one. . . . " When Steven counts 47, a girl asks, "What do you count?" Again, he ignores her and keeps counting. After 49, Steven pauses. Interestingly, Barbara, who interrupted his counting by shouting meaningless words in his ear, rescues him from being stuck at 49. As Barbara says, "fifty," Steven follows her, "fifty, fifty-one, fifty-two. . . . "

When they count "fifty-two," Ruthie comes to the table, picks out one bead, and joins their counting, "fifty-two, fifty-three. . . . " Madonna also wants to play, tries to find a place at the table, picks out one bead, and joins the counting, "fifty-six, fifty-seven. . . . " The girls' counting breaks the one-to-one correspondence between number words and beads; the girls sometimes pick out several beads at once or sometimes don't pick out a single bead, though they correctly say the number words in sequence. They are not engaged in enumeration and instead seem to enjoy the repetitive behaviors of picking up beads and saying the number words in a certain tune and rhythm. Steven does not seem to care about them or what they are doing; he does not exchange a word with them.

After "seventy-nine," Steven again pauses. As the girls say, "eighty," Steven continues the counting, "eighty, eighty-one. . . . " When they count "eighty-five," the girls compete to grab more beads. The plastic container is turned over, and the beads in the container drop on the table and the floor, rolling in every direction. The girls grab the beads, trying to get more than one another. Although their fight over the beads leads to chaos, Steven's persistence is surprising. He keeps counting, "eighty-six, eighty-seven . . . ninety-four." He makes several mistakes but this time does not correct them. He seems to be determined to reach 100 no matter what.

After he picks up the 94th bead, he finds no bead on the table. He bends over and picks out a bead from those on the floor, and continues counting, "ninety-five, ninety-six, ninety-seven. . . . " After a short moment, Madonna shouts, "One hundred!" raising her arm in triumph. Steven, Barbara, and Ruthie say, "One-hundred!" right after her. And Steven says, "We all got one hundred." For them, "one hundred" is a special number and needs to be celebrated.

Steven's counting provides an example of when, why, and how counting is used in young children's everyday activities, not simply to show how high and how well he can count. At first, it was a tool to solve the mathematical problem of how many beads were on the table. I call this a mathematical problem because there was no utility in knowing the number. The situation did not involve getting more beads than someone else or competing in the creation of the largest number of beads. As Steven engaged in this activity, he seemed to become interested in counting as an activity for its own sake. His play with the beads morphed into play with the counting system itself. He corrected mistakes, he wanted his counting to be done right and well (except toward the end), and he wanted to reach 100, a special number. He absorbed himself in counting, ignored all distractions, and finally reached his goal. In most kindergarten classrooms, counting from 1 to 100 is often seen as boring drill and is usually considered to be a difficult task. Indeed, the California academic content standards (California Department of Education, 1998) set 30 as the "developmentally appropriate" highest number to which kindergarten children should be expected to count. But for Steven, counting to 100 appeared to be enjoyable and yet serious "play."

Play With the Mathematics That Has Been Taught

As they play "teacher," children also play with the mathematics they learn from their teachers. Here are some examples provided by my student, Luzaria Dunatov. She writes:

> Background. I teach at PS 51, the Bronx New School, a public school of choice. The children are enrolled by lottery and come from different areas of the Bronx. The student population is very ethnically and socio economically diverse. This is my third year teaching. I teach a class of 26 kindergarten students.
>
> Reading numbers. First thing in the morning, Joanna and Nick are assigned to a literacy "center" called "read around the room." Children in this center take turns

pointing with a yardstick to various words scattered around the room and then reading them. They can choose whatever it is they want to read from charts we have created as a class, labels, signs, graphs, and the "word wall," which contains high frequency sight words alphabetically arranged. When I modeled what to do in this center, I used the pointer to point to and read words on the word wall and letters on the ABC chart (which links the letters of the alphabet with pictures). I did not model the "reading" of any number charts or number lines.

On this day, I observe Joanna and Nick standing in front of the classroom calendar. As she points to different numbers on the January calendar, Joanna pauses and waits for Nick to say the target number. She does not point to the numbers in any particular order. As she points, Nick correctly reads the numbers 15, 23, 11, 5, 8, 14, 17, 9, 23, 10.

A few minutes later I turn to see what they are up to. They are in front of the 100 chart. I have used the 100 chart in my math lessons and daily during morning meeting. It is a well-known resource in our classroom. Joanna is pointing to the numbers as Nick counts. I see them when they are already at the number 79. She points to the numbers in sequence and Nick keeps up with her pointing as he counts. Joanna says, "Say it louder!" She starts pointing too fast for Nick to keep up with so he falls behind by one number. When Joanna points to the number 98, Nick is saying 97. Joanna waits and stays at 98 until Nick says 98, then she continues and points to 99 and 100. They walk away to find something else to read.

Keisha and Derek are also walking around the room with a pointer reading things on the walls around the classroom. Derek is pointing and counting on the number line. Keisha watches and walks with him as he counts higher on the number line. Derek pauses after counting and pointing to the number 79. He points to the number 80 and says, "What number is this?" Keisha tells him it's 80. Derek continues to point and count. He gets stuck again after the number 89. He asks Keisha again, "What number is this?" She tells him 90. Derek continues counting once again. At 110, Derek says, "100 and 0." For 111, he says, "100 and 1." Keisha chimes in to continue counting with him. It is interesting to see how Keisha reacts when he gets off track. She identifies his errors, and quickly begins to correct them by counting with him. When Derek needs help counting, she is quick to supply him with the numbers he can't read. She is aware of his abilities and chimes in when he needs extra support. Derek is comfortable asking his classmate for help when he has trouble.

Pattern. Michelle is busy pointing to her stockings during morning meeting. She is wearing striped colorful stockings and she is saying the colors aloud as she points to the stripes. I ask Michelle what she is doing. She says, "I was figuring out a pattern. It keeps going." She says, "Purple, green, pink, blue, orange, white, purple, green, pink, blue, orange, white, purple. . . . "

We have done a good amount of work around patterns. The children have created and extended patterns made of colors, pattern blocks, and other math manipulatives. Amazed by all the different kinds and complexity of patterns I was observing, I briefly mentioned how some kids were making ABC patterns and how some were making ABB patterns or AB patterns, etc. I read their patterns to the class using letter notation.

I say, "Wow! That's a long and tricky pattern. I point to each of the stripes and say," A, B, C, D, E, F, A, B, C, D, E, F." I proclaim, "It's an A, B, C, D, E, F, pattern."

Base ten. During choice time, Derek has chosen to play at the math manipulatives center. Derek is using linking cubes to make towers of 10. He already had 3 towers of 10 lying next to each other. He says, "Look, Luzaria, I'm doing by 10's. I can make a pattern like brown, green, or A, B." As he makes the fourth tower of 10, he is measuring it up against the other towers of 10 to see how many more cubes he needs. "I need one more."

Derek is transferring knowledge from our math work during morning meeting where we count the days in school using linking cubes. When we have 10 loose cubes, we snap them together into groups of 10. But he modifies the strategy a bit when, instead of counting 10 cubes and then snapping them together, he compares the tower he is building to the other towers of 10.

Measuring. Joan and Shelly are playing with tape measures at the math manipulatives center. Joan is measuring the bin that holds the tape measures. She holds the tip of the measuring tape on one side of the top of the bin and stretches the tape across the bin. She says, "It's 12, it's 12."

Shelly says, "I got 21."

Joan says, "Let me see," and measures it again. See, you made a mistake. It was 12."

Shelly says, "We measure it around like this." Shelly takes the tape and measures from the bottom of the container up to the top, across the top to the other end, and down to the bottom.

Joan says, "It's 12. See, we don't measure it around, we measure it like this." She measures it again, across the top, and says, "It's 12 to me."

In the beginning of the year, we did some work in measurement. We measured each other's heights using paper strips and then I measured each child using a yardstick. Shelly and Joan have transferred this knowledge from these lessons to their own free play. They are very aware of each other's measurements and try to model for each other the "right" way to measure the bin.

SOME MAJOR FEATURES OF EM

Several often overlooked or misunderstood features of EM are important to highlight.

First, it is *comprehensive*. EM involves not only number but also shape, space, measurement, magnitude, and the like. Although researchers have tended to focus on number (for comprehensive reviews, see Baroody, Lai, & Mix, in press; Geary, 1994; Ginsburg, Cannon, Eisenband, & Pappas, 2006; Nunes & Bryant, 1996), children's interests are broader. For example, as is widely observed (Leeb-Lundberg, 1996) in block play, children often create *patterns* evident in constructions symmetrical in three dimensions and involving regular repetitions of shapes. Children also demonstrate competence in spatial relations. Thus, preschoolers can use external guides such as informal x and y axes to help specify location (Clements, Swaminathan, Hannibal, & Sarama, 1999). EM includes *measurement*, too. Young children are vitally concerned with growing both bigger and older (Corsaro, 1985). Preschool students "sometimes discussed eagerly, 'Who is the tallest?' with a keen sense of rivalry" (Isaacs, 1930, p. 41).

In short (a spatial, not numerical metaphor), children's EM is broad, including budding proficiency in number, shape, pattern, space, measurement, and no doubt other topics. It is certainly a mistake to limit our conception of EM to "numeracy." Clearly, children's play reflects the breadth of their mathematical interests.

Second, as we saw, children's EM was often *competent*, as when Steven counted very high or Michelle noted a pattern. Contemporary research has stressed the young child's competence in many aspects of EM (Gelman & Brown, 1986). For example, babies (Wynn, 1998) and children as young as 24 months (Sophian & Adams, 1987) have a basic understanding of adding and taking away. Preschoolers commonly use various strategies to calculate simple addition and subtraction problems (Carpenter, Moser, & Romberg, 1982). Thus, in trying to answer the question "How much is three apples and two apples?" children may not only count on from the larger number ("three, and then four, five") but also use such "derived facts" as "I know that two and two is four, and there is one more, so the answer is five" (Baroody & Dowker, 2003).

Research on children's competence has made an enormous contribution. It has opened our eyes to the fact that young children are surprisingly proficient in at least some aspects of EM and suggests the possibility that young children can learn much more than we previously expected. Indeed, the research has so effectively introduced these insights that we now run the risk of exaggerating young children's competence.

Third, although young children are indeed competent in many ways, their EM suffers at the same time from several weaknesses. Matthew struggles to figure out the meaning of "a lot." Steven makes mistakes in counting. Derek cannot read 110. Researchers concur that competence and limits on competence coexist in young children's minds. They understand principles underlying whole numbers (Gelman & Gallistel, 1986) but exhibit serious misunderstanding of rational numbers (Hartnett & Gelman, 1998). They can correctly locate clusters of model furniture items in a scale model of their classroom but get confused when they must themselves position the items (Golbeck, Rand, & Soundy, 1986).

Also, despite strong critiques (e.g., Donaldson, 1978), we should not forget the substantial body of Piaget's research (e.g., Piaget, 1952a; Piaget & Inhelder, 1967) showing that children do indeed have clear cognitive limitations. The paradigmatic example is the preoperational child who cannot "conserve" numerical or other kinds of equivalence. Shown a line of seven cups, each in a saucer, the preoperational child judges that the numbers of cups and saucers are the same. But when the cups are removed from the saucers and spread apart to form a line longer than the line of saucers, the preoperational child now believes that there are more cups than saucers. Even correctly counting the number in each line does not lead to recognition of the numerical equivalence. Thus, the preoperational child focuses on the *appearance* of the lines of cups and saucers, *centers* only on the dimension of length and ignores the spacing between elements, does not *reverse* thought to reason that because each cup could be returned to its corresponding saucer the numbers must be the same, and does not *understand* the significance of counting the two rows. In brief, Piaget's work shows that at least under some conditions (albeit perhaps more restricted than he originally proposed), young children's mathematical thinking is indeed limited.

Fourth, EM is sometimes very *concrete* or grounded in ordinary activities, as when children compare the heights of two block towers or try to grab the biggest cookie. But it also can be very *abstract* and in a real sense purely mathematical, as when children want to count to 100 or want to know what the "largest number" is (Gelman, 1980). Another way to say this is that young children do not necessarily require "manipulatives" to learn mathematics. They can learn from saying or hearing counting numbers or seeing visual patterns. As Piaget (1970) pointed out, the child may learn from manipulating *ideas*, not necessarily objects: "the most authentic research activity may take place in the spheres of reflection, of the most advanced abstraction" (p. 68).

Fifth, some aspects of EM are *verbal*, the most obvious being counting or knowing the names for the plain plane shapes, like "circle" or "square." But EM may sometimes take *nonverbal* form, as when Chris and Jeff build a block structure. Without speaking, they carefully attend to the lengths of the blocks, the positions where they place the blocks, the arrangement of the blocks (some have to be at right angles to others), and the geometrical nature of the blocks (cylinders are used for some purposes, rectangular prisms for others). Clearly, they do not know the words for many aspects of their EM (e.g., "rectangular prism" and "cylinder"). The clearest example of nonverbal EM involves babies, who, of course, completely lack language but can nevertheless determine that one set of dots is more numerous than another (Antell & Keating, 1983) and may be able to do a form of addition (Wynn, 1998).

HOW COMMON IS EM?

The examples of children's play show that EM is comprehensive and at the same time limited, both competent and incompetent, both concrete and abstract, and both verbal and nonverbal. But the examples do not show how frequently mathematical activity occurs in children's everyday lives. One study attempted to determine the nature and frequency of young children's everyday mathematical activities and the extent to which they are associated with SES (Seo & Ginsburg, 2004). The investigators videotaped (for 15 minutes each) the everyday mathematical behavior of 90 individual 4- and 5-year-old children drawn about equally from lower-, middle-, and upper-SES families during free play in their day care or preschool settings. Inductive methods were used to develop a coding system intended to capture the mathematical content of the children's behavior. Three categories of mathematical activity occurred with some frequency. *Pattern and shape* (exploration of patterns and spatial forms) occurred during an average of about 21% of the 15 minutes, *magnitude* (statement of magnitude or comparison of two or more items to evaluate relative magnitude) during about 13% of the minutes, and *enumeration* (numerical judgment or quantification) during about 12% of the minutes. No significant SES differences emerged in mathematical activity. I do not wish to exaggerate the extent to which mathematical activity occurs in free play: note that several different categories of mathematical activity could occur during any given minute and that each of the activities could be of short duration.

Nevertheless, it is fair to conclude that, regardless of SES, young children spontaneously and relatively frequently (albeit sometimes briefly) engage in forms of everyday mathematical activity, ranging from counting to pattern.

USING PLAY IN EARLY CHILDHOOD MATHEMATICS EDUCATION

We have seen that very young children have an EM that permeates their play. Now the question is: What does all this mean for the goals and methods of early childhood mathematics education (ECME)? How can we use the knowledge gained from this research to improve ECME?

Background

Around the world, there is widespread interest in ECME. In the United States, many states and other education agencies have introduced new literacy and mathematics programs for preschool children. Psychologists and educators have created research-based programs of early mathematics instruction (Casey, 2004; Greenes, Ginsburg, & Balfanz, 2004; Griffin, 2004; Serama & Clements, 2004; Sophian, 2004; Starkey, Klein, & Wakeley, 2004).

One major goal of these programs is to prepare children for school. The primary reason for the contemporary emphasis on this goal is that many education professionals, parents, and policy makers are concerned that American children's mathematics performance is weaker than it should be. East Asian children outperform their American counterparts in mathematics achievement, perhaps as early as kindergarten (Stevenson, Lee, & Stigler, 1986). Also, within the United States, low-income and disadvantaged minority children show lower average levels of academic achievement than do their middle- and upper-income peers (Denton & West, 2002).

Clearly, American children in general, and low-income children in particular, should receive a better mathematics education than they do now. One part of a solution to the problem is high-quality mathematics instruction beginning in preschool. Research shows that a solid foundation in preschool education, including mathematics, can improve academic achievement for all children (Bowman, Donovan, & Burns, 2001). Of course, ECME cannot produce miracles; the mathematics instruction children receive once they arrive in school needs improvement, too.

But what form should ECME take? Research on EM and on its role in children's play can help us answer this question.

Broadening the Goals of ECME

As noted, the main goal cited for ECME has been preparing young children for school in order to improve their later mathematics achievement. No doubt preparation for school is an important goal, especially for low-income children. But an exaggerated focus on the future can be self-defeating. It entails the danger of ignoring and even spoiling the present and thereby ultimately limiting what can be accomplished in the future. As Dewey (1938) put it:

> What, then, is the true meaning of preparation in the educational scheme? In the first place, it means that a person, young or old, gets out of his present experience all that there is in it for him at the time in which he has it. When preparation is made the controlling end, then the potentialities of the present are sacrificed to a suppositious future. When this happens, the actual preparation for the future is missed or distorted. (p. 49)

We have seen that children's EM is exciting and vital. Young children develop mathematical strategies, grapple with important mathematical ideas, use mathematics in their play, and play with mathematics. Young children often enjoy their mathematical work and play. Indeed, despite its immaturity, young children's mathematics bears some resemblance to research mathematicians' activity. Both young children and mathematicians ask and think about deep questions, invent solutions, apply mathematics to solve real problems, and play with mathematics. Clearly, then, one of our goals should be to encourage and foster young children's *current* mathematical activities.

Indeed, if by contrast the exclusive goal is to prepare young children for the future, we run the risk of ignoring and even stifling children's current mathematical development. This can happen if we convert preschool into a miniature version of what passes for mathematics education in the higher grades. As Dewey (1976) put it, "The source of whatever is dead, mechanical, and formal in schools is found precisely in the subordination of the life and experience of the child to the curriculum" (p. 277). The mathematics of the schools is often a dreary chore, preserving little of the excitement and intellectual depth of young children's and research mathematicians' sometimes playful endeavors. Thus, if we drill preschoolers in number facts, we may increase their current and subsequent scores on tests that emphasize this topic (thus achieving high predictive "validity"—the validity of the trivial), but we may at the same time fail to foster their current more genuine mathematical interests and even instill at an earlier age than usual a virulent antipathy for the subject. In other words, a focus on preparation for school may allow us to achieve later success (narrowly defined) at the expense of real mathematics education.

The Content and Challenge of ECME

The research on EM suggests two simple lessons about the content that ECME should cover. One is that it should be broad, dealing not only with number and simple shape but also with space, measurement, operations on numbers, and perhaps other topics as well. If children explore these topics on their own, there is good reason to include them in the curriculum. The second lesson is that the curriculum can be much more challenging than it is now. Children like to count to high numbers, to read and write numerals, and to explore symmetries in three dimensions. There is no need to limit so severely our and their expectations about what they can accomplish, especially when mastery of difficult problems can improve children's motivation to learn (Stipek, 1998).

Understand and Build on Children's EM

One of the major themes of early childhood education is "child-centered instruction." Following this approach, the teacher needs to take the child's perspective, understand the child's current intellectual activities, and build on them to foster the child's learning, whether of mathematics or any other topic. "Teachers need to find out what young children already understand and help them begin to understand these things mathematically" (National Association, 2002, p. 6). Play is an especially promising setting for child-centered teaching. "Play does not guarantee mathematical development, but it offers rich possibilities. Significant benefits are more likely when teachers follow up by engaging children in reflecting on and representing the mathematical ideas that have emerged in their play" (National Association, p. 10).

A popular early childhood program, Creative Curriculum, follows this approach (Dodge, Colker, & Heroman, 2002). Although this is an admirable strategy, it is difficult to implement. It requires, first, that teachers recognize children's EM in real time during play and, second, that they then seize upon the teachable moment to foster children's learning. Clearly, early childhood teachers who by and large have had little acquaintance with or training in ECME require a good deal of help to make child-centered teaching a practical reality.

Introduce a Playful and Organized Mathematics Curriculum

We have seen that a child-centered approach involves recognizing and building upon the EM in children's play and other activities. But this kind of child-centered approach is not sufficient. The teacher must do more than seize upon the teachable moment that arises spontaneously. "In high-quality mathematics education for 3- to 6-year-old children, teachers and other key professionals should . . . actively introduce mathematical concepts, methods, and language through a range of appropriate experiences and teaching strategies" (National Association, 2002, p. 4).

One way to do this is through the project approach (Edwards, Gandini, & Forman, 1993; Katz & Chard, 1989), in which teachers and children engage in large-scale activities like making applesauce, and then exploit and elaborate on the mathematics and science that arise in the course of the activity. The strength of the project method is that it situates the learning of mathematics in a highly motivating investigation. But the weakness of the method is that, alone, it does not constitute a coherent curriculum (Ginsburg & Golbeck, 2004). Projects can be exciting but do not structure the emerging ideas in a systematic way.

Therefore, in addition to building on children's everyday mathematics and introducing conceptually rich projects, teachers should use a curriculum that "is more than a collection of activities; it must be coherent, focused on important mathematics, and well articulated across the grades" (National Association, 2002, p. 2).

The problem, then, is how to teach a mathematics curriculum in a way that is appropriate for young children and in tune with their EM. What does the research on EM tell us about how to do this? Not a great deal, but it does suggest some guidelines. One is that the curriculum should be playful in order to preserve the kind of natural enthusiasm that characterizes children's EM. The curriculum should cover a wide range of mathematics and need not be limited to the concrete. As we have seen, EM may involve abstract ideas. But whether concrete or abstract, the curriculum should be playful.

Big Math for Little Kids (BMLK) (Greenes et al., 2004), a curriculum designed for 4- and 5-year-olds, offers a pertinent example. BMLK offers a planned sequence of activities covering a large range of mathematical topics and is intended for use each day of the school year.

Consider a counting activity that is central to the BMLK approach to number. The activity derived from several observations. One is that children like to say the counting numbers and, in fact, are often interested in counting as high as possible. Recall Steven's attempt to count 100 objects. Given children's interest in counting, we thought that we would foster it and developed an activity, Counting with Pizzazz, designed to teach children, over the course of the year, to count to 100. Why 100? We ask them to count this high because young children see 100 as a big number, and they are very proud to be able to reach it. At the pre-K level, Counting with Pizzazz is done almost every day during the year, often at circle time. It takes only a few minutes, and as we shall see, it is a good physical activity for children (and teacher, too).

We begin the activity by practicing the number words *one* through *ten*. In English, and in virtually all other languages, these numbers must be memorized. There is no sense to the first 10 numbers (and also to *eleven* and *twelve*). After that point, English counting becomes more regular and operates according to system of base 10 rules. We usually say the "decade" word, like *twenty* or *fifty*, and then add on the unit words *one*, *two* . . . *nine*. The numbers from 20 to 99 are fairly regular. In English, the numbers from 11 to 20 are very odd. In fact, most of them are "backward." *Thirteen* should be *teen-three*, just like *twenty-three* and *forty-three*. In brief, the numbers from 1 to 12 or so must be memorized, the numbers from 13 to 19 are backward, and the numbers from 20 to 99 are governed by base 10 rules. From an educational point of view, it is ironic that although the easiest numbers to learn are those 20 and above, we first teach children the number words that make no sense and then the ones that violate the important base 10 rules.

BMLK helps children learn to count by engaging in various physical activities as they say the numbers. For example, they can jump from 1 to 9 or raise the left hand for each number, then hop from 10 to 19, raise their arms from 20 to 29, and so on. Each day, the activity can be varied; sometimes the children choose the activity. Each class does the activity differently and sets its own time schedule. One class may spend a month on the numbers from 1 to 9, and another class may spend 2 months going from 11 to 19. Different classes may make different faces and sounds to mark the decades (the tearful 20s and ferocious 40s).

A second observation that shaped our approach to teaching counting is that children often enjoy playing with written numerals. We observed one 3-year-old who spontaneously chose to put in order a collection of number cards from 1 to 30. He did this day after day and eventually achieved a good amount of success. Given this observation, and given our desire to help children learn the pattern underlying the system of counting numbers, we chose to present written numerals as children count. When they learn a new set of numbers, whether from 1 to 9 or 50 to 59, the teacher helps them construct a new portion of the number chart, with each number on a separate card. Then, as the children count, the teacher points to each number in turn, saying nothing else. After the counting activity is completed, the teacher makes the number chart available to the children during their free play. After a year of these kinds of activities, the children seem to learn both to count and to read most of the numerals to 100.

Is this play? On the one hand, the teacher directs the counting activity and the curriculum developers decided that the reading of numerals should be linked to saying the counting numbers. Clearly, the counting activities are not primarily student generated. At the same time, the material is presented in a playful manner, and the children can play with what the teacher has taught. Recall the example reported by Luzaria Dunatov, whose students enjoyed the game of testing each other on reading numbers as they played teacher and student.

POLICY IMPLICATIONS

Support Development of New and Innovative Curricula and Make Them Available

At the present time, few mathematics curricula for young children are available. Work in this area is just beginning. We should invest in developing new and innovative curricula. We should also make them available to the preschools and child care centers that serve an increasingly large proportion of the preschool population. High-quality preschool education requires funding at least at the level of good elementary education.

Strengthen Teacher Professional Development

Preschool teachers need extensive professional development to learn to implement early childhood mathematics education effectively. Professional development should promote an understanding of children's EM, as well as mathematics itself and pedagogy (Ginsburg, Kaplan, et al., 2005). Students of education in colleges and universities also need to acquire this knowledge, and methods for helping them do so are being developed (Ginsburg, Jang, Preston, Appel, & VanEsselstyn, 2004).

Create New Forms of Evaluation and Assessment

Child-centered teaching and curriculum require deep understanding of children's EM and their learning of mathematics in an organized curriculum. Teachers need to learn effective methods of observation and clinical interview (Bowman et al., 2001). These methods are more valuable than standard tests for the purpose of improving everyday instruction. But some form of appropriate standard testing is required to evaluate the success of curricula. At present, few appropriate tests are available. We need to support their development (Hirsh-Pasek, Kochanoff, Newcombe, & de Villiers, 2005).

Conduct Teaching Experiments in Context

It is a truism to say that more research is needed. But it is. In particular, we need research that focuses not so much on what children know but on what they could know under stimulating conditions. Good teaching experiments (e.g., Zur & Gelman, 2004; Zvonkin, 1992) are rare. We need more of them.

CONCLUSION

Many otherwise intelligent people suffer from fear and loathing of mathematics. One might even say that these feelings have been a cultural imperative in the United States. Perhaps this is one reason that the idea of teaching mathematics to preschoolers arouses antipathy in some quarters. Indeed, many teachers seem to believe that early childhood mathematics education is an unnecessary, unpleasant, and developmentally inappropriate imposition on young children. But we have seen that this need not be the case. Mathematics is embedded in children's play, just as it is in many aspects of their lives; children enjoy playing with everyday mathematics; and children even spontaneously play with the mathematics taught in school. Mathematics education for young children need not be dreadful. Early mathematics education need not focus only on preparation for future ordeals. Teaching mathematics to young children can be developmentally appropriate and enjoyable for child and teacher alike when it is challenging and playful and produces real learning.

References

Antell, S., & Keating, D. (1983). Perception of numerical invariance in neonates. *Child Development, 54*, 695–701.

Balfanz, R. (1999). Why do we teach children so little mathematics? Some historical considerations. In J. V. Copley (Ed.), *Mathematics in the early years* (pp. 3–10). Reston, VA: National Council of Teachers of Mathematics.

Baroody, A. J., & Dowker, A. (Eds.). (2003). *The development of arithmetic concepts and skills: Recent research and theory*. Mahwah, NJ: Erlbaum.

Baroody, A. J., Lai, M., & Mix, K. S. (in press). The development of young children's early number and operation sense and its implications for early childhood education. In B. Spodek & O. Saracho (Eds.), *Handbook of research on the education of young children* (Vol. 2). Mahwah, NJ: Erlbaum.

Bowman, B. T., Donovan, M. S., & Burns, M. S. (Eds.). (2001). *Eager to learn: Educating our preschoolers*. Washington, DC: National Academy Press.

Brosterman, N. (1997). *Inventing kindergarten*. New York: Harry N. Abrams.

California Department of Education. (1998). *The California mathematics academic content standards* (Prepublication ed.). Sacramento: Author.

Carpenter, T. P., Moser, J. M., & Romberg, T. A. (Eds.). (1982). *Addition and subtraction: A cognitive perspective*. Hillsdale, NJ: Erlbaum.

Casey, B. (2004). Mathematics problem-solving adventures: A language-arts-based supplementary series for early childhood that focuses on spatial sense. In D. H. Clements, J. Sarama, & A.-M. DiBiase (Eds.), *Engaging young children in mathematics: Standards for early childhood mathematics education* (pp. 377–389). Mahwah, NJ: Erlbaum.

Clements, D. H., Swaminathan, S., Hannibal, M. A. Z., & Sarama, J. (1999). Young children's concepts of shape. *Journal for Research in Mathematics Education, 30*(2), 192–212.

Corsaro, W. A. (1985). *Friendship and peer culture in the early years*. Norwood, NJ: Ablex.

Denton, K., & West, J. (2002). *Children's reading and mathematics achievement in kindergarten and first grade*. Washington, DC: National Center for Education Statistics.

Dewey, J. (1938). *Experience and education*. New York: Collier.

Dewey, J. (1976). The child and the curriculum. In J. A. Boydston (Ed.), *John Dewey: The middle works, 1899–1924. Volume 2: 1902–1903* (pp. 273–291). Carbondale: Southern Illinois University Press.

Dodge, D. T., Colker, L., & Heroman, C. (2002). *The creative curriculum for preschool* (4th ed.). Washington, DC: Teaching Strategies.

Donaldson, M. C. (1978). *Children's minds*. New York: Norton.

Edwards, C., Gandini, L., & Forman, G. (Eds.). (1993). *The hundred languages of children: The Reggio Emilia approach to early childhood education*. Norwood, NJ: Ablex.

Geary, D. C. (1994). *Children's mathematical development: Research and practical applications*. Washington, DC: American Psychological Association.

Geary, D. C. (1996). Biology, culture, and cross-national differences in mathematical ability. In R. J. Sternberg & T. Ben-Zeev (Eds.), *The nature of mathematical thinking* (pp. 145–171). Mahwah, NJ: Erlbaum.

Gelman, R. (1980). What young children know about numbers. *Educational Psychologist, 15*, 54–68.

Gelman, R. (2000). The epigenesis of mathematical thinking. *Journal of Applied Developmental Psychology, 21*(1), 27–37.

Gelman, R., & Brown, A. L. (1986). Changing views of cognitive competence in the young. In N. J. Smelser & D. Geistein (Eds.), *Behavioral and social science: Fifty years of discovery* (pp. 175–207). Washington, DC: National Academy Press.

Gelman, R., & Gallistel, C. R. (1986). *The child's understanding of number*. Cambridge, MA: Harvard University Press.

Gelman, R., Massey, C. M., & McManus, M. (1991). Characterizing supporting environments for cognitive development: Lessons from children in a museum. In L. B. Resnick, J. M. Levine, & S. D. Teasley (Eds.), *Perspectives on socially shared cognition* (pp. 226–256). Washington, DC: American Psychological Association.

Ginsburg, H. P., Cannon, J., Eisenband, J. G., & Pappas, S. (2006). Mathematical thinking and learning. In K. McCartney & D. Phillips (Eds.), *Handbook of early child development* (pp. 208–229). Oxford: Blackwell.

Ginsburg, H. P., & Golbeck, S. L. (2004). Thoughts on the future of research on mathematics and science learning and education. *Early Childhood Research Quarterly, 19*(1), 190–200.

Ginsburg, H. P., Jang, S., Preston, M., Appel, A., & VanEsselstyn, D. (2004). Learning to think about early childhood mathematics education: A course. In C. Greenes &

J. Tsankova (Eds.), *Challenging young children mathematically* (pp. 40–56). Boston: Houghton Mifflin.

Ginsburg, H. P., Kaplan, R. G., Cannon, J., Cordero, M. I., Eisenband, J. G., Galanter, M., et al. (2005). Helping early childhood educators to teach mathematics. In M. Zaslow & I. Martinez-Beck (Eds.), *Critical issues in early childhood professional development*. Baltimore: Brookes.

Ginsburg, H. P., & Seo, K. H. (1999). The mathematics in children's thinking. *Mathematical Thinking and Learning, 1*(2), 113–129.

Ginsburg, H. P., & Seo, K.-H. (2000). Preschoolers' math reading. *Teaching Children Mathematics, 7*(4), 226–229.

Golbeck, S. L., Rand, M., & Soundy, C. (1986). Constructing a model of a large scale space with the space in view: Effects of guidance and cognitive restructuring. *Merrill Palmer Quarterly, 32*(2), 187–203.

Greenes, C. (1999). Ready to learn: Developing young children's mathematical powers. In J. Copley (Ed.), *Mathematics in the early years* (pp. 39–47). Reston, VA: National Council of Teachers of Mathematics.

Greenes, C., Ginsburg, H. P., & Balfanz, R. (2004). Big math for little kids. *Early Childhood Research Quarterly, 19*(1), 159–166.

Griffin, S. (2004). Building number sense with Number Worlds: a mathematics program for young children. *Early Childhood Research Quarterly, 19*(1), 173–180.

Groen, G., & Resnick, L. B. (1977). Can preschool children invent addition algorithms? *Journal of Educational Psychology, 69*, 645–652.

Hartnett, P. M., & Gelman, R. (1998). Early understandings of number: Paths or barriers to the construction of new understandings? *Learning and Instruction: The Journal of the European Association for Research in Learning and Instruction, 8*(4), 341–374.

Hirsh-Pasek, K., Kochanoff, A., Newcombe, N., & de Villiers, J. (2005). Using scientific knowledge to inform preschool assessment: Making the case for "empirical validity." *Social Policy Report, 19*(1), 3–19.

Isaacs, S. (1930). *Intellectual growth in young children*. London: Routledge & Kegan Paul.

Katz, L. G., & Chard, S. C. (1989). *Engaging children's minds: the project approach*. Norwood, NJ: Ablex.

Klein, A., & Starkey, P. (1988). Universals in the development of early arithmetic cognition. In G. Saxe & M. Gearhart (Eds.), *Children's mathematics* (pp. 5–26). San Francisco: Jossey-Bass.

Leeb-Lundberg, K. (1996). The block builder mathematician. In E. S. Hirsch (Ed.), *The block book* (pp. 34–60). Washington, DC: National Association for the Education of Young Children.

National Association for the Education of Young Children and National Council of Teachers of Mathematics. (2002). *Position statement. Early childhood mathematics: Promoting good beginnings*. From http://www.naeyc.org/about/positions/psmath.asp

Nunes, T., & Bryant, P. E. (1996). *Children doing mathematics*. Oxford: Basil Blackwell.

Piaget, J. (1952a). *The child's conception of number* (C. Gattegno and F. M. Hodgson, Trans.). London: Routledge & Kegan Paul.

Piaget, J. (1952b). *The origins of intelligence in children* (M. Cook, Trans.). New York: International Universities Press.

Piaget, J. (1970). *The science of education and the psychology of the child* (D. Coleman, Trans.). New York: Orion.

Piaget, J., & Inhelder, B. (1967). *The child's conception of space* (F. J. Lunzer and J. L. Lunzer, Trans.). New York: W. W. Norton.

Saxe, G. B., Guberman, S. R., & Gearhart, M. (1987). Social processes in early number

development. *Monographs of the Society for Research in Child Development, 52*(2, serial no. 216).
Seo, K.-H., & Ginsburg, H. P. (2004). What is developmentally appropriate in early childhood mathematics education? Lessons from new research. In D. H. Clements, J. Sarama, & A.-M. DiBiase (Eds.), *Engaging young children in mathematics: Standards for early childhood mathematics education* (pp. 91–104). Hillsdale, NJ: Erlbaum.
Serama, J., & Clements, D. H. (2004). Building blocks for early childhood mathematics. *Early Childhood Research Quarterly, 19*(1), 181–189.
Sophian, C. (2004). Mathematics for the future: Developing a Head Start curriculum to support mathematics learning. *Early Childhood Research Quarterly, 19*(1), 59–81.
Sophian, C., & Adams, N. (1987). Infants' understanding of numerical transformations. *British Journal of Developmental Psychology, 5*, 257–264.
Spelke, E. S. (2003). What makes us smart? Core knowledge and natural language. In G. Gentner & S. Goldin-Meadow (Eds.), *Language in mind: Advances in the study of language and thought* (pp. 277–311). Cambridge, MA: The MIT Press.
Starkey, P., Klein, A., & Wakeley, A. (2004). Enhancing young children's mathematical knowledge through a pre-kindergarten mathematics intervention. *Early Childhood Research Quarterly, 19*(1), 99–120.
Stevenson, H., Lee, S. S., & Stigler, J. (1986). The mathematics achievement of Chinese, Japanese, and American children. *Science, 56*, 693–699.
Stipek, D. (1998). *Motivation to learn: From theory to practice* (3rd ed.). Boston: Allyn and Bacon
Vygotsky, L. S. (1978). *Mind in society: The development of higher psychological processes*. Cambridge, MA: Harvard University Press.
Wynn, K. (1998). Numerical competence in infants. In C. Donlan (Ed.), *The development of mathematical skills* (pp. 3–25). East Sussex, England: Psychology Press.
Zaslavsky, C. (1973). *Africa counts: Number and pattern in African culture*. Boston: Prindle, Weber & Schmidt.
Zur, O., & Gelman, R. (2004). Young children can add and subtract by predicting and checking. *Early Childhood Research Quarterly, 19*(1), 121–137.
Zvonkin, A. (1992). Mathematics for little ones. *Journal of Mathematical Behavior, 11*(2), 207–219.

PART III

Media and Computers

9

Media Use by Infants and Toddlers: A Potential for Play

DEBORAH S. WEBER

Can the media serve as a tool for parents and caregivers to facilitate play among infants and toddlers? A common belief is that television and videos take the place of spending time with others and playing. Another concern is that parents use television as a "babysitter." This may conjure up an image of children spending numerous hours passively watching television or videos with no adult presence or interaction. Is this in fact what is really occurring? Can and do television and videos actually encourage parent–child interactions? Can children use media as a model to incorporate in their imitative play? Do the media enhance play or detract from play? The amount of time that very young children spend watching television and video programs is increasing (Anderson & Pempek, 2005), and unfortunately this most likely detracts from the amount of time they spend playing. We now have data indicating the media-viewing habits of infants and toddlers, what factors influence these media-viewing habits, and the effects of such early viewing on the development of cognitive and social-emotional skills. This chapter discusses research regarding infant and toddler media and places it in the context of children's play and parent–child interactions.

Many professionals in the early childhood field are opposed to the practice of encouraging children under age 2 years to view television or video programs (American Academy of Pediatrics, 2001). Children are particularly vulnerable and influenced by the messages conveyed through television and unable to discriminate between what they see and what is real (Gerbner, Gross, Morgan, & Signorielli, 1994). According to Anderson and his colleagues (2003), recent surveys reveal a widespread presence of violence in today's media, and many children spend an excessive amount of time watching violent media. Extensive research provides clear evidence that media violence increases the likelihood of aggressive and violent behavior in both short- and long-term contexts. Short-term exposure increases the likelihood of physically and verbally aggressive behavior, thoughts, and emotions. Large-scale longitudinal studies present evidence linking frequent exposure to violent media in childhood with aggression later in life (Anderson et al., 2003).

Additionally, researchers have found a significant association between the amount of television watched between ages 1 and 3 and subsequent attention problems at age 7 (Christakis, Zimmerman, DiGiuseppe, & McCarty, 2004). These results held when other factors that may explain this association, such as the amount of cognitive stimulation in the home, were controlled for. One-year-olds watched an average of 2.2 hours of television per day and 3-year-olds 3.6 hours per day. Ten percent of those children had attention problems at age 7.

Huston and Wright (1998) report how infants and toddlers spend their time with media. They also argue that what children attend to on television and video can have critical influences on their development. Very young children have a greater amount of individual variability in how they utilize their time than older children who are involved in school and after-school activities. If this variability in time use relates to significant consequences such as growth in social skills and school achievement, then understanding differences in television and video use in the infant and toddler years is crucial. Those differences in media use could include the content of the programs children watch, how often they watch, and the reason for watching. The effects of television on many aspects of learning are more related to program structure and content than to the medium itself. If children are encouraged to view television primarily for entertainment, even if the content is well designed, they may learn relatively little from it because they do not engage in it purposefully (Huston & Wright, 1998).

According to a policy statement issued by the American Academy of Pediatrics (2001), possible negative health effects of television viewing on children include, but are not limited to, violent or aggressive behavior, decreased school performance, poor body image, and obesity. The statement also provides a list of parental guidelines and recommendations for children's television viewing, such as watching television programs along with children and discussing the content and encouraging more interactive activities that will promote proper brain development (talking, playing, singing, and reading together). It suggests delaying all TV and video viewing until children reach age 2. Infants and toddlers are sensory learners; they need to touch, taste, look at, listen to, and explore objects and have contact with people in their environment (Leach, 1997). Their interactions are what create learning. Motor development is also a significant learning task for these very young children. They need opportunities to push, pull, and manipulate objects, crawl, climb, and pull up to standing positions. These opportunities do not come from passively watching TV or video programs.

In contrast to many professionals in the early childhood field and the academy's position, both child industry companies and parents have been encouraged by popular lore about potential "brain connection enhancement" to foster early age-relevant media exposure. Recently, DVDs, videotapes, and television shows have been marketed directly at infants and toddlers. The majority of companies producing such media claim that viewing these videos and programs can provide young children with stimulating play and learning experiences. Additionally, these companies tend to define learning as narrowly as ABC's, 123's, shapes, and colors.

My intention in this chapter is not to increase infants and toddlers' television viewing or to suggest that media can or should take the place of play as it naturally occurs away from the screen. Instead, this chapter examines existing research on infant and toddler TV and video viewing as it relates to play and offers techniques that could help caregivers and very young children get the most out of media-viewing experiences.

WHAT DOES THE RESEARCH TELL US ABOUT INFANT AND TODDLER MEDIA-VIEWING HABITS?

Commercial rating systems such as Nielsen (1998) generally record the viewing habits of children over the age of 2, but there is increasing evidence that infants and toddlers are being exposed to videotapes or television designed for and aimed to them more today than in the past (Anderson & Pempek, 2005). Not only do these young children view television and videos but also they pay substantial attention to the programs made for them.

Infants as young as 6 to 12 months of age are watching television about 1 to 2 hours per day, according to Hollenbeck and Slaby (1979). A Kaiser Family Foundation study in 2003 indicated that 74% of all infants and toddlers surveyed had watched television before the age of 2; during a typical day in America, 59% of children under age 2 watch television, and 42% watch a video or DVD (Rideout, Vandewater, & Wartella, 2003). Similar to these findings, a more recent survey of parents conducted by Weber and Singer (2004) found that the mean age at which infants and toddlers began watching videos was 6.1 months, and the mean age of television viewing was 9.8 months. The mean number of hours infants and toddlers watched television per day was 1.12 hours, in addition to 0.41 hours for video.

Children's time spent viewing the media increases as their age increases. In 1991, Comstock and Paik found that one in four 2-year-olds spent 2 to 4 hours per day watching television. Nielsen Media Research (1998) specified that children as young as 2 years old were watching more than 3 hours of television daily. Woodard (2000) conducted a national survey including 145 families with 2- and 3-year-olds and found similar results. "Parents reported that their child watches an average of about 2 hours (159 minutes) each day. Children this age also watch nearly 1½ hours (82 minutes) of videotapes" (Jordan & Woodard, 2001, p. 7).

This is a seemingly enormous amount of media viewing for such young children. What is creating this trend? Is it simply the influx of programming aimed at these young viewers? Is it the vast amount of peer pressure that caregivers have to raise a "Baby Einstein," or are they so overscheduled that they need to put children in front of a screen to "get things done"? Is it that babies and toddlers are so responsive to this media and enjoy it so much that parents don't want them to "miss out"? Why are caregivers exposing children to this media to begin with? What are the real reasons they feel compelled to have their children spend so much time watching video and TV versus playing? And how will professionals in the early childhood field continue to respond to this trend?

WHAT PERSPECTIVE DO PARENTS HAVE ABOUT INFANT AND TODDLER MEDIA VIEWING?

The Kaiser Family Foundation report (Rideout et al., 2003) showed that a large portion of parents believe that educational media is "very important" to children's intellectual development, including educational television (58%) and educational videos (49%). More parents (43%) think TV "mostly helps" children learn than think it "mostly hurts" learning (27%) or that it doesn't affect learning at all (21%). Parents' attitudes on this issue of learning are positively related to the amount of time their children spend viewing media. Those in favor of this type of media allow more viewing time than those who do not. Additionally, parents recognize that children's TV watching has a direct effect on their behavior. They are more likely to see positive behaviors such as sharing or helping, rather than negative behaviors such as hitting or kicking (Rideout et al., 2003).

A parent media survey of 221 middle-class Caucasian families found similar results when examining the degree of parent satisfaction and comfort level with infant and toddler media (Weber & Singer, 2004). On a 5-point scale, with 1 signifying not comfortable and 5 signifying very comfortable, 82% of the parents indicated that they were either comfortable or very comfortable with having their children watch television, and 81% were either comfortable or very comfortable with having their children view videos. Eighty-four percent of the parents were satisfied or very satisfied with the quality of television programs, and 89% were very satisfied or satisfied with the quality of videos. Parents readily accept and even accommodate this trend of infant and toddler media use. Why are they so accepting?

DEMOGRAPHIC PREDICTORS FOR MEDIA USE BY VERY YOUNG CHILDREN

A recent study investigating factors that determine how much time young children spent interacting with media focused on potential demographic predictors of media use by children age 6 months to 6 years (Anand & Krosnick, 2005). Using data from a large-scale national survey sponsored by the Kaiser Family Foundation, Anand and Krosnick conducted multiple regression analyses that included predicting time spent watching television and watching videos and/or DVDs. Their findings indicated that a child's age, race, parents' education, and parents' marital status had significant effects. A child's gender, birth order, languages spoken at home, parents' employment status, and parents' age had only occasional, isolated effects, and family income had no impact at all.

These researchers found that children's time spent watching television steadily increased as their age increased up to 4 years, with a slight decline after 4 years. Those children less than 1 year old viewed approximately 35 minutes of television per day, increasing to 55 minutes at 1 year, approximately 70 minutes at 2 years, and more than 70 minutes of viewing time at 3 and 4 years. It's possible that viewing time decreased after 4 years when video and computer games became available to them or simply because these children are not home as much. They are now beginning to participate in preschool programs and may attend extracurricular classes such as music or gymnastics.

Time spent watching video and/or DVDs increased with age up to 3 years, after which it declined. Children less than 1 year old viewed approximately 35 minutes of video or DVDs each day, with viewing time steadily increasing up to 45 minutes per day for 3-year-olds. This steady increase in both TV and video viewing with age may relate to the child's ability to comprehend program content, as well as the larger number of programs offered that are targeted to the preschooler versus those for the infant and toddler.

When investigating parents' education, Anand and Krosnick (2005) found that children of mothers and fathers with less education watched more television. In contrast, children of fathers with moderate levels of education spent more time watching video or DVDs than children of fathers with the most or the least education. Children whose fathers worked part-time viewed less television than did children of unemployed fathers. However, children of retired fathers and mothers viewed more television than those with fathers and mothers who were unemployed. In addition, children with retired mothers watched more video and/or DVDs than those with older parents or with mothers who were unemployed. It seems that children living with retired parents engage in the most screen time. Perhaps these children are simply home more than others, and media viewing is the most readily available choice for activity.

Parental marital status also played a role in television-viewing habits. Researchers discovered that children living with a divorced parent or a parent who never married spent less time watching TV than children living with married adults. However, those children living with a separated parent spent more time watching videos and/or DVDs than children living with married adults (Anand & Krosnick, 2005).

In an earlier study, Jordan and Woodard (2001) also found differences in children's media use patterns according to demographics such as parental education, race, the presence of older siblings, gender, and income. Similar to the Anand and Krosnick (2005) findings, Jordan and Woodard reported that children who have parents with a high school education or less view television an hour more, on average, than children whose parents have more education. Regarding race, children's media use varied only to some extent. Two- to 3-year-olds from nonwhite families spent 23 minutes more per day with TV and 13 minutes more per day with the VCR. For gender, parents reported that their daughters spend more time per day than their sons with videotapes (20 minutes) and television (17 minutes), and those children with older siblings in the homes watched, on average, 20 minutes more per day of TV than children without an older sibling. They also found that children from families with lower incomes typically watch 30 minutes more of television and 22 minutes more of videotaped programming than children from higher income families. It's possible that this is occurring because children from families with lower incomes have less opportunity for organized extracurricular activities that cost money, such as swimming, music, and gymnastics.

In a very recent study, the amount of television use among children from birth to 6 years was examined according to rules caregivers established (Vandewater, Park, Huang, & Wartella, 2005). Parents with "time rules" reported their children watching less television; parents with "program rules" reported their children watching more television. The parents who had established program rules were more likely to have positive attitudes toward television and to be present when their children were viewing. Interestingly enough, parents with both types of rules were more likely to see their children imitating positive behaviors from television, whereas parents with only program rules tended to see their children imitating negative behaviors. It's possible, as well as concerning, that the programs these parents are allowing their children to watch include content that models and encourages this negative behavior they see their children imitating. Additionally, a higher education level was related to rules of both types, and higher household income was related only to having program rules. To summarize, children with parents who restrict the amount of time they spend viewing programs ultimately watch less TV collectively, and parents who enforced program rules were most likely present while the child was watching.

In an earlier study investigating the influence of nonrelated caregivers versus related caregivers, 2-year-olds in care with relatives were found to watch television for longer periods of time than those with nonrelated caregivers. It is interesting to note that children in care with nonrelatives tended to watch more educational and age-appropriate television programs and fewer adult programs than children cared for by relatives (Mullin-Rindler & Fucinga, 1995). Conceivably, the nonrelated caregiver may have a more immediate need to be concerned about the type of content children under his or her care are exposed to. Nonrelated caregivers, perhaps, believe that they are held accountable for what the children do while they are under their care and need to justify the type of program viewing that takes place.

Pierroutsakos, Hanna, Self, Lewis, and Brewer (2004) surveyed 100 parents with children ages 2½ months to 24 months. In this study, parents were asked to complete a diary tracking infants' amount and type of TV exposure. Similar to studies previously mentioned, parents reported that their child was attentive to about 60 minutes of television per day, on average. However, they were exposed to about 120 minutes per day, and not all programs viewed were appropriate for these young children. What is most revealing is that of those 120 minutes of media exposure, 50% included infant and toddler programming, 40% adult programming, and 9% preteen programming. These children are being exposed to inappropriate content that they are particularly vulnerable to and influenced by (Gerbner et al., 1994), and this could potentially cause a variety of negative effects, such as aggressive or violent behavior.

WHAT BEHAVIORS DO INFANTS AND TODDLERS EXHIBIT WHILE WATCHING THE MEDIA?

Despite a recent increase in research on the amount of media viewing among children under 2 years old, its effects and impact on child development remain understudied. In part, this may be due to the fact that children this age cannot articulate how and why they spend their time with media. In addition, researchers may not be able to get accurate measures of these effects without using intrusive and expensive approaches, such as longitudinal studies and intervention experiments (Jordan & Woodard, 2001; Schmitt, 2001). A select number of research studies, however, have been completed.

Lemish (1987), for example, conducted a participant-observation study of families with children ages 6½ to 29½ months old, for a period of 6 to 8 months. The objective was to study babies' viewing behavior in their natural environment. She discovered distinct phases in how children process television. Children ages 0 to 6 months attend to loud voices and sudden noises, whereas 6- to 10-month-olds are attracted to certain sounds (e.g., a character's voice, laughter). The 10- to 18-month-olds' pattern of attention focuses on music, content, and character awareness. What is of special relevance to this chapter is that Lemish reported data suggesting television *encourages* particular forms of play. By the first half of the second year, when babies heard certain sounds, they would stop what they were doing and run to the location of the television to watch, sway, bounce and clap their hands, sing along with the television, and vocalize in excitement. She also found that once children viewed *Sesame Street* repeatedly, they became familiar with and attentive to the characters in the program. Both mothers' reports and participant observations revealed that babies as young as 15 months were able to point out and name most of the major characters, as well as recognize the characters in other contexts, such as books, toys, stores, posters, or clothing. Children showed preference for familiar content as well, favoring commercials and programs that included babies, young children, and familiar animals.

Earlier work by Meltzoff and Moore (1977) found that infants only days old could imitate the facial expressions of an adult. He also reported that 14-month-olds imitate actions they see on television. Later, Meltzoff's (1988) research focused on whether TV viewing simply presented infants with a salient collection of moving patterns or whether they could readily pick up information shown in the two-dimensional (2-D) representation and incorporate it into their own behavior. He wanted to learn more about infants' ability to understand the content of television to the extent that they could direct their behaviors within the context of their own environment accordingly. Meltzoff studied this question by presenting a model via television for infants to imitate. The child's ability to imitate these TV models was explored at 14 and 24 months, under conditions of immediate and deferred imitation. In deferred imitation, infants were exposed to a TV portrayal of an adult manipulating a novel toy in a particular way but were not presented with the real toy until the next day.

Meltzoff indicated that 14-month-olds were able to learn how to manipulate a toy they had never seen before by watching the television demonstration. Results demonstrated significant imitation at both 14 and 24 months and that even the youngest group imitated after the 24-hour delay. This study adds to a growing body of literature on prelinguistic representational abilities: infants can relate 2-D representations to their own actions on real objects in 3-D space. The information picked up through viewing television can be internally represented over lengthy delays before it is used to guide a young child's actions within the context of their own natural environment. In sum, these results imply that even very young children have the potential to learn about different ways to play with toys or objects by watching the media.

Richards and Cronise (2000) also noted that 1-year-olds are able to imitate what they view on television. They studied viewing behavior patterns (attention and heart rate) of infants ranging in age from 6 to 24 months when they showed the children two different samples: an excerpt from a *Sesame Street* movie and a computer-generated display of randomly moving forms and sounds. Infants up to 12 months old showed the same visual behavior patterns and heart rate when watching either display. Eighteen- and 24-month-olds watched the *Sesame Street* movie for longer periods of time and demonstrated heart rate patterns indicative of sustained and focused attention (Richards & Cronise, 2000). This suggests that children 18 months and older can begin to discriminate a comprehensible organized program such as *Sesame Street* from a random display of visuals.

Further work on attention to television among children age 6 to 58 months was carried out by Valkenburg and Vroone (2004). In their homes, children were shown a video including six brief television segments that varied in complexity, such as news, children's commercials, and *Teletubbies*. They indicated that very young children paid more attention to programs with simple content, *Teletubbies*, and older children paid greater attention to more difficult content, *Lion King II*, supporting the premise that attention is highest for content that is within the child's level of comprehension.

Despite evidence that infants and toddlers have a different understanding of television than older children (Schmitt, 1997), the elements that attract their attention to TV have been found to be similar (Schmitt, Anderson, & Collins, 1999). Singing, movement, and portrayals of TV characters such as babies, puppets, or other nonhumans enhance the attention of infants and toddlers. Weber and Singer (2004) also gathered data on the types of program features and activities that were most appealing to this age group. Mentioned most often were music and songs, characters, animals, action or movement, dancing, animation, and babies with children.

Media viewing, according to these studies, appears to have different effects on infants versus toddlers. If a caregiver is to use television or video and DVD programs as a tool to encourage play, choosing the appropriate type of program according to content and age suitability is essential (Lerner, Singer, & Wartella, 2001). The amount of media viewing should remain limited, and the caregiver should be present during viewing time to encourage play, interact with the child, explain concepts, and ask the child questions.

CAN TV AND VIDEO PROGRAMS ENCOURAGE PLAY AND SOCIAL INTERACTION?

Eighteen-month-old Anthony holds up his talking stuffed animal named Barney, smiles as he looks up, and says, "Barney!" His mother is standing behind him as he enters the Play Lab for his toddler playgroup. She emphatically explains that Anthony loves Barney and lately they have been watching the *Dance with Barney* video together at home every day. She mentions that he likes to hold his Barney toy while they dance and sing along with the video together. Once Anthony enters into the Play Lab classroom, he immediately asks to watch what he calls the "Barney Zoo" (*Barney: Let's Go to the Zoo*) video. He moves his hips back and forth and sings along to the beginning theme song, as he watches the large purple dinosaur character on screen and hugs his Barney toy.

Anthony's experiences and actions while viewing a video program are very similar to what was found in an infant and toddler study (Weber & Singer, 2004). That is, this 18-month-old and his mother view the Barney video program together while interacting and playing with one another. The Weber and Singer (2004) data indicated TV and videotapes have the potential to encourage time together for parents and the very young. When referring to their children between the ages of 1 and 23 months, 47% of the parents in the survey said they watch children's television programs with their child at each viewing, and 39% watch each time while viewing children's videos. Only 1% of parents said they never watched television or video programs with their child. As can be seen in figures 9.1 and 9.2, the most frequent activities parents engaged in with their children while viewing TV and videos relate to different elements of play: singing, dancing, and pointing to what is taking place on the screen.

Results related to parent presence while infants and toddlers view media were presented in a Kaiser Family Foundation study of children 0 to 6 years old (Rideout et al., 2003). The majority of parents (85%) reported that most of the time the child watched television with someone else. Additionally, 69% of parents said they were in the room either most or all of the time their child was watching. In

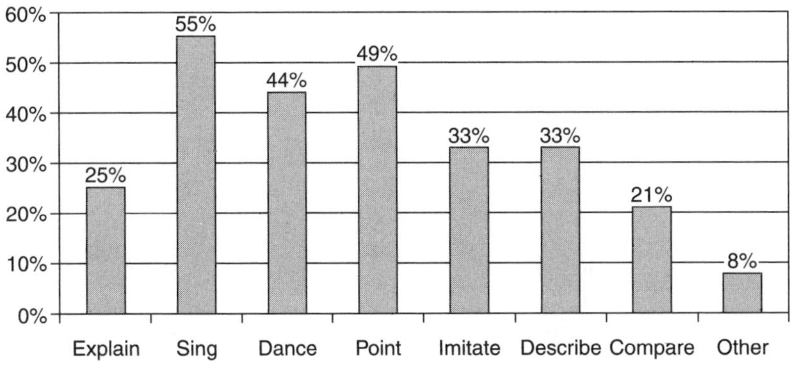

Figure 9.1 Activities With Video (Mother with Child, N = 138)

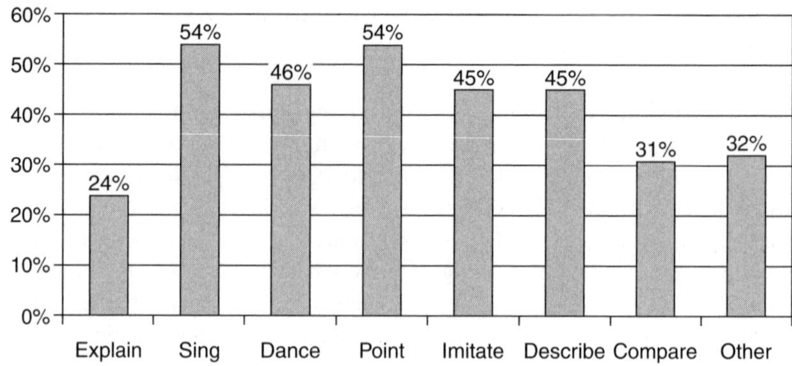

Figure 9.2 Activities With Television (Mother with Child, N = 127)

contrast, 45% of all parents said they would be very or somewhat likely to set their child down with a video or a television program if they had something important to do. In a study by Schmitt (2001) examining 2-year-olds' media-viewing behaviors, nearly half of the toddlers' time viewing television was spent interacting with others, and one third of their time was spent playing. Thus, the common portrayal of solitary television watching among young children is not completely accurate.

Very young children often engage in other activities while viewing media (Weber & Singer, 2004). The most common activities children participated in while watching TV were playing with toys (73%), eating and drinking (23%), moving in a swing or ExerSaucer (18%), crawling, walking, or running (11%), and looking at books (11%). Results for viewing videos were similar, with the most popular activities playing with toys (67%), eating and drinking (22%), dancing (12%), moving in a swing or bouncer seat (13%), walking, crawling, or climbing (11%), and looking at books (9%).

When Schmitt (2001) observed behaviors of 2- to 3-year-olds who were viewing TV, she found similar results. The most frequent nonviewing behaviors were social interaction (39.2%) and playing (32.1%). Other behaviors included eating (7.6%), reading or being read to (2.2%), grooming (1.4%), and writing or drawing (1.3%). These children spent only 40.6% of their viewing time actually watching the screen. Fifty-eight percent of the children's social interactions were with another child, usually a brother or sister. Most common types of play were play with toys (59.4%) and physical activity such as running around the room (15.1%). Approximately one third of the time, toddlers were physically active when they were in the viewing room. Schmitt (2001) reported that the 2- to 3-year-olds were as likely to interact with someone in their environment as they were to look at the TV, and sometimes they did both at the same time. The most common type of social interaction was talking, followed by looking at others. The 2-year-olds also spent some of their viewing time sitting next to another person or cuddling with them, indicating that media viewing is not necessarily a passive and physically isolating activity.

Twenty-two-month-old Jenna is watching the *Little People* video *Big Discoveries* attentively. One of the segments in the video is based on the character Sonya Lee's day visiting her animal friends at the zoo. A few minutes after Jenna watches the segment, she gets up from the child-size couch and quickly gathers a handful of Little People toy figures (including Sonya Lee) and a train that the toys fit inside of. She brings them back to the couch, sets them down, and begins to put the characters and animals into the train. She fills each car with a toy little person or animal and then drives the train in circles. Jenna stops the train, takes the figures out of the car, puts one little person in one hand and an animal in the other, and moves them back and forth to have them "talk" to one another. Jenna was imitating what she had just watched on the video program—engaging in early imitative imaginative play as prompted by viewing the *Little People* video. As observed further in the Play Lab, once children were at the developmental stage to engage in pretend play and sociodramatic play, these videos motivated them to develop their own play scenarios by using the characters or message that was conveyed through the story line.

Many animated television programs are based on products; the characters in the programs are readily available as toys in stores. The combination of product-based television and thematically related toys is potentially stimulating to imitative imagination—play representations where the children use the toy or animated figure in a similar manner as shown in the television program (Greenfield et al., 1993; Singer & Singer, 1990, 2005).

Educational programs such as *Barney & Friends* and *Sesame Street* include fantasy elements and offer solutions to problems. They have been shown in research to foster imagination and creativity (Skeen, Brown, & Osborn, 1982). The presence of live actors in these programs can help convince young children that fantasy episodes can really occur. On many television programs, adult characters talk to the fantasy characters (*Mister Rogers' Neighborhood*, *Sesame Street*, *Barney & Friends*), which adds to the apparent realism of the puppets or animated characters on the program. Having live figures on a television program is important if they clarify information and allow the children to process the story line more easily. Singer and Singer (1998) studied the effects of the children's program *Barney & Friends*, where the host, Barney, and generally four children in each episode indeed provide explanations and clarification of concepts on the program. Toddlers in experimental and control conditions were rated during their free play periods before and after TV viewing by two trained independent observers for 10 minutes over two points in time. Observers rated both groups on imaginativeness of play, persistence, and aggression. The experimental group watched 10 episodes of *Barney* daily, just before their free play periods, and the control group did not see the program at all. Parents filled out questionnaires about their children's language abilities, favorite toys and activities, and degree of television viewing. The toddlers who were exposed to *Barney & Friends* showed more imagination and were more socially appropriate than the control group (Singer & Singer, 1998). The children viewing *Barney* were actively involved with the show as evidenced by their tendency to dance along with the characters and to sing the songs from the show.

Teletubbies was launched on BBC in 1997 and is targeted to 1-year-old children. A series of studies in a special report, *Televizion* (Lohr, 1999), suggested benefits for preschoolers who watch *Teletubbies*. For example, one study indicated that as the *Teletubbies* program becomes increasingly familiar to many children, literacy activities related to the *Teletubbies* could be an incentive for toddlers to learn how to read and write in preschool classes (Marsh, 1999). Most of the data, however, were gathered through observations of children older than 1 year or through anecdotal data from caregivers. The studies report positive effects in the children such as smiling, laughing, and imitating sounds on the screen in Great Britain, Germany, Australia, and Israel.

CAN YOUNG CHILDREN LEARN LANGUAGE SKILLS FROM THE MEDIA?

An example of children benefiting in language usage from viewing television was demonstrated in a longitudinal study by Lemish and Rice (1985), where children's behaviors were recorded while they watched television in their own homes. The children were newborn to 3 years old, actively involved in the process of language acquisition. Observations revealed multiple consistent occurrences of language-related behaviors among children and parents in the viewing situation. The main categories of children's verbalizations were labeling objects on the screen, asking questions about the program, repeating television dialogue or parent comments about the content, and describing the content. Parents acted as mediators, with their verbalizations paralleling their child's. Results of this study indicate that television and video have the potential to serve as a facilitator of children's language development when parents mediate the viewing experience.

It's important to consider that a child's language skills could develop even more rapidly when a caregiver asks questions and encourages conversation, makes up simple rhymes along with a child, defines words using terms that are understandable to the child, repeats words, and uses new words in sentences that a child will comprehend. This type of interaction is rarely integrated into programs designed for infants and toddlers.

In a more recent longitudinal study conducted by Linebarger and Walker (2005), findings supported the importance of content and type of program when describing media effects on language development. The researchers observed 51 babies every 3 months, from 6 months of age to 2 years, and tracked language development as measured by vocabulary and expressive language use (ability to express needs and wants). At 2 years old, watching *Dora the Explorer*, *Blue's Clues*, *Arthur*, *Clifford*, or *Dragon Tales* resulted in bigger vocabularies and higher expressive language scores versus watching *Teletubbies*, which related to fewer vocabulary words and lower expressive language scores. Viewing *Sesame Street* was related only to smaller expressive language scores, and watching *Barney & Friends* was related to fewer vocabulary words and more expressive language. Linebarger (2005) concluded that programs featuring tight narrative structures that used language-promoting strategies predicted positive language development. Infants and toddlers need a very linear narrative with much repetition within the episode, as well as clear sequences and story patterns.

In an earlier report concerning this study, Linebarger (2004) explained that *Arthur*, *Clifford*, and *Dragon Tales* include opportunities to see and hear vocabulary words within the context of everyday conversation. *Dora* and *Blue's Clues* are audience-participation programs that actively seek feedback and comments from children, praise children's responses, and offer explanations and visual demonstrations of various vocabulary words. Linebarger (2004) indicates that these strategies are often used to increase vocabulary and support increased single and multiple word use.

Perhaps a child's vocabulary and expressive language skills could develop all the more with a caregiver who introduces new words in context and explains the word by using meaningful and appropriate terms for the individual child. Caregivers can encourage children to use expressive language within the context of everyday situations. An example that readily comes to mind involves sharing: a child pulls a toy out of another child's hand without asking first and explaining that he wants to play with that toy now, too. The caregiver can explain to the child that he or she has to ask to use the toy versus physically demonstrating his or her needs by pulling it away.

In contrast to the previously mentioned programs, *Teletubbies* uses poor language models that consist of vocalizations, baby talk, and single-word utterances. The children who watched this program tended to produce more vocalizations and fewer single and multiple word utterances than those who did not, suggesting that children will repeat or imitate what they watch on media. Linebarger (2004) surmised that the loose narrative structure and the changing vignettes of *Sesame Street* and *Barney & Friends* may not have provided enough support to maintain interest and learning throughout the show for very young viewers. She noted that *Sesame Street* was completely redesigned in 2001 after data collection was complete and indicated that the new format features tighter narratives with content more suitable for younger viewers. Regarding *Barney & Friends*, other research showed word learning occurred more frequently when there was an adult coviewer present to support program messages (Linebarger, 2004). Support for the importance of adult mediation was demonstrated by Singer and Singer (1998), who found that preschool children who had adult intervention after viewing *Barney & Friends* made stronger gains in vocabulary than a control group who had no such intervention.

Singer and Singer (1981) found modest correlations between language and television viewing in a study with 3- and 4-year-olds. There were positive correlations between the amount of weekly television viewing and imperative sentences of an aggressive nature, such as commands and exclamations, and negative correlations between the amount of weekly television viewing and questions, verbs in the future tense, and adjectives. Children who viewed a great deal of television, 4 hours or more per day, and played less simply were not making gains in vocabulary parallel to light TV viewers of 2 hours or less per day. In addition, light TV viewers revealed slight positive correlations between weekly television viewing and mean length of utterances, suggesting that television may tend to facilitate language.

In sum, the research discussed supports the notion that children's language skills can be enhanced by the media, most likely within the context of a mediated environment, viewing specific developmentally appropriate programming for limited amounts of time.

CAN TODDLERS AND PRESCHOOLERS ACQUIRE SCHOOL READINESS SKILLS FROM THE MEDIA?

In a 3-year longitudinal study named the "Early Window Project" of 2- to 5-year-old children from relatively low-income families, the Center for Research on the Influences of Television on Children investigated the long-term effects of educational television on achievement and school readiness (Bickham, Wright, & Huston, 2001). The researchers found a positive relationship between watching educational TV and tests of achievement and school readiness. "Overall, viewing *Sesame Street* and other similar programs at ages 2 and 3 predicted higher scores at age 5 on measures of language, math, and school readiness" (Bickham et al., 2001, p. 114). These children were rated by their first teachers as more ready to learn, based on attitude and preacademic skills, than their peers who did not watch such programs. The study also indicated that children who repeatedly watch developmentally appropriate educational television programs learn basic concepts and the language needed to use them, they discover that learning is fun, they anticipate going to kindergarten, and they are more prepared for and excited about learning (Linebarger, 2004).

Anderson and Pempek (2005) hold a different perspective when referring to media as a learning tool. They compared a child's ability to learn from a live presentation versus a video presentation and found substantially less learning from videos. They refer to this as the *video deficit*. One study used live and video versions of an experimenter demonstrating the functioning of a puppet. Demonstrations ranged from one-step operations (taking a mitten off) to more complicated operations (taking the mitten off, shaking it to hear a bell inside the mitten, and then taking the bell out). After a 24-hour delay, 12- to 15-month-olds imitate the live demonstrations with little difficulty. However, they are not able to imitate the video demonstrations as easily. The children showed some success with the one-step demonstrations only (Barr & Hayne, 1999). Further study and discussion are needed to better understand what influence the media has on the acquisition of school readiness skills among infants and toddlers, specifically.

TYPES OF MEDIA EXPOSURE

Anderson and Evans (2001) suggest that very young children have two kinds of exposure to television: background and foreground exposure. When a child is incidentally exposed to media, background exposure occurs. For example, a child is in the same room as a parent or older sibling who is viewing a television program. Foreground exposure occurs when the child is attentive to and/or is interacting with a television program, and the program is designed for young children. They found that background TV is a disruptive influence on the amount and quality of toy play and interactions.

Evans, Pempek, Kirkorian, Frankenfield, and Anderson (2004) directly measured the impact of background media on play and parent–child interactions. The researchers observed 12-, 24-, and 36-month-old children's toy play with and without a television program (*Jeopardy!*) playing in the background. Parents were asked to limit interactions with their children so that the researchers could observe the impact of television on toy play independent of parent–child interaction. Background television reduced both the length of play episodes and the degree of focused attention during object play. Results from an ongoing study (Murphy, 2004) indicate that parent–child interactions are substantially decreased in the presence of background television. An analysis of parent interactions with their 24-month-old children showed a 22% reduction when the television was on. Perhaps this decrease in parent–child interaction is one factor causing the reduced length of play episodes and attention during play; it's possible that the parents aren't helping to sustain the play as much as they normally would if the television was off.

The research discussed thus far shows both positive and negative effects of media viewing on our very young children. To speculate in the most simplistic terms, when infants and toddlers are exposed to age-appropriate media with an adult present interacting with the child, explaining the content, and encouraging play, media viewing can result in a positive playful learning experience. Negative outcomes result when the adult is not present and the child is exposed to unlimited amounts of inappropriate program content. With these findings in mind, how might we encourage additional positive media-viewing experiences that facilitate learning through play?

DO PARENTS BELIEVE CHILDREN LEARN THROUGH PLAY?

According to *What Grown-Ups Understand About Child Development: A National Benchmark Survey* (DYG, 2000), most parents see the important connection between play and intellectual, emotional, and social development. The majority of parents see play as crucial to the healthy development of a child. However, there are gaps in adults' knowledge about play. Results of the survey indicate parents as being less likely to see the importance of play when they think about younger children (10-month-olds). Fathers see less benefit in play, regarding the 10-month-olds, than do mothers. Parents with a high school degree or less are less likely to understand the connection between healthy play and development. All adults surveyed see a greater connection between social development and playing than they do between playing and language development.

From a survey questioning 1,160 middle-class mothers of children below the age of 6 and 106 play experts who were mainly professors (74%), data suggest that 95% of the parents indicated it was important for their child to spend time playing each day (Yankelovich, 2005). When asked whether playtime equals learning, both mothers and experts were in fair agreement (86% of the mothers and

81% of the experts). However, 46% of the mothers believed that free unstructured play was the *best way* for children to learn versus 75% of the experts. Although 77% of the experts believed that it was most important for young children to be emotionally and socially prepared for school, only 48% of the mothers agreed.

The majority of mothers in this survey believe that children do learn from play. As previously discussed, we now have data indicating that parents are facilitating media use among infants and toddlers, and there is evidence that children's programs can enhance learning through play. How, then, might we bridge the gap between media viewing and play to help caregivers and children get the most out of each viewing experience?

HOW TO USE CHILDREN'S TELEVISION AND VIDEO PROGRAMS AS RESOURCES FOR PLAY

Television is a special experience that should be a relatively small part of a child's day, but it should offer an opportunity to play, learn, and grow. Lerner, Singer, and Wartella (2001, p. 33) suggest guidelines for parents and caregivers about the use of media with very young children:

1. Screen TV programs before presenting them to a child. (What is the content? Have the producers or manufacturers tested the content for age appropriateness?)
2. Limit young children's time with TV. (Generally 30 minutes of TV a day is reasonable for 2- to 3-year-olds, balancing empathy for the parent with developmental appropriateness.)
3. Be with the child while watching TV. (Mediate the child's experience; that is, help the child focus; discuss what the child is viewing.)
4. Extend learning from media into play at home or in the childcare setting. (Through discussion and pretend play, help young children use their experiences with media to make sense of their real world.)

It's now worth examining some of the advantages of video. Most infant and toddler video programs are designed to encourage discovery and inspire new ways for caregivers and children to interact. The video format is a controlled medium that allows parents to specifically select the content they are sharing with their young children. They can use the pause, stop, and fast forward buttons on media players to tailor the amount of viewing time to the age of their child.

Among the videos on the market that have been prepared for children beginning at age 3 months are, for example, *Baby Einstein*, *BumbleBee-Bee Smart Baby*, *Mommy and Me*, and *The Baby Development Collection*. These videos are produced with animation only, with objects only, with a combination of a live host and animation, with mainly live people with a sprinkling of animation, with only live adults and babies, and with puppets.

For the youngest baby under 12 months old, the adult can talk to the child about what is on screen, playfully animate one's voice, sing along with the songs and encourage the baby to vocalize, and dance and move to the music with the child. Some of the programs offer games and activities to play in addition to the videos. This provides yet another way to foster adult–child interaction through play.

THE BABY DEVELOPMENT COLLECTION: AN EXAMPLE OF USING MEDIA TO ENCOURAGE PLAY

Because the *Little People* video series was designed only for toddlers, the Child Research Department at Fisher-Price decided to develop a new series of home videos targeted to children age 3 months and above, titled *The Baby Development Collection*. This video series features live footage of babies, children, mothers, and fathers interacting and playing with one another, as well as music, poetry, visual imagery, and three puppet characters. The four videos in the collection are *Baby's Day*, *Musical Baby*, *Baby Moves*, and *Nature Baby*. (See appendix A for a description.) Each video includes a 10-minute playgroup segment. The leader for the group invites parents to participate in four or five interactive games they can play with their children. Just as the videos are theme related, each playgroup focuses on activities that help develop specific skills for babies and toddlers: music, sensory, physical, or language (Warner, 1999). (See appendix B for a description.)

In January 2004, a national sample of 44 families with 3- to 18-month-old boys and girls completed an online survey. Respondents were asked to watch the Baby Development Collection's *Musical Baby* and *Baby's Day* prior to completing the survey. Parents were requested to use and evaluate the videos regardless of their children's interest and developmental stage. First they rated on a 4-point scale their overall likeness rating, their likeliness to recommend to a friend with a similar age child, the entertainment value, and the educational value. They were also asked a series of qualitative questions relating to the DVD main programs and playgroup segments: specific likes, dislikes, additional theme suggestions, and sibling viewing patterns.

For the two videos researched, more than a third of the parents gave an excellent or good rating, and less than 4% of the respondents rated the videos as poor. Approximately half of the respondents indicated that they would be likely to recommend the videos, with no one reporting that they would not make a recommendation. The majority of parents felt that the videos were educational, with no one reporting that the videos were not educational. Most important, many parents saw the 10-minute playgroups as a good resource for new activities and games to play with their infants and toddlers.

IMPLICATIONS

This chapter presented research on infant and toddler media use and the media contribution to the development of cognitive and social skills among this age group. It is clear from the data that parents are using videos and television in a playful and active way. The research underscores the importance of choosing television and video programs that are age-appropriate and that have well-developed curricula. Very young children may especially benefit from appropriate media viewing, which can provide opportunities for early language and concept learning not otherwise available. This early learning and experience has the potential to enhance positive developmental outcomes.

More studies are needed to examine whether or not, what type of, and how media should be integrated into the lives of very young children in a developmentally appropriate way. Television is part of children's everyday life, and with the increase in programming and video development, it may become even more prevalent in the near future. Empowering parents to engage in play with children by participating in playgroups or even viewing different types of play as presented in the media may foster play among families today. Media viewing, however, should be limited in terms of hours and kinds of programs children watch, and there should be ample discussion to clarify what children have watched.

References

American Academy of Pediatrics, Committee on Public Education. (2001). Children, adolescents, and television,, policy statement. *Pediatrics, 107*(2), 423.

Anand, S., & Krosnick, J. A. (2005). Demographic predictors of media use among infants, toddlers, and preschoolers. *American Behavioral Scientist, 48*(5), 539–561.

Anderson, C. A., Berkowitz, L., Donnerstein, E., Huesmann, L. R., Johnson, J. D., Linz, D., et al. (2003). The influence of media violence on youth. *Psychological Science in the Public Interest*, *4*(3), 81–110.

Anderson, D. R., & Evans, M. K. (2001). Peril and potential of media for infants and toddlers. *Zero to Three, 22*(2), 10–16.

Anderson, D. R., & Pempek, T. A. (2005). Television and very young children. *American Behavioral Scientist, 48*(5), 505–522.

Barr, R., & Hayne, H. (1999). Developmental changes in imitation from television during infancy. *Child Development, 70*, 1067–1081.

Bickham, D. S., Wright, J. C., & Huston, A. C. (2001). Attention, comprehension, and the educational influences of television. In D. G. Singer & J. L. Singer (Eds.), *Handbook of children and the media* (pp. 101–119). Thousand Oaks, CA: Sage.

Christakis, D. A., Zimmerman, F. J., DiGiuseppe, D. L., & McCarty, C. A. (2004). Early television exposure and subsequent attentional problems in children. *Pediatrics, 113*(4), 708–713.

Comstock, G., & Paik, H. (1991). *Television and the American child.* San Diego, CA: Academic Press.

DYG. (2000). What grown-ups understand about child development: A national benchmark survey. Washington, DC: Zero to Three.

Evans, M. K., Pempek, T. A., Kirkorian, H. L., Frankenfield, A. E., & Anderson, D. R. (2004, May). *The impact of background television on complexity of play*. Paper presented at the Biennial International Conference for Infant Studies, Chicago.

Gerbner, G., Gross, L., Morgan, M., & Signorielli, N. (1994). Growing up with television: The cultivation perspective. In J. Bryant and D. Zillman (Eds.), *Media effects* (pp. 17–41). Hillsdale, NJ: Erlbaum.

Greenfield, P. M., Yut, E., Chung, M., Land, D., Kreider, H., Pantoja, M., et al. (1993). The program-length commercial: A study of the effects of television/toy tie-ins on imaginative play. In G. L. Berry & J. K. Asamen (Eds.), *Children and television: Images in a changing sociocultural world* (pp. 53–72). Newbury Park, CA: Sage.

Hollenbeck, A. R., & Slaby, R. G. (1979). Infant visual and vocal responses to television. *Child Development, 50*, 41–45.

Huston, A., & Wright, J. (1998). Television and the informational and educational needs of children. *The Annals of the American Academy of Political and Social Science, 558*, 9–23.

Jordan, A. B., & Woodard, E. H. (2001). Electronic childhood: The availability and use of household media by 2-to-3-year-olds. *Zero to Three, 22*(2), 4–9.

Leach, P. (1997). *Your baby & child from birth to age five*. London: Dorling Kindersley.

Lemish, D. (1987). Viewers in diapers: The early development of television viewing. In T. R. Lindlof (Ed.), *Natural audiences: Qualitative research of media uses and effects* (pp. 33–57). Norwood, NJ: Ablex.

Lemish, D., & Rice, M. L. (1985). Television as a talking picture book: A prop for language acquisition. *Child Language, 13*, 251–274.

Lerner, C., Singer, D. G., & Wartella, E. (2001). Computers, TV, and very young children: What impact on development? *Zero to Three, 22*(2), 30–33.

Linebarger, D. (2004). Young children, language, and television. *Literacy Today, 40*, 20–21.

Linebarger, D. (2005, March 13). *Language, television, and very young children. Can babies learn from television?* Transferring 2–D information to the real world symposium. Paper presented at Eastern Psychological Association convention, Boston.

Linebarger, D. L., & Walker, D. (2005). Infants' and toddlers' television viewing and language outcomes. *American Behavioral Scientist, 48*(5), 624–645.

Lohr, P. (1999). The world of the "Teletubbies." *Televizion, 2*(12), 2.

Marsh, J. (1999). Learning to speak, read, and write with the "Teletubbies": The UK experience. *Televizion, 2*(12), 31–34.

Meltzoff, A. N. (1988). Imitation of televised models by infants. *Child Development, 59*(5), 1221–1229.

Meltzoff, A. N., & Moore, M. K. (1977). Imitation of facial and manual gestures by human neonates. *Science, 198*, 74–78.

Mullin-Rindler, N., & Fucigna, C. (1995, March–April). *Television use in home-based child care at 24 months.* Paper presented at the biennial meeting of the Society for Research in Child Development, Indianapolis, IN.

Murphy, L. (2004). *The effect of background television on parent–child interactions.* Unpublished honors thesis, University of Massachusetts, Amherst.

Nielsen Media Research. (1998). *1998 report on television.* New York: Author.

Pierroutsakos, S. L., Hanna, M. M., Self, J. A., Lewis, E. N., & Brewer, C. J. (2004, May). *Baby Einsteins everywhere: The amount and nature of television and video viewing of infants birth to 2 years.* Paper presented at the Biennial International Conference for Infant Studies, Chicago.

Richards, J. E., & Cronise, K. (2000). Extended visual fixation in the early preschool years: Look duration, heart rate changes, and attentional inertia. *Child Development, 71*, 602–620.

Rideout, V. J., Vandewater, E. A., & Wartella, E. A. (2003). *Zero to six: Electronic media in the lives of infants, toddlers, and preschoolers.* Menlo Park, CA: Kaiser Family Foundation.

Schmitt, K. M. (1997). *Two- to three-year-olds' understanding of the correspondence between television and reality.* Unpublished doctoral dissertation, University of Massachusetts, Amherst.

Schmitt, K. M. (2001). Infants, toddlers & television: The ecology of the home. *Zero to Three 22*(2), 17–23.

Schmitt, K. M., Anderson, D. R., & Collins, P. A. (1999). Form and content: Looking at visual features of television. *Developmental Psychology, 35*(4), 1156–1167.

Singer, D. G., & Singer, J. L. (1990). *The house of make-believe: Play and the developing imagination.* Cambridge, MA: Harvard University Press.

Singer, D. G., & Singer, J. L. (2005). *Imagination and play in the electronic age*. Cambridge, MA: Harvard University Press.

Singer, J. L., & Singer, D. G. (1981). *Television, imagination, and aggression: A study of preschoolers.* Hillsdale, NJ: Erlbaum.

Singer, J. L., & Singer, D. G. (1998). Barney and friends as entertainment and education: Evaluating the quality and effectiveness of a television series for preschool children. In J. K. Asamen & G. L. Berry (Eds.), *Research paradigms, television, and social behavior* (pp. 305–367). Thousand Oaks, CA: Sage.

Skeen, P., Brown, M. H., & Osborn, D. K. (1982). Young children's perception of "real" and "pretend" on television. *Perceptual & Motor Skills, 54*(3), 883–887.

Valkenburg, P. M., & Vroone, M. (2004). Developmental changes in infants' and toddlers' attention to television entertainment. *Communication Research, 31*, 288–311.

Vandewater, E. A., Park, S., Huang, X., & Wartella, E. A. (2005). No, you can't watch that. *American Behavioral Scientist, 48*(5), 608–623.

Warner, P. (1999). *Baby play and learn: 160 games and learning activities for the first three years.* Minnetonka, MN: Meadowbrook.

Weber, D. S., & Singer, D. G. (2004). The media habits of infants and toddlers: Findings from a parent survey. *Zero to Three, 25*(1), 30–36.

Woodard, E. (2000). *Media in the home 2000: The fifth annual survey of parents and children* (survey no. 7). Philadelphia: The Annenberg Public Policy Center of the University of Pennsylvania.

Yankelovich. (2005). *The power of play: How to change the conversation* (a custom study conducted for Fisher-Price). Chapel Hill, NC: Author.

Appendix A Fisher-Price Baby Development Collection Programs

Title	Program Description
Musical Baby	Introduces babies to varieties of music and musical instruments, demonstrating how children can experience a variety of real musical instruments and toy replicas of instruments, such as the drum, trumpet, violin, piano, and guitar.
Baby's Day	Includes everyday sights and sounds from baby's world. It includes activities such as getting dressed, eating, playing, bath time and bedtime.
Nature Baby	Shows the beauty of the changing seasons, introducing baby to sights, sounds and experiences from the world outside.
Baby Moves	Provides ideas to enhance a child's physical progress and self-discovery. It shows babies and toddlers engaged in a broad range of movement, from reaching, kicking, and crawling, to dancing and playing.

Appendix B Fisher-Price Baby Development Collection: Playgroup with Caregiver and Child

Baby Moves Playgroup

Activity Title	Description
Roll-Overs	Promotes directionality and large motor skill control as children learn how to use their bodies to roll over.
Upsy Daisy	Promotes head and neck control, grasping, anticipation, and social interaction, as adults assist babies to a sitting position by encouraging them to grasp onto their thumbs to pull up.
Tummy Fun	Promotes the strength needed to learn how to crawl as babies lay on their tummies to play with a toy or another person.
Wiggle Worm	Promotes the use of the walking reflex to help babies practice for crawling as they lay on their tummies with a toy within reach in front of them while an adult applies pressure to the bottom of their feet.
Baby On The Bus	Promotes language skills, motor movement and control, as an adult moves different parts of the baby's body according to the lyrics of the "Wheels on the Bus" song.

Baby's Day Playgroup

Activity Title	Description
Tickle Bee	Promotes back and forth conversation while providing babies with a fun game.
Pat-a-cake	Clapping hands to the patty-cake rhyme gives babies practice in coordinating actions with words.
Babble-on	Promotes conversation between babies and another object, as well as sound repetition.
Pony Rides	Singing and moving to the beat provides babies practice in coordinating actions with song lyrics.
Fingers, Toes, Hair and Nose	Promotes language skills while introducing the names of body parts.

Musical Baby Playgroup

Activity Title	Description
Sway Time	Enhances a baby's awareness of rhythm and melody as a caregiver sings and sways baby back and forth rhythmically.
Ball Beat	Promotes listening skills, rhythm and the awareness of cause and effect as a caregiver holds their baby's hand and helps him or her tap the ball to a beat.
Mouth Music	Introduces sound discrimination and imitation, as well as helping with language skills as a caregiver demonstrates different sounds with their mouth and encourages baby to respond.
Clap Time	Allows babies to experience rhythm and tempo as the caregiver demonstrates rhythm and tempo by clapping with baby.
Bells Are Ringing	Promotes awareness of cause and effect, cognitive development and listening skills as a caregiver plays a game of "hide & seek" with the bell.

Nature Baby Playgroup

Activity Title	Description
Water Fun	Introduces different colors and shapes of tub toys. It also provides sensory stimulation and social interaction.
At The Zoo	Enhances a baby's auditory skills and helps with language development and social interaction as a caregiver uses a puppet and makes sounds that relate to the puppet animal.
Nature's Elements	Provides an opportunity for babies to experience elements from outdoors as a caregiver presents different objects to his or her baby.
Snow Scape	Allows babies to experience the different texture and temperature of snow.

10

Computer as Paintbrush: Technology, Play, and the Creative Society

MITCHEL RESNICK

Let's start with a familiar children's game: Which of these things is not like the others? Which of these things just doesn't belong?

Television. Computer. Paintbrush.

For many people, the answer seems obvious: the paintbrush doesn't belong. After all, the television and the computer were both invented in the 20th century, both involve electronic technology, and both can deliver large amounts of information to large numbers of people. None of that is true for the paintbrush.

But, in my view, computers will not live up to their potential until we start to think of them less like televisions and more like paintbrushes. That is, we need to start seeing computers not only as information machines but also as a new medium for creative design and expression.

In recent years, a growing number of educators and psychologists have expressed concern that computers are stifling children's learning and creativity and engaging children in mindless interaction and passive consumption (Cordes & Miller, 2000; Oppenheimer, 2003). They have a point: today, many computers *are* used in that way. But that needn't be the case. This chapter presents an alternate vision of how children might use computers, in which children use computers more like paintbrushes and less like televisions, opening new opportunities for children to playfully explore, experiment, design, and invent. My goal in this chapter is not to provide conclusive evidence but rather, through illustrative examples, to provoke a rethinking of the roles that computers can play in children's lives.

AN EXAMPLE: ALEXANDRA'S MARBLE MACHINE

To provide a clearer sense of how computers can serve as paintbrushes, this section tells the story of Alexandra, an 11-year-old girl who used a tiny computer called a Cricket as a new medium for expression, experimentation, and exploration.

Alexandra wasn't very excited about school, but she loved coming to the Computer Clubhouse in her neighborhood in Boston. Alexandra's local Clubhouse was part of a worldwide network of after-school centers established to help young people (ages 10–18) from low-income communities learn to express themselves creatively with new technologies (Resnick, Rusk, & Cooke, 1998). At Computer Clubhouses, young people become actively engaged in designing with new technologies, creating their own graphic animations, musical compositions, and robotic constructions. Alexandra became particularly excited when two volunteer mentors (from a local university) organized a Clubhouse workshop for building "marble machines"—whimsical contraptions in which marbles careen down a series of ramps and raceways, bouncing off bells and bumpers.

The mentors, Karen Wilkinson and Mike Petrich, brought a variety of craft materials to the Clubhouse: pegboard, wooden slats, bells, string, marbles. They also brought a collection of tiny computers called Crickets, small enough to fit inside a child's hand (Martin, Mikhak, & Silverman, 2000; Resnick, Berg, & Eisenberg, 2000; Resnick, Martin, Sargent, & Silverman, 1996). Crickets can be programmed to control motors and lights, receive information from sensors, and communicate with one another via infrared light. Children can use Crickets to make their constructions come alive—for example, making a motor turn on whenever a touch sensor is pressed or whenever a shadow is cast over a light sensor.

Alexandra became interested in the marble-machine project right away. She cut wooden slats to serve as ramps and inserted the ramps into a pegboard. She began playfully rolling marbles from one ramp to another, trying to create interesting patterns of motion, without the marbles dropping off. As the marbles dropped from one ramp to another, Alexandra giggled with delight.

Next, Alexandra created a Cricket-controlled conveyor belt with a small basket on top. Her plan: the marble should roll down a ramp into the basket, ride along the conveyor belt inside the basket, and then drop onto the next ramp when the basket tipped over at the end of the conveyor belt. How would the conveyor belt know when to start moving? Alexandra programmed the conveyor-belt Cricket to listen for a signal from another Cricket higher up on the pegboard, alerting it that the marble was on its way. The conveyor-belt Cricket waited 2 seconds, to make sure the marble had arrived safely in the basket, before starting to move the conveyor belt and basket.

Alexandra worked on her project for several weeks, experimenting with many different configurations of the ramps and adjusting the timing of the conveyor belt. She playfully tried out new features—for example, putting bells on the ramps, so that the marbles would make jingling sounds as they rolled past.

Alexandra decided to enter her marble machine into her school's science fair. But when she talked to her classroom teacher about it, the teacher said that the marble machine was not acceptable as a science fair project. The teacher explained that a science fair project must use the "scientific method": the student must start with a hypothesis, then gather data in an effort to prove or disprove the hypothesis. The marble machine, said the teacher, didn't follow this approach.

Alexandra was determined to enter her marble machine in the science fair. With support from mentors at the Clubhouse, she put together a sequence of photographs showing different phases of the marble-machine construction. Even though Alexandra never wrote a hypothesis for her project, her teacher ultimately relented and allowed her to enter the marble machine in the school science fair. Much to Alexandra's delight, she was awarded one of the top two prizes for the entire school.

What did Alexandra learn through her marble-machine project? A great deal. Although Alexandra's teacher was concerned that the project did not use the scientific method, the project is, in fact, a wonderful example of the scientific method. True, Alexandra did not start with a single overarching hypothesis. But as she playfully experimented with her marble machine, Alexandra was continually coming up with new design ideas, testing them out, and iterating based on the results. Each of these design ideas can be viewed as a "mini-hypothesis" for which Alexandra gathered data. Over the course of her project, she investigated literally dozens of these mini-hypotheses. While positioning the ramps, for example, Alexandra tested different angles to try to find the maximum range for the marble. Alexandra also experimented to find the right timing for the conveyor belt. She modified the conveyor-belt program so that the basket would make one complete revolution, returning to its original location properly positioned for the next marble.

Through her playful experiments, Alexandra not only improved the workings of her marble machine but also developed a better understanding and appreciation of the process of scientific investigation. In the spirit of John Dewey's "theory of inquiry" (1910), Alexandra began to develop a scientific frame of mind through her playful yet systematic efforts to solve the practical problems that arose in her marble-machine project.

EDUTAINMENT VERSUS PLAYFUL LEARNING

The story of Alexandra's marble machine highlights how new technologies can support playful learning—and how playful activities can help children understand and make full use of new technologies. Of course, the idea of mixing play, technology, and learning is hardly new. In establishing the first kindergarten in 1837, Friedrich Froebel used the technology of his time to develop a set of toys (which became known as "Froebel's gifts") with the explicit goal of helping young children learn important concepts such as number, size, shape, and color (Brosterman, 1997). Other educators, such as Maria Montessori (1912), have built on Froebel's ideas to create a wide range of manipulative materials that engage children in learning through playful explorations.

More recently, there has been a surge of computer-based products that claim to integrate play and learning, under the banner of "edutainment." But these edutainment products often miss the spirit of playful learning. Often, the creators of edutainment products view education as a bitter medicine that needs the sugarcoating of entertainment to become palatable. They provide entertainment as a reward if you are willing to suffer through a little education. Or they boast that you will have so much fun using their products that you won't even realize that you are learning—as if learning were the most unpleasant experience in the world.

Part of the problem is with word *edutainment* itself. When people think about *education* and *entertainment*, they tend to think of them as services that someone else provides for you. Studios, directors, and actors provide you with entertainment; schools and teachers provide you with education. New edutainment companies try to provide you with both. In all of these cases, you are viewed as a passive recipient. But that's not the way most learning happens. In fact, you are likely to learn the most, and enjoy the most, if you are engaged as an active participant, not as a passive recipient (e.g., Bruner, 1963).

The terms *play* and *learning* (things that you do) offer a different perspective from *entertainment* and *education* (things that others provide for you). Thus the phrase *playful learning*, as opposed to *edutainment*, conveys a stronger sense of active participation. It might seem like a small change, but the words we use can make a big difference in how we think and what we do.

Alexandra's playful explorations with her marble machine were not a sugarcoating for science experiments; rather, play and learning were fully integrated in her project. Alexandra experimented with ramp angles and conveyor-belt timing not to get a reward or a grade but as an integral part of her play experience. In other words, Alexandra was driven by "intrinsic motivation," not external rewards. That distinction is critical. Research has found that "self-motivation, rather than external motivation, is at the heart of creativity, responsibility, healthy behavior, and lasting change" (Deci, 1995). Indeed, in our studies, we have found many examples of students who had short attention spans in traditional school classrooms but displayed great concentration when engaged in projects that interested them.

Alexandra's project was far from easy: she worked very hard on it, and parts of the project were very difficult for her. But the challenge of the project was one of the attractions. Too often, designers and educators try to make things "easy" for learners, thinking that people are attracted to things that are easy to do. But that is not the case. Mihaly Csikszentmihalyi (1991) has found that people become most deeply engaged in activities that are challenging but not overwhelming. Similarly, Seymour Papert has found that learners become deeply engaged by "hard fun"; in other words, learners don't mind activities that are hard as long as the activities connect deeply with their interests and passions (Papert, 1993).

LEARNING THROUGH DESIGNING

Unfortunately, projects like Alexandra's marble machine are the exception, not the rule, in children's use of new technologies. Children have many opportunities to *interact* with new technologies—in the form of video games, electronic storybooks, and "intelligent" stuffed animals. But rarely do children have the opportunity to *create* with new technologies, as Alexandra did with the Crickets in her marble machine.

Research has shown that many of children's best learning experiences come when they are engaged not simply in interacting with materials but in designing, creating, and inventing with them (Papert, 1980; Resnick, 2002). In the process of designing and creating—making sculptures out of clay or towers with wooden blocks—children try out their ideas. If their creations don't turn out as they expected or hoped, they can revise their ideas and create something new. It's an iterative cycle: new ideas, new creations, new ideas, new creations.

This design cycle can be seen as a type of play: children play out their ideas with each new creation. In design activities, as in play, children test the boundaries, experiment with ideas, and explore what's possible. As children design and create, they also learn new concepts. When they create pictures with a paintbrush, for example, they learn how colors mix together. When they build houses and castles with wooden blocks, they learn about structures and stability. When they make bracelets with colored beads, they learn about symmetries and patterns.

In my research group at the MIT Media Lab, our goal is to develop new technologies that follow in the tradition of paintbrushes, wooden blocks, and colored beads to expand the range of what children can create, design, and learn. Our Programmable Brick technology, for example, is a natural extension of the LEGO brick. The original LEGO brick, developed in the 1950s, enabled children to build structures like houses and castles. In the 1970s, the LEGO Company expanded its construction kits to include gears, pulleys, and other mechanical parts, enabling children to build their own mechanisms. Programmable Bricks, which we developed in the 1990s in collaboration with the LEGO Company, represent a third generation. With these new bricks, children can program their LEGO creations to move, sense, interact, and communicate. Now, children can build not only structures and mechanisms but also behaviors.

Programmable Bricks are commercially available as part of a robotics kit called LEGO Mindstorms. Over the past decade, there have been hundreds of different robotic toys on the market, but Mindstorms is fundamentally different. With most robotic toys, children simply interact with a prebuilt robot. With Mindstorms, children create their own robots: they use gears, axles, pulleys, and cams to build the mechanisms, connect motors to drive the motion, attach sensors to detect conditions in the world (temperature, light levels, etc.), and write computer programs to guide the robot's behavior (turning motors on and off, based on inputs from the sensors).

By creating their own robots, children gain a deeper understanding of the ideas underlying the workings of robots. In one fifth-grade class, for example, students used a Programmable Brick to create a LEGO dinosaur that was attracted to flashes of light, like one of the dinosaurs in *Jurassic Park*. To make the dinosaur move toward the light, the students needed to understand basic ideas about feedback and control. They wrote a program that compared readings from the dinosaur's two light-sensor "eyes." If the dinosaur drifted too far to the left (i.e., more light in the right eye), the program made it veer back to the right; if the dinosaur went too far right (more light in the left eye), the program corrected it toward the left. This classic feedback strategy is typically not taught until university-level courses. But with the right tools, fifth graders were able to explore these ideas (Resnick, Bruckman, & Martin, 1996).

CRICKETS AND CRAFTS

In her marble machine, Alexandra used a new version of Programmable Brick called the Cricket. Whereas the Programmable Bricks in LEGO Mindstorms were designed primarily for controlling robots, the Crickets are designed for more artistic and expressive projects. The Crickets can control not only motors but also multicolored lights and music-synthesis devices, so children can use Crickets to build their own musical instruments and light sculptures. The Crickets are also much smaller than previous Programmable Bricks, so they are well suited for projects that need to be small and mobile, such as electronic jewelry.

The Cricket was designed to feel more like a craft material than an information-processing machine, in hopes that children would see the Cricket as just another object in their bin of construction parts—and use the Cricket just as playfully and creatively as they use traditional craft materials. One indicator of success: when Alexandra described the parts of her marble machine, she listed Crickets right along with all of the other materials: "slopes, stoppers, Crickets, LEGOs. . . ."

To explore the possibilities of integrating Cricket technology with traditional craft activities, my research group co-organized a hands-on workshop (called Digital Dialogues) with Haystack Mountain School of Crafts, an internationally renowned craft center in Maine (Willow, 2004). At the workshop, artists worked alongside technologists and engineers, sharing ideas, techniques, and materials. Sally McCorkle, a sculptor from Penn State University, used a Cricket, a small fan, and a distance sensor to create an interactive sculpture that blew gold dust in interesting patterns whenever anyone approached. Artist Therese Zemlin created a series of handmade paper lanterns with small lights inside and programmed the lights to change color and intensity based on the movements of the people around the lanterns. Three Media Lab researchers collaborated with blacksmith Tom Joyce to create a vessel that could "talk for itself," telling the story of its own making. When you reached into the vessel, sensors activated videos showing how the metal had been forged and riveted.

We have found that activities integrating computation and craft provide a good context for learning math, science, and engineering ideas—especially for young people who are alienated by traditional approaches to math and science education, which often emphasize abstract concepts and formal systems rather than hands-on design and experimentation. Although screen-based computer applications offer many advantages, Michael and Ann Eisenberg (2000) argued that "something is lost, too, in this move away from the physical—something pleasurable, sensually and intellectually, about the behavior of stuff." Computational crafts, they argue, combine the best of the physical and computational worlds:

> It's a natural desire to employ all one's senses and cognitive powers in the course of a single project. We do not feel that a love of crafts is incompatible with

> technophilia, nor that an enjoyment of computer applications must detract from time spent in crafting. The world is not, or should not be at any rate, a battleground between the real and the virtual. It is instead a marvelous continuum, a source of wonders that blend and knead together the natural and artificial, the traditional and novel, the scientifically objective and the personally expressive, the tangible and the abstract. We anticipate a future in which ever more astonishing things will present themselves to our minds, and ever more astonishing ideas to our hands. (p. 280)

SUPPORTING PLAYFUL LEARNING (AND LEARNINGFUL PLAY)

Regardless of how innovative or evocative they are, new technologies cannot, on their own, ensure playful-learning experiences. Technologies can always be used in multiple ways—including many ways not intended or desired by their designers. LEGO Mindstorms, for example, was designed as a "robotics invention system" to encourage people to develop their own robotic inventions. And certainly, many children (and adults, too) have used Mindstorms in creative and inventive ways. But there are also many classrooms where the teacher assigns students to build a particular robot according to predesigned plans and then grades the students on the performance of their robots.

Our ultimate goal is not creative technologies but rather technologies that foster creative thinking and creative expression. This section discusses several strategies that we have developed over the years to try to maximize the chances that children will use our technologies in creative, playful, and "learningful" ways.

Making It Personal

We have found that children become most engaged with new technologies, and learn the most in playing with these technologies, when they work on projects growing out of their own personal interests. When children care deeply about the projects they are working on, not only are they more motivated but they also develop deeper understandings and richer connections to knowledge.

Consider the case of Jenny, an 11-year-old girl. Jenny loved watching birds, so when she was introduced to the Cricket, she decided to use it to build a new type of bird feeder. Jenny already had a bird feeder in her backyard, but there was a problem: often, the birds would come while Jenny was away at school, so she didn't get to see the birds. With the Cricket, Jenny figured she could build a new bird feeder that would collect data about the birds that landed on it.

Jenny started by making a wooden lever that served as a perch for the birds. The long end of the lever was next to a container with food for the birds. At the other end of the lever, Jenny attached a simple homemade touch sensor consisting of two paper clips. Jenny's idea: When a bird landed near the food, it would push down one end of the lever, causing the two paper clips at the other end to move slightly apart. Jenny connected the paper clips to one of the sensor ports on a Cricket, so that the Cricket could detect whether the paper clips were in contact with one another.

But what should the bird feeder do when a bird landed on it? At a minimum, Jenny wanted to keep track of the number of birds. She also thought about weighing the birds. But she decided it would be most interesting to take photographs of the birds. She began exploring ways of connecting a camera to her bird feeder, built a motorized LEGO mechanism that moved a small rod up and down, and mounted the mechanism so that the rod was directly above the shutter button of the camera.

Finally, Jenny plugged the mechanism into her Cricket and wrote a program for the Cricket. The program waited until the paper clips were no longer touching one another (indicating that a bird had arrived), and then turned on the motorized LEGO mechanism, which moved the rod up and down, depressing the shutter button of the camera. At the end of the day, the camera would have taken pictures of all of the birds that had visited the bird feeder.

Jenny worked on the project for several hours a week over the course of 3 months. By the end, the sensor and mechanism were working perfectly. But when she placed the bird feeder outside her window at home, she got photographs of squirrels (and of her younger sister), not of birds.

Jenny never succeeded in her original plan to monitor what types of birds would be attracted to what types of bird food. But the activity of building the bird feeder provided a rich collection of learning experiences. While building the lever for the bird feeder, Jenny needed to experiment with different lever designs to achieve the necessary mechanical advantage for triggering the paper-clip touch sensor. Jenny also systematically experimented with the placement of her camera, testing it at different distances from the bird perch in an effort to optimize the focus of the photographs. Thus, the bird feeder activity provided Jenny with an opportunity to make use of scientific concepts in a meaningful and motivating context.

The fact that Jenny built the bird feeder herself put Jenny in closer contact with the technology—and with the scientific concepts related to the technology. Crickets provided Jenny with "design leverage," enabling her to create things that would have been difficult for her to create in the past. At the same time, the bricks provided Jenny with "conceptual leverage," enabling her to learn concepts that would have been difficult for her to learn in the past.

Consider Jenny's touch sensor. In general, touch sensors are based on a very simple concept: they measure whether a circuit is open or closed. People interact with touch sensors (in the form of buttons) all of the time. But because most touch sensors appear in the world as "black boxes" (with their internal working hidden from view), most people don't understand (or even think about) how they work. In Jenny's touch sensor, created from two simple paper clips, the completing-the-circuit concept is exposed. Similarly, Jenny's LEGO mechanism for pushing the shutter of the camera helped demystify the control process of the bird feeder; sending an infrared signal from the Cricket to trigger the camera might have been simpler in some ways, but also less illuminating.

Of course, not everything in Jenny's bird feeder is transparent. The Cricket itself can be seen as a black box. Jenny certainly did not understand the inner workings of the Cricket electronics. On the other hand, Jenny was able to directly control the rules underlying the functioning of her bird feeder. Through the course of her project, she continually modified the computer program on the Cricket to extend the functionality of the bird feeder. After finishing the first version of the bird feeder, Jenny recognized a problem: if a bird were to hop up and down on the perch, the bird feeder would take multiple photographs of the bird. Jenny added a wait statement to her program, so that the program would pause for a while after taking a photograph to avoid the "double-bouncing" problem.

This ability to modify and extend her project led Jenny to develop a deep sense of personal involvement and ownership. She compared her bird feeder project with other science-related projects that she had worked on in school. "This was probably more interesting cause it was like you were doing a test for something more complicated than just what happens if you add this liquid to this powder," she explained. "It was more like how many birds did you get with the machine *you* made with this complex thing you had to program and stuff" [emphasis hers]. Jenny cared about her bird feeder (and the photographs that it took) in large part because she had designed and built it. The "fun part" of the project, she explained, "is knowing that you made it; *my* machine can take pictures of birds" [emphasis hers].

Many Paths, Many Styles

While developing an early version of the Programmable Brick technology, we tested some prototypes with a fourth-grade class in Boston. We asked the students what types of projects they wanted to work on, and they decided to create an amusement park, with different groups of students working on different rides for the park.

One group of three students worked on a merry-go-round. They carefully drew up plans and then built the structure and mechanisms according to their plans. After they finished building, they wrote a computer program to control the merry-go-round with a touch sensor. Whenever anyone touched the sensor, the merry-go-round would spin for a fixed amount of time. Within a couple hours, their merry-go-round was working.

Another group, also with three students, decided to build a Ferris wheel. But after working half an hour on the basic structure for the Ferris wheel, they put it aside and started building a refreshment stand next to the Ferris wheel. This decision could be viewed as a positive example of students following their interests. But there was a problem: By focusing on the refreshment stand, which did not have any motors or sensors or programming, the students were missing out on some of the important ideas underlying the activity. The students continued to work on structures (as opposed to mechanisms or programming) for several hours. After finishing the refreshment stand, the group built a wall around the amusement park. Then they created a parking lot and added lots of little LEGO people walking into the park.

Finally, after the whole amusement park scene was complete, the students went back and finished building and programming their Ferris wheel. For this group, building the Ferris wheel wasn't interesting until they had developed an entire story and context around it. In the end, their Ferris wheel worked just as well as the first group's merry-go-round. And, like the first group, they learned important lessons about mechanical advantage as they built the gearing system for the Ferris wheel, and they developed their ability to think systematically as they wrote the programs to control the Ferris wheel. But the two groups traveled down very different paths to get to the same result.

These two groups represent two very different styles of playing, designing, and thinking. Turkle and Papert (1992) have described these styles as "hard" (the first group) and "soft" (the second). The hard and soft approaches, they explain, "are each characterized by a cluster of attributes. Some involve organization of work (the hards prefer abstract thinking and systematic planning; the softs prefer a negotiational approach and concrete forms of reasoning); other attributes concern the kind of relationship that the subject forms with computational objects. Hard mastery is characterized by a distanced stance, soft mastery by a closeness to objects" (p. 9).

In many math and science classrooms, the hard approach is privileged, viewed as superior to the soft approach. Turkle and Papert argue for an "epistemological pluralism" that recognizes the soft approach as different, not inferior. My research group has taken a similar stance in the design of new technologies and activities, putting a high priority on supporting learners of all different styles and approaches. We pay special attention to make sure that our technologies and activities are accessible and appealing to the softs; because math and science activities have traditionally been biased in favor of the hards, we want to work affirmatively to close the gap.

Using the Familiar in Unfamiliar Ways

Over the past 5 years, my research group has collaborated with a group of museums on an initiative called the Playful Invention and Exploration (PIE) Network. The museums have used Crickets to develop a new generation of hands-on activities that combine art, science, and engineering. By taking a playful approach to invention, and integrating engineering with artistic expression, the PIE museums have engaged a broad and diverse population of people in scientific inquiry and invention (Resnick, Mikhak, et al., 2000).

Some of the most popular and successful activities at the PIE museums have been based on the use of familiar objects in unfamiliar ways. At the MIT Museum, for example, Stephanie Hunt and Michael Smith-Welch created workshops in which children turned food into musical instruments. At the core of the activity was a simple Cricket program that measured the electrical resistance of an object and played a musical note based on the resistance. The higher the resistance, the higher the note. Children could put different food items on a plate (with electrical connections to the Cricket) and hear the resistance. A marshmallow (high resistance) would play a high-pitched note, while a pickle (low resistance) would play a low-pitched note. Children could play songs by quickly replacing one piece of food with another.

In one workshop, a 9-year-old named Jonah took several pieces of cantaloupe and lined them up in a row. He attached one wire on the left end of the cantaloupe row and moved a second wire gradually down the row. The musical notes got higher and higher as he moved down the row. The reason: with more cantaloupe pieces between the two wires, there was more resistance, hence higher notes. And thus the melon xylophone was born. Jonah found a xylophone mallet and connected a wire to it. Then, he could tap the cantaloupe pieces with the mallet to play different melodies, just as on a xylophone. As he worked on this playful project, Jonah learned about the workings of electrical circuits, the nature of electrical resistance and conductivity, and the electrical properties of everyday objects.

Inspired by the food-based musical instruments, another 9-year-old named George came up with an idea for a new type of robot. He attached two wires inside the "mouth" of his robot. When the robot bumped into a piece of food, the two wires formed a circuit with the food and measured its resistance. George programmed the robot so that it could tell one type of food from another, based on differences in resistance. George recorded sound clips for the robot to play when it encountered different food. When the robot bumped into a lemon, it would say, "Yuck, a lemon." When it bumped into a pickle, it would say, "Yum, a pickle."

As they ran the musical-food workshops, Stephanie and Michael continued with their own food experiments. They discovered that the resistance of a hot dog changes as you bend it, so a hot dog could be used as a "bend sensor." The more you bend a hot dog, the higher the resistance. They experimented with green beans and string cheese, too. "We never had a enough bend sensors," said Stephanie. "It was great to discover that we could make our own."

The musical-food activities led children (and the workshop organizers) to start to think about food in new ways. Typically, people think of food in terms of its color or texture or taste. Through Cricket music activities, children began to realize that food has other properties—in particular, electrical resistance. And resistance became not just an abstract concept learned in science class but a useful tool for creative expression.

Other PIE workshops used other familiar materials: Q-tips, pipe cleaners, blocks of ice. As they played with familiar materials, children seemed more comfortable experimenting and exploring. At the same time, they were more intrigued when unexpected things happened. If you're playing with unfamiliar or complex materials and something unexpected happens, you're not so surprised. But if you're playing with something simple and familiar (like a hot dog or piece of cantaloupe) and something surprising happens, then you want to find out more. "The familiar doing the unfamiliar stops you in your tracks," said one PIE workshop leader. "It jars you to want to know more."

THE CREATIVE SOCIETY

In the 1980s, there was much talk about the transition from the Industrial Society to the Information Society (e.g., Beniger, 1986; Salvaggio, 1989). No longer would natural resources and manufacturing be the driving forces in our economies and societies. Information was the new king.

In the 1990s, people began to talk about the Knowledge Society (e.g., Drucker, 1994). They began to realize that information itself would not bring about important change. Rather, the key was how people transformed information into knowledge and how they managed and shared that knowledge.

But, as I see it, knowledge alone is not enough. Success in the future—for individuals, for communities, for companies, for nations as a whole—will be based not on what we know or how much we know, but on our ability to think and act creatively. In the 21st century, we are moving toward the Creative Society.

The proliferation of new technologies is quickening the pace of change, accentuating the need for creative thinking in all aspects of our lives. At the same time, some new technologies can foster and support the development of creative thinking. We have seen, for example, how Cricket-based activities at the PIE museums can help children develop as creative thinkers.

In some ways, children can serve as models for the Creative Society. Childhood is one of the most creative periods of our lives. We must make sure that children's creativity is nurtured and developed, providing children with opportunities to exercise, refine, and extend their creative abilities. That will require new approaches to education and learning—and new types of technologies to support those new approaches. The ultimate goal is a society of creative individuals who are constantly inventing new possibilities for themselves and their communities.

A NEW ALLIANCE

In March 2001, I had one of the most frustrating meetings of my life. Three leaders of the Alliance for Childhood came to visit me at the MIT Media Lab. The previous September, the group had published a report called *Fool's Gold: A Critical Look at Computers in Childhood* (Cordes & Miller, 2000). In reading the report, I found myself agreeing with the authors on many issues. The report emphasized the importance of nurturing children's creative abilities, arguing that "creativity and imagination are prerequisites for innovative thinking, which will never be obsolete in the workplace." I certainly agreed. And the report expressed concern that many new technologies restricted rather than encouraged creative thinking: "A heavy diet of ready-made computer images and programmed toys appear to stunt imaginative thinking." Again, I agreed: Most computer-based products for children are like televisions, not paintbrushes, delivering preprogrammed content rather than fostering exploration and expression.

I was pleased that the leaders of the alliance had asked to visit the Media Lab. I looked forward to showing them some of the projects that children had created with our Cricket technology. I felt that our Cricket research was grounded in the same core values expressed in their report. I wanted to show them that some technologies, rather than stunting imaginative thinking, could actually foster and support the development of creative thinking and creative expression.

But the meeting didn't go according to my expectations. After I showed the visitors Jenny's bird feeder and told them the story of how Jenny had built and programmed it, one of the visitors turned to me and said: "Don't you think it's a problem to take children away from creative play experiences?" I couldn't believe it. I had just described what I considered to be an extraordinarily playful and creative project, but the visitor from the alliance didn't see it that way. She saw a project using advanced technology and immediately assumed that the child could not possibly have been doing anything creative.

The interaction made me aware of how polarized our discussions about children and technology have become. There is no doubt, as the *Fool's Gold* report persuasively argues, that the promoters of new technologies make excessive claims and promises, assuming that all technologies must be worthwhile technologies. But it is equally true that the critics of new technologies are too quick to lump all technologies together and dismiss them collectively.

Although I work at one of the world's leading centers of technological innovation, I often find myself sympathizing more with the techno-critics than with the techno-enthusiasts. I resonated with the *Fool's Gold* report when it asserted (p. 68): "Knowledgeable, caring teachers—not machines—are best able to mediate between young children and the world." I, too, am deeply skeptical about "intelligent tutoring systems" that try to put a computer in the place of a teacher. But in the very next sentence, the *Fool's Gold* report argues: "Low-tech tools like crayons, watercolors, and paper nourish children's inner capacities and encourage the child to freely move in, directly relate to, and understand the real world." Why restrict it to "low-tech" tools? Does the ability to "nourish children's inner capacities" really depend on the level of technology? A century ago, crayons were considered advanced technology. Did that make them less able to nourish children's inner capacities?

We need to move away from generalizations about all computers or all technologies and consider instead the specifics of each technology and the context of its use. Some technologies, in some contexts, foster creative thinking and creative expression; other technologies, in other contexts, restrict it. Rather than focusing on the division between techno-critics and techno-enthusiasts, we need to focus on the difference between activities that foster creative thinking and creative expression (whether they use high-tech, low-tech, or no tech) and those that don't.

New alliances are needed. At the Playing for Keeps conference in October 2004, I had the good fortune to meet again with Joan Almon, coordinator and president of the board of U.S. Alliance for Childhood. It was the first time Joan and I had met since the meeting at MIT in 2001. I told Joan how frustrated I had been by the earlier meeting—frustrated not because we disagreed (I disagree with many people) but because we allowed our disagreements to overwhelm and obscure what I thought were deep commonalities. We talked for several hours, and we did, indeed, find many shared values, beliefs, and goals. A few months later, Joan came to MIT and spent 2 days with my research group. We still have our differences, and I'm sure we always will. But those of us who believe in paintbrushes over televisions need to stick together.

Acknowledgments Robbie Berg, Keith Braafladt, Mike Eisenberg, Stephanie Hunt, Fred Martin, Bakhtiar Mikhak, Steve Ocko, Seymour Papert, Mike Petrich, Margaret Pezalla-Granlund, Natalie Rusk, Brian Silverman, Michael Smith-Welch, Karen Wilkinson, and Diane Willow have made important contributions to the technologies and activities described in this chapter. I want to give special thanks to all of the children who have participated in activities with our Crickets and other technologies. (Pseudonyms are used for all children mentioned in this paper.)

I am grateful to members of the LEGO Learning Institute, the Playful Learning Panel, and the PIE Network for many stimulating discussions about the nature and value of playful learning. This research has been supported by generous grants from the LEGO Company, the Intel Foundation, the National Science Foundation (grants CDA-9616444, ESI-0087813, and ITR-0325828), the MIT Media Laboratory's Things That Think and Digital Life consortia, and the Center for Bits and Atoms (NSF CCR-0122419). Portions of this chapter previously appeared in Resnick, Berg, and Eisenberg (2000).

References

Beniger, (1986). *The control revolution: Technological and economic origins of the information society*. Cambridge, MA: Harvard University Press.

Brosterman, N. (1997). *Inventing kindergarten*. New York: Harry N. Abrams.

Bruner, J. (1963). *The process of education*. Cambridge, MA: Harvard University Press.

Cordes, C., & Miller, E. (2000). *Fool's gold: A critical look at computers in childhood*. College Park, MD: Alliance for Childhood.

Csikszentmihalyi, M. (1991). *Flow: The psychology of optimal experience*. New York: Harper-Collins.

Deci, E. (1995). *Why we do what we do: Understanding self-motivation*. New York: Putnam.

Dewey, J. (1910). *How we think*. Boston: Heath.

Drucker, P. (1994). *Knowledge work and knowledge society*. Edwin L. Godkin Lecture, John F. Kennedy School of Government, Harvard University, Cambridge, MA.

Eisenberg, M. (2003). Mindstuff: Educational technology beyond the computer. *Convergence, 9*(2), 29–53.

Eisenberg, M., & Eisenberg, A. (2000). The developing scientist as craftsperson. In N. Roberts, W. Feurzeig, & B. Hunter (Eds.), *Computer modeling and simulation in pre-college science education* (pp. 259–281). New York: Springer-Verlag.

Martin, F., Mikhak, B., & Silverman, B. (2000). MetaCricket: A designer's kit for making computational devices. *IBM Systems Journal, 39*(3–4), 795–815.

Montessori, M. (1912). *The Montessori method*. New York: Frederick Stokes.

Oppenheimer, T. (2003). *The flickering mind: Saving education from the false promise of technology*. New York: Random House.

Papert, S. (1980). *Mindstorms: Children, computers, and powerful ideas*. New York: Basic Books.

Papert, S. (1993). *The children's machine: Rethinking school in the age of the computer*. New York: Basic Books.

Resnick, M. (2002). Rethinking learning in the digital age. In G. Kirkman (Ed.), *The global information technology report: Readiness for the networked world* (pp. 32–37). Oxford: Oxford University Press.

Resnick, M., Berg, R., & Eisenberg, M. (2000). Beyond black boxes: Bringing transparency and aesthetics back to scientific investigation. *Journal of the Learning Sciences, 9*(1), 7–30.

Resnick, M., Bruckman, A., & Martin, F. (1996). Pianos not stereos: Creating computational construction kits. *Interactions, 3*(6), 41–50.

Resnick, M., Martin, F., Sargent, R., & Silverman, B. (1996). Programmable Bricks: Toys to think with. *IBM Systems Journal, 35*(3–4), 443–452.

Resnick, M., Mikhak, M., Petrich, M., Rusk, N., Wilkinson, K., & Willow, W. (2000). *The PIE network: Promoting science inquiry and engineering through playful invention and exploration with new digital technologies.* Proposal to the U.S. National Science Foundation (project funded 2001–2004). MIT Media Laboratory, Cambridge, MA.

Resnick, M., Rusk, N., & Cooke, S. (1998). The Computer Clubhouse: Technological fluency in the inner city. In D. Schon, B. Sanyal, & W. Mitchell (Eds.), *High technology and low-income communities* (pp. 266–286). Cambridge, MA: MIT Press.

Salvaggio, J. (1989). *The information society: Economic, social, and structural issues.* Mahwah, NJ: Erlbaum.

Turkle, S., & Papert, S. (1992). Epistemological pluralism and the revaluation of the concrete. *Journal of Mathematical Behavior, 11*(1), 3–33.

Willow, D. (Ed.). (2004). *Digital dialogues: Technology and the hand.* Haystack Monograph Series. Deer Isle, ME: Haystack Mountain School of Crafts.

PART IV

Play With Dysfunctional Children

11

Pretend Play and Emotion Learning in Traumatized Mothers and Children

WENDY HAIGHT, JAMES BLACK, TERESA OSTLER, AND KATHRYN SHERIDAN

Pretend play is a context that facilitates learning. It facilitates children's learning about emotions, adults' learning about children, and children's and adult's learning together. Indeed, pretend play, a subcategory of play in which actions, objects, and persons are transformed or treated nonliterally (Haight & Miller, 1993), has long been recognized as pivotal in facilitating early social and emotional development. Through pretend play, young children can express and communicate their emerging concerns and interpretations of the social and cultural world. Children's pretend play also allows adults to learn about children. In the words of a young mother of a 2½-year-old:

> I have a tendency of watching how she's pretending. . . . To see if she is having any anxieties or worries or, you know, happiness that she wants to share with me that maybe she, at her age, isn't able to come right out and say, "I'm scared about this. . . ." It's important for me to *see* what's on her mind. (Haight, Parke, & Black, 1997)

When children and adults pretend together, they may spontaneously interpret emotionally important issues as they naturally emerge during everyday life. For example, after his colicky baby brother finally went to sleep, a 3-year-old initiated a pretend game of "bad babies" with his mother. Such mundane communications with parents or other caregivers may be helpful to young children in understanding and responding to the stresses inherent in everyday life. They may be particularly important, however, when young children experience highly stressful or traumatic events such as prolonged separation from parents, violence, death, accidents, or serious illness. Indeed, pretend play has been used extensively by play therapists to facilitate children's recovery from stressful or traumatic events (e.g., see Singer, 1993). Yet, little is known about the roles of spontaneous, everyday pretend play with parents in children's emerging interpretations of stressful events. In this chapter, we present pilot data suggesting that parent–child pretend play is an underdeveloped resource for professionals helping children interpret and recover from traumatic experiences.

EVERYDAY, CAREGIVER–CHILD PRETEND PLAY AS A CONTEXT FOR EMOTION SOCIALIZATION

Developmental research on the role of pretend play in young children's learning has focused largely on cognitive learning, such as symbolic thought or reading readiness. Yet, theorists as diverse as Freud, Winnicott, Piaget, and Vygotsky concur that pretend play is central to emotional development in early childhood. As an interpretive activity, pretend play allows children to explore, practice, and critique emotions they have observed or experienced (e.g., Groves, 2002). By as early as 2 years, children begin to engage in verbal pretense portraying emotionally significant events (Bretherton & Beeghly, 1982; Wolf, Rygh, & Altschuler, 1984). Among the affective functions of pretend play is the construction of meaning from emotionally challenging experiences. Pretend play offers children a safe outlet to express negative emotions, including those they might not ordinarily express, such as intense anger toward a sibling or parent, in a context in which there are no real-world consequences (See Haight & Miller, 1993, for discussion). For example, in a remarkable study of children experiencing illness (diabetes and asthma), Cindy Dell Clark (2003) described the pervasive and spontaneous use of pretend play by children age 5 through 8 as a means of coping with the stress of chronic, serious illness and its treatment. These children engaged in pretend play to reassure themselves about painful treatments and worrisome symptoms and to compensate for vulnerable feelings related to their illness and treatment. Through pretend play, they transformed threatening, painful, or frightening events into occasions for mastery or even celebration.

The safe context of pretend play also may facilitate communication about emotionally charged situations with adults: teachers, parents, and other supportive caregivers. When such communication occurs, adults have the opportunity to provide comfort, guide, and contextualize children's emerging understanding of stressful events and the emotions they evoke (Haight & Sachs, 1995). Indeed, naturalistic research indicates that caregivers from a wide variety of cultural communities spontaneously engage in pretend play with young children (e.g., see Göncü, 1999; Haight & Miller, 1993; Haight, Wang, Fung, Williams, & Mintz, 1999). Such pretend play, typically, is highly enjoyable for children and is associated with secure parent–child attachment relationships (see review by Sutton-Smith, 1994).

Some empirical research suggests that spontaneous, caregiver–child pretend play supports emotion socialization in low-risk, apparently well-functioning middle-class families. In longitudinal research, nine children and their mothers were followed from children's first through fourth birthdays. During 116.5 hours of naturalistic, videotaped observations in and around the home, they produced 320 spontaneous episodes of mother–child pretend play, 79 of which involved the enactment of aggression, illness, and accidents (Haight & Sachs, 1995). Eight of the nine dyads enacted aggression, for a mean of 14% of all episodes of mother–child pretend play. Six dyads enacted illness or accidents, for a mean of 7% of all episodes of mother–child pretend play. Communication about emotion varied in culturally appropriate ways in relation to the themes enacted, for example, enacted anger co-occurred with aggression, and fear with illness and accidents. Furthermore, mothers' participation may have shaped children's portrayals. For example, mothers produced more positive, contingent responses and elaborations to children's initiation of themes involving illness or accident than to themes of aggression. Children's initiations of themes involving aggression sometimes were overtly discouraged by mothers. These findings suggest that mother–child pretend play is a context for the socialization and acquisition of culturally appropriate emotion communication.

Parent–child pretend play also may be a context for co-constructing an emotional understanding of traumatic events in vulnerable children who actually have experienced or witnessed significant aggression, illness, accidents, or other highly stressful or traumatic events. Indeed, play therapy has been one of the few effective means of intervening with young children exposed to trauma. Existing empirical evidence, however, indicates that children's *solitary* pretend play declines considerably during times of stress (Kramer & Schaefer-Hernan, 1994). That is, at the very time when children may benefit most from pretend play, they are less inclined to engage in it. Other children repeatedly reenact traumatic events they have experienced in play with no healing effect (Terr, 2003). To be helpful to children, pretend play during times of extreme stress or trauma appears to require the support, structure, and guidance provided by a trusted adult. Empirical research, however, has not considered the relation of *stress* and social pretend play with parents. This chapter addresses the extent to which and how parents and young traumatized children actually pretend together.

PRETEND PLAY AS A CONTEXT FOR CO-CONSTRUCTING INTERPRETATIONS OF TRAUMATIC STRESS

According to the *DSM–IV–TR*, traumatic stress involves experiencing or witnessing actual or threatened physical injury to the self or another person, especially a family member, accompanied by feelings of fear, helplessness, and horror and, in children, disorganized or agitated behavior (American Psychiatric Association, 1994). Traumatic stress that results from intentional human design, particularly that which occurs within the family and is caused by parents or other attachment figures, is especially challenging for children (Egeland, Weinfield, Bosquet, & Cheng, 2000). Common responses of children to trauma include the development of specific fears, the repetitive reenactment of traumatic events in play, nightmares, separation difficulties, avoidance of reminders of the trauma, and fear arousal to stimuli associated with the trauma, for example, smells and sounds (Webb, 2002).

Traumatic stress may disturb children's emerging understanding of self and other, safety, and protection (e.g., Pynoos, Steinberg, & Goenjian, 1996) and interfere with the development of self-soothing capabilities (Parens, 1991).

Evidence from the trauma literature suggests that not all children exposed to traumatic stress will show significant effects on their mental health. Indeed, there is evidence of individual variation in children's resiliency, with some children showing relatively normal patterns of development despite profound and ongoing stress (e.g., Garmezy, 1985). In their review of the psychiatric literature, Yehuda, McFarlane, and Shalev (1998) conclude that there is no simple relationship between exposure to trauma and the subsequent development of a psychiatric disorder. Children exposed to traumatic stress may vary in whether they experience posttraumatic stress disorder (PTSD) or other psychiatric disorders and in the intensity of any symptoms.

Variation in children's responses to traumatic stress has been attributed, in part, to their quality of relationships and communications with parents (e.g., Bowlby, 1988a,b; Coates & Schechter, 2004; Garmezy, 1985; Lynskey & Fergusson, 1997; Pynoos et al., 1996). Children may rely on parents for interpreting the traumatic events and the feelings they evoke because they trust their parents (Bowlby, 1988a,b) and because children have fewer and less developed psychological resources to respond to trauma (e.g., ability to reason about causes and motivations and to imagine a more hopeful future) (Marand & Adelman, 1997; Pynoos & Eth, 1985). Following exposure to trauma, parents may begin both to soothe their children and to scaffold their emerging interpretation of the event (e.g., Bat-Zion & Levy-Shiff, 1993), for example, through comfort, emotional security, and explanations. Indeed, even infants use emotional cues from parents to assess the meaning of new or stressful situations (Campos & Stenberg, 1981). The crucial role of parents as mediators may be one reason that children often are especially stressed when parents are physically or emotionally unavailable to them in times of trauma, for example, during war or maternal rape (Punamaki, 1987).

Surprisingly little research has addressed caregivers' socialization practices with respect to how and when children are socialized for responses to traumatic stress. Existing evidence suggests that children's resilient responses to traumatic stress are enhanced by calm, comprehensible communication with parents. Parent–child pretend play is one of the contexts in which such communication may occur. For example, parents' spontaneous involvement in children's posttraumatic pretend play after Hurricane Hugo was identified as possibly instrumental in children's constructive resolution of their fears (Cohler, 1991) and in helping young children in New York to come to terms with the aftermath of 911 (Lehmann, 2001). Alternatively, parents' own feelings of trauma may compromise their abilities to support their children (Coates & Schechter, 2004; Marand & Adelman, 1997), including through parent–child pretend play, and thus affect children's subsequent coping. Indeed, the psychological well-being of some children in the years following the Chernobyl catastrophe was attributed, in part, to parents' open communications of their own emotions including anxiety and grief (Bromet et al., 2000). Evidence from disasters (e.g., Bromet et al., 2000; Norwood, Ursano, & Fullerton, 2000; Perry, Silber, & Block, 1956; Vogel & Vernberg, 1993), violence

(Marand & Adelman, 1997), childhood sexual abuse (e.g., Cohen & Mannarino, 1996; Feiring, Taska, & Lewis, 1998; Lynskey & Fergusson, 1997), war (Freud & Burlingham, 1943; Punamaki, 1987), life-threatening illness and painful medical procedures (Ackerman, Newton, McPherson, Jones, & Dykman, 1998; Stuber, Nader, Yasuda, Pynoos, & Cohen, 1991) indicates a relationship between children's and parents' responses to traumatic stressors. For example, the intensity of Israeli schoolchildren's stress responses to SCUD missile attacks was related to parental behaviors and attitudes. Parents' negative emotional manifestations (e.g., confusion, exhaustion, anger) were associated with negative attitudes in children, whereas positive parental emotional manifestations (e.g., holding and soothing) were associated with children's increased coping efforts (Bat-Zion & Levy-Shiff, 1993). After a devastating tornado, some parents argued that the best strategy for helping their children to recover was to avoid discussion of the disaster, a response that the researchers associated with children's acute stress reactions (Perry et al., 1956). Some parents even respond to traumatic events in a disturbed or out-of-control manner as distressing to the children as the precipitating event (Burt, 1943).

One source of individual variation in parents' responses to their children's traumatic stress is their own mental health. Many mothers involved with the public child welfare system have their own unmet mental health needs. They have experienced high levels of stress, and many experience complex trauma, that is, traumatic experiences repeated over time, often from childhood into adulthood, which remain troubling and affect concepts of self, interpersonal relationships, and coping skills (e.g., Haight, Mangelsdorf et al., in press). High levels of ongoing stress and a trauma history may compromise mothers' abilities to buffer children from traumatic stress. In addition, witnessing traumatic stress in her child may reactivate a mother's own past trauma experiences (Banyard, Williams, & Siegel, 2002) and lead to dissociative and other trauma reactions in the mother.

Considerable research does suggest that parents' own complex, unresolved trauma histories negatively affect their interactions and relationships with their own children (Banyard, Williams, & Siegel, 2003). For example, a number of studies have revealed that adults who have experienced trauma in childhood are more likely to be classified as "unresolved" when assessed with the Adult Attachment Interview (AAI) than are adults who do not have such histories of trauma (Hess, 1999). The AAI is a semistructured interview developed by George, Kaplan, and Main (1985) to evaluate a parent's current state of mind about attachment. In the AAI, adults who are unresolved with respect to attachment speak in unusual ways regarding loss experiences or trauma either in childhood or adulthood. Unresolved feelings about loss or trauma often are suggested by lapses in metacognitive monitoring. For instance, a parent may evidence odd slips of the tongue (speaking about a long dead parent in the present tense), change topics abruptly, or have other pronounced difficulties in even speaking about the event. Interestingly, adult unresolved classifications are in turn significantly related to higher rates of insecure attachment, specifically disorganized attachment in their own children (Hess, 1999; van Ijzendoorn, 1995). Infants with disorganized attachment do not develop a coherent strategy for coping with stress and obtaining comfort from their caregiver. Many show overt fear or dissociative-like symptoms under stress. Disorganized attachment is associated with vulnerability to stress as assessed through salivary cortisol (e.g., Hertsgaard, Gunnar, Erickson, & Nechmias, 1995) and is a risk factor for the development of a variety of psychosocial and mental health disorders in childhood and adolescence (e.g., Crittenden & Ainsworth, 1989; Greenberg, Speltz, & DeKlyen, 1993; Lyons-Ruth, Alpern, & Repacholi, 1993; Lyons-Ruth, Easterbrooks, & Cibelli, 1997; see Main, 1996; Zeanah, Mammen, & Lieberman, 1993).

Existing research also suggests considerable variation in traumatized parents' socialization beliefs and strategies for supporting their children's interpretations of traumatic events. For example, during in-depth, semistructured interviews, most battered women involved in the public child welfare system gave specific descriptions of how exposure to domestic violence had harmed their children's psychological well-being, and many also described specific strategies to enhance young children's recovery (Haight, Shim et al., in press). However, mothers' reports varied in their directness in addressing the trauma of domestic violence, their attempts to instill in their children hope for a more positive future, and their efforts to educate their children to prevent their own future involvement with violence. In a survey of battered women, Holden, Stein, Ritchie, Harris, and Jouriles (1998) posed an open-ended question: "What do you say to your child after he/she becomes aware of a violent conflict?" The two most common responses, each provided by approximately 20% of mothers, were to tell their children that their father was angry with the mother and not the child or to explain to their children that their father was sick and needed help, responses that could prevent children from internalizing blame or misconstruing violence (Bowlby, 1988). Another 17% of the mothers indicated that after a violent incident they would reassure their children that they were okay. In contrast to these explanations, some mothers wrote that they would offer other types of comments, including threats ("You better behave before he hits you, too") and excuses for the fathers' violent behavior ("It's not his fault"). These reports suggest some potentially important differences in how mothers interpret traumatic stress with their children and hence in how mothers support or compromise their children's resilient responses. Some responses may be more conducive to children's mental health, whereas others, especially those that are not forthcoming about what happened or place blame elsewhere, may contribute to confusion, disturbance, and psychopathology, particularly when a parent's explanations vary considerably from what a child has observed or seen, a parent denies what has happened, or no explanation whatsoever is provided (Bowlby, 1988b).

Some evidence on mothers' narrative practices with young children in relation to potentially traumatic events also suggests variation across cultural communities. Evidence from North American working-class and middle-class families suggests that such variation is linked, in part, to culturally specific belief systems. Such belief systems are taken-for-granted ideas about the nature of reality that provide a frame of reference within which individuals interpret experience and formulate goals and strategies for living and problem solving within the constraints of culture (Bruner, 1990; Goodnow, 1988; Harkness & Super, 1996).

Many working-class mothers tell stories involving traumatic stress in the presence of, and with, their young children, whereas middle-class mothers typically censor such talk (Burger & Miller, 1999). In addition, working-class mothers generally view such exposure as protective because children need to know about predictable dangers so that they may avoid or handle them effectively in the future. In contrast, middle-class mothers generally believe that shielding children is protective because children are psychologically vulnerable and exposure to topics involving trauma can be harmful (Cho & Miller, in press).

Existing research has not addressed mothers' pretend play with young children related to traumatic themes. Most children in developmental studies of caregiver–child pretend play have been from low-risk, middle-class families with no known trauma history. Hence, any challenging events that children interpreted with their caregivers during pretend play were limited and comparatively mild. By contrast, young children in foster care have experienced traumatic separations from parents. Most have also experienced family violence, maltreatment, exposure to adults' substance abuse, or other traumatic events. Not surprisingly, young children in foster care have 3 to 7 times more chronic emotional disorders than children of similar socioeconomic backgrounds (Blatt & Simms, 1997) and also experience disproportionate rates of developmental delays (Cicchetti & Toth, 1995) and educational underachievement. Effective prevention and intervention strategies for these high-risk children are imperative in the aftermath of traumatic events. Describing and understanding spontaneous beliefs and practices is a first step in developing such interventions. In addition, developmental research on the functions and limitations of parent–child pretend play will be advanced by describing the breadth, diversity, and intensity of events and emotions interpreted, as well as the ways in which stressful or traumatic events are communicated, constructed, and developed during pretend play. This requires observation of children with diverse life experiences. Our preliminary study describing high-risk families, reported later, suggests that spontaneous parent–child pretend play does occur around traumatic themes and that such play can serve as a context for children's positive emotion socialization.

CAREGIVER–CHILD PRETEND PLAY IN HIGH-RISK FAMILIES

Our study focused on mothers and children involved with the public child welfare system in central Illinois. They were part of a larger study of parent–child relationships in high-risk families (Haight, Black, Workman, & Tata, 2001). Children were between the ages of 2 and 4 years (mean = 32 months) and were living in foster homes. Five children were African American, three were white, and one was biracial. Seven were girls. All children had experienced multiple traumas. All had been forcibly separated from their primary caregivers (mothers) within the last year because of maltreatment, five were known to have witnessed repeated and severe domestic violence, three were known to have witnessed parent substance abuse, and three were known to have been physically and/or sexually abused. All mothers and children had regular, weekly contact with one another (described later). Those who did not were excluded, as lack of play in such circumstances could be expected because of grief responses or strong emotional detachment resulting from prolonged separation (Heinicke & Westheimer, 1966).

Mothers were between 16 and 30 years old (mean age 23 years). None of the mothers resided with the target child's father. Four were employed at service or factory jobs, and five were unemployed. One was known to be actively abusing drugs, and one was known to be suffering from clinical depression. With two exceptions, mothers also had experienced significant trauma in addition to the ongoing loss of their children. Five mothers had experienced domestic violence, five reported significant childhood trauma (physical and sexual abuse), four reported unresolved mental health problems, and three struggled with substance abuse.

Children and their mothers were videotaped during 1-hour-long "visits." Visits are the scheduled, face-to-face meetings that occur between parents and their children who are in foster care. For the families in our study, visits were relatively unstructured. Mothers were to be sober and refrain from abusive behavior. Otherwise, they were free to interact with their children as they chose. Parents and children typically visited for 1 hour, once a week. Visits occurred in a well-stocked playroom. The room was comfortable and homelike with furniture, toys appropriate for young children, and refreshments. Available toys particularly suitable for pretend play included a dollhouse with miniature toys, puppets, dolls, toy phones, shopping carts, medical instruments, weapons including a hunting knife and guns, handcuffs, and a sand table with miniature toys. Mothers were asked to interact with their children as they ordinarily would during a visit. They were given no other specific instructions, for example, regarding play. Mothers and children then were videotaped for 1 hour.

Videotapes were transcribed verbatim with notes describing relevant contextual features such as affect, gestures, and objects. Adequate reliability was established for all codes described here. (Details are available upon request from the authors.)

Cross-Case Overview of Mother–Child Pretending

A cross-case overview suggests that mother–child pretend play may be an important context in which young children who have experienced trauma communicate with their parents about traumatic events to understand and clarify events, derive comfort, recover a sense of self independent from the trauma, and/or develop hope for a more positive future. Pretend play in many of the high-risk dyads observed in this study looked very similar to what we have observed in dyads with no known history of trauma (e.g., Haight & Miller, 1993; Haight, Parke & Black, 1997; Haight et al., 1999). Our cross-case overview, however, also suggests considerable variation across high-risk dyads in the propensity to engage in mother–child pretend play, the ways in which pretend play is socially conducted, and the enacted themes. Such variation may have an impact on children's responses to traumatic events and hence their subsequent well-being and mental health (Bowlby, 1988b).

In contrast to reports of children's solitary pretend play following trauma, all mothers and children, even those who had experienced recent trauma, spontaneously pretended together. As with the low-risk, middle-class mothers and children observed in our previous studies of everyday caregiver–child interaction (e.g., Haight & Miller, 1993; Haight et al., 1999), all dyads engaged in some pretend play, but there was variation across dyads in the frequency of pretending. We adopted a conservative approach to determining the amount of pretend play within the visit. Following Garvey (1990), we defined pretend play as a subcategory of play in which actions, objects, persons, places, or other aspects of the here-and-now are transformed or treated nonliterally. For example, a doll is animated, a child is transformed into a superhero, or behaviors conventionally associated with one context are enacted in a different context (e.g., a child says "good night," lies down on the playroom floor, and covers up with a napkin). We defined an episode of pretend play as a continuous stretch of pretending on a given topic or theme. Episodes began with the first action of pretend play produced by, or directed at, the child and continued as long as the chain of transformational actions and supporting responses continued. An episode ended with the final action of play produced by or directed to the child. Actions that were suggested by an object's unique and salient physical properties (e.g., placing a toy biscuit in a toy bowl), unless accompanied by other clearly transformational actions or talk (e.g., discussion of feeding the baby), were excluded on the grounds that they were ambiguous as to whether the child was treating the object nonliterally. (See Haight & Miller, 1993, for further details.) Even using this conservative definition of pretend play, the mean percentage of the visit time spent in pretend play was 21%, ranging across mother–child dyads from 1% to 49% of the visit.

Given that mothers and children spontaneously pretended together, it is important to consider whether such interactions are likely to have affected children's interpretations of, or responses to, emotionally stressful or traumatic events. Clearly, any effects of mothers' participation on children's pretend play will depend on how the play is socially conducted, in particular, the degree to which pretending is constructed as a mutual activity. Maternal involvement that is too passive or too dominating is unlikely to support children's emerging emotion interpretations. Mutual involvement is indicated if both mother and child abide by the conventions of mutuality, that is, initiating joint pretending and pretending in response to the other's initiations. We considered the "initiator" to be the first person to direct pretend play to the other person. We considered a "responsive" reaction to be one that continued the play initiated by the other, for example, through producing a contingent pretend response or by encouraging nonverbal responses such as smiling and nodding. (See Haight & Miller, 1993, for discussion).

Similar to our low-risk dyads, most mothers and children in this study were mutually engaged and responsive to one another's pretending. Both mothers and children actively participated in initiating pretend play with the other (mothers initiated a mean of 44% of all episodes). In addition, children and mothers were generally responsive to one another's initiations. Mothers were responsive to a mean of 95% of children's initiations of pretend play, and children were responsive to a mean of 83% of mothers' initiations.

There was, however, considerable variability in how episodes of pretend play were socially conducted in these high-risk dyads, with some extreme scores not seen in the low-risk dyads of our previous studies. Although children generally were very responsive to their mothers' initiations of pretend play, their responsive reactions ranged from 0 to 100%. The child who did not respond to her mother's initiations of pretend play responded to few of her mother's other social overtures. This mother and child were separated because of the mother's active substance abuse and profound neglect of her daughter. Similarly, although mothers were generally responsive to their children's initiations of pretend play, the range was from 50% to 100%. In accordance with past research (e.g., Tarullo, DeMulder, Ronsaville, Brown, & Radke-Yarrow, 1995), the mother with the lowest rate of responsive reactions was experiencing clinical depression.

The extent to which mutually engaging mother–child pretend play facilitates children's responses to emotionally stressful or traumatic events also depends on the extent to which such themes actually are incorporated into the play. Children and mothers did enact some themes that were related to stressful or traumatic real-life events that they had experienced. Similar to our earlier studies with low-risk families, mothers and children enacted a variety of stressful events including interpersonal aggression, illness, and accidents. They also enacted a theme of traumatic separation (described later) that we did not observe in our low-risk families. (Note that more than one of these themes could and did occur within single episodes of pretend play; for example, the mother and baby are traumatically separated, and the baby then becomes ill.)

We considered interpersonal aggression to be the enactment of intentional physical or psychological harm or threat of harm to persons. It included the enactment of stabbing or obscene name-calling. As with our low-risk, U.S. samples, aggression was the most frequently enacted stressful event. Seven of the nine dyads enacted aggression accounting for a mean of 40% of episodes, ranging from 0 to 100% of all episodes. Again, we saw extreme scores on aggression, which we had not previously seen in our low-risk dyads. For one dyad, all episodes of pretend play involved the enactment of aggression, and for another dyad, 89% of episodes involved aggression. In addition, the aggression enacted by many children was realistic and resembled antisocial, adult behavior. For example, during dollhouse play, Molly made the daddy doll shake the mommy doll while screaming in a "doll" voice, "Stop it! Stop it, bitch!" Clinical studies suggest that such realistic enactments are often linked to behaviors that a young child has observed (Bowlby, 1988; Terr, 2003), for example, at home between his or her parents. In our low-risk dyads, enacted aggression typically involved portrayals of media characters such as Batman and villains.

We considered "illness/accident" to be the enactment of accidental harm, such as getting burned or having a heart attack (Haight & Sachs, 1995). Illness/accident occurred much less frequently than aggression (two dyads enacted accidents or illness accounting for a mean of 16%, ranging across dyads from 0 to 100%).

In addition to these themes, some mothers and children displayed a theme of traumatic separation. This theme involved the forced separation of child and primary caregiver (in these cases, the mothers with whom they were playing). Although we have observed the theme of mother–child separation enacted in low-risk families, this theme typically involves the child's protestations, for example, of the mother's departure for work. In the high-risk samples, the mother's distress is also enacted, and the child's behavior may become disorganized. For example, during play with a dollhouse, May asked her young daughter, "Are you at your new (foster) house?" Molly responded, "No!" Later in the episode, she picked up the mother doll and screamed in a "doll" voice," Stop it! Stop it! Give me back my baby! Don't do that no more!" Molly then became visibly distressed and began throwing the dollhouse props. Three dyads enacted traumatic separations from a parent accounting for a mean percentage of 8%, ranging across dyads from 0 to 25%.

Four Illustrative Cases

The cross-case analysis suggests that traumatized mothers and children regularly engage in spontaneous pretend play together during visits. Because pretend play can provide a "safe" environment for exploring feelings about family experiences, it could potentially be an important resource for intervention with some traumatized children. If a parent can engage the child emotionally in play, allowing for some expression and exploration of the child's feelings and thoughts, a therapist could help the parent provide the child with clear feedback about events and feelings. Such communications could contribute to the healing process for both parent and child. None of the children in the current study, however, were receiving mental health intervention for help in dealing with prolonged separation or with previous traumas leading up to placement in foster care. An analysis of several illustrative cases suggests qualitative differences in styles of mother–child pretend play that may affect children's responses to the literal traumatic stresses they have experienced. These four patterns are not intended to reflect a comprehensive typology. They do suggest that the context of mother–child pretend play may be an important resource for a therapist working with some, but not all, traumatized children. They also suggest different strategies that a therapist might need to employ to support different mothers and children. (Identifying details have been changed to disguise the cases.)

Maternal Proactive Support of Child's Trauma Resolution During Mother–Child Pretend Play

Despite their own difficult histories, a number of mothers in our study displayed remarkable sensitivity and wisdom in responding to their children's reactions to trauma, including the use of pretend play. For example, both 19-year-old Susan and her youngest daughter, 2½-year-old Anna, had experienced significant trauma in their young lives. As a child, Susan was sexually abused by her alcoholic father and later by her stepfather. At the age of 15, her first daughter, Melinda, was born, and at the age of 16, Susan married Melinda's father. Sadly, her husband was an addict and physically abusive. He was primarily abusive to Susan but had begun to abuse the children as well. Susan had been a good student ("when I could concentrate") but did not finish high school. She had recently obtained her GED. Her children were removed 3 months prior to our observation of her visit with Anna. At that time, Susan was engaging in some petty criminal activity and, although she herself did not drink or abuse drugs, she associated with substance abusers. Her children were removed because of endangerment related to the domestic violence and because of abuse. Anna cried inconsolably for her mother at the end of each weekly visit, suffered from nightmares, and displayed withdrawn and regressed behavior in her foster home. At the time of the visit, Susan had filed for divorce and obtained an order of protection. She was in therapy, in her words, "to learn to make better choices."

Despite her own difficult history and youth, Susan was warm, attentive, and remarkably wise in her face-to-face interactions with Anna. In the following excerpt, Susan spontaneously used pretend play to comfort a distraught Anna at the end of their weekly, hour-long visit by reminding her of the dinner and bedtime routines they had shared when they lived together. (Susan and Anna are pretending with a dollhouse. They have chosen dolls to represent Susan, Anna, and Anna's older sister, Melinda.)

Susan: You want to sit at the table with Melinda? (Susan places the Anna doll in a chair at the table.) You know how we used to do it at home? Do we have another chair so Mommy can sit at the table? (They place the Susan doll at the table.) What do we do at home? We put you in a highchair, right? (They change the Anna doll to the highchair, and the dinner play continues.)

Anna: That's you! (Referring to Susan doll.)

Susan: Are you talking to Mama Susan? Hmm?

Anna: That you.

Susan: Yeah.

Anna: Yeah.

Susan: Does Mama Susan read books to you when you go to bed at night?

Anna: Yeah. (Haight et al., 2001)

Pretend play was a favored activity of Anna and Susan in which they spontaneously engaged for 23% of their visit time. In the play episodes, Susan was able to connect with her daughter emotionally and remind her of their shared lives together and of her commitment to their remaining together. By reminding Anna of daily routines they had shared, Susan was reminding Anna that she was her mother and was there to help her. For a young child who is experiencing the trauma of a prolonged and forced separation from a caregiver, this is crucial information that may help to sustain the parent–child attachment relationship. At the time of our study, Anna was not receiving any services to address the traumas that she had experienced, either the trauma at the hands of her abusive father or the traumatic separation from her mother.

Yet, given Susan's "spontaneous maternal proactive support of the child's trauma resolution during mother–child pretend play," a skilled therapist would have a sturdy base on which to build an intervention to support Anna. If Anna and her mother were seen by a skilled therapist, their joint play episodes could potentially provide a safe and powerful environment for exploring and processing past trauma. In this context, Anna's mother could provide her with critical information that could facilitate healing (e.g., confirming what she saw, explaining misconceptions, and reassuring her of her current safety and her commitment to her).

Minimal Communication About Stressful or Traumatic Events During Mother–Child Pretend Play

Not all dyads, however, used mother–child pretend play to communicate about separation experiences or other traumatic events. Some mothers and children simply preferred other forms of expression, such as asking and answering direct questions. Other mothers lacked strategies for communicating with their very young children about the trauma they had experienced. As one mother expressed during a discussion of domestic violence, "How do you talk to a 2-year-old about the fact that Daddy almost killed Mommy? I don't understand it myself." In this latter case, pretend play between the dyad and a skilled therapist could reveal how much difficulty the dyad is having in communicating about powerful and painful events in their lives. Using the play as an impetus for discussion about feelings and events (Fraiberg, Adelson, & Shapiro, 1975; Lieberman & Zeanah, 1999), the therapist could then help the dyad to begin to communicate about the trauma and pain, thereby promoting a healthier developmental trajectory for the mother and child.

In many ways, Dorothy and Clarissa were similar to Anna and Susan. Dorothy, at 20 years old, had two small children and a violent boyfriend. Both Dorothy and 2-year-old Clarissa had experienced significant trauma. Dorothy described a difficult and traumatic childhood. As a young child, she witnessed her mother's boyfriend murder her slightly older sister. She entered foster care and was eventually adopted. Her adoptive father sexually abused her for a number of years until her adoptive mother "threw" her out of the house at age 16. By the age of 17, Dorothy was an emancipated minor, working full time. When she became pregnant with Clarissa, she obtained her GED and advanced to the level of supervisor at a fast-food chain. Unfortunately, the father of her children was physically abusive. Several months prior to our observation, the children were placed in foster care because of risk of endangerment related to the domestic violence. As reported by Dorothy, 2-year-old Clarissa actively fought her father off Dorothy when he "almost killed me." Clarissa was described by her foster mother as "high tempered," difficult, and fearful of men. A beautiful little girl, Clarissa's arms and legs were covered with scabs from nervous picking and scratching at her skin. At the conclusion of each weekly visit, she screamed and had tantrums when separated from her mother.

Like Susan, Dorothy was remarkably warm, attentive, and insightful in her interactions with Clarissa. Although Dorothy and Clarissa engaged in spontaneous pretend play (17% of the visit time), they did not enact trauma themes. Their play focused on domestic routines, such as shopping and cooking enacted by a mommy and her little girl, and social routines such as phoning. As with Anna and Susan, the themes of home routines appeared to connect the two together emotionally, providing a vital link for maintaining their relationship. At the time of our study, Clarissa was not receiving services to help her to interpret the violence she had witnessed at home or the traumatic separation from her mother. Given this "minimal communication about stressful or traumatic events in mother–child pretend play" in a dyad that clearly enjoys sharing pretend play, a skilled therapist might help to open up the possibility of greater communication through play. For example, when Dorothy introduced a male figure into their dollhouse play, Clarissa objected, "No bad man." Although Clarissa resisted the inclusion of the male figure into their peaceful play, her spontaneous identification of the male figure as "bad" suggests the potential for her to explore past traumatic experiences with her mother in play, especially in enactments guided by a skilled clinician. Having a clinician work with the dyad appeared to be important because her mother made no response to Clarissa's comment about the "bad man." Therapeutic interventions that build constructively on the themes that were emerging spontaneously in play could help Clarissa and her mother come to terms with past violence and with the ongoing separation.

Maternal Disapproval of Child's Aggressive Pretend Play

Similar to the low-risk samples we observed in our earlier studies, some mothers in the current study actively discouraged their children's enactment of aggression and other antisocial behaviors during pretend play. The explicit message sent by these mothers during mother–child pretend play was that interpersonal aggression is wrong. Given that many of the children in our high-risk sample had repeatedly witnessed interpersonal aggression, especially domestic violence between parents, pretend play could be a context for resocialization. In some instances, however, disapproval of the child's enactment might foreclose on opportunities to explore and communicate about these traumatic experiences.

May was a 27-year-old high school graduate. Four-year-old Molly entered foster care because of neglect. May was homeless after leaving Molly's father, who was violent. She was struggling to find a job and appropriate housing. She described her childhood history as "boring," with no significant trauma. She did cry, extensively, when telling us about her separation from Molly. During the visit, May and Molly co-constructed a narrative of when Molly was placed by child welfare professionals in protective custody. May also made positive comments about Molly's foster placement, encouraging Molly to get along in her temporary home and reassuring Molly that she was actively seeking a home for them. Molly was doing relatively well at her foster home but had begun to act out aggressively in her preschool. She cried inconsolably at the end of each visit when she had to separate from May. May was the only mother in our study who had regained custody of her child at the 6-month follow-up.

May and Molly pretended extensively during their visit (49% of the visit time). Their play was animated and lively and encompassed many themes. Similar to our low-risk families, pretend play for May and Molly was not only fun but also a context of socialization. In the following excerpt, May responds to Molly's enactment of rough-and-tumble play but explicitly discourages antisocial aggression.

(May and Molly are playing with puppets. Molly initiates pretend rough-and-tumble play and begins tickling May's puppet. May makes her puppet squeal and retaliate. May makes her puppet playfully hit Molly's on the head.)

May: No! No! Stop! Stop! (playfully, while smiling. Molly laughs and reaches for a plastic hunting knife.)

Molly: I'm gonna get that knife. . . . I'm gonna cut her.

May: (no longer playing) No, you ain't gonna get no knife. Knives are bad. Put the knife back.

At the time of our observation, Molly was receiving no services to help her cope with the separation from her mother or other traumas. Given the "maternal disapproval of the child's antisocial enactments" and this dyad's elaborate and imaginative pretend play around other themes, a skilled therapist might help May to both communicate the inappropriateness of interpersonal violence and also open up pretend play as a context for communicating about Molly's feelings evoked by such past traumas and her separation from May. In the play episode, May gave Molly clear verbal feedback regarding the interpersonal aggression she was beginning to enact in her play. Given that anger is a common response to a major separation and exposure to domestic violence, having a therapist present could both support May's legitimate attempts to communicate about interpersonal aggression and her understanding that her daughter's anger is a natural sequela of their separation and exposure to domestic violence.

Maternal Pressure for Antisocial Pretend Play

Mother–child pretend play typically is a context supportive of children's positive socialization and well-being. It may be tempting to encourage all traumatized parents and children to pretend together under the guidance of a skilled therapist. To do so, however, would be naive. Parent–child pretend play does have limitations. If parents are antisocial or enact their own unresolved trauma histories in play, the emotion socialization their children experience during parent–child pretend play may not be conducive to their positive development. In the following case, the mother introduces antisocial themes into the pretend play that are initially resisted by the child. The child's mother, perhaps because of her own unmet needs, failed to create a safe environment within which experiences about past trauma, and the feelings they engendered, could be explored. Indeed, antisocial themes initiated by the mother within the play itself apparently were highly stressful to the child.

Seventeen-year-old Shareese had been in foster care because her stepfather was known to have sexually molested her sister. Prior to that time, she had lived with her 2½-year-old son, Robert, with her family in a public housing facility notorious for its violence. Before and after participation in this study, Robert had visited Shareese in jail, where she was beginning a sentence for selling drugs. At the time of the study, Robert had been in foster care for 10 months.

Shareese's interactions with Robert were complex. There was a sense of warmth and playfulness in their interactions. On the other hand, Shareese rushed from toy to toy with little attention to Robert's interests or emotional cues. On several occasions, she made him cry by scaring him with a stuffed snake or threatening to end the visit if he did not comply with her frequent demands. Although this dyad did engage in frequent, spontaneous pretend play (25% of the visit), the episodes were very short, and all were initiated by Shareese. Furthermore, in many of these episodes, Shareese seemed to pressure Robert to enact antisocial themes that he apparently found distressing.

Shareese: Look. I'm gonna handcuff you. (Picking up play handcuffs. Smiling, she takes Robert by the arm and tries to lead him back to the chair. Robert whimpers and resists.)

Shareese: C'mere. (Robert whines. Shareese frowns.) Gun—C'mere! C'mere! (She pulls Robert back to the chair, sits in the chair, and stands Robert in front of her.)

Shareese: C'mere. Turn around. Put your hands behind your back. (Shareese puts a toy gun in her lap and handcuffs Robert.) OK, we're goin' to take you to jail. Gonna take you to jail. . . . You're gonna go to jail. We're gonna shoot you. (Shareese takes a toy gun, puts it to Robert's chest, and pulls the trigger.) Pow! (Robert starts to shake and whine.)

Shareese: Break out! (Robert shakes his hands to free his wrists from the handcuffs. Shareese holds the gun near Robert's head and pulls the trigger. He whines.)

Shareese: OK. Here. (She holds out the gun for Robert to take. Robert takes it and stands watching as Shareese takes another gun. She puts a holster on her waist and returns to the chair.)

Shareese: You want it [the gun]?

Robert: No (whining).

Shareese: C'mere. (She points her gun at Robert and shoots twice. Then, smiling, she hands it to Robert, pointing it at herself.) Shoot it. Shoot it.

Shareese: OK, give me your knife. I'm gonna stab you. (Shareese pretends to stab Robert to death. The play continues, and eventually, Robert joins in as a willing partner pretending to shoot and stab his mother.) (Haight et al., 2001)

Like the other children in our study, Robert was receiving no intervention to help him to deal with past traumas and the current separation from his mother. Given "maternal pressure for antisocial pretend play," any joint therapy could proceed only if Shareese has access to, and successfully responds to, counseling. In this episode, Shareese was unable to create a sense of safety for Robert in their shared play. Instead, her behaviors only frightened her son. Her comments also served the function of inculcating antisocial behavior by teaching him to respond to aggression with aggression. Under the guidance of a skilled clinician, pretend play might provide an important venue for this vulnerable and at-risk dyad to connect in a more positive way with each other and to communicate about the trauma and violence. To do so, however, it would first be important for the therapist to help Shareese consider the origins of her angry feelings and to connect her anger to the events and experiences that conditioned them (Bowlby, 1988b). It would also be important for the therapist to help Shareese empathize with her own sense of vulnerability and with Robert's need for empathy and love (Fraiberg et al., 1975; Lieberman & Zeanah, 1999).

CONCLUSION

In this chapter, we have explored the pretend play of mothers and children from high-risk families who have experienced recent trauma. Despite the facilitating role accorded to pretend play in emotional development and socialization in early childhood, previous empirical research has focused on the cognitive and linguistic functions of pretend play. In addition, much of the existing empirical research focuses on children in low-risk groups, which may restrict our understanding of the range of emotion themes enacted during mother–child pretend play.

In many respects, the mothers and children from the high-risk families described in this chapter resembled those from low-risk families we have observed in our previous studies. In a supportive context, all mothers and children spontaneously pretended together. Much of this play displayed mutuality: episodes were initiated by both mothers and children, and mothers and children were generally very responsive to one another's initiations of pretend play. There was, however, variation across our high-risk, mother–child dyads. In one of the dyads, the mother dominated the pretend play with little regard for the child, and in another, she was minimally responsive to the child's initiations of pretend play. Such variation may affect the extent to which mother–child pretend play supports children's positive development.

Similar to the pretend play we have observed in low-risk families, mothers and children from high-risk families enacted a range of themes, including those related to trauma such as interpersonal aggression. In some of the high-risk dyads, however, aggression dominated the play or contained realistic enactment of adult aggression such as that experienced or observed by the children in their actual lives, for example, the daddy punching and swearing at the mommy. In contrast, much of the aggression we observed in many low-risk dyads involved fantasy aggression, for example, superheros fighting bad guys. The pretend play of some high-risk dyads also contained themes infrequently observed in low-risk families, such as the traumatic separation of babies from their mothers in which mothers as well as babies display distressed and disorganized behavior.

This exploratory research has two primary implications. First, understanding the role of pretend play in emotion learning requires the study of diverse families experiencing a range of emotional events. Past research suggested that children experiencing stress do not engage in solitary pretend play, or they pretend much less frequently. This exploratory study suggests that some traumatized children do pretend frequently in the supportive context of mother–child interaction. Future research on pretend play as a context for emotion socialization should recruit diverse families to consider the range of emotion enacted during parent–child pretend play, as well as consider the role of parent–child pretend play in children's recovery from trauma. Unanswered questions for future research include: Do traumatized children who spontaneously engage in parent–child pretend play display better developmental and mental health outcomes than those traumatized children who do not have this resource? What are the characteristics of mother–child pretend play that do or do not support more positive developmental outcomes in traumatized mothers and children?

The second implication is for intervention with traumatized children. Although play therapy is commonly used to support the recovery of traumatized children, rarely are parents utilized directly. For some of the dyads in the current exploratory study, mother–child pretend play was an unutilized resource for children's recovery from trauma. Such play was mutual and included culturally appropriate messages about stressful or traumatic events. Furthermore, unlike play that is elicited in the context of therapy, spontaneous pretend play emerges in the context of the child's everyday life, as issues and reactions related to trauma actually emerge and the child is motivated to communicate about them. For example, in the hands of a skilled play therapist, the pretend play routines that Susan, Dorothy, and Anna had spontaneously developed could be used to systematically support their children's recovery from trauma.

Clearly, any use of parent–child pretend play by therapists would need to be utilized with discretion. Some dyads might simply prefer other expressive activities. Clarissa and her mother, for example, seemed to prefer drawing and other forms of creative play, which might be a more natural context for this mother and child to begin communicating about traumatic events. In addition, not all mother–child pretend play has the potential to be therapeutic. Antisocial tendencies, unresolved trauma, active substance abuse, or unmet mental health needs, for example, may prevent some parents from pretending in an emotionally supportive manner with their young children.

Acknowledgment This project was supported by the School of Social Work, University of Illinois, Urbana-Champaign.

References

Ackerman, P. T., Newton, J. E. O., McPherson, W. B., Jones, J. G., & Dykman, R. A. (1998). Prevalence of posttraumatic stress disorder and other psychiatric diagnoses in three groups of abused children (sexual, physical, and both). *Child Abuse and Neglect*, *22*(8), 759–774.

American Psychiatric Association. (1994). *Diagnostic and statistical manual of mental disorders* (4th ed.). Washington, DC: The Author.

Banyard, V. L., Williams, L. M., & Siegel, J. A. (2002). Retraumatization among adult women sexually abused in childhood: Exploratory analyses in a prospective study. *Journal of Child Sexual Abuse, 11*, 19–48.

Banyard, V. L., Williams, L. M., & Siegel, J. A. (2003). The impact of complex trauma and depression on parenting: An exploration of mediating risk and protective factors. *Child Maltreatment, 8*, 334–349.

Bat-Zion, N., & Levy-Shiff, R. (1993). Children in war: Stress and coping reactions under the threat of Scud missile attacks and the effect of proximity. In L. Lewis & N. Fox (Eds.), *The psychological effects of war and violence on children* (pp. 143–161). Hillsdale, NJ: Erlbaum.

Blatt, S., & Simms, M. (1997). *Foster care: Special children, special needs.* Contemporary Pediatrics, 14*(4), 109–129.*

Bowlby, J. (1988a). *A secure base: Parent-child attachment and healthy human development.* London: Routledge.

Bowlby, J. (1988b). On knowing what you are not supposed to know and feeling what you are not supposed to feel. In J. Bowlby (Ed.), *A secure base: Clinical applications of attachment theory* (pp. 99–118). London: Routledge.

Bretherton, I., & Beeghly, M. (1982). Talking about internal states: The acquisition of an explicit theory of mind. *Developmental Psychology, 18,* 906–921.

Bromet, E. J., Goldgaber, D., Carlson, G., Panina, N., Golovakha, E., Gluzman, S. F., et al. (2000). Children's well-being 11 years after the Chernobyl catastrophe. *Archives of General Psychiatry, 57*(6), 563–571.

Bruner, J. (1990). *Acts of meaning.* Cambridge, MA: Harvard University Press.

Burger, L. K., & Miller, P. J. (1999). Early talk about the past revisited: Affect in working-class and middle-class children's co-narrations. *Journal of Child Language, 26*, 133–162.

Burt, C. (1943). War neuroses in British children. *Nervous Child, 2*, 324–337.

Campos, J., & Stenberg, C. (1981). Perception, appraisal, and emotion: The onset of social referencing. In M. E. Lamb & L. R. Sherrod (Eds.), *Infants' social cognition: Empirical and social considerations*. Hillsdale, NJ: Erlbaum.

Cho, G., & Miller, P. J. (in press). Personal storytelling: Working-class and middle-class mothers in comparative perspective. In M. Farr (Ed.), *Ethnolinguistic Chicago: Language and literacy in Chicago neighborhoods.* Mahwah, NJ: Erlbaum.

Cicchetti, D., & Toth, S. (1995). Developmental psychopathology perspective on child abuse and neglect. *Journal of American Academy of Child and Adolescent Psychiatry, 34,* 541–565.

Clark, C. (2003). *In sickness and in play: Children coping with chronic illness.* New Brunswick, NJ: Rutgers University Press.

Coates, S., & Schechter, D. (2004). Preschoolers' traumatic stress post-9/11: Relational and developmental perspectives. *Psychiatric Clinics of North America, 27,* 473–489.

Cohen, J., & Mannarino, A. (1996). Factors that mediate treatment outcome of sexually abused preschool children. *Journal of the American Academy of Child and Adolescent Psychiatry, 34*(10), 1402–1410.

Cohler, B. (1991). Overcoming adversity: Family response to natural disaster. In J. Vofel (Chair), *Children's responses to natural disasters: The aftermath of Hurricane Hugo and the 1989 Bay Area earthquake.* Symposium conducted at the meeting of the Society for Research in Child Development, Seattle.

Crittenden, P., & Ainsworth, M. (1989). Child maltreatment and attachment theory. In D. Cicchetti & V. Carlson (Eds.), *Child maltreatment: Theory and research on the causes and consequences of child abuse and neglect.* New York: Cambridge University Press.

Egeland, B., Weinfield, N. S., Bosquet, M., & Cheng, V. K. (2000). Remembering, repeating, and working through lessons from attachment-based interventions. In J. D.

Osofsky & H. E. Fitzgerald (Eds.), *Infant mental health in groups at high risk: Vol. 4. WAIMH handbook of infant mental health* (pp. 35–89). New York: Wiley.

Feiring, C., Taska, L., & Lewis, M. (1998). Social support and children's and adolescents'adaptation to sexual abuse. *Journal of Interpersonal Violence, 13*(2), 240–260.

Fraiberg, S., Adelson, E., & Shapiro, V. J. (1975). Ghosts in the nursery. A psychoanalytic approach to the problems of impaired infant–mother relationships. *American Academy of Child Psychiatary, 14*(3), 387–421.

Freud, A., & Burlingham, D. (1943). *War and children.* London: Medical War Books.

Garmezy, N. (1985). Stress-resistant children: The search for protective factors. In J. Stevenson (Ed.), *Recent research in developmental psychopathology* (pp. 213–233). Oxford: Pergamon.

Garvey, C. (1990). *Play.* Cambridge, MA: Harvard University Press.

George, C., Kaplan, N., & Main, M. (1985). *The adult attachment interview.* Unpublished manuscript, University of California at Berkeley.

Goodnow, J. (1988). Parents' ideas, actions, and feelings: Models and method from developmental and social psychology. *Child Development, 59*, 286–320.

Göncü, A. (Ed.). (1999). *Children's engagement in the world: Sociocultural perspectives.* New York: Cambridge University Press.

Greenberg, M., Speltz, M., & DeKlyen, M. (1993). The role of attachment in the early development of disruptive behavior problems. *Development and Psychopathology, 5*, 191–213.

Groves, B. M. (2002). *Children who see too much: Lessons from the child witness to violence project.* Boston: Beacon.

Haight, W., Black, J., Workman, C., & Tata, L. (2001). Parent–child interaction during foster care visits: Implications for practice. *Social Work, 46,* 325–338.

Haight, W., Mangelsdorf, S., Black, J., Szwczyk, M. Shoppe, S., Giorgio, G., et al. (in press). Enhancing parent–child interaction during foster care visits: Experimental assessment of an intervention. *Child Welfare.*

Haight, W., & Miller, P. (1993). *Pretending at home: Early development in a sociocultural context.* Albany: State University of New York Press.

Haight, W., Parke, R. & Black, J. (1997). Mothers' and fathers' beliefs about and spontaneous participation in their toddlers' pretend play. *Merrill-Palmer Quarterly, 42,* 271–290.

Haight, W., & Sachs, K. (1995). The portrayal of emotion during mother–child pretend play. In L. Sperry & P. Smiley (Eds.), *Exploring young children's concepts of self and other through conversation* (pp. 33–46). San Francisco, CA: Jossey-Bass.

Haight, W., Shim, W., Linn, L., & Swinford, L. (in press). Promoting children's psychological resilience in violent families: The perspectives of battered women involved in the public child welfare system. *Child Welfare.*

Haight, W., Wang, X., Fung, H., Williams, K., & Mintz, J. (1999). Universal, developmental, and variable aspects of young children's play: A cross-cultural comparison of pretending at home. *Developmental Psychology, 70,* 1477–1488.

Harkness, S., & Super, C. (1996). Introduction. In S. Harkness and C. Super (Eds.), *Parents' cultural belief systems: Their origins, expressions, and consequences.* New York: Guilford.

Heinicke, C., & Westheimer, I. (1966): *Brief separations.* New York: International Universities Press.

Hertsgaard, L., Gunnar, M., Erickson, M. F., & Nechmias, M. (1995). Adrenocorticol responses to the strange situation in infants with disorganized attachment relationships. *Child Development, 66*(4), 1100–1106.

Hess, E. (1999). The adult attachment interview. In J. Cassidy & P. Shaver (Eds.), *The handbook of attachment* (pp. 395–433). New York: Guilford.

Holden, G., Stein, J., Ritchie, K., Harris, S., & Jouriles, E. (1998). Parenting behaviors and beliefs of battered women. In G. Holden, R. Geffner, & E. Jouriles (Eds.), *Children exposed to marital violence: Theory, research and applied issues.* Washington, DC: American Psychological Association.

Hughes, F. (1998). Play in special populations. In O. Saracho & B. Spodek (Eds.), *Multiple perspectives on play in early childhood education.* Albany: State University of New York Press.

Kramer, L., & Schaefer-Hernan, P. (1994). Patterns of fantasy play engagement across the transition to becoming a sibling. *Journal of Child Psychology and Psychiatry, 35,* 749–767.

Lehmann, C. (2001). Psychiatrists advise parents in responding to children's concerns *Psychiatric News, 3*, 8–28.

Lieberman, A. F., & Zeanah, C. (1999). The influence of attachment theory on infant–parent psychotherapy and other interventions with young children. In P. Shaver & J. Cassidy (Eds.), *Handbook of attachment theory and research.* New York: Basic Books.

Lynskey, M., & Fergusson, D. (1997). Factors protecting against the development of adjustment difficulties in young adults exposed to childhood sexual abuse. *Child Abuse and Neglect, 21*(2), 1177–1190.

Lyons-Ruth, K., Alpern, L., & Repacholi, B. (1993). Disorganized infant attachment classification and maternal psychosocial problems as predictors of hostile-aggressive behavior in the preschool classroom. *Child Development, 64*, 572–585.

Lyons-Ruth, K., Easterbrooks, M., & Cibelli, C. (1997). Infant attachment strategies, infant mental lag, and maternal depressive symptoms: Predictors of internalizing and externalizing problems at age 7. *Developmental Psychology, 33*, 681–692.

Main, M. (1996). Introduction to the special section on attachment and psychopathology: 2. Overview of the field of attachment. *Journal of Consulting and Clinical Psychology, 64*, 237–243.

Marand, S., & Adelman, A. (1997). Experiencing violence in a developmental context. In J. Osofsky (Ed.), *Children in a violent society* (pp. 202–222). New York: Guilford.

Norwood, A., Ursano, R., & Fullerton, C. (2000). Disaster psychiatry: Principles and practice. *Psychiatric Quarterly, 71*(3), 207–226.

Parens, H. (1991). A view of the development of hostility in early life. *Journal of the American Psychoanalytic Association, 39*(Suppl.), 75–108.

Perry, S., Silber, E., & Block, D. (1956). *The child and his family in disaster: A study of the 1953 Vicksburg tornado* (Publication 394). Washington, DC: National Academy of Sciences, National Research Council.

Punamaki, R. (1987). Psychological stress response of Palestinian mothers and their children in conditions of military occupation and political violence. *The Quarterly Newsletter of the Laboratory of Comparative Human Cognition, 9*, 76–79.

Pynoos, R., & Eth, S. (1985). Children traumatized by witnessing acts of personal violence: Homicide, rape, or suicide behavior. In S. Eth & R. Pynoos (Eds.), *Posttraumatic stress disorders in children* (pp. 17–44). Washington, DC: American Psychiatric Press.

Pynoos, R., Steinberg, A., & Goenjian, A. (1996). Traumatic stress in childhood and adolescence: Recent developments and current controversies. In B. Van der Kolk, A. McFarlane, & L. Weisaeth (Eds.), *Traumatic stress: The effects of overwhelming experience on mind, body and society* (pp. 331–358). New York: Guilford.

Silverman, R., & Lieberman, A. F. (1999). Negative maternal attributions, projective identification, and the intergenerational transmission of violent relational patterns. *Psychoanalytic Dialogues, 9*(2), 161–187.

Singer, D. (1993). *Playing for their lives: Helping troubled children through play therapy.* New York: Free Press.

Stephens, D. L. (1999). Battered women's views of their children. *Journal of Interpersonal Violence, 14*(7), 731–746.

Stuber, M., Nader, K., Yasuda, P., Pynoos, R., & Cohen, S. (1991). Stress responses after pediatric bone marrow transplantation: Preliminary results of a prospective longitudinal study. *Journal of the American Academy of Child and Adolescent Psychiatry, 30*(6), 952–957.

Sutton-Smith, B. (1994). Paradigms of intervention. In J. Hellendoorn, R. van der Kooij, & B. Sutton-Smith (Eds.), *Play and intervention* (pp. 3–22). Albany: State University of New York Press.

Tarullo, L. B., DeMulder, E. K., Ronsaville, D. S., Brown, E., & Radke-Yarrow, M. (1995): Maternal depression and maternal treatment of siblings as predictors of child psychopathology. *Developmental Psychology 31*, 395–405.

Terr, L. (2003). "Wild child": How three principles of healing organized 12 years of psychotherapy. *Journal of the American Academy of Child and Adolescent Psychiatry, 42*(12), 1401–1409.

van Ijzendoorn, M. H. (1995). Adult attachment representations, parental responsiveness, and infant attachment: A meta analysis on the predictive validity of the Adult Attachment Interview. *Psychological Bulletin, 117*, 387–403.

Vogel, J. M., & Vernberg, E. M. (1993). Psychological responses of children to natural and human-made disasters: I. Children's psychological responses to disasters. *Journal of Clinical Child Psychology, 22*(4), 464–84.

Webb, N. (Ed.). (2002). *Helping the bereaved child: A handbook for practitioners* (2nd ed.). New York: Guilford.

Wolf, D., Rygh, J., & Altschuler, J. (1984). Agency and experience: Representations of people in early play narratives. In I. Bretherton (Ed.), *Symbolic play: The development of social understanding.* New York: Academic Press.

Yehuda, R., McFarlane, A., & Shalev, A. (1998). Predicting the development of posttraumatic stress disorder from acute response to a traumatic event. *Biological Psychiatry, 44*(12), 1305–1313.

Zeanah, C., Mammen, O., & Lieberman, A. (1993). Disorders of attachment. In C. Zeanah (Ed.), *Handbook of infant mental health.* New York: Guilford.

12

Play and Autism: Facilitating Symbolic Understanding

MELISSA ALLEN PREISSLER

Autism is a pervasive developmental disorder characterized by impairments in three discrete domains: communication, social abilities, and imagination (resulting in repetitive interests and behavior) (American Psychiatric Association, 2000). The incidence of autism has dramatically increased in recent years, with estimates between 1:500 and 1:1,000 births in the United States (Volkmar, 2005). According to the Centers for Disease Control, recent estimates are as high as 1:166 births. Autism spectrum disorder (ASD) is now considered a national epidemic. The spectrum has been expanded to include autism, Asperger's syndrome, pervasive developmental disorder–not otherwise specified (PDD-NOS), and the rarer Rett's syndrome and child disintegrative disorder.

There are varying degrees of impairment among subtypes across the spectrum, but the more "classic" symptoms of ASD occur in autism, Asperger's syndrome, and PDD-NOS, rather then Rett's syndrome and child disintegrative disorder, which appear to have a different etiology. There is a fairly specific profile generally seen in these former three subtypes, which will be referred to here collectively as ASD. There is a reduced sensitivity to language and a decreased response to the child's own name, so much so that many children are suspected of having hearing impairments because they often fail to orient to words, even if spoken in close proximity. Expressive language deficits are also quite severe, with almost a third of individuals with ASD remaining functionally nonverbal. Those with verbal language often have bizarre linguistic output, with frequent pronoun reversal, limited social reciprocity, and scripted or echolalic speech. Children with ASD tend to engage in ritualistic or obsessive behaviors (e.g., lining up cars, having to put books away in a specific order, or insisting on wearing a particular hat at all times), possibly because such behaviors are routine and familiar and therefore bring comfort. An overwhelming environment or a change in an established routine could result in temper tantrums, anger attacks, and often severe resistance.

Lower functioning individuals with autism often have comorbid mental retardation that manifests itself not only in impairment in the three major diagnostic domains but also in diminished cognitive capacities. These individuals are also more likely to have nonfunctional speech or limited spontaneous speech. Children with ASD vary individually in terms of severity of impairment within each of the domains. Although all children with this diagnosis share the core features of the diagnostic criteria, symptoms and degree of severity differ from individual to individual.

As of yet, there is no cure for ASD. There is some evidence to suggest that genetics plays a role in the proliferation of the disorder (Folstein & Santangelo, 2000; Hallmayer et al., in press; Ingram et al., 2000). Parents with one child with ASD have a 5% chance of having a second affected child, compared with a baseline incidence rate of 0.05%. In addition, the greater incidence of ASD in boys to girls (4:1) and more variance in alternative forms of a gene (alleles) indicate that chromosomes play a role (Ingram et al., 2000). A common biological or environmental causal mechanism has not been identified, and with the rise in incidence of the disorder, due in part to increased awareness by physicians and alert parents and to the sensitivity of diagnostic measures, it is paramount to address the treatment of this increasing population with special needs. The primary form of treatment is educational therapy, combined with other specific therapies as needed (e.g., physical, occupational, speech and language). The most frequently implemented educational treatment with consistent proven results is behavioral therapy (McEachin, Smith, & Lovaas, 1993), in which the principles of operant conditioning are applied to teach new skills across a broad domain. There are a growing number of alternative treatments, such as restrictive diets, prism glasses, sensory integration, and chelation (an invasive treatment to rid the body of metals such as mercury). However, the efficacy of these treatments has not been established. One increasingly recognized and legitimate component of therapeutic interventions involves play, because play skills are staggeringly different in children with ASD than in typically developing children.

THE IMPORTANCE OF PLAY

The act of play extends far beyond the recreational factor. It enables children to learn many skills, such as decision making, turn taking, and, significantly, language skills and social interaction, monitoring, and reciprocity. Both Piaget (1962) and Vygotsky (1966, 1978) acknowledged the significance of symbolic play for normal development. According to Vygotsky, play is not parallel to development but rather a central driving force to its unfurling. Recent research emphasizes that rather than being possibly superfluous, a view endorsed by many parents, particularly in a Baby Einstein-laden society, play is rather a disguised opportunity to learn (for reviews of the importance of play in learning, see Hirsh-Pasek & Golinkoff, 2003; Zigler, Singer, & Bishop-Josef, 2004). It provides children with a creative outlet, where they have the power to create a fantasy world or make decisions affecting what and whom they play with. It increases problem-solving abilities, encourages spontaneity, and promotes intellectual growth (Hirsh-Pasek & Golinkoff, 2003). It also becomes a foundation for acquiring and practicing joint attention skills—a shared, coordinated visual interaction between two individuals and an object or event (Tomasello, 1995). Encouraging play breaks in a school environment allows children to maximize their attention during lesson hours (chapter 3; Pellegrini & Smith, 1993).

Pretend play bridges the gap between real events in the changing world and imagination within one's head. Marilyn Segal notes that pretending "represents a critical step in passing from the sensory-motor intelligence of infancy to the symbolic thinking of adulthood" (Zigler, Singer, & Bishop-Josef, 2004, p. 42). It also provides children with the opportunity to learn vocabulary and complex language (Ervin-Tripp, 1991), story comprehension (Pellegrini, 1985), and an understanding of literal and nonliteral meaning (Garvey, 1977; Howes, Unger, & Matheson, 1992) that in turn underlies the capacity to develop theory of mind skills (Baron-Cohen, Leslie, & Frith, 1985).

According to Piaget, there are discrete stages of a child's play across development. Initially, young children exhibit sensorimotor play. In this kind of play, infants and toddlers experiment with the interaction of their bodily movements with people and objects. They may explore toys by mouthing them or throwing them to the floor (and learning about the principles of gravity). During this time, children learn cause-and-effect contingencies. This type of play is important but falls short of symbolic. Importantly, it is a building block for more sophisticated skills.

Symbolic play requires imagination, as children learn to substitute one object for another, such as using a banana as a telephone or setting up a pretend tea party. More advanced stages include mastery, when a child is in full control of his or her actions and can flexibly switch from reality to make-believe. Finally, children can explore games that require turn taking and rule following. Symbolic play remains a critical foundation for normal social growth.

LINK BETWEEN SYMBOLIC PLAY AND SYMBOLIC LANGUAGE

There is a critical link between the development of symbolic play and the use and understanding of symbolic language. Children's ability to use language in a functional or flexible manner coincides with the emergence of predictable symbolic play routines (Westby, 1980). Supporting this is Deacon's view that what sets humans apart from the rest of the species is our ability to conceptualize symbolically (Deacon, 1997). Without such ability, one might be restricted to learning via associative based strategies, like those seen in autism (Preissler, under review; Preissler & Carey, 2004, 2005). In fact, many children with ASD appear to have an associative learning style, reflected in scripting, contextual based responding, and difficulties with generalization.

Longitudinal research indicates that early joint attention, receptive language, and symbolic play are predictors of long-term outcome in autism (Sigman et al.,

1999). Westby (1980, 1991) asserts that she has not seen an evaluation in which a child's meaningful use of language has been above his or her cognitive play level. It is also imperative that children have the necessary cognitive prerequisites for the linguistic structures they are learning; otherwise, they will not utilize them in actual social situations.

Although many recent interventions focus on teaching symbolic skills, the interventions are inconsistently administered between children and by different therapists working with the same child. Therefore, teaching language use and promoting symbolic play skills should co-occur in a standard fashion. Westby (1980) points out that interventions for ASD that incorporate only operant conditioning based behavioral therapy, *without* a component of symbolic development, fall short of providing children with the symbolic cognitive skills to foster language development. This argument can be traced back to Piaget (1962), who suggested a common underlying structure behind cognitive and other areas of development. More recent theories specifically suggest a direct link between symbolic play and symbolic understanding (Doswell, Lewis, Sylva, & Boucher, 1994; Lewis, Boucher, & Astell, 1992). What are the skills necessary to support the development of symbolic understanding?

PRECURSORS TO SYMBOLIC UNDERSTANDING

To attain symbolic understanding, one must first master basic communicative behaviors beyond mere instrumental responding and appropriately begin to track the intentions of others. To succeed at these actions, an individual must show proficiency in using the joint attention skills, as they are the "precursors" to symbolic representation. Joint attention encompasses a variety of behaviors, including gaze following (following the direction of a person's eye movements as a cue to reference), social referencing (looking at another individual to share an experience), joint engagement (looking at a stimulus, then at another person to include them in the social experience), and imitation (copying the motor moves or vocalizations of another). During the time these skills develop, typical children also begin to point protoimperatively (for the purpose of requesting) and protodeclaratively (for the purpose of commenting), and they additionally show objects to adults. As speech develops, this behavior extends into verbal commenting on stimuli in the environment ("Look Mommy, a car!" or "It's red!") for the mere sake of sharing the experience. These joint behaviors are essential to learn language effectively and to learn about participation in the social world. They enable one to initially share attention, to encode social and linguistic input from the environment, and then, as skills develop, to connect interpersonally and become an effective communicator and engaging participant in the social world.

Joint attention skills are compromised in individuals with ASD and remain one of the core symptoms of the disorder. There is evidence for impairments in both production and comprehension of these behaviors (Charman, 2003). Abundant research reveals that children with ASD are notoriously poor at following another person's eye gaze (Baron-Cohen, 1995). Children with ASD both have difficulty recognizing complex facial expressions such as fear and surprise and find it problematical to infer what someone wants based on where he or she is looking. Even adults with ASD in Baron-Cohen's gaze task struggle with monitoring intent from the eye region. One reason they are not following acts of others is that they are missing the subtle cues eye expression affords (Baron-Cohen, 1995; Klin et al., 2002a, 2002b). Klin and colleagues showed that whereas typical adolescents focus on the eye region of the face to infer the content of a situation, adolescents with autism instead focus on irrelevant details, such as a light switch or the mouth region. This eye-tracking research is concordant with behavioral measures. Aspects of a scene that may appear irrelevant to a typical person may maintain relevance for a child with ASD. For instance, children with ASD will sort pictures of faces on the basis of the presence or absence of a hat, whereas typically developing children will sort them by emotional expression (Hobson, 1986). Thus, there is a fundamental deficit in seeking the relevant social stimuli in the environment, and this deficit constrains the way children with ASD learn about the world. It also affects how children with ASD expressively communicate.

Children with ASD usually begin to get their needs met by using an adult as a tool to achieve a desired item, rather than interacting with an adult as a socially responsive being. In many cases, children with ASD can use gestures for the purpose of requesting or within the context of a scripted social routine (e.g., the "itsy-bitsy spider" song). However, they do not use pointing to share their interest or comment on the environment (Mundy et al., 1993; Wetherby & Prutting, 1984).

Imitation, another joint attention skill, is either absent or quite delayed among very young children with ASD. The relation between imitation and theory of mind has been studied by several researchers (Meltzoff, 1990; Meltzoff & Gopnik, 1993; Rogers & Pennington, 1991). The ability to imitate is essential, as it allows children to make a connection between their own internal states and stimuli out in the real world (Tomasello, 1999). Early imitation involves vocalizations, body movements, and facial expression, and it allows one to communicate and get needs met without the requirement of functional speech. As more complex imitation skills develop, children use these behaviors to socially engage with others and feel a sense of connectedness. Typically developing children begin advancing on this trajectory of imitation at a very young age. If you stick out your tongue at a newborn, you will be delighted to find that the baby will mimic the action (Meltzoff & Moore, 1977, 1983). The existence of other early imitative gestures suggests that this is an innate ability. Children with ASD, however, show deficits in any gestural imitation even at later ages, including tongue protrusion, supporting the idea that the disability is present at birth, rather than acquired as a toddler. After their first birthday, young, normally developing children will imitate a bizarre act, such as turning off a light with their head, and complete actions based on the intent of an adult, such as trying to pull apart dumbbells or hang something on a peg, even when the adult's action failed (Meltzoff, 1988, 1995). Even 12-month-old typically developing infants can identify the goal of an agent and interpret its actions causally in relation to it (Gergely, Nadasdy, Csibra, & Biro, 1995). Imitation studies in ASD tend to focus on facial motor imitation, actions of objects, and manual motor movements, such as clapping hands. The results are consistent and reveal deficits across all these domains in ASD (see Charman et al., 1997).

When one has difficulty recognizing the connection between one's own movements and the movements of others, the result is impairment in social functioning, as seen in both chimpanzees and some children with autism (Tomasello, 1999). According to Tomasello, children with ASD fail to establish a "like me" connection, which is required for understanding that oneself and others possess intentions. If this connection is not established, one cannot expect an individual to ever be able to track the intentions of another.

Other joint attention skills include social referencing and joint engagement. Young, typically developing children are likely to look up at a parent when they are happily engaged in playing with a toy. The purpose of this behavior is to share the child's experience, and it is of a purely social quality (see Vygotsky, 1978). Joint engagement occurs when the child is able to look at an adult, for instance, then look at an object, and then check back to make sure the adult is attending to what the child wants her or him to attend to. This occurs a bit later in development, but both behaviors are strikingly impaired in children with ASD. Often a child with ASD fixates on an object for a long time, and adults can come and go without protest, as they appear to be irrelevant to the child's world.

In total, these joint attention skills can be considered building blocks for a formation of a "theory of mind," which includes utilizing pragmatic information, being aware of one's own mental state, and being able to monitor others' intentions. Children with autism have a general deficit in attaining a theory of mind (Baron-Cohen, 1995, 1997, 2001; Baron-Cohen et al., 1985; Frith, 2003; Gopnik, Capps, & Meltzoff, 2000; Klin, Schultz, & Cohen, 2000; Lord & Paul, 1997; Tager-Flusberg, 1997). Essentially any task related to theory of mind, such as those examining the appearance–reality distinction, gaze following, intention tracking, and false belief, reveals robust deficits in children with ASD (for a review, see Baron-Cohen, 2001).

Very young, typically developing children are sensitive to cues about referential intent such as speaker's gaze. These cues are successfully utilized to constrain the meanings of newly heard words. In a task by Baldwin (1993), children as young as 18 months of age were able to look at and follow a speaker's gaze for the referent of a novel word, even when the children were staring at an unnamed, unfamiliar object in their own hands during the labeling phase. Young, typically developing children naturally seek out social cues for language acquisition and semantic identification. The same paradigm was replicated and extended to children with ASD, who failed to use intention as a clue for word-referent identity (Baron-Cohen, Baldwin, & Crowson, 1997; Preissler & Carey, 2005). Children with ASD were more likely to map the novel word to the item they were looking at during the labeling phase. Acquiring and using language symbolically is impaired in those with ASD; to foster a natural understanding of symbols, the role of play must be examined, as the development of symbolic language arises with the development of symbolic play.

PLAY IN AUTISM

When Leo Kanner (1943) first described the symptoms of the "autistic syndrome," he included deficits in pretend play as a core feature of the disorder. As mentioned previously, play enhances social, communicative, and linguistic competence, all of which are impaired in children with ASD (Bruner, 1986). The play of children with ASD is less innovative, less symbolic, and more developmentally immature than normally developing peers (Sigman & Ungerer, 1984). As suggested by Rogers and Pennington (1991), delay in these abilities may lead to executive function deficits such as coordination and planning. Consistent with a spectrum disorder, the play skills of individual children with ASD vary widely. Compared with mental-age matched populations, children with ASD have much less restricted symbolic play in free play scenarios, but the degree of impairment of functional play is debatable (see Jarrold, Boucher, & Smith, 1993, for a review; Charman et al., 1998). Children with ASD often are passive participants in play. They offer limited initiation and approach peers in an awkward, one-sided manner (Lord, 1984; Wolfberg, 1999).

If you were to observe a child with ASD in an unstructured play situation, you would see something quite different than what you would witness if you watched a normally developing peer. The child would prefer solitude to social interaction, at times being on his or her own in the corner of the room potentially engaged in self-stimulatory behavior such as hand posturing or rocking back and forth. The child might line up toys such as blocks or cars in a particular order, rather than playing with them in an appropriate or functional manner. In this population, play is often routine and scripted instead of spontaneous and creative, and imitation skills are diminished (Frith, 2003). There are few attempts to show others the objects in their focus of attention or to share enjoyment with another person. Eye contact is limited, and therefore social referencing during play is dismally low or absent in many cases. These behaviors are far different from the seemingly effortless way typical children express themselves through play.

Children can play in a variety of ways and enact a myriad of scenarios. Some solitary play occurs with every young typical child; however, this becomes the preferred mode of play for many children with ASD, which clearly does not promote the benefits of social interaction. In parallel play, children play side by side without interaction. This is a popular form of play for children with ASD who already have the capacity for functional play. A child with ASD might be interested in other children but lack the ability for spontaneous social engagement and therefore play next to others without communication or reciprocity. With a quick glance, you might see what appears to be a normal play scenario with a child with ASD and typical peers. Upon closer inspection, you might find that the typically developing children are interacting with each other and the child with ASD is playing close by, but by himself. Notably absent is the sharing of this experience with peers. Often, a young child with ASD will even use other children as tools, climbing over them like a ladder to obtain a particular toy.

Researchers have termed the repetitive, unimaginative qualities of play as "echoplaylia" (Schuler & Wolfberg, 2000), as the same qualities apply to echolalia, a property of expressive language often seen in ASD. The quality of speech in verbal children with ASD is often bizarre, ranging from execution of memorized "scripted" material, pronoun reversals, and frequent repetitions of pieces of language heard before. This repetition of recently heard speech typifies echolalia, which has the quality of unimaginative, nonsymbolic repetition of speech sounds. It is in this way that echolalia and echoplaylia seem like parallel deficits. The play behaviors rely less on imagination and more on repeated actions, as the language relies on previously heard speech and lacks creativity.

Spontaneous pretend play in children with ASD is certainly very impoverished or noticeably absent (Charman & Baron-Cohen, 1994; Ungerer & Sigman, 1981). These play deficits in ASD have been explained by two distinct theories. One of the prevailing theories of autism is that it is a deficit in theory of mind (Frith, 2003; Baron-Cohen, 1995). According to this theory, the deficit arises from a child's failure to reflect on one's own imagination (Leslie, 1987). An executive function explanation instead posits a deficit from flexibly switching attention from reality to a pretend state (Rogers & Pennington, 1991). Regardless of the origin, the deficits in spontaneous pretend play reflect a general deficit in symbolic understanding.

SYMBOLIC UNDERSTANDING IN AUTISM

The ability to manipulate symbols, such as pictures and words, helps humans reason abstractly and process the variety of stimuli in the world efficiently, as it permits categorization and flexible use of symbols to represent items in the world, without the necessity of their physical presence. The emergence of such representational abilities is considered an adaptation (Greenspan & Lieberman, 1994). It provides children the freedom to move past mere somatic behavioral responses to environmental occurrences and form mental representations, a much more efficient method of communicating.

The process by which children with ASD acquire potentially symbolic stimuli such as words and pictures differs greatly from how typical children acquire language. Symbolic understanding of words arises in parallel with symbolic play, so fostering one affects development of the other (McCune, 1995). Therefore, the impoverished play abilities of those with ASD should affect communication strategies and the acquisition of words and pictures. Although many children with ASD can acquire a fairly substantial vocabulary, they have difficulty using this language in a flexible, spontaneous manner (as a symbolic system would predict) and fail to use it to appropriately engage socially with peers.

Consider what life might be like if you lacked the ability to understand the symbolic connection between arbitrary stimuli such as words or pictures and real objects in the world. In terms of language, if you were to encounter a new word (such as *monkey*) in the presence of a detailed scene of a zoo, you would have no way of knowing what or who the word referred to, because you are not equipped with sensitivity to social cues such as gaze and gesture. You would require many pairings of that word and its referent to learn an association between the two. According to such an account, consistent with associative learning, one would have to initially encounter the word or picture in the same context as the real-world entity (Plunkett, 1997). This may make word learning especially difficult in that words are generally spoken without their referents in plain sight, and one would expect some associatively based errors. This is precisely what happens in some cases of autism (see Frith & Happé, 1994, p. 98; Kanner, 1943), but such errors do not occur during the course of normal development (Bloom, 2000).

Empirical evidence supports this associative account (Preissler, under review; Preissler & Carey, 2004). Children with ASD and mental-age matched, typically developing toddlers were taught to pair a new word (e.g., *whisk*) with a picture of a novel stimulus (a real whisk). After several pairings, children were then given the picture they just learned a label for and the previously unseen object the picture depicted. When asked to show the experimenter "a whisk," children with autism selected the picture alone 55%. This is in contrast to typically developing children who *never* indicated the picture alone and always indicated the real object. The interpretation is that normally developing children understand that the purpose of a picture is as a symbolic representation of a real world object; when a picture is named, what is really being identified is a real referent in the world. Children with ASD are instead constructing associative pairings between pictures, words, and objects in the world and fail to connect such stimuli in a symbolic manner. Verbalizations made by some typical toddlers support the notion that symbolic understanding is developing by 2 years of age. For instance, children often labeled both the picture and object as a "whisk," which is consistent with the way adults use language. One child indicated that the real object was a "whisk" whereas the flat, two-dimensional stimulus was a "picture of whisk." Results of the population with ASD are consistent with an associative learning system, rather than a referential, symbolic system of representation. Such statistical models have been frequently endorsed in animal learning since the days of Thorndike (1898) and Pavlov (1957) and can be examined in a closely parallel situation of lexigram learning by chimps (see Savage-Rumbaugh, 1982; Savage-Rumbaugh, McDonald, Sevcik, Hopkins, & Rubert, 1986, for a referential view; Seidenberg & Petitto, 1987, for an associative explanation).

According to Vygotsky, abstract thought is initially unattainable for young children because meaning and objects are fused together as one (Vygotsky, 1978). It is therefore difficult for young children to think about a stimulus (such as a ball) when not in the presence of the real, tangible object. As children engage in pretend play, the ability to use objects or pictures to stand for other things in the world arises, and meaning is thereby separated from the physical objects themselves. This is the very conceptualization that children with ASD fail to accomplish naturally. When one uses something to stand for something else (e.g., the word *ball*, picture of a "ball," or some other entity that stands for a ball), the meaning of the substitute stimulus serves to separate the meaning between the symbolic representation and the real referent. As a result, children soon become able to think about meanings independently of the objects they represent. Hence, symbolic play maintains a crucial role in the development of abstract thought.

How to foster the development of symbolic play remains a challenge for interventionists and therapists. A key problem is the inconsistency in administration of play interventions between schools and home programs, across individual children, and even between different therapists for the same child. There is a paucity of literature about play intervention and children with ASD. Most of the literature describes case reports, which are difficult to generalize to a population already so variable (Schuler, 2003). There have been several reported interventions for preschoolers to evoke symbolic play in particular (Goldstein et al., 1988; Rogers & Lewis, 1989; Thorp, Stahmer, & Schreibman, 1995), and these represent a starting point for intervention change, but research needs to be more widespread, with a significant sample size.

When considering an educational intervention, it is essential for parents to remain aware of their child's program to ensure consistency in behavior and progress in the home. However, parents should not have to bear the burden of being 24-hour therapists. It is often difficult for parents of children with ASD to take a step back from administering therapy and just take time to be a parent and enjoy interactions with their child. Play is one way parents can interact with their children in a natural and supportive way, while fostering cognitive and social development. To facilitate play, parents can assist by organizing a specific area to address and practicing these activities. Because children with ASD respond better to a structured environment, parents can set up an activity board to select the items for play; although the setting may be initially structured, the interactions themselves should promote creativity and flexible use of materials. Siblings also play an important role and can be effective social partners and models of correct social behavior.

INTERVENTION

The National Research Council recommends targeting cognitive development and play skills as part of any effective intervention for ASD (Lord & McGee, 2001, p. 6). A child's capacity for symbolic behavior is significant in determining appropriate intervention (Sparrow, 1997). One can use imagination-provoking strategies for normal toddlers, but such indirect or independent techniques must be adapted to capture the interest of those with ASD.

It is also useful to classify the depth of social impairment to devise an appropriate level of intervention. Three subcategories of social impairment are described further by Lorna Wing (1992). The first type pertains to children who do not appear at all interested in others. They will accept necessary items such as food and drink yet use instrumental responding (e.g., using a person as a tool rather than a social being) to get their needs met. A second type of social impairment is "socially passive," in which children rarely initiate social interactions but can respond when others do the initiating. They also tend to imitate peer movements and behaviors without actually understanding what the behaviors mean. In the third type of social impairment, children with ASD may initiate interactions, but the interactions are often scripted and appear strange to others. It is important to design different therapeutic interventions for social and play skills to meet the varied needs of these children.

Many social skills training sessions fail to foster reciprocity and initiations by the child (Shuler & Wolfberg, 2000). In the current state of the art, play therapy for children with ASD tends to target individual skills that are the presumed developmental building blocks and fails to emphasize flexible modes of communication. For example, a child may be taught to look up at a person's eye region upon hearing a greeting but is unable to use this skill naturally in less structured settings or with unfamiliar individuals. This flexibility and ability to generalize skills from one setting to another work together to promote social interaction, as people are the most unpredictable stimuli one could encounter and the world is full of a myriad of environments. Wolfberg and Schuler (1993) suggest that children with ASD are more capable of interacting in play sessions than has typically been observed, and that it is the limited scope of intervention programs that fails to enhance these spontaneous play skills.

One of the most heavily followed interventions, behavioral therapy, targets a multitude of skills, including language, behavioral issues, social interaction, and social skills. This type of program is commonly referred to as applied behavioral analysis (ABA) (Lovaas, 1987; McEachin et al., 1993). This therapy is based on the principles of operant conditioning and provides a heavily structured, adult-driven environment. According to its proponents, it addresses a multitude of problems that are manifest in children with ASD, including issues of motivation, attention to task demands, and using concrete rather than abstract examples to teach skills. Reinforcement such as a child's favorite snack, access to a preferred toy, or verbal praise is administered for correct behavior throughout each session. Ideally, motivation issues are addressed on an individualized basis to maximize a child's learning potential. ABA therapy also breaks steps into small components to account for failing attention and increased levels of frustration. The therapy is usually administered in a very structured and adult-controlled environment, which tends to minimize distraction and reduce a child's overstimulation in an unpredictable setting.

In terms of play therapy, ABA therapists tend to focus on discrete, individual skills, and the therapists themselves provide the opportunities for children to play rather then allowing children the freedom to make decisions. Particular skills are taught in the context of very specific routines, such as turn taking in a certain card game with the same players or introducing a scripted line for children to rely on to initiate conversation. The skills taught may include all the precursors to symbolic understanding. However, the execution of such skills occurs in a tight environment, and as generalization is a problem for those with ASD (Tager-Flusberg, 1981), sometimes these skills that are wonderfully executed in a single environment do not translate to unfamiliar settings or unfamiliar individuals (Hadwin, Baron-Cohen, Howlin, & Hill, 1997). The goal of ABA is to provide a direct example of correct behavior and require the same performance from the child, because learning by observation alone is poor among this population. Play skills are taught so that children with ASD can be busy independently, rather than slipping into a self-created world of isolation. Again, it is important to note that ABA tends to focus on structured behavior patterns rather than spontaneous behaviors, which requires a closely regulated environment.

Another popular intervention is pivotal response training (PRT) (Koegel & Koegel, 1999). In this treatment protocol, the precursors to symbolic understanding and other capacities, such as learning contingencies, are referred to as "pivotal behaviors." Acquisition of such important behaviors allows a child to learn subsequent skills more readily. The main pivotal behaviors include motivation and responsivity to multiple cues (Koegel & Koegel, 1999). The program intends to teach children the rules of engagement, how to join in with other activities, and how to communicate. PRT can be taught to typically developing children in order to help children with ASD maintain effective social interactions and sustain attention to social stimuli. Koegel and colleagues argue that PRT has been successful in fostering language, play, and social interaction skills in children with ASD. Research on the successful generalization of such skills and applicability to unpredictable social situations is limited or characterized by the results of a few subjects (Koegel & Frea, 1993; Pierce & Schreibman, 1997). However, targeting the essential pivotal skills, which, if lacking, interfere with the acquisition of precursor symbolic skills, does emphasize the importance of an early social intervention and play behaviors. PRT also acknowledges the importance of peer interaction for developing such abilities.

A third method of play and social skills intervention is a scaffolding approach. Schuler and Wolfberg (2000) advise that for interactions with peers to be more effective, the inclusion of more able peers provides social models and ample opportunities to learn by imitation. The interventions that focus on play are driven by individual skill accomplishment, without a more cohesive conceptual framework, which the authors feel underestimates the play capacities of children with ASD. They argue that a behavioral type of approach does not acknowledge child initiatives but rather focuses on accuracy and compliance. Essentially, a therapist is likely to overlook or dismiss a child's spontaneous action if it is not expressly dictated by the behavioral program.

Of course, many educators do incorporate typical peers into play scenarios. Although this is a step in the right direction, Schuler and Wolfberg (2000) note that it is difficult to teach other professionals to implement the same supports, and there is no recourse when such scaffolding efforts fail. Essentially, there is no consistency in the interventions, and they are centered on particular cues and stimuli and driven by adult instruction, reinforcing repetitive behavior rather than encouraging spontaneous actions or expressions. Another limitation of current play skills programs incorporating behavioral techniques is the restricted environment, which does little to contradict the compulsion of children with ASD to remain isolated. This, in turn, leaves them ill prepared for inclusion in the unpredictable real social world. A final possible limitation of such direct approaches is that they may not be compatible with the reciprocal nature of symbolic representation and communication, the very skills such interventions are intended to target.

In a scaffolding approach, the use of peer models in play scenarios is essential. Typical children and novice (children with ASD) players are guided to coordinate play, with the former being both models and facilitators for shared activities. The role of the adult varies; at times, the adult sets the scene for play scenarios, and in other cases, the adult takes a step back and allows the children to build interactions. It is a guided form of intervention, but it allows for spontaneity on the part of the play participants. Of critical importance is the proper training of both the adult and the peer models so they can be effective partners for children with ASD.

RECOMMENDATIONS FOR INTERVENTION

Regardless of which intervention is implemented (and there are certainly many more not discussed in this chapter) to enhance social and play skills, children with ASD would benefit from both individual and group social skills training. Of particular importance is the role of a therapist or peer to model appropriate behavior. Peer groups should include a mix of special needs children and typically developing peers without social difficulties, so children with ASD can learn and practice appropriate social skills. As children with ASD do not have the natural inclination to pay attention to and monitor social stimuli in the world, they must therefore be specifically taught the skills that are the foundation of social interaction: imitation, gaze following, the interpretation of facial expression, and how to modify others' and their own social behaviors. The venues to teach such skills include social stories, role modeling, and videos, all coupled with extensive positive reinforcement and intermodal supports (e.g., visual and verbal). Consistent with each child's therapeutic intervention plan, distinct target behaviors need to be identified and addressed in a stepwise fashion. It is essential to teach these skills in a variety of manners and settings to promote generalization of the acquired skills and reduce dependence on particular cues and stimuli. It is also imperative to use toys appropriate for a child's mental age rather than chronological age and to begin with scenarios that are not more advanced than a child's current capacity.

The format of both group play and social skills training should be initially quite structured, because children with ASD typically fare better in a predictable and familiar environment (Dawson & Osterling, 1997; Harris & Handleman, 1985). It is important to specifically let the child know what behavior is required and then to heavily reinforce that behavior when observed. For a child who has learned the precursors to symbolic functioning and has emerging language, a play program emphasizing the flexible use of such skills should be implemented. The level of structure can be faded out gradually, but children at any stage must be allowed to make decisions themselves and be given every opportunity for spontaneous play interactions.

There are several stages in typical development that children naturally progress through to attain linguistic communication. The first transition is to intentional communication, which is using conventional behaviors to affect another person, as when a baby uses eye gaze to express desires. The second transition is to symbolic communication, where children use words and gestures to represent objects. The final stage is linguistic communication, incorporating syntax, multiword constructions, and semantic relevance. If children with ASD have difficulty with the initial stage, how can we expect them to naturally proceed to effective linguistic communication?

Interventionists must be careful to target a child's specific needs to develop an appropriate program. Initiation strategies in general are appropriate for preverbal children with ASD, whereas teaching verbal initiations should obviously be focused only on children with speech. Despite the commonsense aspect of the previous statements, many interventions simply overreach a child's communicative abilities and therefore affect a child's social progress either minimally or not at all.

Speech and language skills are typically paramount in therapeutic interventions, and the importance of peer play is frequently underrated. When supported by an adult or peers, studies show that children with ASD can engage in more complex forms of play (Greenspan & Wieder, 1997; Lord & Hopkins, 1986; Wolfberg & Schuler, 1993). These research reports suggest the essential nature of structured supports for promoting play behavior, with the full acknowledgment that intervention research studies testing these hypotheses are limited.

POLICY IMPLICATIONS

Public policies are standards by which scarce public resources are allocated to almost unlimited needs (Gallagher, 1994). This is especially valid in the case of ASD, as the incidence of the disorder is at an all-time high, prompting the classification of national epidemic. Parents of children with ASD often fight an uphill battle to gain appropriate services for their children, and the money is stretched tight within educational districts.

Currently, policy items for children with ASD include zero reject (a free public education), nondiscriminatory evaluation, an individualized education program (IEP), the least restrictive environment, due process, and parental participation. The least restrictive environment clause specifies that, when appropriate, children with ASD should be included in typical classrooms. One pitfall to this clause is that many children with ASD often are not yet equipped to make the transition to a classroom flooded with stimulation, and sometimes the precursors to effective communication have not been established.

One significant challenge to the execution of policy items is the actual implementation of successful IEP programs, because many parents are uninformed of their rights and the IEP varies from district to district. If not specifically argued for, the programs that are implemented for many children are impoverished, and the services provided meet only the minimum required standards. There is tremendous variation in the quality of the program and the flexibility of the district.

Because we know that early intervention provides the best possible outcome for those with ASD, it is essential that the early intervention programs target each child's specific needs but also follow a standard protocol for targeting the skills we now know are critical for giving children the best possible outcome over time. The precursors to symbolic knowledge that enable children to engage socially with peers are particularly important and require a specific mandate.

One policy implication regards free early screening for all children at risk, specifically siblings of children already identified with ASD and families with a history of social disabilities, mental retardation, or mental disorders. Retrospective research based on videotapes of affected children at their first birthday party, before they were diagnosed, shows impairments that skilled psychologists and other professionals can detect. This type of research, coupled with the recent onslaught of research targeting siblings of those with autism and the efficacy of early intervention programs, indicates that early detection is not only feasible but also imperative (Klin et al., 2000; Werner, Dawson, Osterline, & Dinno, 2000). Screening instruments used to diagnose the disorder, such as ADI, ADOS, and the Mullen Scales of Early Learning, have been applied to children under the age of 3 and recently under the age of 2. These early diagnoses tend to be stable over time.

Another implication is the specificity of early intervention programs. Joint attention skills such as gaze monitoring, imitation, and social referencing are imperative for the development of symbolic and abstract thought and the proper development of linguistic competence, thus these skills must be targeted in all early intervention programs. The power of play in assisting the development of such skills is well established (Hirsh-Pasek & Golinkoff, 2003). Incorporating a standard play and social skills intervention is essential to provide a child with ASD the best possible chance of developing language and symbolic thought.

A third policy implication should mandate appropriate peer training for social skills groups, as research indicates that peers can be invaluable for offering support, reinforcing social interactions, and helping to elicit social initiations. Often, typical peers are included with children with ASD with good intentions, but the interventionists fail to prepare the typical peers with the appropriate skills to effectively interact and elicit interaction from such children with special needs. Because the least restrictive environment clause tends to move children with ASD into typical classrooms at times prematurely, the normally developing peers must be equipped to interact with this population with special needs.

CONCLUSION

Children with ASD have impairments in social, behavioral, and communicative domains. The ability to detect ASD autism has increased in recent years, and although it may be tentative, children under the age of 2 can now be given the diagnosis of autism spectrum disorder (Lord & McGee, 2001). This early detection is critical, given the wealth of information revealing that early intervention predicts a better outcome (Dawson & Osterling, 1997; Gallagher, 1994; McEachin et al., 1993). Children with ASD provided with early therapeutic interventions are more likely to become verbal, have fewer behavioral problems, and have an opportunity to learn many more daily adaptive and educational skills.

The most effective mode of treatment is a very specific, intense program of intervention administered as early as possible. There are many direct behavioral treatments proven to effectively teach children skills such as compliance, increase receptive and expressive language, and target motor skills in an ordered, structured environment. However, these skills are often not generalized to novel settings and stimuli and lack a certain social quality. An effective part of any therapeutic program should incorporate play therapy. Play is an effective modality to teach children the precursors to symbolic thinking and the dynamics of social interaction. With structured supports and trained peers to enhance and facilitate communication, play can be an immense resource to build symbolic and social skills in children with ASD.

References

American Psychiatric Association. (2000). *Diagnostic and statistical manual of mental disorders* (4th ed.). Washington, DC: Author.

Baldwin, D. A. (1993). Infants' ability to consult the speaker for clues to word reference. *Journal of Child Language, 20*, 395–418.

Baron-Cohen, S. (1995). *Mindblindness: An essay on autism and theory of mind*. Cambridge, MA: MIT Press.

Baron-Cohen, S. (2001). Theory of mind and autism: A review. *Special Issue of the International Review of Mental Retardation, 23*, 169.

Baron-Cohen, S., Baldwin, D. A., & Crowson, M. (1997). Do children with autism use the speaker's direction of gaze strategy to crack the code of language? *Child Development, 68*, 48–57.

Baron-Cohen, S., Leslie, A., & Frith, U. (1985). Does the autistic child have a "theory of mind"? *Cognition, 21*, 37–46.

Bloom, P. (2000). *How children learn the meanings of words*. Cambridge, MA: MIT Press.

Bruner, J. (1986). *Actual minds, possible worlds*. Cambridge, MA: Harvard University Press.

Charman, T. (2003). Why is joint attention a pivotal skill in autism? *Philosophical Transactions of the Royal Society, 358*, 315–324.

Charman, T., & Baron-Cohen, S. (1994). Another look at imitation in autism. *Development and Psychopathology, 6*, 403–413.

Charman, T., Swettenham, J., Baron-Cohen, S., Cox, A., Baird, G., & Drew, A. (1997). Infants with autism: An investigation of empathy, pretend play, joint attention, and imitation. *Developmental Psychology, 33*, 781–789.

Charman, T., Swettenham, J., Baron-Cohen, S., Cox, A., Baird, G., & Drew, A. (1998). An experimental investigation of social-cognitive abilities in infants with autism: Clinical implications. *Infant Mental Health Journal, 19*(2), 260–275.

Dawson, G., & Osterling, J. (1997). Early intervention in autism. In M. J. Guralnick (Ed.), *The effectiveness of early intervention* (pp. 307–326). Baltimore: Paul H. Brookes.

Deacon, T. W. (1997). *The symbolic species: The co-evolution of language and the brain*. New York: W. W. Norton.

Doswell, G., Lewis, V., Sylva, K., & Boucher, J. (1994). Validational data on the Warwick symbolic play test. *European Journal of Disorders of Communication, 29*, 289–298.

Ervin-Tripp, S. (1991). Play in language development. In B. Scales, M. Almy, A. Nicolopoulou, & S. Ervin-Tripp (Eds.), *Play and the social context of development in early care and education* (pp. 84–97). New York: Teachers College Press.

Folstein, S. E., & Santangelo, S. L. (2000). Does Asperger syndrome aggregate in families? In A. Klin, F. R. Volkmar, & S. S. Sparrow (Eds.), *Asperger syndrome* (pp. 159–171). New York: Guilford.

Frith, U. (2003). *Autism: Explaining the enigma* (2nd rev. ed.). Oxford, UK: Blackwell.

Frith, U., & Happé, F. (1994). Language and communication in autistic disorders. *Philosophical Transactions of the Royal Society, series B,* 346, 97–104.

Gallagher, J. (1994). Policy designed for diversity: New initiatives for children with disabilities. In D. Bryant & M. Graham (Eds.), *Implementing early intervention* (pp. 336–350). New York: Guilford.

Garvey, C. (1977). *Play*. Cambridge, MA: Harvard University Press.

Gergely, G., Nádasy, Z., Csibra, G., & Bíró, S. (1995). Taking the intentional stance at 12 months of age. *Cognition, 56,* 165–193.

Goldstein, H., Wickstrum, S., Hoyson, M., Jamieson, B., & Odom, S. L. (1988). Effects of sociodramatic play training on social and communicative interaction. *Education and Treatment of Children, 11,* 97–117.

Gopnik, A., Capps, L., & Meltzoff, A. N. (2000). Early theories of mind: What the theory can tell us about autism. In S. Baron-Cohen, H. Tager-Flusberg, & D. Cohen (Eds.), *Understanding other minds: Perspectives from autism and other disorders* (pp. 50–72). New York: Oxford University Press.

Greenspan, S. I., & Lieberman, A. F. (1994). Representational elaboration and differentiation: A clinical-quantitative approach to the clinical assessment of 2-to-4 year olds. In A. Slade & D. Wold (Eds.), *Children at play* (pp. 3–32). New York: Oxford University Press.

Greenspan, S. I., & Wieder, S. (1997). Developmental patterns and outcomes in infants and children with disorders in relating and communicating: A chart review of 200 cases of children with autistic spectrum diagnoses. *The Journal of Developmental and Learning Disorders, 1,* 87–141.

Hadwin, J., Baron-Cohen, S., Howlin, P., & Hill, K. (1997). Does teaching theory of mind have an effect on the ability to develop conversation in children with autism? *Journal of Autism and Developmental Disorders, 27,* 519–539.

Hallmayer, J., Rogers, T., Kalaydjieva, L., Petersen, P. B., Nicholas, P., Pingree, C., et al. (in press). Absence of linkage to chromosome 15q11-q13 markers in ninety multiplex families with autism. *American Journal of Human Genetics: Neuropsychiatric Genetics.*

Harris, S. L., & Handleman, J. S. (1985). *Preschool education programs for children with autism.* Austin, TX: PRO-ED.

Hirsh-Pasek, K., & Golinkoff, R. (2003). Einstein never used flash cards. Emmaus, PA: Rodale.

Hobson, R. P. (1986). The autistic child's appraisal of expressions of emotion. *Journal of Child Psychology and Psychiatry, 27,* 321–342.

Howes, C., Unger, O., & Matheson, C. C. (1992). The collaborative construction of pretend: Social pretend play functions. Albany: State University of New York Press.

Ingram, J. L., Stodgell, C. J., Hyman, S. L., Figlewicz, D. A., Weitkamp, L. R., & Rodier, P. M. (2000). Discovery of allelic variants of *HOXA1* and *HOXB1*: Genetic susceptibility to autism spectrum disorders. *Teratology, 62,* 393–405.

Jarrold, C., Boucher, J., & Smith, P. (1993). Symbolic play in autism: A review. *Journal of Autism and Developmental Disorders, 23*(2), 281–307.

Kanner, L. (1943). Autistic disturbances of affective contact. *Nervous Child, 2,* 217–250.

Klin, A., Jones, W., Schultz, R. T., Volkmar, F. R., & Cohen, D. J. (2002a). Defining and quantifying the social phenotype in autism. *American Journal of Psychiatry, 159*(6), 895–908.

Klin, A., Jones, W., Schultz, R., Volkmar, F., & Cohen D. (2002b) Visual fixation patterns during viewing of naturalistic social situations as predictors of social competence in individuals with autism. *Archives of General Psychiatry 59,* 809–816.

Klin, A., Schultz, R., & Cohen, D. (2000). Theory of mind in action: Developmental perspectives on social neuroscience. In S. Baron-Cohen, H. Tager-Flusberg, & D. Cohen

(Eds.), *Understanding other minds: Perspectives from developmental neuroscience* (2nd ed.). (pp. 357–388). Oxford: Oxford University Press.

Koegel, L. K., & Koegel, R. L. (1999). Pivotal response intervention I: Overview of approach. *Journal of the Association for the Severely Handicapped, 24*, 174–185.

Koegel, R. I., & Frea, W. D. (1993). Treatment of social behavior in autism through the modification of pivotal social skills. *Journal of Applied Behavioural Analysis, 26*, 369–377.

Leslie, A. M. (1987). Pretense and representation: The origins of theory of mind. *Psychological Review, 94*, 412–426.

Lewis, V., Boucher, J., & Astell, A. (1992). The assessment of symbolic play in young children: A prototype test. *European Journal of Disorders of Communication, 27*, 231–245.

Lord, C. (1984). The development of peer relations in children with autism. In F. J. Morrison, C. Lord, & D. P. Keating (Eds.), *Advances in applied developmental psychology* (pp. 165–229). New York: Academic Press.

Lord, C., & Hopkins, J. M. (1986). The social behavior of autistic children with younger and same-age nonhandicapped peers. *Journal of Autism and Developmental Disorders, 16*, 249–263.

Lord, C., & McGee, J. P. (2001). *Educating children with autism.* Washington, DC: National Academy Press.

Lord, C., & Paul, R. (1997). Language and communication in autism. In D. J. Cohen & F. R. Volkmar (Eds.), *Handbook of autism and pervasive developmental disorders* (12th ed., pp. 195–225). New York: John Wiley & Sons.

Lovaas, O. I. (1987). Behavioral treatment and normal educational and intellectual functioning in young autistic children. *Journal of Consulting and Clinical Psychology, 55*, 3–9.

McCune, L. (1995). A normative study of representational play at the transition to language. *Developmental Psychology, 31*, 198–206.

McEachin, J. J., Smith, T., & Lovaas, O. I. (1993). Long-term outcome for children with autism who received early intensive behavioral treatment. *American Journal on Mental Retardation, 97*, 359–372.

Meltzoff, A. (1988). Infant imitation after a 1–week delay: Longterm memory for novel acts and multiple stimuli. *Developmental Psychology, 24*, 470–476.

Meltzoff, A. (1990). Towards a developmental cognitive science: The implications of cross-modal matching and imitation for the development of representation and memory in infancy. In A. Diamond (Ed.), *The development and neural bases of higher cognitive functions. Annals of the New York Academy of Sciences,* Vol. 608, 1–31. New York: New York Academy of Sciences.

Meltzoff, A. N. (1995). Understanding the intentions of others: Re-enactment of intended acts by 18-month-old children. *Developmental Psychology, 31,* 838–850.

Meltzoff, A. N., & Gopnik, A. (1993). The role of imitation in understanding persons and developing theories of mind. In S. Baron-Cohen, H. Tayer-Flusberg, & D. Cohen (Eds.), *Understanding other minds: Perspectives from* autism (pp. 335–366). Oxford, UK: Oxford University Press.

Meltzoff, A. N., & Moore, M. K. (1977). Imitation of facial and manual gestures by human neonates. *Science, 198*, 75–78.

Meltzoff, A. N., & Moore, M. K. (1983). Newborn infants imitate adult facial gestures. *Child Development, 54,* 702–709.

Mundy, P., Sigman, M., & Kasari, C. (1993). The theory of mind and joint attention deficits in autism. In S. Baron-Cohen, H. Tayer-Flusberg, & D. Cohen (Eds.), *Understanding other minds: Perspectives from autism* (pp. 181–201). Oxford, UK: Oxford University Press.

Pavlov, I. P. (1957). *Experimental psychology and other essays.* New York: Philosophical Library.

Pellegrini, A. D. (1985, March). *The effects of age and play context on the narrative organization of children's play.* Paper presented at Society for Research in Child Development, Toronto.

Pellegrini, A. D., & Smith, P. K. (1993). School recess: Implications for education and development. *Review of Educational Research, 63,* 51–69.

Piaget, J. (1962). *Play, dreams, and imitation in childhood.* New York: W. W. Norton.

Pierce, K., & Schreibman, L. (1997). Multiple peer use of pivotal response training to increase social behaviors of classmates with autism: Results from trained and untrained peers. *Journal of Applied Behavioural Analysis, 30,* 157–160.

Plunkett, K. (1997). Theories of early language acquisition. *Trends in Cognitive Sciences, 1,* 146–153.

Preissler, M. A. *Associative learning of pictures and words by children with autism.* Manuscript submitted for publication.

Preissler, M. A., & Carey, S. (2004). Do both pictures and words function as symbols for 18- and 24-month-old children? *Journal of Cognition and Development, 5,* 185–212.

Preissler, M. A., & Carey, S. (2005). The role of inferences about referential intent in word learning: Evidence from autism. *Cognition, 97,* B13–23.

Rogers, S. J., & Lewis, H. (1989). An effective day treatment model for young children with pervasive developmental disorders. *Journal of the Academy of Child and Adolescent Psychiatry, 28,* 207–219.

Rogers, S. J., & Pennington, B. F. (1991). A theoretical approach to the deficits in infantile autism. *Development and Psychopathology, 3*(2), 137–163.

Savage-Rumbaugh, S. (1982). Acquisition of functional symbol usage in apes and children. In H. L. Roitblat, T. G. Bever, & H. S. Terrace (Eds.), *Animal cognition* (pp. 291–310). Hillsdale, NJ: Erlbaum.

Savage-Rumbaugh, S., McDonald, K., Sevcik, R. A., Hopkins, W. D., & Rubert, E. (1986). Spontaneous symbol acquisition and communicative use by pygmy chimpanzees (*Pan paniscus*). *Journal of Experimental Psychology: General, 115*(3), 211–235.

Schuler, A. (2003). Beyond echoplaylia: Promoting language in children with autism. *Autism, 7,* 455–469.

Schuler, A., & Wolfberg, P. (2000). Promoting peer play and socialization. In A. Wetherby & B. Prizant (Eds.), *Autism spectrum disorders: A transactional developmental perspective* (pp. 251–278). Baltimore: Paul H. Brooks.

Seidenberg, M. S., & Petitto, L. A. (1987). Communication, symbolic communication, and language: Comment on Savage-Rumbaugh, McDonald, Sevcik, Hopkins, and Rupert (1986). *Journal of Experimental Psychology: General, 116,* 279–287.

Sigman, M., Ruskin, E., Arveile, S., Corona, R., Dissanayake, C., Espinosa, M., et al. (1999). Continuity and change in the social competence of children with autism, Down syndrome, and developmental delays. *Monographs of the Society for Research in Child Development, 64,* 1–114.

Sigman, M., & Ungerer, J. A. (1984). Cognitive and language skills in autistic, mentally retarded, and normal children. *Developmental Psychology, 20,* 293–302.

Sparrow, S. (1997). Developmentally based assessments. In D. J. Cohen & F. R. Volkmar (Eds.), *Handbook of autism and pervasive developmental disorders* (pp. 911–947). New York: John Wiley & Sons.

Tager-Flusberg, H. (1997). The role of theory of mind in language acquisition: Contributions from the study of autism. In L. Adamson and M. A. Romski (Eds.), *Research on communication and language disorders: Contributions to theories of language development* (pp. 133–158). Baltimore: Paul Brookes.

Tager-Flusberg, H. (1981). On the nature of linguistic functioning in early infantile autism. *Journal of Autism and Developmental Disorders, 11,* 45–56.

Thorndike, E. L. (1898). Animal intelligence: An experimental study of the associative processes in animals. *Psychological Review Monograph Supplements, No. 8.* New York: Macmillan.

Thorp, D. M., Stahmer, A. C., & Schreibman, L. (1995). Effects of sociodramatic play training on children with autism. *Journal of Autism and Developmental Disorders, 25,* 265–282.

Tomasello, M. (1995). Joint attention as social cognition. In C. Moore and C. J. Dunham (Eds.), *Joint attention: Its origins and role in development* (pp. 103–130). Hillsdale, NJ: Erlbaum.

Tomasello, M. (1999). *The cultural origins of human cognition.* Cambridge, MA: Harvard University Press.

Tomasello, M. (2000). Perceiving intentions and learning words in the second year of life. In M. Bowerman & S. Levison (Eds.), *Language acquisition and conceptual development* (pp. 132–158). Cambridge: Cambridge University Press.

Ungerer, J., & Sigman, M. (1981). Symbolic play and language comprehension in autistic children. *Journal of the American Academy of Child Psychiatry, 20,* 318–337.

Volkmar, F. R. (2005). *Handbook of autism and pervasive developmental disorders.* New York: Wiley.

Vygotsky, L. S. (1966). Development of higher mental functions. In A. N. Leontyev, A. R. Luria, & A. Smirnov (Eds.), *Psychological research in the USSR* (pp. 11–45). Moscow: Progress.

Vygotsky, L. S. (1978). *Mind in society.* Cambridge, MA: Harvard University Press.

Werner, E., Dawson, G., Osterline, J., & Dinno, N. (2000). Brief report: Recognition of autism spectrum disorder before one year of age: A retrospective study based on home videotapes. *Journal of Autism and Developmental Disorders, 30,* 157–162.

Westby, C. (1980). Assessment of cognitive and language abilities through play. *Language Speech and Hearing Sciences in Schools, 11,* 154–168.

Westby, C. (1991). A scale for assessing children's pretend play. In C. Schaefer, K. Gitlin, & A. Sandgrund (Eds.), *Play diagnosis and assessment* (pp. 131–161). New York: Wiley.

Wetherby, A. M., & Prutting, C. A. (1984). Profiles of communicative and cognitive-social abilities in autistic children. *Journal of Speech and Hearing Research, 27,* 364–377.

Wing, L. (1992). Manifestations of social problems in high functioning autistic people. In E. Schopler & G. Meisbov (Eds.), *High functioning individuals with autism.* New York: Plenum Press.

Wolfberg, P. (1999). *Play and imagination in children with autism.* New York: Teachers College Press.

Wolfberg, P., & Schuler, A. L. (1993). Integrated play groups: A model for promoting the social and cognitive dimensions of play in children with autism. *Journal of Autism and Developmental Disorders, 23,* 467–489.

Zigler, E., Singer, D. G., & Bishop-Josef, S. J. (2004). *Children's play: The roots of reading.* Washington, DC: Zero to Three.

13

Epilogue: Learning to Play and Learning Through Play

JEROME L. SINGER

The editors of this book posed a challenge at the outset. In effect, is children's obvious enjoyment of play a pleasant pastime with little significance for effective cognitive and social skill development? Or can play be viewed as an intrinsic learning process, actually a critical method for learning? Chapter 2 provided a thought-provoking review of the way the government call for the No Child Left Behind program and its legislative implementation led many early childhood educators to emphasize drill-based literacy instruction even in preschool settings. Many preschool directors have therefore cut the time commitment for play as a part of children's early experience. Although there is reasonably good evidence that guided forms of pretend and sociodramatic play have proven useful in school settings (J. Singer & Lythcott, 2002), the survey of Head Start programs and other early childhood care settings provided in chapter 2 points to a zeitgeist that constrains or completely eliminates various forms of play in favor of formalized instruction.

The succeeding chapters of this book then address the theoretical and empirical relevance of children's games of mastery, rule play, or pretending for the admittedly important task of preparing preschool children for effective school entry and for the smooth transition to skills in reading, arithmetic, and civic knowledge. In this closing chapter, I attempt to establish a broader context for the role of play in child development and point to implications from the separate chapters that offer answers on the value of children's play as a feature of effective learning through early and middle childhood.

PLAY AS A CRITICAL FEATURE OF CHILDHOOD ADAPTATION

Consider the tasks and confrontations with the "booming, buzzing confusion" of the world that a growing infant and preschool child must cope with early on. We may roughly classify coping mechanisms and tasks to be mastered as "givens" or "wired-in" abilities, versus those abilities that emerge through the child's learning and practice alone or with the aid of adult caregivers. The relatively innate mechanisms include crying to signal distress and, within about 2 months, smiling to signal pleasure, sucking, grasping, and visual and other forms of sensory exploration. Direct contact with the physical surroundings is critical, as the neurologist Frank Wilson (1998) has shown in his fine study of how touching and various forms of manual contact influence brain function and even language or culture. Of course, children must also learn to crawl, to stand, to walk, to respond to facial expressions of the people around them, to laugh reciprocally, and to signal their major needs early on by pointing, directed gazing, or means other than screaming and weeping. These kinds of abilities involve solitary practice but also benefit from the assistance, informal guidance, or even sometimes direct instruction of parents, other caregivers, or siblings.

In contrast to these innate sensory-motor activities, a new form of behavior, play, emerges in the second and third years. Early writers such as Vygotsky (1978), Lewin (1935), Piaget (1962), and Luria (1932) and many recent researchers propose that play is an adaptive, organized means by which children learn to make sense of their physical and social environment. Through play, they gain a feeling of control over the bigness and complexities they confront. They also learn to overcome fears as they create manageable *frames* to enclose scary situations, animals, or people they encounter in real life or on the TV screen. Consider the difference between children's random running, jumping, and repetitive mastery efforts, on one hand, and the apparently greater efficiency of cognitive and social skill mastery that is consequent on their introducing game structure into their movements, on the other. Chapters 4 and 5 point up the self-regulatory and literacy readiness facilitations produced by the special properties of game play, especially pretending and make-believe. More reviews of theory and research on the adaptive significance of imaginative or symbolic play (to use Piaget's term) may be found in Johnson, Christie, and Wardle (2005) and D. Singer and J. Singer (1990, 2005). Early pretend play, when well practiced and joined with constructive interactions with other children, enhances awareness of reality–fantasy distinctions. It also contributes to the child's development of a theory of mind (Harris, 2000; Leslie, 1987; Schwebel, Rosen, & Singer, 1999). This much-researched construct deals with the emergence around age 4 of children's awareness that their own perceptions or beliefs may not be the same as those of other children or adults. It also seems linked to some degree to the experience of make-believe play with other children.

As the talking aloud of children fades in the middle childhood period, we see the fuller emergence of private imagery and the child's awareness of his or her own stream of consciousness. Such awareness of one's private ability to control or vary one's thoughts may prove in the interest of planfulness, enjoyable fantasy, or heightened self-knowledge (D. Singer & J. Singer, 1990; J. Singer, 1973, 2006; Vygotsky, 1978).

Play, then, may well serve a variety of evolutionary adaptive features for the growing child. As Pellegrini and Holmes's (see chapter 3) own research and their review of the literature suggests, at a basic level, the chance for children to break out of the structured school regimen for a brief period to create their own games enhances their learning opportunities. Many years ago, the research directed by Kurt Lewin on authoritarian, laissez-faire, and democratic classrooms demonstrated that more constructive classroom atmospheres resulted when children's school behavior in recess and free play had moderate adult guidance (Lewin, Lippitt, & White, 1939). Further support for Pellegrini and Holmes's research is suggested by an international study of educational systems that ranked the Finnish schools as the world's best, based on students' test performance. Among several distinctive features of these schools is the requirement of a 15-minute recess with play opportunities every hour (Alvarez, 2005). Actually, as our own research and work described by Berk and her colleagues in chapter 5 suggests, the opportunities to shift from adult guidance to self-guided play may be critical in creating attitudes conducive to self-regulation of behavior and emotion in children (see also chapters by Biblow and by Freyberg in J. Singer, 1973; D. Singer & J. Singer, 1990).

The child-controlled storytelling of pretend and make-believe play in the preschool years, carried over either silently or in group play form in middle childhood, not only may be associated with greater delay of gratification or reduced aggression in children but also yields benefits in effective language usage and literacy readiness and may as well be associated with increased creative ability (Russ, 1993, 2004). (See chapters 4 and 6, as well as J. Singer & D. Singer, 1981.)

LEARNING TO PLAY

Almost all of the chapters of this book describe research studies and observational evidence attesting to the adaptive learning that may be a consequence of children's play. Before we review these conclusions, however, we must recognize that children's play itself in its most constructive forms requires enhancement chiefly through various forms of adult intervention. Most child development specialists would agree that the tendency to play is innate and that it emerges naturally and sequentially in children who are free of serious brain disorders like autism (see chapter 12) social neglect, and trauma (see chapter 11). For play to flourish as a truly enjoyable, cognitive, and socially adaptive human ability, it requires (to use Vygotsky's term) the scaffolding support of one or more concerned adults. This seems especially true for imaginative play because its delicate, internalized structure seems to feed on a combination of parental approval and support, guidance into plot content, and, at least initially, modeling of parental playfulness and storytelling (Levenstein, 2005; Shmukler, 1981; D. Singer & J. Singer, 1990, 2005; J. Singer, 1993). In a study I conducted more than 40 years ago with 9-year-olds, those children who showed more imaginative play skills and self-regulatory ability proved to have a close association with at least one parent who had engaged in storytelling and play modeling (J. Singer, 1961).

Our contributors bring out the importance for children of learning to play with some adult guidance in various ways. Chapter 5 builds on Vygotsky's concept of the proximal zone of development but describes further recent studies pointing to how adult interventions can enhance imaginative playfulness. Chapter 6 calls attention to the fact that many parents from disadvantaged backgrounds reported that no one played with them as children and that it did not occur to them to play with their own preschoolers. They benefited from brief training sessions, which they then transferred to their children. Chapter 4 calls attention to a series of studies such as those directed by Eli Saltz (Saltz, Dixon, & Johnson, 1977) in Detroit and Sara Smilansky (1968) in Israel, where children from impoverished or culturally disadvantaged backgrounds increased their sociodramatic play following adult-guided instructions. Chapter 11 describes careful observational study of mother–child dyads in families exposed to traumatic experiences, where adults use a playful interaction that evokes valuable responses in the children. Chapter 9 calls attention to some ways that parents are increasingly using TV viewing or home videos with very young children to stimulate playful behavior as well as cognitive learning. Chapter 10 carries this emphasis further with older children and early teens, who are eased into constructive computer usage and play as a part of club activities at the Massachusetts Institute of Technology. Chapter 7 carries teaching a playful orientation to children a step further toward developing an internalized narrative orientation by the use of journal keeping and by fostering creative self-descriptions. Chapter 12 addresses the problem of dealing with children who have various forms of autism that are known to limit natural imaginative play. Through carefully guided interventions, the children gain new abilities for playfulness.

In summary, our contributors make clear that a critical first step in helping children use play situations for effective learning is for adults to guide them into enriching and varying their inborn interest in and desire to play. Children eagerly responded to such guidance. We can benefit from more research that identifies particular approaches to enhancing play at different ages, for children at different stages of cognitive development, and for children exposed to socioeconomic stressors or to brain disorders. Although books describe specific approaches for teaching play to children at home (D. Singer & J. Singer, 2001) or in school (McCaslin, 1984; Rosenberg, 1987), I believe the time may be ripe for a handbook or comprehensive review presenting a series of age- and condition-appropriate guides for parents, teachers, or other concerned adults who want to teach children to enhance their play, whether in its mastery, pretense, or rule-game forms.

LEARNING THROUGH PLAY

I have stressed the importance of adult intervention to enhance children's play skills because many children from educationally or economically disadvantaged families may be especially at risk in sustaining effective utilization of their natural play tendencies. A majority of children, perhaps because of early parental attachment and encouragement, may be ready to respond to play opportunities for learning. Let us turn now to how parents, teachers, and other caregivers may make use of play, especially in its pretend and make-believe form, to foster learning that is aimed, first of all, at fundamental school readiness skills and then toward broader features of cognitive and social adaptation.

We have already seen in chapter 5 that a critical beginning for children's readiness to sustain the civility and orderliness needed in the classroom may emerge through role-playing and other make-believe play. Their grasp of sequencing, of cooperation, and of attention to others is enhanced by the miniature plots and necessary characterizations of an unfolding imaginative narrative. Chapters 4 and 7 also demonstrate ways in which journal keeping (even in scribbling or drawing form) or extended sociodramatic and role-playing games point children toward sequencing and toward sharing, cooperation, and other good-citizen behaviors. Chapters 6 and 9 emphasize the importance of politeness modeling by real adults or children in videos that many children now watch at younger and younger ages. Our own research at Yale on the *Mister Rogers' Neighborhood* television show, along with other work on the late Fred Rogers's fine series, has demonstrated the importance of children's exposure to thoughtful, responsible, and cooperative actions in a storytelling and play context (Tower, Singer, Singer, & Biggs, 1979). Our studies of the *Barney and Friends* Public Broadcasting preschool series demonstrate that independent raters can document regular instances of politeness and cooperative play behavior in every episode. These studies also attest to how exposure, even in the vicarious TV world, carries over into children's play and classroom activities (J. Singer & D. Singer, 1998). In several of our earlier studies, observers scoring children's spontaneous floor play in preschool found that children who engaged more frequently in imaginative play were also more likely to be cooperative with adults and capable of persistence and less likely to be aggressive or disruptive in that setting or at home (D. Singer & J. Singer, 1990; J. Singer & D. Singer, 1981).

Imaginative play opportunities, both in spontaneous occurrence and as a consequence of adult guidance, also help prepare children for the necessary discipline, self-restraint, and delayed gratification of the school, as chapter 5 makes clear. What, then, of the very specific content areas that are critical in the early schooling of the very young? Chapter 4 examines the specifics of beginning literacy, which include acquisition of new vocabulary, understanding how printed words go with speech sounds and meanings, the beginning of word sounding, an early sense of numeracy, and other features of reading and writing. That chapter suggests a series of ways in which imaginative play opens the child to curiosity about written material and to the linkages of words, sounds, and meanings. It also affords practice opportunities through well-motivated play reenactments that may be more efficient than formal drill in reinforcing memory for the processes involved in reading. Words are then more naturally fitted into contexts, a demonstrably superior form of spoken or written vocabulary or number acquisition and retention. Chapter 7 carries this further by fostering journal keeping and encouraging children to take control of writing and storytelling. In chapter 6, the pretend games, such as Rhyme Store, Octopus Treasure, and Trip to Mars, provide the children with demonstrations and practice opportunities for new vocabulary, phonemic sounding through rhyming, and counting. Chapter 8's creative play opportunities show how even subtler features of arithmetic or mathematics can be inculcated to children in delightful playful formats. A spoonful of make-believe sugar does indeed help the medicine of math go down!

In chapter 10, Resnick's work with somewhat older children uses imaginative game play in the context of introducing and encouraging computer skills. The establishment of a club atmosphere and the involvement of the children in playful and cooperative group play interactions demonstrate in vivid fashion that computer skills can be acquired even by children whose family backgrounds have been impoverished, stressful, and lacking a computer-ready atmosphere.

Chapters 11 and 12 focus even more on at-risk children, the socially traumatized, and the brain disordered. Carefully managed mother–child interactions that take on a playful form provide children exposed to violence new meaning structures and vocabulary, as well as readiness to use literacy skills and emotional awareness. The work with children who have Asperger's syndrome and autism that Preissler describes points to the ways playful teaching by extrafamilial caregivers may not only enhance vocabulary and reading skills but also help these children and adolescents improve their ability to identify their own and others' emotions.

It should be clear from the chapters in this book that children's play yields numerous learning opportunities, creates conditions conducive to reading readiness and to acquisition of basic school skills, and suggests broader potentialities for adaptive functioning. An example of a formal curriculum available to children at the preschool or kindergarten levels that integrates imaginative play with literacy preparation and early reading is the Letter People (Landry & Abrams, 2005). In this commercially distributed program, each letter of the alphabet is given a humorous name and characterization, and the sounds and uses of the letters are woven into story sequences, songs, and interesting interactions that foster the basis for phonemic and other literacy skills. Research on the effectiveness of classroom utilization of this well-organized but play-centered curriculum is beginning to appear (Abrams & Company, 2003).

We need more research that can help us evaluate the benefits of play in a systematic, quantitative fashion. Some of the positive outcomes described in these chapters are based on observations and anecdotes. Even the more extensively documented formal research studies described or reviewed here are often based on short-term interventions or follow-up studies. We especially need more longitudinal work. I would also look for broader efforts to follow up early adult–child situations, such as forms of attachment to parents, and how these yield different degrees of children's readiness to initiate pretend play. A recent area of interest in the study of parent–child relations is observations not only of attachment but also of maternal attentiveness to children's thought patterns (mind-mindedness). We need research on both attachment styles in children and mind-mindedness in mothers to see if such attitudes foster early imaginative play (Borelli & David, 2003–2004; Fonagy, Gergely, Jurist, & Target, 2002; Meins et al., 2003). I would hypothesize that those mothers, fathers, or other adult caregivers who are especially sensitive to their children's thinking processes may be subtly, if not directly, fostering the child's curiosity, storytelling, and narrative play. For some adults, such stimulation may come in religious storytelling; others recount fairy tales, family histories, or even fantasy epics like Tolkien's *Lord of the Rings*, the Harry Potter series, the *Star Wars* films and videos, or C. S. Lewis's Narnia books.

A FINAL WORD: SOME BROADER IMPLICATIONS OF IMAGINATIVE PLAY

Children who engage in constructive, imaginative play in childhood are mastering a heightened awareness of reality–fantasy distinctions. They also gradually learn to recognize the *reality* of human thought processes, which are private, individualized, and potentially useful for self-entertainment, for self-examination, and ultimately for effective scientific and artistic creativity. Let me elaborate on this feature of play-derived imagination. The chapters in this book are persuasive in pointing to the usefulness, indeed, the importance of imaginative play as a feature of specific aspects of school readiness, literacy, numeracy, general knowledge acquisition, and even civility. They are thus responsive to the editors and early chapter contributors. They call for a defense of recess and play opportunities for children in the face of certain governmental or other educators' misguided demands for excessive drill-focused, "teaching to the test" emphases in early education. We need to see early play as potentially valuable in even a broader context.

With all due respect to the cognitive skills of our primate cousins or to the seeming intelligence of whales and porpoises, the stream of consciousness identified in 1890 by William James (1950) as a central feature of our psychology may be specific to our species. Our brains are wired to generate sensory-derived images that recur and are shaped into a virtual reality world. This world we experience privately in ongoing thought, in vivid memories, in day and sleeping dreams, and in anticipatory representations of possible future events or social interactions. Just as we must adapt over time to the social and physical demands of our "real" environment, we must also acquire abilities to recognize, to accept, and to control, at least to some degree, the reality of our ongoing consciousness. Cave paintings that date back about 20,000 years, well before we have any evidence of human literacy, attest to art as an early means of human imagery control. Through multiple forms of religious worship and ritual, spirituality, myths, and legends, the seven or eight millennia of human written records attest to ways in which we have learned to regulate and share the memories, speculations, and fantasies that characterize ongoing thought.

In the 20th century and already in the start of our new millennium, we have witnessed an amazing acceleration not only in worldwide literacy but also in the devising of electronic technologies that reflect aspects of our conscious memories, fantasies, and narrative capacities. These media may also serve as vast systems to distract us from the insistent, often painful, or existentially threatening nature of our private streams of thought (D. Singer & J. Singer, 2005). I propose that those of us who, early on, learned through imaginative play and pretend games to recognize and control our imagery may have at least gained an important resource for adapting to the increasing and inevitable complexities of adult life. Years of practice in the playful exercise of make-believe games, which then become internalized into a form of control of one's thought processes, may have significant coping value in many practical life situations. Let's consider, for example, how such self-regulatory manipulation of one's ongoing conscious thought may actually be useful not only for confronting real-life dilemmas but also for addressing personal conflicts and interpersonal difficulties once one is involved in some form of psychotherapy.

At a modest level, individuals who have learned to attend to and reexamine their memories and future fantasies may have certain advantages in daily life or in working effectively in various psychotherapies (J. A. Singer, 2005; J. L. Singer, 2006). Children who early on engaged in imaginative play or who have been encouraged to use play during therapy have been shown in early clinical studies and in controlled research to function more effectively in psychotherapeutic situations (Reddy, Files-Hall, & Schaefer, 2005; Russ, 2004; D. Singer, 1993; J. Singer, 1973). Sandra Russ's recent examination of child development research, for example, leads to her conclusion that pretend play will facilitate insightful problem solving, divergent thinking ability, the likelihood of developing alternative coping strategies, richer and more complex emotional expressiveness, and higher levels of empathetic responses or adaptive perspective taking (Russ, 2004, p. 32). Russ then examines further evidence from child psychotherapy and other play intervention studies and indicates that play interventions, if they are focused and controlled, do reduce fears and anxieties such as those about undergoing medical procedures or enduring separation or loss. Her analysis of the research also points to the specific aspects of imaginative play as critical features of anxiety-reduction interventions. The evidence supports the notion that well-developed make-believe play skills are more likely to yield effective play behaviors in child psychotherapies or interventions (Russ, 2004, p. 75). Dorothy Singer's (1993) clinical reports of play therapy exemplify some of these research findings.

One of the most recently published and probably one of the most carefully evaluated forms of child psychotherapy is the parent management training method, developed over decades by Alan Kazdin (2005). This method and its manual are based on operant conditioning and positive reinforcement learning principles for use by a therapist-trained parent with an oppositional, aggressive, or antisocial child or early adolescent. Much of the treatment involves parent recognition and practice of behavior-contingent positive reinforcement, avoidance of physical punishment, and employment of well-planned time-outs. Regular use is made of role play as part of the process in training parents and also in the parent's subsequent directional involvement with the child. Pretend activities are regularly employed to identify in advance the child's constructive behaviors that will be rewarded in the play and then are later actually rewarded when they occur in "real time."

A similar method termed parent child interaction therapy (PCIT), also empirically supported, was developed by Brinkmeyer and Eyberg (2003). These investigators trained parents in a set of interaction and communication procedures they labeled P.R.I.D.E. for Praise, Reflection of children's verbalization, Imitation of the child's play activity, Description of the child's play, and Enthusiasm in responding to constructive behaviors or responses (Brinkmeyer & Eyberg, 2003). The PCIT approach obviously relies heavily on playful interactions between the parent and the troubled child. Both of these well-researched treatment approaches for extremely difficult children, while clearly behaviorally focused, still rely on the basic usefulness of play.

Play, then, can be seen to have life-adjustment implications that go well beyond the school readiness and cognitive learning that have been the chief focus of this volume. Let me take this point a step further by a suggestion, admittedly speculative at this time, but with implications for further research on the broader learning value of pretend play. Robert Sternberg and his research group at Yale have generated a considerable body of data around the concept of *successful intelligence*. This work is premised on the notion that intellectual competence is broader than the individual's ability as measured by standardized IQ tests, which are constructed statistically to measure the *g* factor or, basically, abstract thinking in verbal and mathematical forms. Sternberg's research has shown that such abstract intellectual skill, although undoubtedly important, has limited predictive value in areas of effective human functioning beyond school grades.

To predict a greater array of effectiveness not only in broader school performance but also in vocational and career adjustment and in social interactions, one must measure at least two other ability dimensions, practical or "street-smart" intelligence and creative intelligence. Successful intelligence as measured by combining these three dimensions has been shown to be more effective than IQ measurement alone in predicting competent performance in business, military leadership, and other social and school settings (Sternberg, 1985, 1997, 1999; Sternberg & Grigorenko, 2000). Beyond the measurement value of the theory, there is evidence that actually teaching elementary and high school students to heighten the three skills can be effective. Training procedures with adults have also been shown useful (Grigorenko, Jarvin, & Sternberg, 2002; Sternberg et al., 2000). Sternberg and his numerous collaborators have provided, through research and observation, indications of how so-called tacit knowledge or street-smart skills, as well as creative attitudes, prove useful in a variety of personal and professional dilemmas or challenges.

For our purposes, we can take note that much of the measurement, as well as the training procedures, in this growing body of research depends on the use of vignettes of daily life scenes and on role-playing or other imaginative performances by the children or adult participants. There has not yet been a systematic effort to tie early childhood pretend play specifically into this work on successful intelligence. This area deserves exploration in future research. Consider how much of the time children's imaginative play involves thinking of alternative solutions to plot dilemmas. Some of these solutions are certainly fantastic, but, very often, some have practical value. The creative aspects of intelligence are, of course, more obviously linked to the divergent thought capacities or abilities to "think outside the box." Longitudinal research with children and studies of creative adults have linked original thinking and novel achievements in the arts to a history of early make-believe play (Russ, 1993, 2004; D. Singer & J. Singer, 1990).

Reviewing this book's examples of learning to play and learning through play encourages us to consider in how many ways children's play may be tied to the dimensions of practical and creative intelligence. Indeed, children's play may provide important precursors of a broadly adaptive, "successful intelligent" lifestyle. The thoughtful investigator of children's imagination, Paul Harris, has called attention to the "roughly synchronous emergence of pretend play and language in young children." This leads him to propose that at some phase of evolution this "explosive fusion" of language and imagination laid the basis for our great human capacity to conceive of a variety of events, many never actually "witnessed but all imaginable," and to find words to communicate them to others as well as to entertain them ourselves (Harris, 2000, p. 195).

Our book began with a challenge raised that children's play might not be relevant for adaptive development. Our chapters contradict that implication. Rather, we can summarize the reviews of theory and research by our authors as providing an impressive body of evidence that children's play may well be a critical contributor to the development of a literate, creative, and socially effective society.

References

Abrams & Company. (2003). Efficacy study of The Letter People programs, 2000–20003. Waterbury, CT: Author.

Alvarez, L. (2005, April 9). Educators flocking to Finland, land of literate children. *New York Times*, p. A4.

Borelli, J. L., & David, D. H. (2003–2004). Attachment theory and research as a guide to psychotherapy practice. *Imagination, Cognition and Personality, 23*(4), 257–288.

Brinkmeyer, M. Y., & Eyberg, S. M. (2003). Parent–child interaction therapy for oppositional children. In A. E. Kazdin & J. R. Weisz (Eds.), *Evidence-based psychotherapy for children and adolescents* (pp. 204–223). New York: Guilford.

Fonagy, P., Gergely, G., Jurist, E., & Target, M. (2002). *Affect regulation, mentalization and the development of the self.* New York: Other.

Grigorenko, E. L., Jarvin, L., & Sternberg, R. J. (2002). School-based tests of the triarchic theory of intelligence: Three settings, three samples, three syllabi. *Contemporary Educational Psychology, 27*, 167–208.

Harris, P. (2000). *The work of the imagination*. Malden, MA: Blackwell.

James, W. (1950). *The principles of psychology.* New York: Dover. (Original work published 1890)

Johnson, J., Christie, J., & Wardle, F. (2005). *Play, development, and early education.* Boston: Pearson Education.

Kazdin, A. E. (2005). *Parent management training: Treatment for oppositional, aggressive, and antisocial children and adolescents*. New York: Oxford University Press.

Landry, S. A., & Abrams, R. (2005). *Classroom literacy interventions and outcomes study: Report on* The Land of the Letter People. Houston, TX: The Center for Improving the Readiness of Children for Learning and Education, Division of Developmental Pediatrics, University of Texas, Houston, Health Sciences Center Medical School.

Leslie, A. (1987). Pretense and representation: The origins of "theory of mind." *Psychological Review, 94*, 412–422.

Levenstein, P. (2005). The parent–child home program turns forty! *The Parent Child Home Program Newsletter, 5*(3), 1.

Lewin, K. (1935). *A dynamic theory of personality*. New York: McGraw-Hill.

Lewin, K., Lippitt, R., & White, R. (1939). Patterns of aggressive behavior in experimentally created "social climates." *Journal of Social Psychology, 10*, 271–299.

Luria, A. R. (1932). *The nature of human conflicts*. New York: Liveright.

McCaslin, N. (1984). *Creative drama in the classroom*. New York: Longman.

Meins, E. C., Fernyhough, R., Wainwright, D., Clark-Carter, M., Das Gupta, M., Fradley, E., et al. (2003). Pathways to understanding mind: Construct validity and predictive validity of maternal mind-mindedness. *Child Development, 74*(4), 1194–1211.

Piaget, J. (1962). *Play, dreams, and imitation in childhood*. New York: Norton.

Reddy, L. A., Files-Hall, T. M., & Shaefer, C. E. (2005). *Empirically-based play interventions for children*. Washington, DC: American Psychological Association.

Rosenberg, H. S. (1987). *Creative drama and imagination*. New York: Holt, Rinehart, and Winston.

Russ, S. W. (1993). *Affect and creativity: The role of affect and play in the creative process*. Hillsdale, NJ: Erlbaum.

Russ, S. W. (2004). *Play in child development and psychotherapy*. Mahwah, NJ: Erlbaum.

Saltz, E., Dixon, D., & Johnson, J. (1977). Training disadvantaged preschoolers on various fantasy activities: Effects on cognitive functioning and impulse. *Child Development, 48*, 367–380.

Schwebel, D., Rosen, C., & Singer, J. L. (1999). Preschoolers' pretend play and theory of mind: The role of jointly conducted pretense. *British Journal of Developmental Psychology, 17*, 333–348.

Shmukler, D. (1981). Mother–child interaction and its relationship to the predisposition of imaginative play. *Genetic Psychology Monographs, 104*, 215–235.

Singer, D. G. (1993). *Playing for their lives*. New York: Free Press.

Singer, D. G., & Singer, J. L. (1990). *The house of make-believe: Children's play and the developing imagination*. Cambridge, MA: Harvard University Press.

Singer, D. G., & Singer, J. L. (2001). *Make-believe: Games and activities for imaginative play*. Washington, DC: American Psychological Association.

Singer, D. G., & Singer, J. L. (2005). *Imagination and play in the electronic age*. Cambridge, MA: Harvard University Press.

Singer, J. A. (2005). *Memories that matter*. New York: New Harbinger.

Singer, J. L. (1961). Imagination and waiting ability in young children. *Journal of Personality, 29*, 396–413.

Singer, J. L. (1973). *The child's world of make-believe*. New York: Academic Press.

Singer, J. L. (1993). Experimental studies on ongoing conscious experience. In *Experimental and theoretical studies of consciousness* (Ciba Foundation Symposium 174) (pp. 100–122). Chichester, England: Wiley.

Singer, J. L. (2006). *Imagery in psychotherapy*. Washington, DC: American Psychological Association.

Singer, J. L., & Lythcott, M. (2002). Fostering school achievement and creativity through sociodramatic play in the classroom. *Research in the Schools, 9*(2), 43–52.

Singer, J. L., & Singer, D. G. (1981). *Television, imagination and aggression: A study of preschoolers*. Hillsdale, NJ: Erlbaum.

Singer, J. L., & Singer, D. G. (1998). *Barney & Friends* as entertainment and education: Evaluating the quality and effectiveness of a television series for preschool children. In J. Asamen and G. Berry (Eds.), *Research paradigms in the study of television and social behavior* (pp. 305–367). Beverly Hills, CA: Sage.

Smilansky, S. (1968). *The effects of sociodramatic play on disadvantaged children*. New York: Wiley.

Sternberg, R. J. (1985). *Beyond IQ: A triarchic theory of human intelligence*. New York: Cambridge University Press

Sternberg, R. J. (1997). *The theory of successful intelligence*. New York: Plume.

Sternberg, R. J. (1999). The theory of successful intelligence. *Review of General Psychology, 3*, 292–316.

Sternberg, R. J., Forsythe, G. B., Hedlund, J., Horvath, J. A., Wagner, R. K., Williams, W. M., et al. (2000). *Practical intelligence in everyday life*. New York: Cambridge University Press.

Sternberg, R. J., & Grigorenko, E. L. (2000). *Teaching for successful intelligence*. Arlington Heights, IL: Skylight.

Tower, R., Singer, D. G., Singer, J. L., & Biggs, A. (1979). Differential effects of television programming on preschoolers' cognition and play. *Journal of Orthopsychiatry, 49*(2), 265–281.

Vygotsky, L. S. (1978). *Mind in society: The development of higher mental processes*. Cambridge, MA: Harvard University Press.

Wilson, F. (1998). *The hand: How its use shapes the brain, language, and human culture*. New York: Pantheon.

Index